CELEBRATING ROMANS

Robert Jewett

CELEBRATING ROMANS

Template for Pauline Theology

⚜ ESSAYS IN HONOR OF ROBERT JEWETT ⚜

Edited by

Sheila E. McGinn

WILLIAM B. EERDMANS PUBLISHING COMPANY
GRAND RAPIDS, MICHIGAN / CAMBRIDGE, U.K.

Wm. B. Eerdmans Publishing Co.
255 Jefferson Ave. S.E., Grand Rapids, Michigan 49503 /
P.O. Box 163, Cambridge CB3 9PU U.K.
www.eerdmans.com

Printed in the United States of America

09 08 07 06 05 04   7 6 5 4 3 2 1

Library of Congress Cataloging-in-Publication Data

Celebrating Romans, template for Pauline theology: essays in honor of Robert Jewett /
    edited by Sheila E. McGinn
        p.   cm.
    ISBN 0-8028-2839-6 (cloth: alk. paper)
    1. Bible, N.T. Romans — Theology.
    I. Jewett, Robert.   II. McGinn, Sheila E.

    BS2665.52.C45   2004
    227′.106 — dc22

                                    2004053278

The essay by James D. G. Dunn, "Did Paul Have a Covenant Theology? Reflections on
Romans 9:4 and 11:27," appeared in a slightly different form in *The Concept of the Covenant
in the Second Temple Period,* edited by Stanley Porter and Jacqueline de Roo (Leiden: Brill,
2003), and is reprinted here by permission.

ave Doctore

Contents

Contents

Preface

This *Festschrift* volume has been a long time coming. Brain child of Robert Atkins, it originated as a response to Bob Jewett's retirement from Garrett-Evangelical Theological Seminary. Atkins rounded up some of "the usual suspects," a handful of former students of Jewett from the Northwestern University–Garrett joint Ph.D. program, and one of Jewett's most recent Garrett colleagues. All told, the group included Atkins, Keith Burton, Frank Hughes, K. K. Yeo, and myself. We each were to choose one of the many approaches to Scripture that have characterized Jewett's work and take charge of soliciting essays from other scholarly associates of Jewett who shared that particular approach and could make a significant contribution to our thinking on Romans. The collected essays thereby would be a tribute to the interest Jewett's writing and teaching have triggered in his students and in fellow members of the Academy.

The five basic approaches which were to characterize this collection of essays represent five categories of studies about Paul's letter to the Romans. Atkins was to compile essays from scholars who took a social-historical approach; Burton was in charge of the section which put Romans in dialogue with contemporary culture; Hughes would gather essays from rhetorical critics; I was in charge of feminist approaches; and Yeo was to compile essays using a theological approach. We agreed to look for a mix of junior and senior scholars to contribute to the volume. Most importantly, we decided to ask that they all address some aspect or section of Paul's letter to the Romans, a long-time interest of Jewett's and subject of the *Hermeneia* commentary he was writing.

Bob Jewett is known to the academic world as a scholar, but to those who compiled this volume he is known as a teacher as well. In addition, all of us are teachers in academic and church settings. We recognize the need for analyses of the Bible which are substantial contributions to scholarship but also intelligible to the non-specialist reader. These essays are intended to provide such a bridge, challenging the thinking of students and scholars alike. We envision the collection being used as a secondary text for the upper-level college and seminary classroom — e.g., as a companion to Jewett's anticipated new commentary on Romans in the *Hermeneia* series — but the essays should be accessible to the educated lay audience in general.

Because the volume is intended for both students and scholars alike, certain accommodations have been made in the text. Foreign language terms are translated in the text when they first occur; where important, the original language is given either in brackets in the text or in a footnote. Standard abbreviations for Biblical books are used, and wherever practicable such references are included as parenthetical notes in the body of the text. Unless otherwise noted, Bible translations are taken from the NRSV. Rather than using the customary abbreviations for scholarly journals and classical texts, full titles have been used for the first mention in each essay; these revert to the standard abbreviations when that text appears in later reference in the same essay. Technical terms and references to scholarly positions are explained in the text or in footnotes. Separate bibliographies have been omitted, although those readers who wish to investigate a topic further will find a wealth of bibliographic material in the footnotes — and in Bob Jewett's Vita which can be found in the Appendix.

The essays are arranged according to the primary method used to engage the letter to the Romans, but the reader will observe a certain amount of overlap from one section to another given that many of the contributors have used more than one method or approach to the letter. (For example, William Campbell's essay uses rhetorical criticism but raises deeply theological issues as well. Sheila McGinn and Pamela Thimmes take a feminist approach, but also make use of rhetorical theory to illuminate the discussion.) Within each section the essays are simply arranged in alphabetical order according to author; by no means should the arrangement of the essays be read as a judgement on their relative importance. The Introduction offers a quick review of some of the recent trends in New Testament scholarship that are pertinent to Pauline studies, particularly the study of Romans, in order to provide a context for the articles that follow it.

This volume is the work of many hands. I would like to thank my colleagues who helped in the compilation and preparation of this volume. Without the efforts of Bob Atkins, Keith Burton, Frank Hughes, and K. K. Yeo, this collection would never have been started, no less completed. Several people from John Carroll University assisted in preparing the final manuscript. Eric Abercrombie and Trisha Williams tracked numerous references and, with Sylvia Lister, acted as a "student test-audience" for the essays. Mary Jane Ponyik and her student assistants, especially Colleen Cain, provided meticulous copy-editing. Jackie Bluett assisted in compiling the indices. Reinder Van Til, of Eerdmans Publishing, was a tremendous support in the long process from proposal to submission. Last of all but first in importance, on behalf of all the contributors to this volume, I would like to thank Robert Jewett — teacher, mentor, colleague, friend. May this volume be a celebration of scholarship that continues for many years to come. Peace, friend.

SEM
Gaudete Sunday 2003

Introduction

Sheila E. McGinn

Perhaps the most preposterous assertion that students hear in the first few weeks of their introductory college New Testament courses is that one can continue to learn new things about texts that are nearly 2,000 years old. After all, those books have been around so long and studied by so many people — scholars, ecclesiastics, laypersons — how could there possibly be anything new "in there"? And is it not even a bit silly to think we could learn more than already is known about the authors and audiences of those ancient texts? Ecclesiastical tradition provides as much information as we need or can expect to have about the people and authors in the earliest churches. Perhaps if there were a new archaeological find that unveiled writings formerly hidden from public view or that provided physical evidence of some church structure or practice previously unknown, then maybe one could understand how new knowledge could be constructed, but otherwise all this talk about ancient texts seems merely a library debate or "retirement plan" for ivory tower specialists. Developing new methods or approaches to ancient documents (like the Pauline letters) just provides new wrappings for long-established ideas. New methods do not really create new knowledge, they just create more "things we have to learn" about how to read the texts — to find the same old information we could have found without any of those sophisticated tools. Students in Bible courses, like Alice in Wonderland, can begin to feel like "however fast they went, they never seemed to pass anything."[1]

Helping students break out of this mindset is one of the more difficult

---

1. Lewis Carroll, *Through the Looking Glass,* chapter 2.

tasks of the course. It helps somewhat for them to learn that, in fact, there have been three major finds of documents in the last century or so — the Cairo Geniza in 1897, the Nag Hammadi corpus in 1945, and the Dead Sea Scrolls in 1948. While none of these hoards included anything as remarkable as an unknown letter of Paul of Tarsus, they did include unknown gospels and other documents that have changed our understanding of the context in which the New Testament materials were produced — including the context in which Paul wrote his letters. The Dead Sea Scrolls in particular, with their emphasis on the community of the New Covenant, broke apart previous assumptions about the univocal nature of first-century Judaism and revealed the anachronism of imputing a second-century "orthodoxy" where there really was a pluriformity of belief and practice. Recently uncovered material evidence has had a less dramatic but no less significant impact on our understanding of the world in which the New Testament arose, especially the Jewish world, with such discoveries as synagogues with images of the zodiac depicted in the mosaic floor, inscriptions naming women as "president" of synagogues (ἀρχισυνάγωγος), and documents attesting to the fact that other Jewish "missionaries" besides Paul believed a Gentile man could convert without undergoing circumcision.[2] Among the essays in this collection, a good review of how such findings have affected Pauline studies is Graydon Snyder's historical survey of theological motifs and interpretive trends in regard to Paul's letter to the Romans, while James Dunn's discussion of Paul's "covenant theology" is a fine example of how such treasures as the Dead Sea Scrolls can transform our understanding of early Christian writings like Paul's letters.

Especially for students who are new to the New Testament materials, learning about literary and archaeological discoveries like these helps them to see that perhaps these texts are not so "dead" or static in meaning as they initially thought. Peter Lampe's essay investigating the inscriptional evidence and Carolyn Osiek's reading of such texts as *the Shepherd of Hermas* are examples of how such literary and material evidence can be brought into play to advance

---

2. Bernadette Brooten, *Inscriptional Evidence for Women as Leaders in the Ancient Synagogue* (Ph.D. diss.; Harvard University, 1982); *Women Leaders in the Ancient Synagogue: Inscriptional Evidence and Background Issues* (*Brown Judaic Studies* 36; Chico, Calif.: Scholars Press, 1982); "Female Leadership in the Ancient Synagogue," 215-23 in *From Dura to Sepphoris: Studies in Jewish Art and Society in Late Antiquity* (ed. Ze'ev Weiss and Lee Levine; *Journal of Roman Archaeology Supplement* 40; Portsmouth, Me.: JRA Press, 2000). On synagogue mosaics with images — e.g., Dura Europos and Sepphoris — see several other essays in that volume, especially Bianca Kuhnel, "The synagogue floor mosaic in Sepphoris: Between paganism and Christianity," 31-43. For the conversion of the king of Adiabene without circumcision, see Josephus, *Antiquities of the Jews* 21.2.1-4.

our understanding of the social history of early Christianity, while Reta Finger's discussion of her simulation of the Roman house-churches presents a particularly effective way to help students grasp the significance of such social-historical information.

Keith Burton and L. D. Hurst take quite a different tack toward responding to the assumption that such ancient texts are "dead" and offer nothing useful or relevant for contemporary life. Following in the footsteps of scholars such as Robert Jewett, they bring Paul's letter to the Romans into conversation with contemporary films. If "art imitates life," it is equally true that art can illuminate life and uncover meaning in a busy world where that purpose is not self-evident. Paul's letters and contemporary films are two distinct media, but they both use persuasive strategies and symbolic language and imagery to engage the audience in attending to and adopting the message conveyed in that particular work of art. That being the case, Burton and Hurst show how analyzing popular films can be another way to help a contemporary audience recognize the value and significance of Paul's message.

Even when students have begun to grasp the importance of literary and archaeological finds in re-shaping the existing understanding of a corpus of ancient texts like the Pauline letters, it is difficult for them to recognize the profound effect new methods or approaches can have on what we can learn from these texts. Analytical methods are not mere "window dressing" but actually construct knowledge. What one finds in a text is largely contingent upon the questions one raises in evaluating it. This is no less true of the Biblical materials, including the Pauline corpus, than it is of contemporary writings.

For example, rhetorical analysis of the Pauline materials has raised the question of how Paul goes about persuading his audiences. Even before the rise of rhetorical criticism of the New Testament, there was a long-standing scholarly consensus that Paul's letters were "occasional" documents, written to respond to a particular need at a particular place and time. Rhetorical critics have contributed to our understanding of the Pauline corpus, first and foremost, by illustrating that these documents also are rhetorical constructions. If Paul uses rhetoric, "the art of persuasion," it must be because he aimed to persuade his audience. This may seem a very simple and insignificant finding, until one realizes its implications. Paul did not write these letters simply to divulge timeless theological truths, but to motivate individual audiences to affirm his proclamation and act on it in specific ways. If Paul's letters do contain timeless truths, those truths are selected to meet what Paul perceived to be the needs of the precise audience he addressed in a given letter and are couched in terms designed to have persuasive effect on that specific audience. If Paul has to persuade his audience, then what he is teaching or claiming in a particular letter must not have been universally accepted by the intended audience. Ergo, there were some early Christians — perhaps even many — who disagreed with Paul's theology. Suddenly the traditional image of idyllic harmony and unity of belief among early Christians has to be rejected, and this is the result not of a new archaeological or textual find but simply the use of a new method for analysis of the texts.

The adage "form fits function" is no less true of texts than it is of architecture. Studying how it is that Paul argues his case in a given letter also reveals elements of the letter's content that previously were overlooked. In the present volume, the essays by William Campbell, James Hester, and Wilhelm Wuellner are examples of how this can work. And the fact that each letter is crafted for a particular rhetorical context means, for example, that apparent contradictions between two or more of his letters have to be re-evaluated, taking into account the differences in their rhetorical situations. Not all scholars use rhetorical analysis to understand Paul's writings, but the simple fact that some have begun to use this method has had a significant impact upon how the letters are understood. Jeffrey Gibson's analysis of the Pauline "dying formula" is an example of how rhetorical considerations can illuminate and re-shape a theological analysis of Paul's letters. Rhetorical critic or not, no contemporary reader can ignore the implications inherent in the simple fact that Paul's letters were intended to persuade.

Feminist criticism is another example of how a new method can expand our understanding, not simply gloss previously existing knowledge. For centuries Paul's letters were read as if there were no women in his audiences, and certainly no women in real leadership roles in the Pauline churches. Scholars employing a feminist hermeneutic began to ask new questions of the texts, and thereby uncovered data that had never been noticed before. When Paul uses a masculine plural for a collective noun — for example, when addressing the members of one of his churches as "brethren" (ἀδελφοί) — in which cases, if any, should this be read as including the women in the congregation, and when should it be read exclusively? Were there sections of Paul's letters where he simply was not even thinking of the women in the audience, no less aiming his writing toward them? Who actually were the women in Paul's audience? How might they have heard a particular letter? What were they doing in the churches? (Even the idea that they might have been playing a role in the churches rather than passively watching the men fill all the leadership functions was a radical departure from previous interpretations.) And what ought contemporary women make of a given teaching from Paul?

In the present volume, the essays by Sheila McGinn, Elsa Tamez, and Pamela Thimmes illustrate what a significant difference a feminist reading can make in our understanding of the text and its context. The feminist strategy of "using women to think with" leads to challenging interpretations of the marriage/adultery analogy in Rom 7, the "righteousness of God" in Rom 1–8, and Paul's perception of Jew-Gentile relations in Rom 9–11. Just as rhetorical criticism of the Pauline corpus has now made it impossible to think about the letters without keeping in mind their persuasive purpose, the rise of feminist hermeneutics has made it impossible to continue to read Paul's letters as if there were no women in the audience.

By now the reader will have gathered that the essays in this collection are illustrative of several of the "new approaches" to Paul, both in terms of their methods and the assumptions undergirding the investigations. Whether one is new to Pauline studies or already familiar with the Pauline writings, having studied them in church school or academic contexts some years ago, knowing a few of the other significant trends in Pauline studies is quite helpful — even essential — to understanding the shape of the field today. No doubt one could multiply this list, but then this introductory essay might easily expand to the size of an entire New Testament text. The following three examples should suffice to convey the shifting ground over the last few decades of Pauline studies.

Less than a generation ago, one could make the claim that Paul was a "convert" to Christianity from Judaism, or even that he himself was the "founder" of Christianity, and simply state these views as truisms, never expecting to be challenged to provide evidence for such claims.[3] Today one would be hard pressed to find a scholar who would make such dramatic claims. Because of the advances in our understanding of the varieties of first-century Judaism, most scholars now recognize that, born a Jew, Paul continued to understand himself as a Jew throughout his life, even after his Damascus Road experience — which careful scholars would now label a "call" experience rather than a "conversion" to emphasize that Paul's only "conversion" is from one type of Judaism to another (i.e., from Pharisaism to messianic Judaism). When we read the letters of Paul, as is true when we read any of the New Testament texts, we are engaging the analyses and creative ventures of a first-century Jewish theologian. "Christianity" as we understand it today was only beginning to come into existence at the turn of the century, after the New Testament was essentially finished. Paul was a Jewish theologian preaching the good new of Jesus as the long-awaited messiah of Israel. When Paul took to the road with this gospel

3. E.g., Wilhelm Wrede, *Paul* (London: Green, 1907). The idea is by no means dead, however. See, e.g., Gerd Lüdemann, *Paul: the Founder of Christianity* (Amherst, N.Y.: Prometheus, 2002); also Hyam Maccoby, *The Myth-Maker: Paul and the Invention of Christianity* (New York: Harper Collins, 1987).

message and began preaching it to non-Jews, it was precisely as a *Jewish* missionary that he did so.[4]

Again, as recently as the 1960s interpreters could simply attribute to Paul a Law (Torah) v. Gospel dichotomy, reading Christ as the "end of the Law" (Rom 10:4) in a supercessionist way such that the gospel of Christ nullifies the Law and invalidates God's covenant with Israel. No longer could one make such an assertion without providing a substantial argument in its defense. In the face of the Nazi Holocaust — a large part of the propaganda for which derived from Christian theologians interpreting Paul in this manner — scholars were compelled to take another, much closer look at the evidence. Passages such as Rom 9–11, where Paul provides his most extensive discussion of Jew-Gentile relations in the churches, began to receive more careful scrutiny, and scholars began to recognize (a) that Paul insists on the enduring validity of the covenant with Israel, even after Christ, and (b) that there is much more complex interplay between Law and Gospel in Paul's theology than previous generations assumed. The "new consensus" on Paul that has been developing over the last two decades rejects the supercessionist interpretation of Paul, and questions the previous interpretation of Paul as radically opposed to Torah-observance for the followers of Jesus.

For centuries Paul was understood as radically opposing leadership roles for women in the churches. Under the influence of the Pastoral Epistles (1 Timothy, 2 Timothy, and Titus) and such texts as the "household codes" in Col 3:18–4:1 and Eph 5:22–6:9, interpreters consistently claimed that Paul supported exclusively male leadership in church and family. They understood Paul's demand as grounded in his understanding of the "order of nature" ordained by God, and therefore not subject to human controversy.[5] Since the development of widespread consensus that the Pastoral Epistles are post-Pauline rather than authentic letters of Paul, this understanding of Paul as opposed to women's leadership and equality with their Christian brothers has required serious reconsideration. The dubious authorship of Colossians and Ephesians, which

---

4. Nor was he the only Jewish missionary of that time — for example, some as yet unknown missionaries are responsible for founding the churches in Rome already before the 40s. See Peter Lampe's essay in the present volume.

5. One oddity of this interpretation is that it presumes a Paul who continues to hold the validity of both Torah and the "order of creation" over against the "order of grace" made present in Christ, yet the same interpreters — without the slightest hint that they were aware of the incongruity — could argue that Paul took a supercessionist view of the Law being overturned, invalidated by the grace of God manifest in Christ and the Gospel. Essentially their view was that Christians live under grace — until we look at male-female relations; then male Christians live under grace and female Christians live under Law, as interpreted by those male Christians.

now more frequently are considered to be products of one or more of Paul's disciples rather than Paul himself (i.e., "Deutero-Pauline" letters), makes such sweeping claims about Paul's opposition appear very tenuous indeed. On top of that, scholars have become more attentive to the sheer number of women leaders Paul mentions in the seven undisputed letters, which has led to widespread rejection of that earlier understanding of Paul. There certainly is no consensus that Paul himself took an egalitarian view of male-female relations in church and society, but one is much more hard-pressed to defend either claims or accusations of "male chauvinism" on his part. More often now it is the later interpreters of Paul (in the Deutero-Pauline letters and the Pastoral Epistles) who are viewed as back-pedaling on the range of rights and privileges Paul himself accorded to women.

This brief overview cannot describe all of the advances in Pauline studies over the last few decades nor illuminate all of the key issues that are being debated by contemporary Pauline scholars, but the three shifts just outlined should signal enough of the changes to lay the groundwork for the remaining essays in this *Festschrift,* which both reflect and advance those discussions. Readers who would like more complete exposition of the changes in interpretation of Romans might find it helpful to begin with the essays by Campbell, Dunn, and Snyder. Teachers who are interested in exposing their students to some of these interpretive questions for the first time may choose to begin with Finger's contribution. Those who would like more detail on the trends in feminist interpretation of Romans can look to the essay by McGinn to fill this gap. There are many ways to use this volume and many entry points to fit the needs of readers of differing backgrounds and levels of familiarity with the Pauline corpus. Our hope is that, in honoring Robert Jewett with this contribution to Pauline studies, we spark or re-kindle in our readers the love for the Scriptures and for God's people that has been at the heart of Bob's career as scholar, pastor, and teacher.

THEOLOGICAL APPROACHES TO ROMANS

compiled by K. K. Yeo

Did Paul Have a Covenant Theology?
Reflections on Romans 9:4 and 11:27

James D. G. Dunn

The covenant motif plays a rather puzzling role in Paul's theology. The problem is not simply that Paul uses the term covenant relatively infrequently.[1] In addition, his usage seems to be more reactive than systematic, and consequently it is difficult to derive a coherent "covenant theology" from the passages where the term occurs. The tension is reflected in the two principal streams of the Reformation, both of which drew their theological inspiration from Paul. Is "covenant" for Paul a means of expressing continuity between the Old Testament and the New, as for John Calvin? Or does it succumb to the antithesis between law and gospel (*new* covenant) so paradigmatic for Lutheran theology? The problem is magnified by the hundred-year-old scholarly debate as to whether the covenant is a late (Deuteronomic) concept or an early one, fundamental to Israel's self-consciousness more or less from the beginning.[2] Each of these alternatives in its own way can give scope either to the Lutheran antithesis or to Calvin's continuity. To put the question in terms more directly applicable to our present concerns: Against what aspects of his heritage did Paul react? What elements did he accept and develop? And where does the theology of covenant fit? Was it part of that against which Paul reacted, or part of that upon which he drew?

---

1. Rom 9:4; 11:27; 1 Cor 11:25; 2 Cor 3:6, 14; Gal 3:15, 17; 4:24; also Eph 2:12.

2. E.g., for the former, see Julius Wellhausen, *Prolegomena zur Geschichte Israels* (2nd ed., Berlin: G. Reimer, 1883; 6th ed., 1927; repr. Berlin/New York: Walter de Gruyter, 2001; first published in 1878 as *Geschichte Israels*); *Israelitische und jüdische Geschichte* (Berlin, 1894; 10th ed., Berlin/New York: Walter de Gruyter, 2002); etc. For the latter, see Walther Eichrodt, *Theology of the Old Testament* (trans. John Baker; 2 vols.; Philadelphia: Westminster, 1961, 1967).

Since E. P. Sanders' revisioning of Second Temple Judaism in terms of "covenantal nomism,"[3] the pendulum of Pauline interpretation has swung again in favor of emphasis on continuity with Judaism rather than the traditional portrayal of Paul reacting against a legalistic Judaism. In this reassessment, "covenant" usually has been taken as a motif of continuity.[4] It was a leading term in my own statement of the new perspective on Paul.[5] However, I now wonder whether the category is being used too casually in descriptions of Paul's theology, in a way that glosses over the ambivalence of his usage, which reflects also Paul's ambivalence toward his ancestral religion.[6] Particularly striking are the two references to covenant in Romans, which do not seem to reflect the familiar Christian contrast of "old covenant" and "new covenant." How should one understand them in relation to a Pauline covenant theology?

It is appropriate to offer these further reflections in a volume focusing on Romans, where two of Paul's most intriguing covenant references occur — and in a volume presented to Bob Jewett, who has contributed so much to the study of Paul and whose commentary on Romans is eagerly awaited.

Is Paul's a "Covenant Theology"?

From one perspective there can be little doubt that Paul's theology may justifiably be described as covenant theology. In this line of thought, "covenant" denotes the fundamental character of Israel's religion, emphasizing particularly a people chosen by divine initiative and sustained by the merciful love of God (*chesed*). And it is precisely this emphasis which Paul's gospel brings to fresh focus. The God who created the cosmos and made free choice of Israel is the God of Paul's theology.[7] The central term in Paul's most characteristic teaching, justification (δικαιοσύνη) by faith, draws directly on Israel's covenant theology as

3. E. P. Sanders, *Paul and Palestinian Judaism* (London: SCM Press, 1977), 75, 420, 544.

4. E.g., N. T. Wright, *The Climax of the Covenant: Christ and the Law in Pauline Theology* (Edinburgh: T&T Clark, 1991); David Kaylor, *Paul's Covenant Community: Jew and Gentile in Romans* (Atlanta: John Knox, 1988).

5. James D. G. Dunn, *Romans 1–8* (Dallas: Word, 1988), lxviii. See also W. L. Lane, "Covenant: The Key to Paul's Conflict with Corinth," *Tyndale Bulletin* 33 (1982): 3-29; W. J. Webb, *Returning Home: New Covenant and Second Exodus as the Context for 2 Corinthians 6:14–7:1* (*Journal for the Study of the New Testament* Supplement 85; Sheffield: JSOT Press, 1993).

6. This line of reflection was stimulated particularly by the research of E. J. Christiansen, *The Covenant in Judaism and Paul: A Study of Ritual Boundaries as Identity Markers* (Leiden: E. J. Brill, 1995).

7. See James D. G. Dunn, *The Theology of Paul the Apostle* (Grand Rapids: Eerdmans, 1988), §2.

expressed most clearly by the Psalmist and Second Isaiah.[8] What has marked out the new perspective on Paul is precisely this recognition of the extent to which Paul's gospel presupposes these fundamental features of Israel's covenant religion.

It is all the more surprising, then, that the concept of covenant seems to play so little part in Paul's theology. The more fundamental the concept in describing the manner of divine grace, the more we might have expected Paul to make it central to his own exposition. But he did not do so. Why not?

A likely explanation soon offers itself. The covenant theology to which Paul was undoubtedly indebted is never formulated within Paul's scriptures in terms of what we may call the Calvinist abstraction of the "covenant of grace." It always appears within more specific contexts and in more concrete terms. As the history of discussion of the subject has shown, questions and problems begin to mount when these different facets of covenant theology are brought into juxtaposition. For example, how ought we to relate the concept of "covenant" to what are usually described as *different* covenants — those with Noah; Abraham and the patriarchs; Moses at Sinai; Phinehas; David; and so on? Given the spectrum — from the universal perspective of the Noah covenant[9] to the particularism of the Phinehas covenant[10] — how should each of these covenants be related to the others? Is one of them (e.g., Sinai) to be regarded as more definitive than the others? Is the book of Deuteronomy to be regarded as the paradigmatic statement of Israel's covenant theology? Was there a shift in emphasis from the model of an unconditional royal grant (the promissory covenant) to that of a conditional suzerain-vassal treaty (the obligatory covenant)[11] as the religion of Israel grew into early Judaism? How does the "new covenant" prophesied by Jeremiah (Jer 31:31-34) relate to its predecessors? Above all, is there a single "covenant theology" which embraces all these different facets, or are we left with only a sequence of shifting emphases and tensions?

We cannot hope to discuss all these questions here, but the issues which

---

8. Ibid., §14.2.

9. The universal aspect of the covenant with Noah is emphasized in the contexts where the term *bᵉrith* [בְּרִית = διαθήκη] occurs (Gen 6:18; 9:9-17) — although Gen 9:4-6, the basis for the subsequent Noahide Laws which rabbinic Jews regarded as applicable to non-Jews, omits the term and implies conditions to the covenant.

10. Num 25:6-13; Sir 45:23-24; 1 Macc 2:54; Pseudo-Philo 46-48; Phinehas was the great paradigm for the Zealots (see Martin Hengel, *The Zealots: Investigations into the Jewish Freedom Movement in the Period from Herod I Until 70 A.D.* [trans. David Smith; Edinburgh: T&T Clark, 1989], 149-77).

11. See, e.g., Moshe Weinfeld, "בְּרִית *bᵉrith*," *Theological Dictionary of the Old Testament*, Vol. 2 (ed. G. Johannes Botterweck and H. Ringgren; Grand Rapids, Mich.: Eerdmans, 1975), 253-79.

they pose obviously impact upon any covenant theology affirmed by Paul. Was he himself working with an abstracted theology of covenant, or did he simply seize on one strand of the tradition and make only one emphasis his own? Is the election of Israel as God's particular people — such a prominent theme within the covenant theology of the Hebrew Bible — also a feature of Paul's theology, or rather a stumbling block for it?[12] Is Paul's use of the concept of covenant an arbitrary, idiosyncratic development of the covenant theology which he inherited, or an appropriate expansion of the Scriptural theme?

It is important to bear such questions in mind as we approach the passages where Paul speaks of "covenant." Otherwise we may hear them with ears too preconditioned by the traditional New Testament/Old Testament Christian perspective, by previous debates on the theme, and by the more casual talk of "covenant" which has been a feature of recent discussion. Since our goal is to make best sense of the two Romans references, our obvious procedure is to work up to them through the earlier Pauline references. We proceed, then, by examining Paul's usage in what may be regarded as the most probable chronological sequence.

Paul uses the term διαθήκη (the usual word for "covenant") twice in Galatians, in 3:15-17[13] and 4:24.[14]

In Gal 3:15-17, Paul uses the term διαθήκη primarily because it also means "will, testament," and so allows an effective wordplay.[15] Central to the wordplay is the unilateral nature of a human will or testament: what it determines or disposes (within its own competence) no one else can alter.[16] Hence, the wordplay reinforces the divine initiative in and the unilateral nature of the commitment

12. It is notable, for example, that whereas those who make much of Paul's covenant theology tend naturally to speak in terms of "the people of God," Paul himself uses the term "people" (λαός) only in Scriptural quotations (Rom 9:25, 26; 10:21; 11:1-2; 15:10, 11; 1 Cor 10:7; 14:21; 2 Cor 6:16).

13. "Even a human διαθήκην once ratified, no one sets aside or adds to. But the promises were spoken to Abraham and to his 'seed.' It does not say, and to his 'seeds,' as to many, but as to one: 'and to your seed' — who is Christ. My point is this: a διαθήκην ratified beforehand by God, the law which came four hundred and thirty years later does not make void so as to render the promise ineffective (καταργῆσαι)" (Gal 3:15-17).

14. "Such things [i.e., Abraham's two sons: one by a slave girl, the other by a free woman; the one born in accordance with the flesh, the other born through promise] are to be interpreted allegorically. For these women are two covenants; one from Mount Sinai gives birth into slavery — such is Hagar. This Hagar-Sinai . . . belongs to the same column as the present Jerusalem, for she is in slavery with her children. But the Jerusalem above is free; such is our mother" (Gal 4:24-26).

15. On the various translations of διαθήκη offered by commentators, see Christiansen, *The Covenant in Judaism and Paul*, 235-36.

16. For the nuances necessary in the assertion see R. N. Longenecker, *Galatians* (*Word Biblical Commentary* 41; Dallas: Word, 1991), 128-30.

God made to Abraham. To that extent, it serves to reinforce a fundamental feature of covenant theology, but it would be a mistake to conclude that Paul had in mind the Abrahamic covenant as such.[17] Rather Paul sees the promise to Abraham as a kind of *will* or *testament* — hence the formulation of 3:17 as "a will ratified by God" rather than "the covenant made with Abraham."

The key term in the passage is actually "promise" (eight times in 3:14-29).[18] That is the term which provides the cutting edge of Paul's exposition in Gal 3. That is the term which carries the contrast with law (νόμος),[19] as the sequence 3:17-22 clearly indicates. In 3:17 the διαθήκη is simply the carrier of the promise.[20] Had the concept of covenant been more central to his exposition of Abraham, one would have expected it to reappear with some prominence in Paul's reworking of the same theme in Romans 4. But there too it is the theme of "promise" which carries the heavy theological freight (Rom 4:13-21); the term διαθήκη does not even appear.

The fact that Paul chose to build his theological argument round the theme of promise, despite the term covenant being close to hand and actually in use within the immediate context of his argument, must tell us something about Paul's theology. That theology is better described as "promise theology" rather than "covenant theology." Moreover, we note that "covenant" is not used in reference to the law, the other partner in the contrast.[21] But neither was Paul

---

17. It may be of relevance to recall that the term בְּרִית does not occur in the unconditional promise of Gen 12:1-3. The term occurs for the first time in reference to Abraham in Gen 15:18 and is prominent in Gen 17:1-21 (eleven times) — with particular emphasis on circumcision as a condition (17:9-14).

18. The text Paul had in mind (3:16) was presumably the repeated promise of Gen 13:15, 17 LXX; 15:18; 17:8; 24:7.

19. In contrast, no doubt, to the other missionaries in Galatia who would assume that the law was simply the outworking of the promise, as the covenant language of Genesis actually suggested. See esp. J. L. Martyn, *Galatians* (*Anchor Bible* 33A; New York: Doubleday, 1997), 337; idem, "The Abrahamic Covenant, Christ, and the Church," 161-75 in *Theological Issues in the Letters of Paul* (Edinburgh: T&T Clark, 1997), 165-67.

20. Again it may be important to recall that the term "promise" had no equivalent in Hebrew and was a fairly recent coinage in Greek. This does not invalidate Paul's usage here, although it is noteworthy that when the term does begin to feature in Jewish theology it is much more integrated with the law (2 Macc 2:17-18; *Psalms of Solomon* 12.6; *Sibylline Oracles* 3.768-769), a tendency which Paul seems deliberately to cut across; see Dunn, *Romans,* 212.

21. In the imagery which Paul uses the law at best could be regarded as a codicil; despite the usage of the Torah, Paul did not seem to think of circumcision or the law (Exod 19:5; 24:7-8; 31:16; 34:28; Lev 26:15; Deut 4:13, 23; 5:2-3; 7:9, 12; etc.) as potentially a superseding will/covenant. E. Grässer links the treatment here too quickly into the discussion of "new covenant" and "old covenant" (*Der Alte Bund im Neuen* [*Wissenschaftliche Untersuchungen zum Neuen Testament* 35; Tübingen: Mohr, 1985], 68).

referring to the Abrahamic *covenant* as such. On the contrary, he was evidently not thinking of covenants, properly speaking, at all — whether the covenant with Abraham or with Moses. "Covenant" as such was neither a leading nor an organizing category in his thought at this point.[22] This suggests that the features and emphases within Paul's theology which some have labeled "covenant theology" may have been categorized misleadingly, with misleading consequences for our understanding of Paul's "covenant theology."

In Gal 4:24-26, Paul speaks explicitly of "two covenants." The passage seems to invite the conclusion that Paul thus recognized two of what have regularly been designated as "covenants" within the Hebrew Bible — the covenant with Abraham and the covenant made on Sinai. And of course Paul does explicitly identify the first covenant as the "one from Mount Sinai" (Gal 4:24). The way is then open for an exegesis which contrasts old covenant/law with new covenant/promise, and we at once find ourselves back in a classic formulation of "law v. gospel" covenant theology.

A key problem with this, however, is that "covenant" is used on both sides of the contrast. Slave Hagar-Sinai is as much to be identified with covenant as free Sarah. Hence, "covenant" cannot be used to distinguish a theology of promise, grace, and gospel, from a theology of law. This covenant theology embraces both. In Gal 3:15-18 it was possible to draw the inference that Paul wanted to reserve the language of covenant for the promise to Abraham. By implication, the law given through Moses would then fall into a different category — at best an unauthorized codicil. But if Gal 4:24-26 is to be read as saying that the later covenant (Sarah's freeborn child) supersedes or takes higher priority than the earlier (Hagar's slave-born child), this would throw the Gal 3 argument into total confusion; there Paul argued precisely the reverse: the prior promise could *not* be annulled by the later law (Gal 3:17). These observations reinforce the previous conclusion that the imagery of "covenant" is incidental to the argument of Gal 3:15-18, and they strongly suggest that neither is it central to the argument of Gal 4. In neither passage is Paul attempting to develop a "covenant theology" as such.

The primary category in this case is neither "covenant," nor "law" (Sinai), nor "gospel," but relation to Abraham (the two wives) — particularly descent from Abraham (the two sons). That was the category which the other (Jewish-Christian) missionaries had evidently introduced to the Galatians,[23] with the

---

22. Quite probably the close link between covenant and circumcision made "covenant" too dangerous a category for Paul, too connected with a "covenant *of circumcision*" mindset. By contrast, "promise" evoked no such overtones.

23. C. K. Barrett, "The Allegory of Abraham, Sarah, and Hagar in the Argument of Galatians," 154-70 in *Essays on Paul* (London: SPCK, 1982); Martyn, *Galatians,* 302-6.

corollary that (in their view) the Galatians illegitimately were claiming sonship from Abraham. To be more precise, the primary category is the sonship *of Isaac,* for the promise came to effect only through him. There was no covenant made with Hagar or Ishmael (Gen 17:18-21 is quite explicit on the point); and none of the parties in the Galatian churches was interested in claiming sonship of Abraham through Ishmael.[24] The problem was that both sides were laying claim to the determinative sonship, sonship through Isaac. The theological problem which Paul's treatment leaves us is that, in responding to the other missionaries' attempts to exclude the Gentile Galatian believers from that sonship, Paul himself seems to exclude his fellow native-born Jews: the sonship of Ishmael actually means not another covenant but exclusion from the determinative covenant relationship.[25]

In short, there was really only one covenant in question: the covenant of sonship as promised to Abraham (Gen 17:19-21). What Paul describes as two covenants for the purposes of his argument are in effect two different ways of understanding the one covenant-promise of God to Abraham regarding "seed." As with the category "Jerusalem," where Paul refracts the one category of "Jerusalem" into two contrasting columns (Gal 4:25-26), so here Paul refracts the one category of covenant into the two contrasting columns.[26] "Covenant" is the common ground, not part of the argument itself. The issue is not "covenant v. X" (e.g., law), nor is it "new" covenant v. "old" covenant (despite the explicit reference to Sinai).[27] It is how the one covenant with and through Abraham is to be understood and realized.

Here again, then, we see Paul taking up a category which lay conveniently

24. Martyn, *Galatians,* 436: "Nothing is clearer in those stories than the singularity of the covenant God made with Abraham and the passing down of that covenant through Isaac and not through Ishmael. There is, thus, no Hagar covenant."

25. This surprising turn of the tables is reinforced by Paul's re-use of Sarah's harsh words in Gen 21:10, "Throw out the slave girl and her son; for the son of the slave girl will never inherit with the son of the free woman" (Gal 4:30).

26. Cf. Martyn, *Galatians,* 447-57 (= "The Covenants of Hagar and Sarah," 194-204 in *Theological Issues in the Letters of Paul* [Edinburgh: T&T Clark, 1997]).

27. Christiansen, *The Covenant in Judaism and Paul,* 243-44, *contra* the traditional exegesis in such terms as may divert the point of the "allegory" too quickly into another discussion (e.g., Hans Dieter Betz, *Galatians: A Commentary on Paul's Letter to the Churches in Galatia* [*Hermeneia;* Philadelphia: Fortress, 1979], 243-44; Longenecker, *Galatians,* 211). Cf. Grässer, who transposes Paul's context-specific polemical antithesis into an enduring theological antithesis: "Paul's theme is not the fulfilment of the Old Covenant in the New. Rather, it is that the Old Covenant is nullified in light of the New. . . . [Paul makes a] diametric contrast between Old and New Covenant" (*Der Alte Bund im Neuen,* 74, 76 [editor's translation]). Cf. H. Merklein, "Der (neue) Bund als Thema der paulinischen Theologie," *Theological Quarterly* 176 (1996): 290-308, esp. 302-3.

to hand as a means of developing the difficult argument he has to make in order to counter the more obvious claim of his opponents, that sonship to Abraham is secured through natural descent. His usage reflects the traditional Jewish emphasis both on the promises made to the patriarchs and on the covenant made at Sinai. And in the immediate context Paul was certainly concerned to prevent his readers from putting themselves "under the law" (4:21; 5:1). But the idea of covenant as such and an explicit "covenant theology" is not at the forefront of his argument. And the casualness of his usage here, cutting across his earlier usage a few paragraphs earlier as it does, simply confirms that "covenant" was not a major theological category for Paul's own theologizing.[28]

Corinthians

Somewhat curiously, the two Corinthians passages are the only ones within the Pauline corpus to use the concept of the "new covenant" (1 Cor 11:25; 2 Cor 3:6), as also the contrasting talk of "old covenant" (2 Cor 3:14). This is all the more striking since of the four major letters of the Pauline corpus, it is Galatians and Romans that are most immediately and fully concerned with what elsewhere would be described as the relation between the old covenant and the new. The fact that talk of "new covenant" is confined to the Corinthian letters may therefore be significant.

We need not spend too much time with the first reference — the words remembered as spoken by Jesus in inaugurating the Lord's Supper: "Likewise also the cup after dinner, saying, 'This cup is the new covenant in my blood. Do this, as often as you drink it, in remembrance of me'" (1 Cor 11:25). The key point of interest here is that the phrase "the new covenant" appears only in a quotation. Paul was familiar with the Lukan version of the "words of institution," in which the emphasis falls on the cup as a symbol and expression of the new covenant rather than on the blood (Luke 22:20; cf. Matt 26:28//Mark 14:24).[29] The tradition Paul knew portrayed the death of Jesus as the sacrifice (cf. Exod 24:8) that established a new covenant, or *the* new covenant (Jer 31:31), between God and the followers of the Christ, Jesus.[30]

Significantly, Paul nowhere else makes this link. He nowhere speaks of the

28. Cf. Dieter Lührmann, *Die Brief an die Galater* (Zürich: Theologischer Verlag, 1978, 2nd ed. 1988), 79; Grässer, *Der Alte Bund im Neuen*, 56, 77.

29. On the much-discussed issue of the form of the Lukan text and Scriptural echoes in it, see, e.g., J. A. Fitzmyer, *Luke* (Anchor Bible 28; New York: Doubleday, 1985), 1386-95.

30. Once again, Grässer, *Der Alte Bund im Neuen*, 119-21, questions any allusion to Jer 31:31-34 in Paul's treatment of the "new covenant."

Lord's Supper in covenant terms. That might seem a small matter since he says so little about the Lord's Supper as such (1 Cor 11:17-32). But it could have provided a point of substance and leverage in his contrast between participation in Christ and partnership with idols, between "the cup of the Lord" and "the cup of demons" (1 Cor 10:14-22). Did not the fact that the table of the Lord was a covenant meal give it an extra weight, which should have underlined the exclusiveness of the commitment to the Lord expressed by the Lord's Supper? Did the idea of "new covenant" not underline the outmoded nature of the old ways?[31] But Paul brings in the thought of "new covenant" merely as part of the tradition authorizing the meal and not as an item of his own theologizing.

The same point emerges when we think of the other passages where Paul speaks of the death of Jesus. In most cases the imagery is of sacrifice, but of sacrifice for sin, not covenant sacrifice.[32] Here again the link between Christ's death and thought of the new covenant is not one which is central to Paul's theologizing about Christ's death, itself so fundamental to his theology. Here again, in other words, we have confirmation that "covenant" was not a primary category for Paul, and even that the link between his gospel and the idea of the "new covenant" lay somewhat on the periphery of his thought.

But does the picture change with the second Corinthians reference?

> Our qualification [as ministers] is from God, who also qualified us as ministers of a new covenant (διαθήκη), not of letter but of Spirit; for the letter kills, but the Spirit makes alive. But if the ministry of death carved in letters of stone came with glory, so that the children of Israel were unable to gaze on the face of Moses, because the glory of his face was being set aside (καταργουμένην), how much more will the ministry of the Spirit be with glory. . . . For if what is being set aside (καταργούμενον) is through glory, how much more shall what remains be with glory. . . . Moses put a veil over his face to prevent the children of Israel gazing at the end of what was being set aside (καταργουμένου). But their minds were hardened. For, up to the present day the same veil remains unlifted over the reading of the old covenant, because in Christ it is set aside (καταργεῖται). (2 Cor 3:5b-8, 11-14)

Here we seem to have a clear exposition of what is usually regarded as the normal Christian covenant theology, that is, of the contrast between old covenant and new. The old covenant is evidently related to Moses and the law, the new cov-

---

31. In contrast, Paul parallels "the table of the Lord" with "Israel *according to the flesh*" eating the sacrifices of the table as "partners of the altar" (1 Cor 10:18).

32. See Dunn, *Theology of Paul*, §§9.2-3.

enant to the life-giving Spirit claimed by the first Christians. The contrast is heightened by correlating the old covenant/new covenant antithesis with the further antitheses, death/life (3:6-7) and condemnation/saving righteousness (3:9). Most striking of all is the use of καταργεῶ, a popular term with Paul, to indicate the current status (in Paul's eyes) of the old covenant. Unfortunately the force of the verb is not entirely clear. Central to its usage is the sense "make ineffective, abolish, set aside," so the implication is that in some sense the old covenant has been "made ineffective, abolished, set aside" in favor of the new (3:11, 13).[33] That is as close as Paul comes to the more emphatic language of Hebrews: "In saying 'new [covenant]' he has declared old/rendered obsolete (πεπαλαίωκεν) the first [covenant]; and what has become obsolete (παλαιούμενον) and growing old is close to disappearing" (Heb 8:13). The language certainly seems, at first glance, to support a fairly straightforward supersessionist covenant theology.

Yet the issue is more complex. For one thing, "covenant" is, once again, not the primary category. That is "ministry" — the key concept which links 2 Cor 3 to its context (4:1; cf. 2:14-17) — and the question of "sufficiency/competence" for ministry.[34] The contrast is between two kinds of ministry — that represented by Moses and that represented by Paul himself. Moreover, it is notable that the contrast between the two does not arise immediately out of the preceding discussion. Paul introduces the contrast here because those engaged in the *other* ministry, which he contrasts with his own, were making so much of Moses as precedent and norm (2:14–3:1). Quite likely, it was these other ministers who referred to the immediacy of Moses' authorization as a spokesman for God.[35]

---

33. It is noticeable that the same verb (καταργέομαι) seems to have different referents within the scope of a few verses. The first refers to the glory on Moses' face (3:7); see, e.g., M. E. Thrall's comments (2 *Corinthians*, [International Critical Commentary; Edinburgh: T&T Clark, 1994], 1: 243-44), which conclude with the relevant note: "It is essential to note that the participle of *katargeomai* here specifically refers to the radiance on Moses' face, and is to be understood within the context of what is said to have happened at Sinai. If Paul were alluding to the eventual abolition of the Mosaic covenant, the participle would have been attached to *diakonia*, not to *doxa*. Moreover, his argument in this chapter is concerned as much with the personal agents of the two covenants as with the covenants themselves in the abstract." For a critique of the RSV's inadequate rendering "fading (away)," see S. J. Hafemann, *Paul, Moses, and the History of Israel* (*Wissenschaftliche Untersuchungen zum Neuen Testament* 81; Tübingen: J. C. B. Mohr, 1995), 301-309. The same verb in 3:11 and 13 probably refers to "the entire ministry of the old covenant symbolized by Moses" (Victor Paul Furnish, 2 *Corinthians* [Anchor Bible 32A; New York: Doubleday, 1984], 205), or to "the Mosaic covenant in general" (Thrall, 2 *Corinthians*, 1: 252-53, 257). In 3:14 the same term probably refers to the veil (ibid., 264-66).

34. Διακονέω (2 Cor. 3:3); διακονία (2 Cor. 3:7, 8, 9[2x]; 4:1); διάκονος (2 Cor. 3:6). Ἱκανός (2 Cor. 2:16; 3:5); ἱκανότης (3:5); ἱκανόω (3:6).

35. As is alluded in 2:17 and 3:1. Note the parallels: "not as so many" (2:17), "not as some" (3:1); "not just as Moses" (3:13). Presumably they documented their claims by referring to the ac-

This conclusion suggests why Paul introduced talk of "covenant" and of the contrast between two covenants. The texts validating the ministry of Paul's opponents spoke of covenant (Exod 34:10, 12, 15, 27-28; 2 Cor 3:6), so Paul took up the term in refutation of their claims. The words that Moses spoke (his ministry) were "the words of the covenant" (Exod 34:28). Paul also picked up Exodus 34's identification of the Moses/Sinai covenant with "stone (λίθινος) tablets" (2 Cor 3:3; cf. Exod 34:1, 4, 28-29), which must have prompted both the contrasts which he echoes in 2 Cor 3:3 and 3:6: stone v. fleshly heart[36] and Sinai v. "new" covenant.[37] In other words, Paul introduced the talk of covenant and the contrast of new covenant/old covenant not because it was a primary feature of his own theology and gospel, but because it was a way of countering a glorification of Moses' ministry in denigration of his own.

Indeed, the contrast between the two covenants is not so sharp as might first appear.[38] First of all, Paul acknowledges the claim (presumably made by the other ministers) that Moses' ministry was one of "glory" (2 Cor 3:7-11), and counters that this glory is now being set aside.[39] But then he goes on to treat Moses' going into the presence of the Lord (Exod 34:34) as a type of Christian conversion (2 Cor 3:16);[40] the unveiled face of Moses reflecting the glory of the Lord can still serve as the archetype of believers being transformed into the same image from glory to glory (2 Cor 3:18).

Secondly, Paul betrays some ambivalence in regard to what is being or has been "set aside."[41] This should be a warning to us that Paul has a much more nuanced view than is generally recognized of precisely *what* it is of the old covenant that is passé.

Thirdly, recall that the promise of the "new covenant" in Jer 31:31-34 was not of a different covenant so far as the law was concerned. On the contrary, the promise is of the law being "written on their hearts" — that is, of the more ef-

---

count of Moses coming down from Mount Sinai, his face all aglow "because he had been talking with God" as "he gave them in commandment all that the Lord had spoken with him on Mount Sinai" (Exod 34:29-35). Cf. particularly Dieter Georgi, *The Opponents of Paul in Second Corinthians* (Philadelphia: Fortress, 1986), ch. 3. The debate Georgi occasioned is reviewed briefly by Thrall, *2 Corinthians*, 1: 238-39, 246-48.

36. Cf. the "new spirit"/"my [God's] Spirit" of Ezek 11:19 and 36:26-27.

37. Cf. Jer 31:31-34, where God's law is inscribed in the heart. See Dunn, *Theology of Paul*, 147, with further bibliography in n. 103.

38. Dunn, *Theology of Paul*, 148-49.

39. Paul evidently read into the text the idea that the glow on Moses' face was not permanent.

40. See Dunn, *Theology of Paul*, 326, n. 40; 421-22.

41. He variously refers to the glory, the Mosaic covenant in general, and the veil covering the face of those who belong to the old covenant.

fective keeping of the law.[42] Here is no simple contrast between gospel and law, nor Spirit and law.[43]

This ties in, fourthly, with a recognition that the word "law" is never used in the passage. What Paul places on the passé side of the antithesis is "letter" (γράμμα). But γράμμα is not simply a synonym for "law" (νόμος). Γράμμα focuses rather on the law as written, visible to sight in the written letter. Paul seems to connect this with Israel's inability to understand Moses properly. Israel failed to grasp the temporary nature of the Mosaic epoch, and therefore of the ministry represented by Moses and regarded as still valid by the other ministers (3:15-16).[44] Presumably it is this shortfall in understanding which gave the "letter" its deadly character, in contrast to the writing of the Spirit in the human heart (3:3, 6-7).[45] Γράμμα, in other words, is the law, the Torah, misunderstood as to scope and continuing relevance. The "old covenant" here is not the law itself, but γράμμα, the law misunderstood. The "new covenant," in contrast, is the law in its divine intention; the law written in the heart, as Jeremiah promised; the Spirit operating in the fleshly heart, as Ezekiel predicted.[46]

In short, Paul's talk of covenant is not central to his theologizing, nor a point of distinction within Second Temple Judaism.[47] Any conclusion that

---

42. Deut 10:16; Jer 4:4; 9:25-26; Ezek 44:9; *1Q Pesher Habbakuk* [*1QpHab*] 11.13; *Rule of the Community* [*1QS*] 5.5; *Thanksgiving Hymns* [*1QH*] 10[= 2].18-19; 21[= 18].20; Philo, *Spec. Leg.* 1.305.

43. Cf. the Qumran community, which regarded itself as having already entered into "the new covenant" (*Cairo Geniza Damascus Document* [*CD*] 6.19; 8.21; 19.33-34; 20.12) and its more rigorous *halakha* as given by the Spirit (*1QH* 20[= 12].11-12). It is precisely because Jer 31:31-34 does *not* set new covenant and law in antithesis that Grässer doubts the allusion to Jeremiah's "new covenant" (*Der Alte Bund im Neuen,* 81). J. Murphy-O'Connor ("A Ministry Beyond the Letter [2 Cor 3:1-6]," 105-29 in *Paolo Ministro del Nuovo Testamento (2 Cor 2:14–4:6)* [ed. L. De Lorenzi; Roma: Abbazia di S. Paolo, 1987], 116-17) can even argue that "Paul is not making a distinction between the Old and New Covenant, but between *two types of New Covenant,* one that he perceives as being characterized by Letter and the other by Spirit" [emphasis added].

44. See Dunn, *Theology of Paul,* §6.4-5.

45. If there is no life for the law to regulate, then its primary function becomes one of condemnation (ibid., §§6.3 and 6.6).

46. Cf. Merklein, "Der (neue) Bund," 294; Christiansen, *The Covenant in Judaism and Paul,* 253-59, who argues that "'new' is that which brings the potential of the 'old' into existence by adding a new Christological and Pneumatological dimension" (259); Hafemann, *Paul,* 156-73, who argues that "the letter/Spirit contrast is between *the Law itself without the Spirit* . . . and *the Law with the Spirit*" (171; his emphasis). See also S. J. Hafemann, "The 'Temple of the Spirit' as the Inaugural Fulfilment of the New Covenant within the Corinthian Correspondence," *Ex Auditu* 12 (1996): 29-42; here 32-33, 36-39. In contrast, Grässer (*Der Alte Bund im Neuen,* 84, 95), in simply identifying the point here with that of Gal 4:21-31, misses the nuances which distinguish the two passages.

47. *Contra* Hafemann, "Temple of the Spirit," 34.

2 Cor 3 implies a strong gospel v. law antithesis in Paul's theology is at best premature and probably misconceived.

Romans

And so we reach the last of the "covenant" references in the undisputed Pauline letters, Rom 9:4-5 and Rom 11:25-27.[48] How do these two passages fit with our findings so far? What light do our findings shed upon the covenant references in what was undoubtedly Paul's most elaborate and carefully developed statement of his theology?

In regard to Rom 9:4-5, two features immediately catch the eye.[49] One is the plural usage, "covenants." Does this mean that Paul had in view the sequence of covenants mentioned at the beginning — with Abraham (Gen 15, 17), with Israel at Mount Sinai (Exod 19:5-6), in the plains of Moab (Deut 29-31), and at Mounts Ebal and Gerizim (Josh 8:30-35), with Phinehas (Num 25:12-13; Sir 45:24; 1 Macc 2:54), and with David (2 Sam 23:5; Jer 33:21)?[50] More likely, the thought was of the covenants with the fathers — the covenant as first given to Abraham and then renewed with Isaac and Jacob.[51] Another possibility, not least in view of the two passages from Corinthians, is that he was referring to the two covenants, old and new, since the latter as well as the former had been given to Israel.

The second feature to catch the eye is precisely this fact, that this reference to "covenants" appears in a list of the blessings given to Israel. At the same time, it is evident that the blessings listed are those into which believers in Jesus Messiah, Gentiles as well as Jews, had been entering. This was implicit from the first

---

48. The only other reference in the Pauline corpus is Eph 2:12, whose plural ("the covenants of promise") provides an immediate comparison with Rom 9:4. It is noteworthy that there too "covenant" describes Jewish privilege and is not developed as a specific theme of Ephesians.

49. "Inasmuch as they are Israelites: theirs are the adoption, the glory and the covenants, the law, the service and the promises; theirs are the fathers and from them came the Christ insofar as the flesh is concerned" (Rom 9:4-5).

50. C. E. B. Cranfield, *Romans* (2 vols.; *International Critical Commentary;* Edinburgh: T&T Clark, 1979), 2: 462; D. J. Moo, *Romans* (*New International Commentary on the New Testament;* Grand Rapids, Mich.: Eerdmans, 1996), 563. See also J. A. Fitzmyer, *Romans* (*Anchor Bible* 33; New York: Doubleday, 1993), 546. Christiansen, *The Covenant in Judaism and Paul,* 220-25, argues vigorously for the reading διαθήκη (singular).

51. Deut 4:31; 7:12; Wis 18:22 (plural); 2 Macc 8:15 (plural); *Psalms of Solomon* 9.10; *CD* 6.2; 8.18; *War Scroll* [*1QM*] 13.7; 14.8; *Testament of Moses* 4.5; Ps-Philo 10.2 (plural); 13.10 (plural); 19.2.

in Paul's letter to Rome, in the designation of Gentile believers as "beloved of God, called as saints" (Rom 1:7) This implication is reinforced in 8:27-33 where we find the Galatians called "saints," "those who love God," "the called," "first-born," "God's elect" — all terms drawn from traditional epithets for Israel.[52] And the inclusion in the list of 9:4 of key words like "adoption," "glory," and "promise," so important in the preceding argument,[53] reinforces the point still more. These blessings are *Israel's* blessings in which Gentile believers have been given part. They have not been transferred from Israel to some other body, nor have Gentiles been given a share in them at Israel's expense.

The same applies in the case of the "covenants" of 9:4. The covenants in view here are Israel's, and continue to be Israel's.[54] Gentile believers have been given a share in Israel's covenant blessings.[55] There is no thought that Gentile believers have superseded Israel, that Israel has forfeited these covenants, or that a new covenant excludes Israel. For Gentile believers to have received a share in the covenants means that they have been given to share in Israel. The observation ties in to a further point which is often mistaken: that Rom 9–11 are not about Israel and another entity, the church; the sole entity in view is Israel itself, the definition of Israel and membership of Israel, who and how the branches of the olive tree of Israel (11:17-24) are constituted.[56]

This finding confirms our earlier hesitation about speaking of a covenant theology as something which distinguished Paul's theology from that of his Jewish contemporaries, or which marked it as distinctively Christian. On the contrary, it is precisely as a Jew — or, to be more exact, as an Israelite (11:1) — that Paul speaks here. And as such he affirms the continuing blessings of Israel, including not least the covenant(s) from which believers now benefit. Israel held primacy in the covenant, and the covenant blessings continue to belong to Israel. Here is a "covenant theology" indeed, but one at some remove from the traditional, Christian supersessionist theology.

The last of our Romans passages, Rom 11:25-27, is in some ways the most distinctive of all Paul's covenant references.[57] For one thing, it is the only "cove-

---

52. Dunn, *Romans,* 19-20, 481-82, 485, and 502.

53. "Adoption" (8:15, 23; 9:4); "glory" (5:2; 8:18, 21); "promise" (4:13-14, 16, 20).

54. Paul uses the correlative concept of "election" almost exclusively in Rom 9–11 (ἐκλογή — 9:11; 11:5, 7, 28); elsewhere only 1 Thess 1:4; though note also ἐκλεκτός (Rom 8:33; 16:13; Col. 3:12); ἐκλέγομαι (1 Cor. 1:27-28).

55. Paul does not attempt to distance talk of "covenants" from "the giving of the law," the very next item in the list of 9:4, nor does he attempt to deny the law's continuing relevance for Gentile believers.

56. See further Dunn, *Theology of Paul,* §19, esp. §19.2.

57. "I do not want you to be unaware, brothers, of this mystery, lest you be wise in your

nant" reference in Paul which appears in and as a Scriptural citation.[58] More to the point, it seems to envisage an *ad hoc* covenant, "covenant" as a way of speaking about God's proposed dealings with his people, and not any of the specific covenants normally designated as such.[59] On closer inspection, however, it becomes evident that the covenant language on which Paul draws here (Isa 59:20-21) itself presupposes the more familiar covenant imagery.[60] Isaiah 59:21 speaks of teaching handed on to children and children's children, which naturally recalls the exhortation attached to the Sinai covenant (Deut 4:9-10; 6:6-7). The variation which Paul incorporates into the final line of his quotation ("when I take away their sins"),[61] probably is intended to echo Jer 31:34 ("I will forgive their iniquity and remember their sin no more").

Two important points emerge from these observations. First, all the elements just mentioned are intended to ensure effective keeping of the covenant — by careful instruction, by the law written on the heart, by the new spirit within. Second, the promise of the new covenant explicit in the allusion to Jer 31:31-34 is that the law written on the heart will be a more effective way of keeping the law, a more effective way of fulfilling the covenant obligation.[62] In other words, the covenant envisaged in Isa 59:21 is a variation of the new covenant of Jer 31:33, and both are better described as renewals of the Sinai covenant or indeed as the promise of a more effective implementation of the earlier covenant by divine initiative.[63]

More important still, the promise is explicitly to Israel: its fulfilment is what will constitute the eschatological salvation of "all Israel" (Rom 11:26). The inference drawn from Rom 9:4 is thus confirmed: the covenant in view is still Israel's. Israel's promised salvation is not to be brought about by a

---

own estimation, that a hardening in part has come over Israel, until the full number of the Gentiles has come in; and so all Israel shall be saved, as it is written: 'Out of Zion will come the deliverer; he will turn away ungodliness from Jacob. And this will be my covenant with them, when I take away their sins'" (Rom 11:25-27).

58. Grässer, *Der Alte Bund im Neuen*, 22.

59. But such a usage was familiar enough in the Old Testament, particularly in Second and Third Isaiah (Isa 42:6; 49:8; 55:3; 59:21; 61:8).

60. And it may be no coincidence that Isa 59:21 refers to "My spirit that is upon you," which sounds very like the equivalent promise of Ezek 36:27 ("I will put my spirit within you").

61. The last line of the quotation seems to be drawn from or modeled on Isa 27:9 — thus the consensus (see Dunn, *Romans*, 682-84).

62. Similarly Ezek 36:27 ("I will put my spirit within you and make you careful to observe my ordinances").

63. D. Zeller, *Der Brief an die Römer* (*Regensburger Neues Testament*; Regensburg: Pustet, 1985), 199, notes the association of forgiveness of sins and covenant renewal in *Jubilees* 22.14-15; *Psalms of Solomon* 18.5; and Qumran. See also Moo, *Romans*, 729.

switch to a covenant other than that already given to them and reaffirmed to them.[64]

This obvious conclusion has posed such a puzzle to traditional Christian covenant theology that many have been encouraged to resolve the puzzle by splitting Paul's covenant theology into two covenants: a covenant with Israel which endures, and the new covenant which is Christianity's means of salvation; Israel will be saved in terms of its own covenant, whereas Christians will be saved by gospel grace through faith.[65] But that cannot be right. It would run counter to Paul's universal assumption elsewhere that the gospel is the eschatological unfolding of the saving righteousness of God, not least in the thematic statement of Romans itself (Rom 1:16-17). In Paul's perspective the "redeemer out of Zion" could hardly be other than Christ.[66] Which is also to say that the effective covenant in view in Isa 59:21 can hardly be different from the "new covenant" of 1 Cor 11:25 and 2 Cor 3:6. In other words, it is the same covenant which is in view — not two covenants, not a Jewish covenant different from a Christian covenant, but one and the same. The covenant in terms of which relationship with God is established for Christians is the covenant given to Israel, whose more effective implementation was anticipated by Jeremiah and Ezekiel.[67]

A striking feature thus emerges from this most Pauline of Paul's letters: that Paul does not speak of the covenant in Rom 1–8, but only in Rom 9–11; that the only two covenant references in Romans are to the covenant(s) with Israel; that Paul uses the concept of covenant in Romans only when talking about his own people. Which is also further confirmation that Paul does not make use of covenant terminology as a major building block of his own theology as apostle to the Gentiles.[68] Or to be more precise, he does not use covenant language except to reinforce what was evidently an important claim for him, that Gentiles who believe in Jesus Christ are accepted by God on no other terms than the covenant with the fathers, the promise of Isaac and the call of Jacob (Rom. 9:7-12).

---

64. Cf. Merklein, "Der (neue) Bund," 306; Christiansen, *The Covenant in Judaism and Paul*, 226-27. Grässer, *Der Alte Bund im Neuen*, 18-19, disputes the link/equation between the covenant of 9:4 and that of 11:27, despite recognizing that 9:4 could include a reference to Jer 31:31, 33.

65. See Dunn, *Romans*, 683; idem, *Theology of Paul*, 528, n. 138.

66. Despite the suggestion of some that "the deliverer" in view was Yahweh (e.g., C. D. Stanley, "'The Redeemer Will Come *ek Sion*.' Romans 11:26-27," 118-42 in *Paul and the Scriptures of Israel* (ed. C. A. Evans & J. A. Sanders; *Journal for the Study of the New Testament Supplement* 83; Sheffield: JSOT Press, 1993), 137-38.

67. Once again in dispute with Grässer, *Der Alte Bund im Neuen*, 24-25.

68. Covenant is not a category of changed identity (Christiansen, *The Covenant in Judaism and Paul*, 232).

What May We Say in Conclusion?
Does Paul Have a Covenant Theology?

Paul's use of the term "covenant" is surprisingly casual when we consider the weight of significance subsequent theology invested in it. He drew it in because it provided a word-play in Gal 3, and in Gal 4 because a view of Abraham's sonship was being argued which ran counter to his gospel. In the Corinthian correspondence he twice speaks of the "new covenant": in the one case because it was given to him in the tradition of the Last Supper, but without making any more of it on his own account; and in the other case probably to counter a reading of Moses' ministry which was being used to diminish his own. Finally in Romans he used the term twice, both references within his exposition of Israel, but never in the earlier exposition of his gospel. In other words, the covenant theme was not a central or major category within his own theologizing.

In every case the reference is determined by Israel's Scriptures and focuses on a central aspect of Israel's self-identity and hope: the promise to Abraham of seed; the new covenant promise of Jeremiah, that is, the promise of a more effective implementation of Israel's covenant; the covenants of and with Israel, including the promised covenant of eschatological salvation. It is important to appreciate that Paul's talk of covenant is restricted within these themes. He did not use it to develop a theology of a different covenant for Christians. Even his talk of "new covenant" is much more nuanced than is usually recognized. And in his single most important letter, Romans, the only covenant in view is that with Israel. The consequences for Israel's identity within Paul's theology are of exceeding importance, and the consequences for Christian identity as essentially sharing in Israel's identity are still more profound.

If, then, we are to speak of Paul's "covenant theology," it must be not just in terms of Paul taking over the categories of Israel's covenant and applying them to Christians, but in terms of Paul affirming Israel's covenant, and doing so in terms which Israel could recognize. It must be in terms of believers, Jews first but also Gentiles, being given share in the covenant relationship of God with Israel. Where that heritage was disputed, as its terms certainly were between Paul and other missionaries, it was a dispute within that heritage, not dissimilar in terms and claims to the dispute between the Qumran new covenanters and the rest of Israel. The dispute was not over the fact of the covenant, nor that it was Israel's covenant, nor that it was open to Gentiles. The dispute was rather over its terms and timing, of how sonship to Abraham was determined and sustained, of how Moses functioned as a paradigm of ministry, and of how its eschatological promise would be implemented. Paul's covenant theology is an in-house contribution to Israel's understanding of itself as God's covenant people.

Paul's "Dying Formula": Prolegomena to an Understanding of Its Import and Significance

Jeffrey B. Gibson

As is well known, the particular Pauline rhetorical "topic" *(topos)* which Martin Hengel has labeled Paul's "dying formula" — namely, a confession or declaration which involves the use of a form or a variant of the stereotyped expression "X died/gave himself for Y" and which conveys the idea that the death of X is salvific for Y — appears frequently within Paul's writings.[1] We find it at 1 Thess 5:9-10; Gal 2:21; 1 Cor 8:11; 1 Cor 15:3; Rom 5:6, 8; Rom 14:9; and twice in 2 Cor 5:15. Indeed, given this frequency, there is good reason to say that the "dying formula," applied to Jesus, is the most important of all the confessional formulae in the Pauline Epistles, if not within Paul's theology itself.[2]

But it should be noted that the formula was not one peculiar to Paul, let alone something that originated with him. More significantly, *it was not an expression which would have been new to Paul's audiences.* Instances of the use of the expression "X died/gave himself for Y" — and/or the propounding and explication of the theme embodied within it — appear not only in non-Pauline New Testament letters,[3] but also numerous times in secular works written long

---

1. Martin Hengel, *The Atonement: The Origins of the Doctrine in the New Testament* (London: SCM Press, 1981), 36.

2. So Hengel: "[W]ith the best will in the world one cannot claim that statements about the vicarious death of Jesus 'for us' play only a minor role in the letters of Paul. . . . Along with the resurrection formula Θεὸς ἤγειρεν τὸν Ἰησοῦν ἐκ νεκρῶν, the ['dying formula'] is . . . the most important confessional statement in the Pauline Epistles . . ." (*Atonement,* 34, 37).

3. E.g., Jn 11:50-51; 1 Pet 3:18.

before Paul — works such as the *Iliad* of Homer, the elegies of Callinus and Tyrtaeus, the speeches of Isocrates, the tragedies of Euripides, and then again with some frequency up through Paul's time in a variety of compositions that stem from a gamut of writers which includes statesmen and orators, moralists and biographers, historians, mythographers, rhetoricians, playwrights, satirists, and ethnographers.[4] Indeed, in the Pauline era alone secular examples of the use of or the appeal to versions of the "dying formula" are to be found well over thirty-five times within the works of such writers as Philo, Plutarch, Josephus, Epictetus, Dionysius of Halicarnassus, Cassius Dio, Polyaenus, and Pseudo-Apollodorus, not to mention that of the Scholiasts and the anonymous commentators on (especially Aristotelian) philosophical works, let alone of Roman writers like Horace, Seneca, Caesar, Tacitus, and especially Cicero for whom the question *"Honestum sit pro patria mori?"* was a rhetorical exercise.[5] In short, the "dying formula" (a) had been used in the Greco-Roman world long before Paul's time,[6] and (b) had been taken up sufficiently widely and often enough *by and through Paul's time so as to be something already quite well known to those to whom Paul wrote*. The question then arises: *What is Paul up to when he uses it?*

A Way In

To determine this, it first will be necessary to establish what purpose the formula had in its extra-canonical uses. And the best way of doing this is — after noting all the secular instances in which the formula or its explication occurs — is to analyze the various extra-canonical instances of the use of the formula and/or the propounding of the idea embodied within it:

1. Who is the subject of the "dying formula" — that is to say, who is it who is noted as having died?
2. Who is the object of the formula — that is, *for whom* do those who die undergo death?
3. Toward what end do those who die do so?
4. With what result?

4. See below for a listing of these instances as well as the methodology I employed in finding them.

5. On this, see Hengel, *The Atonement*, 12, who cites Cicero, *Topica* 22.84.

6. Albeit applied to figures other than Jesus.

5. For those whose death is commemorated in the "dying formula," in what activity were they engaged when they died?
6. When or in what context was the expression "X died/gave him/herself for Y" typically employed? and
7. With what intended purpose or effect?

Secular Greek Instances of the "Dying Formula"

To find examples of the "dying formula" which parallel the wording and/or thematic substance of Paul's claims regarding the vicarious nature of Jesus Christ's death, I searched the corpus of Greek literature available on the *Thesaurus Linguae Graecae* "D" disk using as my search terms the various forms of the vocabulary Paul himself employs — that is, forms both of (a) the phrases (ἀπο)θνῄσκειν ὑπέρ/περί/πρό/ἀντί and (ἐπι)δίδωναι (ἑαυτὸν) ὑπέρ/περί/πρό/ἀντί and (b) the verb ὑπεραποθνῃσκειν.[7] Excluding the two examples of the "dying formula" in the *Anonymi in Aristotelis Artem Rhetoricam Commentarium* (18.12, 45.34) and those in the *Scholia*[8] (which may post-date Paul), I found that equivalents to Paul's "dying formula" occur well over one hundred times in Greco-Roman literature.[9]

7. I set my word limits in my search, i.e., the number of words between the basic elements of the phrases searched for, to five. So, for instance, in searching for occurrences of the expression ἀπέθανεν ὑπέρ, I set my search engine to find not only all instances of the exact phrase, but also examples in which ὑπέρ and ἀπέθανεν were separated by up to six Greek words. No attempt was made to search the epigraphical and papyrological data outside of that which appears in the *TLG* D Disk, let alone the corpus of Latin literary works or the Latin inscriptional evidence (e.g., the *Epigrammata sepulcralia*).

8. I.e., *Scholia in Aeschinem* 2.8.2; *Scholia in Aeschylum Th.* 17, *Th.* 17b, *Th.* 17.5, *Th.* 477-479; *Scholia in Euripidem* sch *Alc.* 648, *Alc.* 717, *Alc.* 724, *Ph.* 902, *Ph.* 940.2; *Scholia in Homerum, Scholia in Iliadem* 22.71-3.7; and *Scholia in Platonem Lg.* 865b.6.

9. At least once in Homer (*Iliad* 15.495-498; cf. 12.242-245), twice in Tyrtaeus (*fr.* 10.1-2, *fr.* 12.22-34), once in Callinus (*fr.* 1.5-20), eight times in Isocrates (*To Philip* 135; cf. 55; *Against Lochites* 20; *Archidamus* 93-94, 107; *Panegyrics* 75, 77, 83, 94-95; cf. 62; *Panathenicus* 185-186), at least twenty-seven times in Euripides (*Alcestis* 18, 175, 280-300, 434 [cf. 472], 524, 620, 645-652, 682, 690, 698-705, 710, 1002; *Helen* 750; *Heraclidae* 500-510, 532, 545, 550; *Hercules* 578-582; *The Phoenician Women* 914, 969, 997-1018, 1054-1055, 1090; *The Trojan Women* 386-387; *Erectheus* Fr. 79.38-39; 360.32-42; *Phrixis* Fr. 1-2+4.18; *Iphigenia at Aulis* 1543-1560), at least once in the various epitaphs written by Simonides (*Lyrica Graeca* 14. 129; cf. 14.127, 129, 130); once in Pindar (*Fragment* Dith. 78), once in Xenophon (*On Hunting* 1.14), at least three times in Plato (*The Symposium* 179.b; 208.d; cf. 207.b; *Menexenus* 237a; cf. 243b, 246a); four times in Lysias (*Funeral Oration* 68; *Against Eratosthenes* 78; *On the Confiscation of the Property of the Brother of Nicias* 68-69; *Fragment* 345.4 [*Against Theozotides*]), twice in Isaeus (*On the Estate of Dicaeogenes* 42, 46), four times in Demosthenes (*Against Leptines* 82; *Funeral Speech* 29; *On the Crown* 289; cf. 204-205; *Against*

1. Who is the subject of the "dying formula"?

The list is extensive. It includes the Trojans who braved the Achean siege in the age of heroes,[10] the common but valiant citizens of Athens,[11] their forefathers,[12] the friend,[13] the spouse,[14] the lover,[15] the Maccabean martyr Eleazar and the seven stalwart brothers tortured to death by Antiochus Epiphanes,[16] and even the plebians of Rome during the time of Gnaeus Marcius Coriolanus.[17] But more often than not it is either (a) a legendary warrior or stalwart campaigner;[18] (b) heroes of desperate campaigns against the enemies of Hellas;[19] (c) heroic

---

Aristogiton II.23), six times in Lycurgus (*Against Leocrates* 47-50, 82, 86, 88, 103-104, 107); three times in Hyperides (*Demosthenes* frg. 7.30; *Funeral Oration* 24-25, 35), twice in Aristotle (*Nichomachean Ethics* 1169a.19; 1169a.25), once in an epitaph written by Mnasaclas of Sicyon (*Greek Anthology* 7.242), twice in Polybius (*Histories* 6.24.9; 15.10); twice in Dionysius Halicarnassus (*Antiquities of Rome* 11.57.2; *Rh.* 6:4), twice in Diodorus of Sicily (8.12.8; 21.6.2 [cf. 15.52.4]); three times in Philo (*On Husbandry* 156.3; *Abraham* 179; *The Special Laws* 4.15; cf. *On the Change of Names* 40), at least eleven times in Plutarch (*Corialanus* 6:1-2; *Aristides* 21.4; *Cato Minor* 5.2; *Otho* 15.4; *Brutus* 40.8-9; *Phocion* 17.3; *Pericles* 8.6; *Tiberius Gracchus* 9.5; *Sayings of the Spartans* 219.B, 222.A, 225.A, 238A; *On the Fame of the Athenians* 349.7), twice in 1 Macc (1:50; 6:44), twice in 2 Macc (7:37; 8:21); at least five times in 4 Macc (6:22, 27, 30; 11:14; 13:9), five times in Josephus (*Antiquities* 12.281, *Antiquities* 13.1, 6, 198-199; *Ap* 2.218-219), twice in Epictetus (*Diatribai* 2.7.3; 4.1.154), three times in Cassius Dio (14.57.4; 53.8.3; 53.9.4), once in Polyaenus (*Excerpta* 14.8), once in Pseudo-Apollodorus (*Library* 1.106), once in Lucian (*Cont.* 10.17 [cf. *My Native Land* 12]); once in Hermogenes Tarsensis (*Progymnasmata* 7.44), once in (Pseudo) Aelius Aristides (*Panathenaic Oration* 132 [191D, 87]), once in Pausanius (*Description of Greece* 9.17.1), and several times in various inscriptions on Greek sepulchers (*Epigrammata sepulcralia* 19, 20, 406; *Greek Anthology* 7.245). The list of occurrences of the formula in 4 Maccabees would be extended if we took into account the instances of the use of ἀποθνῄσκειν with the preposition διά. Cf., e.g., 4 Macc 6:30; 9:5.

    10. Euripides, *Trojan Women* 386-387.

    11. Isocrates, *Philip* 135; *Against Lochites* 20; *Arch.* 107; Pindar, *Fragment* 78; Plutarch, *Pericles* 8.6. Cf. also the *Epitaphios* attributed to Pericles by Thucydides (2.34-46) and the Funeral Speeches of Demosthenes (on Athenians who were killed at Chaeronea), Lysias (on those who fell in the Corinthian War), and Hyperides (on the Athenian heroes of the Lamian War).

    12. Isocrates, *Archidamus* 94.

    13. Cf. Aristotle, *Nicomachean Ethics* 1169a; Epictetus, *Diatribai* 2.7.3.

    14. I.e., Euripides, *Alcestis, passim.*

    15. See Plato, *Symposium* 179.b.

    16. 4 Maccabees, *passim.*

    17. Cf. Plutarch, *Coriolanus* 6:1-2.

    18. E.g., Achilles (Xenophon, *On Hunting* 1.14); Horatius, Mucius, Curtius, Regulus and the Decii (Dio Cassius, *History* 53.3; Diodorus of Sicily 21.6.2); Otho (Plutarch, *Otho* 15.4); Judas Maccabeus, his brother Jonathan, and their followers (Josephus, *Antiquities* 13.5-6; 2 Macc 4:6); the Spartans Hippodamas, Leonidas, and Astycradius (Plutarch, *Sayings of the Spartans* 222, 225.4, 219b).

    19. E.g., defenders of Platea (*Greek Anthology* [Mnascales] 7.242; *Lyra Graeca* [Simonides] 126; 130; cf. 127; 129), Thermopylae (*Lyra Graeca* [Simonides] 121), and other Greek *poleis* (Pindar, *Fragment* 78; *Lyra Graeca* [Simonides] 135; Isocrates, *Panegyricus* 75; Plutarch, *Aristides* 21).

kings and nobles of old;[20] or (d) the members of these worthies' or other nobles' households.[21]

2. Who or what is the object of the formula?

These people died for such expected objects of affection as a lover, friend, spouse, and heirs, as well as certain higher principles such as "piety" and "the laws" of the ancestors.[22] But in the overwhelming number of extra-canonical instances of the use of the "dying formula," those who died gave up their lives either for their *polis* and all that was sacred within it[23] or for their native land (πατρίς).[24] Such a death consistently is viewed as "the noblest and most resplendent of struggles,"[25] a "holy sacrifice" if not an actual duty to God.[26]

20. E.g. Cordrus (Lycurgus, *Leocrates* 86, 88); Creon (Euripides, *Phoenician Women* 969); and Tellus (Lucian, *Cont.* 10.17), of whom Herodotus notes: "His life was prosperous by our standards, and his death was most glorious: when the Athenians were fighting their neighbors in Eleusis, he came to help, routed the enemy, and died very finely. The Athenians buried him at public expense on the spot where he fell and gave him much honor" (*Histories* 1.30-31 [trans. A. D. Godley, *Loeb Classical Library* 117]).

21. E.g. Creon's son Menoeceus (Euripides, *Phoenician Women* 997-998, 1010-1012); Nestor's son Antilochus (Xenophon, *On Hunting* 1.14); Agamemnon's daughter Iphigenia (Lycurgus, *Against Leocrates* 100; Euripides, *Iphigenia at Aulis* 1543-1560); Heracles' daughter Macaria (Euripides, *Heraclidae* 528-532); the Leokorai (Demosthenes, *Funeral Speech* 29). Cf. also Diodorus 17.15.2; Aelius Aristides, *Panathenaic Oration* 132 [191D, 87]); the daughters of Antipoenus, ruler of Thebes (Pausanius 9.7.1); and the daughter of Erectheus of Athens (Aelius Aristides, *Panathenaic Oration* 132 [191D, 87]; Euripides, *The Erectheoi* as quoted in Lycurgus, *Against Lochites* 88; cf. Demosthenes, *Funeral Oration* 28).

22. E.g., for the lover: Plato, *Symposium* 179; friend: Aristotle, *Nicomachean Ethics* 1169a, line 19; 1169a, line 25; Epictetus, *Diatribai* 2.7.3; 4.1.154; spouse: Euripides, *Alcestis, passim*; cf. Ps. Apollodorus, *Library* 1.106; heirs: Philo, *On Husbandry* 156; piety: Philo, *Abraham* 179; 4 Macc 6:22; 9:29; cf. 9:23-24; ancestral laws: Josephus, *Antiquities* 15.288; 4 Macc 6:27, cf. 6:30; 11:14-15, cf. 11:12; 13:9.

23. Plutarch, *Sayings of the Spartans* 222; 219b; e.g., the sacred shrines of the *polis* or the ancestral graves (Plutarch, *On the Fame of the Athenians* 349.7 [C]).

24. Philo, *Abraham* 179; *Greek Anthology* 7.2.42; Plutarch, *Otho* 15.4; *Sayings of the Spartans* 225.4; *On the Fame of the Athenians,* 349.7 (C).

25. Homer, *Iliad* 15.495-498; Callinus fr. 1.5-7; Tyrtaeus fr. 10, 12; Lycurgus, *Against Leocrates* 49; Plutarch, *Aristides* 21. Indeed, the measure of how resplendent "dying for one's *polis* or *patris*" was thought to be is indicated in its frequently being categorized as "the noble death" (εὐκλεῆ/καλὸν θάνατον). Cf., e.g., Alcaeus, fr. 23 (400); Plutarch, *Moralia* 192c, which has the Theban general Epaminodas declare τὸν ἐν πόλεμον θάνατον εἶναι κάλλιστον. Cf. Lysias, *Funeral Speech* 79. See also Pericles' proclamation in the *Epitaphos* over the Fallen in the early stages of the Peloponnesian War ascribed to him by Thucydides, that "they are fortunate who draw for their lot a death as glorious as that which these now have" (Thucydides 2:44.1). Compare this with Cassandra's declaration at Euripides, *Trojan Women* 386-387 that the death of the Trojans, a death for their fatherland, was the "noblest glory of all" (τὸ κάλλιστον κλέος).

26. Pindar, *Fragment* 78; Euripides, *Iphigenia at Aulis* 1397; 1553-1555; Philo, *Abraham* 179.

3. Toward what end do they die?

Apart from a few instances in which those who have died for others are said to have done so solely with the thought of what it might do for their reputation as defenders of the city (πόλις) or πατρίς,[27] otherwise they are said to have been concerned with one thing: protecting and saving from danger *that which has fostered them*. This may be one's parents or one's spouse,[28] but more often than not it is one's πόλις or one's πατρίς.[29] More importantly, *never* does the one to whom the dying formula is applied die for an adversary or an enemy.[30] The death for others, especially the "noble death," is always undertaken in an attempt to rescue or defend *one's own*.

4. What is the result of such a death?

In virtually all instances of the theme the result is not only the salvation (σωτηρία) of the person or thing for which the deceased has died but, notably, the eventual, if not immediate, defeat or destruction of the persons or the powers that have caused the death or which threatened that for which the deceased died. For example, according to Mnascales, by their deaths, those who died for their πατρίς at Thermopylae not only delivered Hellas from "the tearful yoke" that the Persians had "rested on her neck" but also paved the way for the victory of Greece over Xerxes and his forces.[31] Diodorus of Sicily (following Durus, Diodore, and Cassius Dio) notes that it was by devoting himself to death for the sake of his fellow Romans that the Roman consul Decius brought about the slaughter of one hundred thousand of Rome's enemies.[32] In *Iphigenia at Aulis*,

27. Philo, *On the Change of Names*; Dio Cassius, *History* 50.3.

28. Xenophon, *On Hunting* 1.14; Euripides, *Alcestis, passim*.

29. Euripides, *Phoenician Women*, 997-98; cf. 948. 2 Macc 7:37; 8:21; 4 Maccabees; Euripides, *Iphigenia at Aulis* 1383-87; cf. 1420; 1446; 1472-73; Lycurgus, *Against Leocrates* 49-50, 82; Plutarch, *Cato Minor* 5.2; *Otho* 15; Josephus, *Antiquities* 12.281-282; *Greek Anthology* 7.242; Pindar, *Fragment* 78.

30. There is at first glance one exception to this, found in Lysias' declaration at *Funeral Oration* 68 that in the Corinthian War (395-387 B.C.E.), Athenians "had the courage, not merely to imperil themselves for their own preservation, but also to die for their enemies' freedom." But it should be noted that here those designated as the "enemies" of Athens (i.e., Corinth, Argos, and Thebes) were actually Athens' allies against Sparta during the Corinthian War. The designation πολέμιος is used here because these city states are *former* enemies of Athens.

31. *Greek Anthology* 7.242.

32. Diodorus, 21.6.2. Cf. Cassius Dio, *Roman History* 53.3. Cf. Philo, *Abraham* 179: "They say that many other persons [like Abraham], full of love for their kinsfolk and offspring, have given their children, some to be sacrificed for their country to serve as a price to redeem it from wars. . . . Indeed they say that among the Greeks men of the highest reputation, not only private individuals but kings, have with little thought of their offspring put them to death, and thereby saved armed forces of great strength and magnitude when enlisted as their allies."

Iphigenia's willingness to give her "body . . . to be sacrificed for [her] country's sake and all of Hellas-land" is what gives the Greeks "delivery victorious" over the Trojans and "saves Hellas" from the threat they represent to the freedom of her countrymen.[33] And the author of 2 Maccabees records that the deaths of the seven brothers who, during the persecutions of Antiochus Epiphanes, gave up "body and life for the laws of [their] fathers," not only brought about "an end of the wrath of the Almighty which has justly fallen on our whole nation" but accelerated the Jewish victory over Antiochus and his armies (2 Macc 7:1-45).[34]

5. What were those commemorated doing when they died?

In several instances of the use of the formula, what those who die are doing at the time of their death is offering themselves up upon an altar of a god in accordance with a divine demand for the sacrifice of a life.[35] In some others, namely, those that appear in 4 Maccabees, those who die are having to endure tortures and persecutions designed to break them of their devotion (πίστις) to that which they hold dear.[36] In another, the one who dies is carrying out a ruse that he knows will result in his being killed by those among his city's foes who were trying to avoid doing him any harm.[37] But in the majority of cases the one who dies has been plunging headlong and voluntarily into deadly and death-dealing combat, waging war against the enemy on the ramparts, in the siege, or on the open battlefield.[38] Each death is presented — and often is appealed to — not

33. Euripides, *Iphigenia at Aulis* 1553-55; cf. 1420; 1472-73; 1383-84.

34. See also 4 Macc 1:11 and 9:11; 17:2, 20-21, where the deaths of these martyrs are placarded as "the cause of the downfall of [the] tyranny [of Antiochus Epiphanes] over their nation"; these deaths "nullified the violence of the tyrant," "frustrated his evil designs," and ultimately brought God to rid the land of the enemies of Israel. See Sam K. Williams, *Jesus' Death as Saving Event: The Background and Origin of a Concept* (Missoula, Mont.: Scholars Press, 1975), 165-83.

35. I.e., Moneoceus, Iphigenia, Macaria, the Leokorai, Abdrocleia and Aleis (the daughters of Antipoenus of Thebes), and the daughters of Erectheus, respectively. See Euripides, *Phoenician Women* 1015-18; *Iphigenia at Aulis* 1379ff; *Heracleidae* 500-558; Demosthenes, *Funeral Speech* 29; Diodorus 17.15.2; Aelius Aristides, *Panathenaic Oration*, 132 [191D, 87]; Pausanius 9.7.1.

36. 2 Macc 7:1-42; 4 Maccabees *passim*.

37. Cordrus, in Lycurgus, *Against Leocrates* 85-87.

38. Actually, when we examine the context in which the stories about Menoeceus, Iphigenia, Macaria, the Leokorai, Abdrocleia and Aleis, the daughters of Erectheus, Cordrus, and the Maccabean Martyrs appear, not to mention the use to which the stories of their deaths are put, there are several reasons to say that this was presumed to be the case with these figures as well, even though they themselves were not on the battlefield or directly engaged in combat with the enemy when they gave themselves up to death. (1) Each dies when the safety or the lib-

only as an example that should be imitated by those who find themselves called upon to fight and die for *polis* or *patris* but also as an illustration that *death in battle* is a noble death. Space prevents a full listing of such cases. Let one example suffice. Leosthenes and his men, as Hyperides proclaims, "gave their lives for the freedom of the Greeks, convinced that the surest proof of their desire to guarantee the liberty of Greece was to die in battle for her."[39]

> [10] For Leosthenes perceived that the whole of Greece was humiliated and ... cowed, corrupted by men who were accepting bribes from Philip and Alexander against their native countries. He realized that our city stood in need of a commander, and Greece herself of a city, able to assume the leadership, and he gave himself to his country and the city to the Greeks, in the cause of freedom. [13] ... The circumstances subject to his will he mastered, but fate he could not overpower.[40]

6. When or in what context was the expression "X died for Y" employed?

The "dying formula" occasionally is employed when philosophers — such as Plato, Aristotle, and Epictetus — turn their attention to the nature of love or true friendship.[41] It also appears when Hellenistic historians are intent to give descriptions of such things as the motive behind a city's or an army's resolve not to surrender to a conquering foe,[42] the customs of the Spartans,[43] orders of command of the Roman army and the qualities sought in candidates for certain military offices,[44] or

---

erty or the way of life of their city or their nation is severely imperiled by an "enemy." (2) Each dies in order to ward off, if not destroy, the "enemy" and to bring salvation (σωτηρία) to their city or the nation or their homeland's way of life. (3) The manner of their death or the way they face it is shrouded in military language and imagery. E.g., Eleazar, the elderly Maccabean martyr who dies for the sake of his "religion" (ὑπὲρ εὐσέβειας) and the Law of Moses (cf. 4 Macc 6:22, 27), is compared to a city besieged by machines of war; and by his death he is said to have "conquered his besiegers with the shield of his devout reason" (4 Macc 7:4). The deaths for the "laws of their fathers" accepted by the seven brothers who expired under the tortures of Antiochus Epiphanes are labeled a "fight" (στρατεία) and are identified as part of "a sacred and noble battle" (4 Macc 9:23-24). (4) Those named above are regarded as Σωτήρ and/or Εὐεργέτης, titles given primarily to warriors who have delivered their πόλις or πατρίς from the ravages of war.

39. Hyperides, *Lycurgus* 10.

40. Hyperides, *Lycurgus* 10, 13 (trans. J. O. Burt, *Minor Attic Orators*, 2 vols.; Cambridge, Mass.: Harvard University Press; London: William Heinemann, 1962).

41. For Plato, see *Symposium* 179b. For Aristotle, see *Nicomachean Ethics* 1169a. For Epictetus, *Diatribai* 4.1.154.

42. Polybius, *Histories* 16.34.11; Plutarch, *Crassus* 29.7; *Tiberius and Caius Gracchus* 9.5 [cf. *Pelopidas* 4.5]; Appian, *Roman History (Civil Wars)* 1.48.6; Diodorus of Sicily 18.22.3.

43. Plutarch, *Customs of the Spartans (Moralia)* 238 A.14.

44. Polybius, *Histories* 6.24.9.

the complaints of the Roman plebeians in the time of Coriolanus against their treatment by the rich.[45] But in the overwhelming majority of cases, the formula is found employed either

1. Within, and as an integral part of, the celebration of the civic cult;
2. As a *topos* in *symbouleutic* speeches — speeches given in or addressed to an ἐκκλησία or council — when the issue under debate is the wisdom of going to war;
3. As a *topos* in forensic speeches given, or written to be delivered, in the law court;
4. In testamentary addresses and epitaphs;
5. In the military commander's address to his troops who either are about to go into battle or, already there, are on the brink of suffering a catastrophic defeat;
6. In the battlefield declarations of intent made by individual soldiers to their superiors or their comrades in arms; or
7. In inscriptions on public monuments and war memorials erected to commemorate and honor those "fallen" in battle.

6.1. The Formula within the Context of the Civic Cult

A notable instance of the use of the "dying formula" within the context of the civic cult and as an integral part in its celebration is Isocrates' declaration (at *Panathenaicus* 185-186) that the ancestors of the Athenians who chose "to risk their lives for their country" are "much more deserving of our praise than [the Spartans] who, while ready and willing to face death to gain the possessions of others, are yet in no wise different from hireling soldiers." The *Panathenaicus* — an encomium on the glory of Athens — was intended to be delivered at the *Panathenaea*, the great late summer civic festival at Athens in honor of its patron goddess Athena which, given the required participation of Athenian allies in the festival's core event (the procession from the Ceramicus through the agora to the acropolis), celebrated Athen's imperial power.[46] Since it was most likely composed for recitation at the Panathenaea, Pindar's *Fragment* 78 provides another instance.[47]

Also to be placed within the cultic context are most of the instances of the

45. Plutarch, *Coriolanus* 6:1-2.
46. R. C. T. Parker, "Panathenaea," in *The Oxford Classical Dictionary* (3rd ed.; Oxford: Oxford University Press, 1996), 1104.
47. "Hearken, Spirit of the War Shout, Alala, daughter of War, Thou prelude of the clashing spears, Whose beasts of sacrifice are men who die the hallowed death for their fatherland."

"dying formula" found in Euripides, who created his speeches for the Great Dionysia, a cult festival where, at some point before the tragedies performed there began, the sons of those who had fallen in battle for Athens and Hellas were paraded in front of the audience in full battle array.[48] It was for the attendees and celebrants of this civic cult that Euripides first placarded for admiration and imitation the willingness of the likes of his Macaria and Menoeceus, or of his Erectheoi and Iphigenia, to "die for the city," to give up their lives for Hellas. Indeed, these figures' willing sacrifice continued to be placarded for such audiences long after Euripides died.

The most prominent of the extant examples of the use of the dying formula within the context of the civic cult is found in Plutarch:

[21.1] After this, there was a general assembly of the Hellenes, at which Aristides proposed a decree to the effect that deputies and delegates from all Hellas convene at Plataea every year, and that every fourth year festival games of deliverance be celebrated — the Eleutheria; also that a confederate Hellenic force be levied, consisting of ten thousand shield, one thousand horse, and one hundred ships, to prosecute the war against the Barbarian; also that the Plataeans be set apart as inviolable and consecrate, that they might sacrifice to Zeus the Deliverer in behalf of Hellas.

[21.2] These propositions were ratified, and the Plataeans undertook to make funeral offerings annually for the Hellenes who had fallen in battle and lay buried there. And this they do yet unto this day, after the following manner. On the sixteenth of the month Maimacterion (which is the Boeotian Alalcomenius), they celebrate a procession. This is led forth at break of day by a trumpeter sounding the signal for battle; [21.3] wagons follow filled with myrtle-wreaths, then comes a black bull, then free-born youths carrying libations of wine and milk in jars, and pitchers of oil and myrrh (no slave may put hand to any part of that ministration, because the men thus honored died for freedom); [21.4] and following all, the chief magistrate of Plataea, who may not at other times touch iron or put on any other raiment than white, at this time is robed in a purple tunic, carries on high a water-jar from the city's archive chamber, and proceeds, sword in hand, through the midst of the city to the graves; [21.5] there he takes water from the sacred spring, washes off with his own hands the gravestones, and anoints them with myrrh; then he slaughters the bull at the funeral pyre,

---

48. R. A. S. Seaford, "Dionysia," in *The Oxford Classical Dictionary*, 476; cf. Isocrates, *On the Peace* 82; Aeschines, *Against Ctesiphon* 154.

and, with prayers to Zeus and Hermes Terrestrial, summons the brave men who died for Hellas to come to the banquet and its copious draughts of blood; next he mixes a mixer of wine, drinks, and then pours a libation from it, saying these words: "I drink to the men who died for the freedom of the Hellenes." These rites, I say, are observed by the Plataeans down to this very day.[49]

6.2. The Formula in the Assembly

Besides the civic cult as its "home," the "dying formula" also figures prominently in the political discourses addressed to the assembly — particularly assembly discourses which deal with the issue of the wisdom or necessity of committing the πόλις to war. We find it, for instance, in the deliberative address by Isocrates entitled *To Philip*, ostensibly an open letter to Philip of Macedon, but directed to the ἐκκλησία of Athens,[50] which was written to gain the support of Philip and the Athenian Assembly for a war of revenge against the Persians.

> [134] No, it is not with a view to the acquisition of wealth and power that I urge this course, but in the belief that by means of these you will win a name of surpassing greatness and glory. . . . [135] You may observe that even common citizens of the best sort, who would exchange their lives for nothing else, are willing for the sake of winning glory to lay them down in battle; and, in general, that those who crave always an honor greater than they already possess are praised by all men, while those who are insatiable with regard to any other thing under the sun are looked upon as intemperate and mean. [5.136] But more important than all that I have said is the truth that wealth and positions of power often fall into the hands of our foes, whereas the good will of our fellow countrymen and the other rewards which I have mentioned are possessions to which none can fall heir but our own children, and they alone. I could not, therefore, respect myself if I failed to advance these motives in urging you to make this expedition and wage war and brave its perils.[51]

---

49. Plutarch, *Aristeides* 21.1-4, in *Plutarch's Lives* (trans. Bernadette Perrin; Cambridge, Mass.: Harvard University Press; London: William Heinemann, 1914).

50. M. M. Markle, "Support of Athenian Intellectuals for Philip: A Study of Isocrates' *Philippus* and Speusippus' *Letters to Philip*," *Journal of Hellenic Studies* 96 (1976): 80-99, esp. 81-82.

51. Isocrates, *To Philip* 134-36 (trans. George Norlin, *Isocrates with an English Translation in Three Volumes* [Cambridge, Mass.: Harvard University Press; London: William Heinemann, 1980]).

We also find the "dying formula" twice taken up as a *topos* in the *Panegyricus*, the appeal made by Isocrates to all the assemblies of Greece, in the wake of the peace of Antalcidas, to engage in a pan-Hellenic crusade against Persia with Athens as the leader in this proposed "war of deliverance." Towards this end Isocrates reminds his hearers that:

> [T]he men who are responsible for our greatest blessings and deserve our highest praise are, I conceive, those who risked their bodies in defense of Hellas; and yet we cannot in justice fail to recall also those who lived before this war and were the ruling power in each of the two states. . . . For they did not slight the commonwealth, nor seek to profit by it as their own possession, nor yet neglect it as the concern of others . . . nor did they cultivate recklessness in themselves, but thought it a more dreadful thing to be charged with dishonor by their countrymen than to die honorably for their country (ὑπὲρ τῆς πόλεως ἀποθνήσκειν); and they blushed more for the sins of the commonwealth than men do nowadays for their own.[52]

After calling the character of the ancestors of the Athenians to mind, Isocrates asks:

> For what words can match the measure of such men, who so far surpassed the members of the expedition against Troy that, whereas the latter consumed ten years beleaguering a single city they, in a short space of time, completely defeated the forces that had been collected from all Asia, and not only saved their own countries but liberated the whole of Hellas as well? And from what deeds or hardships or dangers would they have shrunk so as to enjoy men's praise while living — these men who were so ready to lay down their lives for the sake of the glory they would have when dead (οἵ τινες ὑπὲρ τῆς δόξης ἧς ἔμελλον τελευτήσαντες ἕξειν οὕτως ἑτοίμως ἤθελον ἀποθνήσκειν)? Methinks some god out of admiration for their valor brought about this war in order that men endowed by nature with such a spirit should not be lost in obscurity nor die without renown, but should be deemed worthy of the same honors as are given to those who have sprung from the gods and are called demi-gods; for while the gods surrendered the bodies even of their own sons to the doom of nature, yet they have made immortal the memory of their valor.[53]

---

52. Isocrates, *Panegyricus* 75-77 (trans. George Norlin, ibid.).
53. Ibid., 83-84.

The ἐκκλησία focus of the "dying formula" is also to be found in Isocrates' *Archidamus*. Isocrates wrote this speech for Archidamus III, the son of the Spartan king Agesilaus, to be delivered during a congress of Sparta and its allies convened in the wake of the battle of Leuctra and subsequent Theban incursions into the Peloponnesus to debate the issue of war and peace with Thebes. The aim of the speech was not only to counter a proposal made there by the Corinthian delegation that Sparta should surrender to Thebes and accede to its peace terms, but also to exhort all gathered at the congress to vote for going to war against Thebes.[54] To do this, Archidamus first reminds the congress:

> [T]he cowardice of states is made manifest in deliberations like these no less than in the perils of war; for the greatest part of what takes place on the battle-field is due to fortune, but what is resolved upon here is a token of our very spirit. Wherefore we should strive for success in the measures to be adopted here with an emulation no less keen than we show in the lists of war. I marvel at those who are willing to die for their personal glory (ὑπὲρ μὲν τῆς ἰδίας δόξης ἀποθνήσκειν) but have not the same feeling for the glory of the state, for which we may well suffer anything whatsoever to avoid bringing shame upon our city, nor should we permit it to abandon the post in which it was established by our forefathers. It is true that many difficulties and dangers beset us; these we must avoid, but first and foremost we should be careful that we are never found doing any cowardly deed or making any unjust concessions to the foe; for it would be shameful if we, who once were thought worthy to rule the Hellenes, should be seen carrying out their commands, and should fall so far below our forefathers that, while they were willing to die in order that they might dictate to others, we would not dare to hazard a battle in order that we might prevent others from dictating to us.[55]

He goes on to note that they must not

> forget that the attention of the whole world is fixed upon this assembly and on the decision which you shall reach here. Let each one of you, therefore, govern his thoughts as one who is giving an account of his own character in a public theater, as it were, before the assembled Hellenes. Now it is a simple matter to reach a wise decision on this question. For if we are willing to die for our just rights (ἀποθνήσκειν ὑπὲρ τῶν δικαίων), not only shall we gain

---

54. On this, see Norlin, *Isocrates*, Vol. 1: 343-44.
55. Isocrates, *Archidamus* 93-94 (trans. George Norlin, ibid.).

renown, but in time to come we shall be able to live securely; but if we show that we are afraid of danger, we shall plunge ourselves into endless confusion. Let us, therefore, challenge one another to pay back to our fatherland the price of our nurture, and not suffer Lacedaemon to be outraged and contemned, nor cause those who are friendly to us to be cheated of their hopes, nor let it appear that we value life more highly than the esteem of all the world.[56]

Josephus tells us that the reminder that Judas Maccabeus had "died for the Jewish nation's liberty" was an integral part of the appeal made by his companions. Seeing that Israel was leaderless at a time when it was suffering a national calamity not seen by Jews since their return from exile in Babylon, Judas' companions assembled in a war council with Jonathan and began to urge him "to imitate his brother, and that care which he took of his countrymen, . . . and that he would not permit the nation to be without a governor, especially in those destructive circumstances wherein it now was," and lead them to victory over their Syrian enemies.[57]

6.3. The Formula in Forensic Rhetoric

Judging by the frequency of its usage — some ten times[58] — in speeches written for delivery in the law court by such noted Attic logographers as Isocrates, Isaeus, Demosthenes, and Lysias, the dying formula was a favorite *topos* in forensic rhetoric. It appears consistently in appeals to pity designed to play upon the patriotic sentiment of the judges or the jurors to whom the speech is addressed. For instance, in *Against Lochites* — Isocrates' plea for heavy damages against a rich young citizen (Lochites) who had struck the orator — the formula is employed in two ways. First, Isocrates likens the insolence behind the physical assault to the spirit and attitude of the oligarchs who, during the Peloponnesian war, twice overthrew the democracy (which the judges Isocrates addresses had defended). Second, he portrays the assault as something which, if left unpunished, would implicate the judges in a betrayal of the ideals for which citizens of Athens had always been ready to lay down their lives. As Isocrates notes,

56. Ibid., 106-8.

57. Josephus, *Antiquities* 13:5.

58. Isocrates, *Against Lochites* 19-21; Isaeus, *On the Estate of Dicaeogenes* 41-47; Lysias, *On the Confiscation of the Property of the Brother of Nicias*, 9-13.21-26; *Against Eratosthenes*, and *Against Theozotides*; Demosthenes, *On the Crown* 82-83; *Against Aristogiton, Against Leptines*; Lycurgus, *Against Leocrates*; Plutarch.

[I]t would be a most shocking state of affairs if in a democratic state we should not all enjoy equal rights; and if, while judging ourselves worthy of holding office, yet we deprive ourselves of our legal rights; and if in battle we should all be willing to die for our democratic form of government (ἀποθνήσκειν ὑπὲρ τῆς πολιτείας) and yet, in our votes as judges, especially favor men of property.[59]

Isaeus' speech, *On the Estate of Dicaeogenes,* is another example. This appeal was to be delivered by a nephew of the Athenian war hero Dicaeogenes II on behalf of himself and his first cousin, Cephisodotus, and their mothers. The speaker argues that their recognized claim to the hero's estate had been undermined by the illegal actions of both another of the hero's heirs, Dicaeogenes III, and Leochares, a man who had promised to stand as surety for the discharge of the testator's will. He urges that the judges regard as a sham Dicaeogenes III's appeals for sympathy on the grounds of patriotism to absolve himself of his failure to restore to these rightful heirs what he had illegally taken from the estate.[60] Isaeus has Dicaeogenes II's nephew expressly point out that, unlike their forefathers, who gave great contributions of time and money to the well-being of the city, Dicaeogenes III has never done anything of the sort. Quite contrary to his claim for acquittal, he has never proved himself a soldier, let alone a good one. He has not "served at all in the whole course of the long and critical war, during which the Olynthians and the islanders are dying fighting against the foe in the defence of our land." Moreover, the property that he inherited only to squander "wickedly and disgracefully" was that of men who "died fighting for their country (ὑπὲρ τῆς πατρίδος πολεμοῦντες ἀπέθανον)."[61]

And in the speech of Lysias entitled *On the Confiscation of the Property of the Brother of Nicias,*[62] Isocrates has the son of Eucrates argue his case primarily by pointing out that it would be "strange" for jurors whose own fathers had

59. *Against Lochites* 19-21 (trans. Norlin).

60. On the background and intent of the speech, see E. S. Forster, *Isaeus* (London: William Heinemann; New York: G. P. Putnam's Sons, 1927), 153-57. The translation of Isaeus that follows is from this volume.

61. Cf. Isaeus, *On the Estate of Dicaeogenes* 41-47.

62. A speech written for delivery by the son of the Athenian political martyr Eucrates (and also nephew of the Athenian general Nicias) which was aimed at persuading a jury constituted by citizens who had survived the terrors of the oligarchies of 404/403 B.C.E. not to accede to the demand made by a demagogue Poliochus that the son of Eucrates should be stripped of his inheritance and his patrimony for his (or his father's) alleged disloyalty to the state. On the background and intent of this speech, see S. C. Todd, *Lysias* in *The Oratory of Classical Greece* (Austin: University of Texas Press, 2000), 2:190-93.

"given their lives for the democracy"[63] to confiscate the property of someone who, in character with his ancestors and other members of his family's household, had always been devoted to Athens[64] — indeed, even saved it from those who had originally thought to bring "succor" to the oligarchs.[65] In addition, it would be a violation of the Athenian constitution for which Eucrates and his brother Nicias and others of their kinsmen "gave their lives." Isocrates has Lysias cap off his defense by an appeal to the Commissioners of Finance to "remember that time when, expelled from your native land and deprived of your property, you esteemed most highly the men who gave their lives for you (ὑπὲρ ὑμῶν ἀποθνῇσκοντας), and you prayed to the gods that you might be able to show your gratitude to their children."[66]

6.4. The Formula in Testamentary and Funeral Speeches

Under this heading can be placed not only the instances of the formula that appear in the various *Epitaphioi* of Demosthenes, Hyperides, Pericles (on those who had fallen in the Samian War),[67] and Lysias, but also the ones (a) in the deathbed address of Mattathias to his sons as reported in 1 Macc 2:50 and by Josephus;[68] (b) of the youngest of the seven Jewish brothers martyred by Antiochus for the law (2 Macc 7:1-42); and (c) in Augustus' farewell address as reported by Cassius Dio. Augustus declares that his last act of renouncing power and turning over the administration of the Roman state to the Senate is a course from which having to die a thousand deaths could not have dissuaded him, so great was his concern for the welfare of his people. In addition, his choice to become a private citizen under the circumstances in which he has arranged it will bring him renown, since he will then be one who "not only did

---

63. Lysias, *On the Confiscation of the Property of the Brother of Nicias*, 12.

64. Cf. ibid., 21.

65. Ibid., 9-13.

66. Ibid., 26.

67. See Plutarch, *Pericles* 9.6.

68. "'O my sons, I am going the way of all the earth; and I recommend to you my resolution, and beseech you not to be negligent in keeping it, but to be mindful of the desires of him who begat you, and brought you up, and to preserve the customs of your country, . . . and so to dispose your souls, as to be ready, when it shall be necessary, to die for your laws. . . . Your bodies are mortal, and subject to fate; but they receive a sort of immortality, by the remembrance of what actions they have done. And I would have you so in love with this immortality, that you may pursue after glory, and that, when you have undergone the greatest difficulties, you may not scruple, for such things, to lose your lives'" (Josephus, *Antiquities* 12.279-83; trans. Whiston).

not deprive another of his life in order to win that office, but went so far as to even give up my life to avoid being king."[69]

6.5. The Formula in the Military Commander's Address to His Beleaguered Troops

Among the instances of this use of the "dying formula" are four of note: First is that of *Aelian* 2.28 which speaks of Themistocles giving courage to the men he was leading to fight the Persians at Salamis by ordering them to note that cocks they saw fighting to the death along the way were, unlike his men, "not fighting for their country or their father's gods; they are not enduring pain to defend the tombs of their ancestors, their reputation, freedom, and children; [and yet] each of them [still] aims to avoid defeat and not yield to another."

Second, Plutarch, *Otho* 15.4, records how Otho, seeing his men remain steadfastly loyal to him even as his cause crumbled around them, exhorted himself to courage in the face of defeat. "But do not rob me of a greater blessedness — that of dying nobly in behalf of fellow citizens so many and so good. If I was worthy to be Roman emperor, I ought to give my life freely for my country."

Third, in *Polybius* 15.10, Polybius reports Scipio's address to troops on the eve of their battle with Hannibal:

> Those of you who fall will meet a death that is made for ever glorious by this sacrifice for your country. . . . And so now that Fortune has given us the choice of the most glorious of prizes according to which way the battle is decided, we should be the most mean-spirited and in a word the most witless of all mankind if we were to reject the most splendid rewards and choose the worst of misfortunes merely in order to cling to life. So when you go to meet the enemy, there are two objects only to keep before you, to conquer or to die.

And fourth, Dionysius of Halicarnassus records that "the Roman Dictator," Posthumus Albius Regellensus, on the eve of the battle of Lake Regillus, exhorted to valor the younger members of his vastly outnumbered troops by pointing out that the principal members of the Senate, who were exempt from military service by virtue of their age, had nevertheless come out to the battlefield to share the fortunes of war with them; therefore it would be shameful "if

---

69. Cassius Dio, *Roman History* 53.9.1-6.

you who are in the vigour of life should flee from what is formidable, while these who are past the military age pursue it."[70]

6.6. The Formula in Battlefield Declarations of Intent Made by Individual Soldiers to Their Superiors or Their Comrades in Arms

According to Plutarch, the formula is used in this context by Astycratidas, Hippodamus, and Leonidas. Astycratidas was a soldier in the army of Agis, King of Sparta. When asked what he and others like him would do after Agis' army suffered defeat at the hands of Antipater and thus apparently were about to find themselves subject to the Macedonians, Astycratidas replied, "What? Is there any way in which Antipater can forbid us to die fighting for Sparta?"[71] The aged Hippodamas had taken up arms on the field of battle beside King Agis. In the instant before he fell, he proclaims: "I shall meet no more honourable death than in playing the part of a brave man for Sparta's sake."[72] As the King was leading his men out to the plain of Thermopylae to confront the Persians, the Ephors of Sparta asked Leonidas if he had decided to do anything other than keep the barbarians from getting by the pass there. Leonidas' answer was that he actually was "expecting to die for the Greeks."[73]

---

70. Even worse "if the zeal of the old men, since it lacks the strength to slay any of the enemy, should at least be willing to die for the fatherland, while the vigour of you young men, who have it in your power, if successful, to save both yourselves and them to be victorious, or in case of failure, to suffer nobly while acting nobly, should neither make trial of fortune nor leave behind you the renown that valor wins" (Dionysius of Halicarnassus 6.9.2). Cf. Dio Cassius, *Roman History* 14.4.

If this is not enough to show that "the eve of the battle" was a primary context for the use of the "dying formula," consider the testimony of Lycurgus that the Spartans were taken with the ability of the elegies of Trytaeus to inspire courage in their young men — elegies which proclaim that "he who so falls among the champions and loses his sweet life, so blessing with honor his city, his father, and all his people, . . . why, such a man is lamented alike by the young and the elders, and all his city goes into mourning and grieves for his loss. . . . As a result, the men of Sparta, after taking the field, shall be summoned to the king's tent to hear the verses of Tyrtaeus all together, holding that this of all things would make them most ready to die for their country." Lycurgus, *Against Leocrates* 107 (trans. J. O. Burt, *Lycurgus; Minor Attic Orators*, 2 vols.; Cambridge, Mass.: Harvard University Press; London: William Heinemann, 1962).

71. Plutarch, *Sayings of the Spartans* 219B.

72. Ibid., 222.

73. Ibid., 225.4.

6.7. The Formula in Inscriptions on Public Monuments and War Memorials Erected to Commemorate and Honor Those "Fallen" in Battle

One fine example of the use of the formula in this context is the Epitaph written by Mnasacles of Sicyon for the Greeks who took up arms against the Persian invasion: "These men delivering their country from the tearful yoke that rested on her neck, clothed themselves in the dark dust. High praise win they by their valor, and let each citizen looking on them dare to die for his country."[74]

Similarly, on monuments to the Spartan and Athenian heros of Platea we find the following from the hand of the poet Simonides: "If the greatest part of virtue is to die well, that hath Fortune given, of all men, unto us; we lie here in glory unaging because we strove to crown Greece with freedom."[75]

7. What was the intended purpose or effect of using the "dying formula"?

We come finally to the question of the function or functions that the "dying formula" has in its extra-canonical contexts. Given the evidence at our disposal, what were the cult leaders, politicians, testamentarians, war memorial eulogists, hard-pressed battlefield commanders, beleaguered soldiers, and epigraphers trying to accomplish by employing the formula?

In the light of the evidence above, the answer is: to inculcate, confirm, or reinforce the values that stood at the very heart of Greco-Roman, Imperial ideology — values that were accepted by Jews, Greeks, and by those whom Paul called "the rulers of this age" as essential for maintaining "peace and security" — namely, that the warrior is the ideal citizen; that war is "glorious"; that violence is a constructive force in the building of civilization; and that "salvation" from that which threatens to harm or destroy a valued way of life is ultimately achieved only through the use of brute force. What, for instance, does the chief magistrate of Platea do in the annual gathering of Hellenes founded there by Aristides when, after marching with sword in hand through the city to the graves of those who "fell" at Platea, with his own hands he washes off their gravestones and anoints them with myrrh, summons the brave men who died for Hellas to come to the banquet he prepares there, and then consecrates a libation he prepares and pours out there with the institutional words "I drink to the men who died for the freedom of the Hellenes"? What else than to *pay homage and dedicate his community to imperial values*, confirming their ultimate worth? What else does Isocrates do when, in his goad to a pan-Hellenic war

---

74. *Greek Anthology* 7.242.
75. *Lyra Graeca* 14.127; see also 14.126; 14.129; 14.130.

against the Persians, he calls to mind the fact that "even common citizens of the best sort, who would exchange their lives for nothing else, are willing for the sake of winning glory to lay them down in battle" except to underscore the warrior ideal? What does Lysias or Demosthenes or Hyperides or Pericles do in eulogizing those who went off to battle to save their *polis* or *patris* and, in "giving their lives," brought "glory on themselves and their city" and became the "authors of many benefits conferred upon their country and the rest of Greece"[76] or saved all that makes for liberty? What are they doing except to hold up for all to emulate the idea that honor and peace and security ultimately come through readiness for war and the willingness to kill? What else was Mnascales trying to do (when he penned his Epitaph to the fallen who, for Greece's sake, fought against the Persian hordes and in "clothing themselves in the dark dust" won the prize of memorials and high praise) other than shame others into being willing to do likewise when their country's liberty was threatened by the enemy?

What, then, was Paul doing by using this "dying formula"?

We return now to the question of what Paul was trying to do when he proclaimed that "Christ died for us/our sins." Paul designates the one who died as "the Christ," Jesus of Nazareth. The nature and character of the historical figure whom God designated "Lord" and "Son of God in power according to the Spirit of holiness by his resurrection from the dead" was that of one who "though he was in the form of God, did not count equality with God a thing to be grasped, but emptied himself, taking the form of a servant, being born in the likeness of men. And being found in human form he humbled himself and became obedient unto death, even death on a cross" (Phil 2:6-8). Given these facts, I would suggest that in using this "dying formula" Paul was engaged in a profound polemic against the prevailing values of his day with respect to what ordinarily was thought to create personal and public "salvation" (σωτηρία). The one whose death Paul proclaims as salvific is the very antithesis of those who in the secular instances of the "dying formula" are known, proclaimed, and honored as having brought about peace and security through their deaths. Instead of seeking or grasping δόξα, he shuns it (Phil 2:6-8). Instead of engaging in or advocating war when he dies, he embraces defenselessness. Instead of dying for his own, he dies for his enemies.

It would take far more space than is available to conclusively demonstrate that Paul was mounting a counter-argument about what kind of death is salvific when he proclaimed that Christ Jesus (not the warriors of Hellas or

76. Hyperides, *Funeral Oration* 9.

those who imitated them) "died for us." But that my contention has merit seems clear from three facts.

First, as demonstrated by N. T. Wright[77] and Neil Elliot[78] among others, the center of Paul's Gospel involved a major challenge to the validity of the ideology of the imperial cult and the values of the *Pax Romana* which were part of the air Paul and his converts breathed.

Second, Paul's missionary work, which called for the acceptance of Jesus' death as a "death for others," was not so much that of "a traveling evangelist offering people a new religious experience" as of an ambassador for a king-in-waiting; his goal was establishing cells of people loyal to this new king, ordering their lives according to his story, his symbols, and his praxis, and their minds according to his truth.[79]

Third, Paul himself notes that to the wider Greco-Roman world (whom Paul identifies as "those who perish") — those who, certain in their "worldly wisdom" that strength (ἡ ἰσχύς) rules the world, despise weakness — his "word of the cross," his proclamation about Jesus' death being a (if not "the") death that brings salvation (σωτηρία) is both the height of "foolishness" (μωρία)" and a "scandal" (σκάνδαλον).[80]

Finally, there is the evidence of Celsus who took pains to deny the Christian claim that Jesus' death could have the salvific significance of a "death for others." As Origen notes (*Against Celsus* 1.30.31), Celsus denies this not because he rejects the idea that a life laid down for others could "remove those evils which have fallen upon cities and countries." On the contrary, this is something Celsus affirms. Rather it is because the one whose death was claimed by Christians as achieving this end was one who, in the manner of his dying, *was of no account in word or deed* when compared to the Greco-Roman heroes of old. But why would Celsus deny this unless he recognized that behind the declaration that Jesus' death was a "death for others" stood a critique of the claim, pervasive in Greco-Roman thought and self-evident to those who were wise according to

---

77. N. T. Wright, "Paul's Gospel and Caesar's Empire," 160-83 in *Paul and Politics: Ekklesia, Israel, Imperium, Interpretation. Essays in Honour of Krister Stendahl* (ed. R. Horsley; Harrisburg, Pa.: Trinity Press International, 2000).

78. Neil Elliott, *Liberating Paul: The Justice of God and the Politics of the Apostle* (Maryknoll, N.Y.: Orbis, 1994).

79. Wright, "Paul's Gospel and Caesar's Empire."

80. 1 Cor 1:18-27. According to contemporary philosophy, the *only* causes for which the giving up or making exit of one's life was "reasonable," and therefore in conformity with "wisdom," were the good of one's country or one's friends or to escape intolerable pain, mutilation, or incurable disease. Dying for one's enemies was the height of irrationality. Cf. Diogenes Laertius, 7.130 (Zeno).

"worldly wisdom," that the death-dealing death for others that is a constant theme in "the many accounts current both among Greeks and Barbarian, of persons who have laid down their lives for the public advantage" was really what brought salvation (σωτηρία), peace, and security to the world?

Major Motifs in the Interpretation of Paul's Letter to the Romans

Graydon F. Snyder

From the beginning the theology of Paul has been difficult to understand. His letter to the Romans, while arguably the primary manifesto of the Christian faith, has been particularly puzzling to readers through the centuries.[1] In this essay many problems will, of necessity, remain untouched. Our intent will be to lift up for the general reader those major theological motifs that have derived from the reading and study of Paul's letter to the Romans.[2]

One New Testament author had already noted the complexity of Romans. The author of 2 Peter expressed appreciation for the wisdom given to Paul, but admitted that some things were difficult to understand: "So also our beloved brother Paul wrote to you according to the wisdom given him, speaking of this as he does in all his letters. There are some things in them hard to understand, which the ignorant and unstable twist to their own destruction, as they do the other Scriptures" (2 Pet 3:15-16).

While 2 Peter does not mention any specific problems, eventually the Romans debate centered on (1) the meaning of "righteousness of God" (δικαιοσύνη τοῦ Θεοῦ); (2) the purpose of the letter; (3) the addressees (Jews or Gentiles); (4) the situation of the Roman church; (5) the doctrinal nature of the letter; and (6) the importance of Paul's Jewish background.[3]

1. Alan Segal, *Paul the Convert: The Apostolate and Apostasy of Saul the Pharisee* (New Haven: Yale University Press, 1990), xi-xii.

2. Given Robert Jewett's extensive involvement in Paul's Letter to the Romans, to outline the history of interpretation for his Festschrift has been a daunting assignment. Nevertheless, this article is dedicated to a long-time close friend and colleague.

3. L. Ann Jervis, *The Purpose of Romans: A Comparative Letter Structure Investigation* (Sheffield: JSOT Press, 1991), 11-28.

Faith and Works

A more specific critique may come from the author of James who complained about those who depended on faith: "What good is it, my brothers and sisters, if you say you have faith but do not have works? Can faith save you?" (Jas 2:14) For many readers this seems to be a direct attack on the "faith" stance of Paul, so strongly stated in Rom 1:16-17.

James favors what is called a "Two-Ways" theological system. The reader or listener is urged to take the Way of Life rather than the Way of Death. Choice or "Two-Ways" theology has deep roots in the theology of Israel. One finds it even in Joshua's final exhortation before the Israelites enter the promised land (Josh 24:15). By the time of the New Testament, "Two-Ways" theology was prominent. In *The Testament of Asher* (2nd century b.c.e.), the author writes: "God has granted two ways to the sons of men, two mind-sets, two lines of action, two models and two goals" (1:3); every person must choose. In *The Testament of Judah,* we are told that this choice is a free one: "[T]wo spirits await an opportunity with humanity: the spirit of truth and the spirit of error. In between is the conscience of the mind which inclines as it will."[4]

Both ways are described by a series of virtues or vices. The Way of Death exhibits hate, greed, self-centeredness, for example, while the Way of Life is characterized by such virtues as hope, love, and joy.[5] The author of James (perhaps the earliest book of the New Testament) may not have known the letters of Paul.[6] For our study it does not matter. The point here is that first-century Judaism inherited and developed a free-choice doctrine. Paul himself reflected this Two-Ways theology, as did other early church writers.[7] As time went on, Two-Ways theology was combined with Hellenistic Virtue and Vice lists.[8] We can see Paul using parallels to the Two-Ways/Virtue-Vice list in Gal 5:17-23a:

---

4. *The Testament of Judah* 20:1b-2; reading of Recension B.

5. See *Didache* 1-6; *Barnabas* 17; *Shepherd of Hermas* 36; Carolyn Osiek, *Shepherd of Hermas: A Commentary on the Shepherd of Hermas* (Minneapolis: Augsburg Fortress, 1999), 31-34, 124-25; Graydon F. Snyder, *The Shepherd of Hermas* (ed. Robert M. Grant, *Apostolic Fathers* 6; Camden, N.J.: Thomas Nelson, 1969), 76-83.

6. Luke Timothy Johnson, *The Letter of James* (New York: Doubleday, 1995), 111-14, 118-21.

7. Odette Mainville, in her *Un Plaidoyer en faveur de l'unité: La Lettre aux Romains* (Montréal: Médiaspaul, 1999), proposes that Romans was written as an ethical treatise designed to unite the various factions of the Roman church (see esp. 111-35).

8. M. J. Suggs, "The Christian Two Ways Tradition: Its Antiquity, Form, and Function," 60-74 in *Studies in New Testament and Early Christian Literature* (ed. David Aune; Leiden: Brill, 1972).

For what the flesh [σάρξ] desires is opposed to the Spirit [κατὰ τοῦ πνεύματος], and what the Spirit desires is opposed to the flesh; for these are opposed to each other, to prevent you from doing what you want. But if you are led by the Spirit [εἰ δὲ πνεύματι ἄγεσθε] you are not subject to the law [ὑπὸ νόμον]. Now the works of the flesh are obvious: fornication, impurity, licentiousness, idolatry, sorcery, enmities, strife, jealousy, anger, quarrels, dissensions, factions, envy, drunkenness, carousing, and things like these. I am warning you, as I warned you before: those who do such things will not inherit the kingdom of God. By contrast, the fruit of the Spirit is love, joy, peace, patience, kindness, generosity, faithfulness, gentleness, and self-control.

Christology

Pauline theology was not only difficult to understand, but lacking in broad popular acceptance. The second century has been described as a "dark time" or "tunnel period" as far as the theology of Paul is concerned. Ignatius of Antioch (fl. C.E. 110) and Marcion of Sinope (ca. 85–ca. 160) seem the exceptions that prove the rule. Until Irenaeus of Lyons (ca. 125–ca. 200) and Tertullian of Carthage (ca. 160–ca. 225), the influence of Paul was seriously diminished.[9]

The Pastoral Epistles exemplify some of the alterations that took place in Pauline theology. One area in which such changes can be seen is the understanding of Jesus. The confession in Rom 1:2-4 stresses Jesus' human origins, his fulfillment of prophetic promises, his humanity, his death and resurrection, and his acclamation as Son of God. On the other hand, a primary confession in the Pastorals states that Jesus was revealed in the flesh, confirmed as divine by heavenly beings, and shared with the world who believed; then he returned to his heavenly home (1 Tim 3:16). Gone are the human origins of Jesus, the human ministry, the death and resurrection, and the adoption as God's Son.[10]

9. E.g., Karl Hermann Schelke, *Paulus Lehrer der Väter: Die altkirchliche Auslegung von Römer 1–11* (Düsseldorf: Patmos-Verlag, 1956).

10. Eduard Schweizer, "Two New Testament Creeds Compared," 166-77 in *Current Issues in New Testament Interpretation* (ed. William Klassen and Graydon F. Snyder; New York: Harper, 1962).

There is no consensus as to the reasons for such a shift in theology. E.g., is it because fewer Christians had a Jewish background? Because Christians were entering the Hellenistic thought-world? Because there was a need for a less complex view of Christian origins?

Church and State

While the Pastoral Epistles altered the theological worldview of Romans, yet another New Testament writer strongly objected to Paul's view of ἐξουσία (power, authority) in Rom 13. In what might be the most influential passage he ever penned, Paul writes:

> Let every person be subject to the governing authorities [ἐξουσίαις ὑπερεχούσαις ὑποτασσέσθω]; for there is no authority except from God, and those authorities that exist have been instituted by God [ὑπὸ θεοῦ τεταγμέναι εἰσίν]. . . . It is the servant of God to execute wrath on the wrongdoer. (Rom 13:1, 4b)

Whatever Paul meant by these words, they were taken as a call to obey the Roman government — a call rejected by at least one later New Testament writer, the author of the Apocalypse of John.

The Seer compared Rome with the beast of Dan 2:31-45. The image of the beast in Daniel was taken from an Ancient Near Eastern divine-combat myth that involved sea monsters. In Daniel, what had been a cosmological myth is transformed into a political commentary. The sea monsters become oppressive empires. Continuing this line of development, the Seer of Revelation (Rev 12:17–13:7) utilizes the political imagery from Daniel to rebut Rom 13:1-7. According to the Seer, Rome does not use its ἐξουσία for the benefit of the "saints" (ἅγιοι) but to make war against them. To obey is to be complicit in blasphemy.

Grace and the Justice of God

Marcion of Sinope (ca. 85–ca. 160) was the son of a bishop. About C.E. 140 he joined a Roman church and, as a wealthy ship-owner, became known as a generous philanthropist. He came under the influence of the Gnostic teacher, Cerdo, and was excommunicated in 144. (The church returned his money!) Marcion then started a new church so popular it soon could be found throughout the Roman Empire.

Theologically, Marcion rejected the Creator-God of the Hebrew Scriptures as imperfect, ignorant, and responsible for the intrusion of evil. The Supreme God, instead, was the one described in Marcion's New Testament, a collection (canon) that included an abridged Gospel of Luke and ten altered letters of Paul (*Apostolicon*).[11] A number of readers have concluded that Marcion ac-

---

11. [Editor's note: Marcion's *Apostolicon* included ten of Paul's letters, which were listed

tually did adopt the theology of Paul. For Adolf von Harnack, Marcion was the first Protestant.[12] No writings of Marcion are extant, so we cannot be certain about his use of Paul. From his opponents' reports, however, it appears that Marcion created a radical dichotomy between a gospel of love and a covenant of law. If this is accurate, it seems that Marcion sought to establish Paul's doctrine of grace or love over against law and judgment.[13]

Against Marcion, Tertullian, a presbyter from North Africa, argued that Paul did not separate the God of the Hebrew Scriptures from the God of the New Testament.[14] In Rom 1:16-17, the δικαιοσύνη τοῦ Θεοῦ (a possessive genitive) included God's judgment as well as God's right-wising.[15]

Augustine: Grace and Free Will

At key moments in the history of Christianity, the Letter to the Romans has given direction to the church. Augustine of Hippo (C.E. 354-430) was involved in three major controversies — against the Manichees, the Donatists, and Pelagius (ca. C.E. 354-418) — each of which had to do with interpretations of Romans. Much of the debate revolved around the question of divine "justification by faith" in contrast to human free will.

Against the Manichees' doctrine of an evil material world, Augustine stressed the goodness of the Creator-God and creation.[16] The fault does not lie with the created world, but with human impiety.[17] Augustine developed a doc-

---

in this order: Gal, 1-2 Cor, Rom (1–14, only), 1-2 Thess, Eph, Col, Phlm and Phil; it also contained part of the *Epistle to the Laodiceans.* Marcion's canon of the New Testament was prepared and published soon after his arrival at Rome, probably about C.E. 145.]

12. Adolf von Harnack, "Marcion: das Evangelium vom Fremden Gott," *Texte und Untersuchungen* 45 (1921): 231: "the work and struggle of the Apostle as a true 'Reformer' was resumed in this 'younger Paul'" [Editor's translation].

13. R. Joseph Hoffman, *Marcion: On the Restitution of Christianity: An Essay on the Development of Radical Paulinist Theology in the Second Century* (Chico, Calif.: Scholars Press, 1984), 307-9.

14. Tertullian, *Against Marcion* 5:13.

15. Schelke, *Paulus Lehrer der Väter,* 41.

16. See Simon J. Gathercole, "A Conversion of Augustine: From Natural Law to Restored Nature in Romans 2:13-16," 147-72 in *Engaging Augustine on Romans: Self, Context, and Theology in Interpretation* (ed. Daniel Patte and Eugene TeSelle; Harrisburg: Trinity Press International, 2002).

17. Augustine, *Expositio quarundam propositionum ex epistola ad Romanos* 3.3: "Nam sapientes gentium quod invenerint creatorem manifeste idem apostolus. . . ." See *Augustine on Romans: Propositions from the Epistle to the Romans, Unfinished Commentary on the Epistle to the Romans* (ed. and trans. Paula Fredriksen Landes; Chico, Calif.: Scholars Press, 1982). Cf. idem, *Augustine's Early Interpretation of Paul* (Ann Arbor: Landen, 1980).

trine of human will, a human faculty informed by both knowledge and experience. Originally the human will was oriented toward that which was most desirable — God. But the primordial sin was to shift that desire from God to self. God's grace can restore the will's orientation toward God,[18] but human perfection lies beyond time and space. The creation is not evil, as the Manichees believed; still, in this life we cannot know the perfect joy of the original creation.

The second controversy occurred with the Donatists, who believed sacraments were valid only when administered by ministers who essentially were without sin. Augustine, in turn, argued that the sacraments were valid as acts of the Church and therefore did not depend on the sanctity of the minister.[19] For Augustine, Divine grace, not human perfection, is what makes the sacraments efficacious.

Most important for our discussion of Romans, however, is the controversy with Pelagius concerning the nature of sin.[20] A British or Irish monk who lived in Rome toward the end of the fourth century, Pelagius rejected the idea that human mortality was the punishment on Adam and all his descendants because of original sin. For Pelagius, Adam was a mortal subject to death even before his sin, and he certainly did not bequeath a sinful nature to the rest of the human race. Every newborn child enters the world without sin and can make choices in life that might lead to perfection.[21]

Pelagius objected to Augustine's prayer, "Command what you will and give what you command."[22] It seemed to eradicate any opportunity to cooperate with God or even to choose to obey God. A pivotal point of the debate concerned the interpretation of Rom 5:12:

> Therefore, just as sin came into the world through one human [Διὰ τοῦτο ὥσπερ δι' ἑνὸς ἀνθρώπου ἡ ἁμαρτία εἰς τὸν κόσμον εἰσῆλθεν], and death came through sin [καὶ διὰ τῆς ἁμαρτίας ὁ θάνατος], and so death spread to all human beings [καὶ οὕτως εἰς πάντας ἀνθρώπους ὁ θάνατος διῆλθεν] inasmuch as all have sinned [ἐφ' ᾧ πάντες ἥμαρτον].[23]

18. Augustine, *Confessions* 7.14.

19. Augustine, *On Baptism, Against the Donatists*.

20. J. Patout Burns, "The Interpretation of Romans in the Pelagian Controversy," *Augustinian Studies* 10 (1979): 43-54.

21. Alexander Souter, *Pelagius's Expositions of Thirteen Epistles of St. Paul* (2 vols.; *Text and Studies* 9; Cambridge: The University Press, 1926), 2: 46. See also Graydon F. Snyder, *Irish Jesus, Roman Jesus* (Harrisburg: Trinity Press International, 2002), 216-30.

22. Augustine, *On the Predestination of the Saints* 2.53.

23. Editor's translation.

Augustine followed the Vulgate version of the Bible, whose translation of ἐφ᾿ ᾧ πάντες ἥμαρτον read *"in quo omnes peccaverunt,"* so that the verse would read, "Therefore, just as sin came into the world through one human, *in whom all have sinned,* so death came through sin, and death spread to all." Because of the sin of Adam, every human enters the world incapable of avoiding sin *(non posse non peccare).*

On the other hand, Augustine found in the theology of Paul a strong sense of grace which made it possible for those so destined to live by faith (Rom 1:16-17). Through grace, the faithful are free to avoid sin *(posse non peccare).*[24] Augustine's reading of Rom 5:12 and the doctrine of original sin became standard for later theology.

The Powers of the State

As we have seen, Paul's discussion of the powers in Rom 13:1-7 was a source of controversy, even from the first century. Despite the immeasurable importance of Paul's teaching on "justification by faith," it may well be that Paul's advice to submit to the governing authorities has influenced Western civilization even more. Ernst Bammel writes, "Chapter 13:1-7 of Paul's letter to the Romans became perhaps the most influential part of the New Testament on the level of world history. This happened in spite of the fact that the interpretation of the passage has never been found easy and nowadays is more disputed than ever before."[25] Bammel is quite correct about modern scholarship. The meaning of and reason for Rom 13 has not — perhaps cannot — be settled.[26]

It would be tempting to review the exegetical history of Rom 13:1-7, but it is the theological/political impact that concerns us here.[27] Briefly, the text reflects a deep sense of monotheism. The ultimate authority or ἐξουσία belongs to and derives from God (13:1b). Social and community organization is a God-

---

24. J. Patout Burns, *Augustine's Discovery of Operative Grace* (Paris: Études Augustiniennes, 1980).

25. Ernst Bammel, "Romans 13," in *Jesus and the Politics of His Day* (ed. Ernst Bammel and C. F. D. Moule; Cambridge: Cambridge University Press, 1984), 365.

26. Jan Botha, *Subject to Whose Authority? Multiple Readings of Romans 13* (Atlanta: Scholars Press, 1994).

27. The possibility that Romans 13:1-7 is an interpolation appeals to many readers who assume the separation of church and state in the first centuries of Christianity. For a review of the arguments, see Vilho Reikkinen, *Römer 13: Aufzeichnung und Weiterführung der exegetischen Diskussion* (Helsinki: Suomalainen Tiedeakatemia, 1959), 7-24; J. C. O'Neill, *Paul's Letter to the Romans* (London: Penguin Books, 1975), 14.

function, not the product of an opposing demonic force (13:3). Not to submit to social organization results in anarchy and unacceptable individualism.[28]

Needless to say, early Christians did wish to affirm that God was the ultimate ἐξουσία. However, they usually were unwilling to say that an unfriendly, pagan government (e.g., Rome) ought to be obeyed without question. To be sure Ignatius, Bishop of Antioch (d. ca. 110), submitted willingly to the decisions of the Empire. But his contemporary, Polycarp of Smyrna (ca. 70–ca. 155), when asked to submit, replied: "To you indeed I have considered myself accountable; for we have been taught to render fit honor to rulers and authorities appointed by God in so far as it is not injurious to us; as for these, I do not consider myself bound to make my defense before them."[29] Polycarp accepted the teaching of Rom 13, but not when the State attacked Christians.

Other early Christian writers differ, perhaps according to the intensity of persecution they suffered. Irenaeus of Lyons dissociates the ἐξουσία of God from that of Rome, but then assumes the Christian will be obedient to the State.[30] Most ancient commentators assume that Rom 13 calls for good citizenship and obedience to the State but, like Polycarp, they make an exception when it conflicts with the Christian faith or endangers the faith community.[31] Tertullian especially insists that Rom 13 does not call for any compromise of one's faith, even if it means martyrdom.[32]

When the Christian Roman Empire was formed, attitudes toward the State changed significantly. Eusebius of Caesarea (ca. 260–340), the earliest Church historian, wrote during the reign of the first Christian Emperor, Constantine the Great. Eusebius says that Christians "gave honour first of all to God the universal King, for this they had been instructed to do, and then to the pious Emperor with his sons beloved of God."[33] Echoing Rom 13, Eusebius equates Constantine with the ἐξουσία τοῦ Θεοῦ [Divine authority] and applauds him as the servant of God.[34]

Approval of the State as a divine gift continued after Eusebius and Constantine. The doctrine of the "divine right of kings," based on Rom 13, began with Charlemagne (C.E. 742-814) and Otto the Great (C.E. 912-973). The

28. Graydon F. Snyder, *Power and Violence* (*Colloquium* 1; Oak Brook, Ill.: Bethany Theological Seminary, 1971), 27-60. Cf. Walter Wink, *Naming the Powers: The Language of Power in the New Testament* (Philadelphia: Fortress, 1984), 104-13.

29. *Martyrdom of Polycarp* 10.2.

30. See Irenaeus, *Against Heresies* 4.36.6; 5.24.1, 3.

31. E.g., Origen, *Commentary on Romans* 9.24-28; Cyprian, *Treatises* 5.37-39.

32. Tertullian, *Antidote for the Scorpion's Sting* 14; *The Crown*.

33. Eusebius, *Church History* 10.9.7.

34. Eusebius, *Life of Constantine*.

Graydon F. Snyder

Holy Roman Empire was divided by the Reformation (1517), yet neither Luther nor Calvin broke with the divine right of the State. It took the Left Wing of the Reformation to see that the ἐξουσία τοῦ Θεοῦ could not be found in any State, friendly or unfriendly. Either Rom 13 had been misunderstood, or other Biblical texts (e.g., Rev 13) obviated the words of Paul. Jesus himself did not submit to the authority of the State, nor even to the Jewish authorities. So Jesus-oriented Anabaptists saw him as a Martyr rather than a redeemer or revelator.[35] That break with the divine right of the State, and the concomitant stress on obedience to God alone, created a theological atmosphere in which the American experiment (with its separation of church and state) could occur.

Martin Luther: Justification by Faith

It is probably inevitable, perhaps even necessary, that the existential moment of faith *(fides)* should take on concrete forms such as creedal formulations and community disciplines *(credentia)*. In the period following Augustine, ecclesiastical authors refined and expanded the meaning of faith in order better to inform the Christian world, to define appropriate behavior, to establish right forms of worship, and also to determine where variations in the Christian faith had become improper and misleading. For some, the concern for *credentia* became sterile and oppressive. Faith was no longer a vibrant trust in God but a tradition to which one must adhere.

Martin Luther (1483-1546), a German Augustinian friar, was deeply dissatisfied with Scholasticism, the Inquisition, and disciplinary abuses such as the selling of indulgences. Sometime between 1513 and 1519, Luther had his famous conversion experience *("Turmerlebnis")* in which he realized that "the righteousness of God" did not refer to our God-like righteousness, but the gracious gift of God accepting us as righteous. Luther's 1515-1516 lectures on Romans contain an exegesis of Rom 1:17 and 3:21-26 in light of the *Turmerlebnis.*

Luther's reading of Romans can best be seen in his treatise *On the Bondage of the Will,* which was written in response to criticisms leveled by the Dutch theologian, Desiderius Erasmus Roterodamus (1466-1536), in *On the Freedom of the Will.* For Luther, all humans were so caught in the sin of self-centeredness that they were incapable of cooperating with God and participating in their own salvation. "[T]he whole purpose and intention of the apostle in this epistle

35. E.g., Thieleman J. van Braght, ed., *The Bloody Theater or Martyrs' Mirror of the Anabaptists or Defenseless Christians* (Holland: 1660; Scottdale, Pa., and Waterloo, Ont.: Herald, 1972), 67.

is to break down all righteousness and wisdom of our own, to point out again those sins and foolish practices."[36] Salvation depended solely on God's justification of sinners by the gift of faith. So, although humans remained sinners, they participated in the divine gift of justification — that is, they were simultaneously sinners and justified *(simul peccator et iustus).*

This reading of Romans in terms of "justification by faith alone" was a key "fault line" of the Reformation. Although other Reformers expressed marked differences with Luther, on this point they agreed: salvation was a gift acquired by faith, not produced by correct doctrine or obligatory actions.

Historical Purpose — The Enlightenment

Despite the ongoing power of "justification by faith" as a rallying point for Pauline Christianity, following the Enlightenment, with its insistence on historicity, other perspectives became more prominent. In particular, nineteenth-century Protestant scholars maintained that Paul's letters were not theological documents *per se,* but were written for a specific purpose.[37] Ferdinand Christian Baur (1792-1860), Professor at the University of Tübingen in Germany, argued that the meaning and theology of Romans could be understood only when its historical situation was understood: "The origin and aim of the Epistle are generally determined from the purely dogmatic point of view. Scholars have failed to inquire carefully into the historical occasion and the circumstances in the Roman Church on which the Epistle proceeds."[38]

Historical critics examined the language of the letter, its rhetorical form, the Roman context, Paul's intention in writing the letter, the nature of the Roman congregations, and the development of the Pauline churches. Generally, though not always, those who read Romans as a historical document disparaged its use as a source of theology. Historians tended to find meaning in human relationships and behavior rather than the God perspective. Baur himself, following Hegelian idealism, saw in Jesus and Paul a Western anthropology of autonomy (self-rule) that eventually was compromised by a Jewish/Eastern heteronomy (rule by others).[39]

36. Martin Luther, *Lectures on Romans* (ed. H. C. Oswald; *Luther's Works* 25; St. Louis: Concordia, 1972), 3.

37. For the continuing discussion see Karl P. Donfried, ed., *The Romans Debate* (Peabody, Mass.: Hendrickson, 1995), especially Donfried's "False Presuppositions in the Study of Romans" (102-25).

38. F. C. Baur, *Paul the Apostle of Jesus Christ,* Vol. 1 (trans. from the 2nd German edition; ed. E. Zeller; rev. A. Menzies; London: Williams & Norgate, 1876), 310.

39. F. C. Baur, "Die Christus partie in der korinthischen Gemeinde, der Gegensatz des

Christ-Mysticism

The discovery of countless papyri in Egypt made it abundantly clear that the language of the New Testament was that of the common people of the Ancient Near East. Theologically it destroyed the ancient thesis that the New Testament was written in God-language. Words, phrases and ideas could be examined in the context of the Greek of the first century. The impact on New Testament studies was immeasurable. One important religious affirmation was made by the person who pioneered *Koine* studies, Adolf Deißmann (1866-1937). In his doctoral study at Marburg, he proposed that the phrase "in Christ" (ἐν Χριστῷ; e.g., Rom 8:1-2) referred to the immersion of the individual person into the mystical being of Christ.[40] The Greek preposition ἐν implied "being inside" the object of the preposition (i.e., Christ). The center of Paul's faith was then a Christ-mysticism.

Christ-mysticism was picked up by Albert Schweitzer (1875-1965) as a way of saving Pauline theology from his own radical view of Jewish apocalypticism. Having shown that the misguided Jesus expected an immediate, cataclysmic end to the world, Schweitzer proposed that the first Christian, Paul, was a mystic rather than an apocalypticist.[41]

In the English language, the major proponent for Christ-mysticism was James Stewart in his book, *A Man in Christ*.[42] Basically Christ-mysticism holds that Paul made available to his converts a relationship with Jesus Christ which paralleled the relationship of Jesus to God the Father. One's relationship to God is a religious experience in Christ.

Eschatology: God Who Acts

The reading of Jesus as a radical apocalypticist, proposed by Albert Schweitzer and Johannes Weiss (1863-1914), also had a significant impact on the study of

---

petrinischen und paulinischen Christentums in der ältesten Kirche, der Apostel Petrus in Rom," *Tübinger Zeitschrift für Theologie* 4 (1831): 61-206. Available also in Baur's *Ausgewählte Werke in Einzelangaben,* Vol. 1 (Stuttgart: Fromann, 1963), 1-146.

40. Gustav Adolf Deißmann, *Die neutestamentliche Formel "in Christo Jesu"* (Marburg: N. G. Elwert, 1892).

41. Albert Schweitzer, *The Mysticism of Paul the Apostle* (trans. W. Montgomery; London: Black, 1931); Edward Newman Mozley, "The Conception of the Kingdom of God in the Transformation of Eschatology," in *The Theology of Albert Schweitzer for Christian Inquirers* (London: Black, 1950).

42. James Stewart, *A Man in Christ: The Vital Elements of St. Paul's Religion* (New York: Harper, 1935). Also Johannes Schneider, *Die Passionsmystik des Paulus* (*Untersuchungen zum Neuen Testament* 15; Leipzig: J. C. Hinrichs, 1929).

Paul, and especially Romans.[43] Instead of a God who offered a right relationship by means of grace and mercy (Luther), God was seen as the God of history, a God who could be trusted to fulfill the promises given to the Jewish people and, in turn, to all people (Gen 12:1-3).[44] God is a God who acts and who also asks of us end-time action.[45] Paul understood his mission in Rome as an eschatological act.[46] Rom 9–11 especially made the end-time point clear.[47] Paul's mission to the Gentiles was understood as the way in which God would not only bring salvation to the nations, but also consummate the promise to the Jews.

Rather than focusing on a God who reveals the Law of relationships and offers mercy (Gospel) for those who have been alienated, the eschatological approach emphasizes that God is the Creator who acts to complete Creation. Christ on the cross is more the fulfillment of promises than an act of salvation.[48]

The argument "to the Jew first and then the Gentile" (Rom 1:16) had a profound effect. Even though the theology of *Heilsgeschichte* and "God who acts" has fallen prey to post-modern thinking, many Christians still assume that the Jews, and Israel, are integral to world mission.[49]

God's Promise Has Been Thwarted

Shortly after the rise of the Tübingen school and its historical-critical approach, a brilliant British scholar by the name of John William Colenso

43. Albert Schweitzer, *The Quest of the Historical Jesus: A Critical Study of Its Progress from Reimarus to Wrede* (trans. W. Montgomery; London: Black, 1954); Johannes Weiss, *Jesus' Proclamation of the Kingdom of God* (trans. R. H. Hiers and D. L. Holland; London: SCM Press, 1971).

44. Otto A. Piper, *God in History* (New York: Macmillan, 1939); Werner G. Kümmel, *Promise and Fulfillment: The Eschatological Message of Jesus* (trans. Dorothea M. Barton; Naperville, Ill.: A. R. Allenson, 1957).

45. George Ernest Wright, *God Who Acts: Biblical Theology as Recital* (Chicago: Regnery, 1952).

46. Oscar Cullmann, "Le caractère eschatologique du devoir missionaire et de la conscience apostolique de S. Paul. Étude sur le κατέχον de II Thess. 2.6-7," *Revue d'histoire et de philosophie religieuses* 16 (1936): 210-45.

47. Johannes Munck, *Christus und Israel: Eine Auslegung von Romans 9–11* (*Acta Jutlandica* 7; Copenhagen: Universitetsforlaget, 1956), and *Paul and the Salvation of Mankind* (trans. F. Clarke; London: SCM Press, 1959).

48. Anton Fridrichsen, "Jesus, St John and St Paul," 37-62 in *The Root of the Vine* (London: Dacre, 1953); *The Apostle and His Message* (*Uppsala Universitets Årsskrift*, 1947); "Nya Testaments enhet," *Svensk Exegetisk Årsbok* 6 (1941): 43-54.

49. Werner E. Lemke, "Revelation through History in Recent Biblical Theology," *Interpretation* 36 (1982): 34-46.

(1814-1883) went to study in Germany. He then took an assignment as a missionary-teacher in what is now northern South Africa. Colenso learned Zulu, eventually making a translation of the Bible, and wrote commentaries on various sections. His Romans commentary set a new direction in studies of the epistle.[50] Although there is conflicting evidence regarding the addressees, Colenso assumed that the letter was addressed to Jews who considered themselves the "chosen people." Despite the political situation of the first century, Colenso interpreted the Gentiles as marginalized people who were scorned by God's Chosen and not fully accepted as participants in salvation history. He identified the Jews in Romans with the British (and Calvinists) in South Africa, who considered themselves the superior people; the Gentiles he identified with the Zulus, a "savage," uncultured group of black Africans.[51]

Colenso paid dearly for his analysis of Romans. His attack on the British as the self-righteous Jews eventually brought his condemnation as a heretic. His commentary has received little notice in academic circles, but his analysis, based as it was on newly developed historical criticism, pre-figured the Romans debate by nearly 100 years. Romans was a missionary document; Paul's intent was to include those who were outside the covenant made with the Jews. In more recent years, writers have understood the God of Romans to be the God of the poor and the marginalized.[52] Colenso was the first to start down this path.

---

50. John William Colenso, *St. Paul's Epistle to the Romans: Newly Translated and Explained from a Missionary Point of View* (New York: Appleton, 1863).

51. For example, writing on Rom 9:13 ("Jacob I loved, but Esau I hated"), Colenso says: "St. Paul is not speaking at all of eternal salvation and perdition, but of the temporal privileges and blessings, by which it pleased God to distinguish some more than others, and by the proper use of which they would have gained, doubtless, a higher place in the Heavenly Kingdom, whereas, by the abuse of them, they have sunk proportionally lower than others. As regards their state in the eternal world, Ishmael and Esau and their descendents, (among whom we may reckon the Zulus and Kafirs,) stand on the same level, and will be judged with the same righteous judgment, as others more highly favored in this world with the means of grace and the hope of glory, as their brethren in the Jewish Church of old, in the Christian now. All will be judged according to their works, and according to the light vouchsafed to them. With reference to the Light, which we, Christians of England, have received, it might be said, in like manner, 'England God has loved, and Africa has He hated.' Yet not all English Christians are children of the Light, nor are all African heathens children of Satan; but those, who have received most, shall have most required of them." Ibid., 195-96.

52. Gottlob Schrenk, "Der Römerbrief als Missionsdokument," in *Studien zu Paulus* (Zurich: Zwingli-Verlag, 1954), 82-87; Robert Jewett, "Romans as an Ambassadorial Letter," *Interpretation* 36 (1982): 5-20; Steve Mosher, *God's Power, Jesus' Faith, and World Mission: A Study in Romans* (Scottdale, Pa.: Herald, 1996); John Howard Yoder, *The Fullness of Christ: Paul's Revolutionary Vision of Universal Mission* (Elgin, Ill.: Brethren, 1987).

Universal Toleration — A God of Peace

Literary and rhetorical critics have argued that Paul wrote the letter to the Roman church in what might be called a diatribe style, a literary strategy to engage both Jew and Gentile in dialogue.[53] Despite the efforts of Colenso and later writers to find in Romans a concern for the disadvantaged, the purpose of Romans was actually to build a community that shared the missionary eschatology of the apostle Paul.[54] Paul's intent was to place Jews and Gentiles on the same plane. It did not matter whether or not you had the Law; all those who have sinned will be judged accordingly (Rom 2:8-9). On the other hand, both Jew and Greek may receive "glory and honor and peace" (2:10), for "God shows no partiality" (2:11).

On the basis of this equality Paul builds a unified community. He writes that, even though the members of the community have differing functions and skills, "we, who are many, are one body in Christ, and individually we are members one of another" (Rom 12:5). Paul describes how they can be one body by including echoes of the Jesus-tradition regarding mutual care: "Live in harmony with one another; do not be haughty, but associate with the lowly; do not claim to be wiser than you are. Do not repay anyone evil for evil, but take thought for what is noble in the sight of all. If it is possible, so far as it depends on you, live peaceably with all" (Rom 12:16-18). In the case of specific problems, such as vegetarianism on the part of some and not others, or the preference of one day for fasting rather than another, Paul asked the Roman Christians to "pursue what makes for peace and for mutual upbuilding" (14:19).[55] God in the Letter to the Romans is a God of peace. Paul ends the body of his letter with the blessing: "The God of peace be with all of you" (15:33).

The unity of the community expresses itself in mission. The Roman community should share with the poor in Jerusalem, and should support Paul, and probably Phoebe as well, on a mission trip to Spain. In other words, not only did the new community of Roman Jews and Gentiles find in Christ a way to be one, but that oneness should energize them to include Jewish Christians of Jerusalem and Gentiles in the far reaches of the Mediterranean world.[56]

53. Stanley Stowers, *The Diatribe and Paul's Letter to the Romans* (Chico, Calif.: Scholars Press, 1981), 115-17.

54. Gottlob Schrenk, "Der Römerbrief als Missionsdokument," in *Studien zu Paulus* (Zurich: Zwingli-Verlag, 1954), 82-87. Robert Jewett, "Romans as an Ambassadorial Letter," *Interpretation* 36 (1982): 5-20.

55. Robert Jewett, *Christian Tolerance: Paul's Message to the Modern Church* (Philadelphia: Westminster, 1982), 62-63.

56. Luke Timothy Johnson, *Reading Romans: A Literary and Theological Commentary* (New York: Crossroad, 1997), 6.

Graydon F. Snyder

Karl Barth: The Word of God

Despite the advances made by historical research, in 1919 a bombshell hit the world of Biblical studies. It has been difficult to determine just why the revolution occurred. Was it the failure of "liberal" theology to deal with a devastating world war? Was it because the thoroughgoing application of historical criticism would actually produce something other than what had been anticipated (the mysticism of Albert Schweitzer)? Was it the need for a faith more deeply rooted in the Other?[57] Whatever the reason, a pastor in Safenwil, Switzerland, wrote a commentary on Romans that turned Biblical scholarship upside down.[58] For Karl Barth, the Epistle to the Romans was the Word of God communicated by the Apostle Paul as he wrote of Jesus Christ.

Historical critics were horrified by this apparent return to a theological reading of Romans, but Barth did not go away. Following his Romans commentary, he taught theology at the University of Basel where he produced a *Church Dogmatics,* surely the most prodigious theological undertaking since the Reformation.

At stake is the nature of the Bible. From Barth's perspective, it is not the product of given historical or sociological situations, but is God's Word brought to us through linguistic analogy. Barth is far from Fundamentalism, though he does not shy away from terms like "divine inspiration." He recognizes the relativity of language and human thinking, but he also insists that we should read the Bible to discover the intent of the author. Our reading is not to be clouded by asking our own questions or seeking historical explanations. When we read Romans, we hear the Word even through imperfect communication. Subject encounters Object. The conversation has been called dialectical theology or *Krisis* theology, with a nod toward the Danish philosopher Søren Kierkegaard.[59] The Bible may have been written centuries ago, but the Word speaks to us now. For that reason, Barth was often seen with a Bible in one hand and a newspaper in the other.

The theology of Romans does not consist of any content (grace, peace,

---

57. Robert Jewett, "Major Impulses in the Theological Interpretation of Romans Since Barth," *Interpretation* 34 (1980): 17-31.

58. Karl Barth, *The Epistle to the Romans* (trans. E. C. Hoskyns; London: Oxford University Press, 1933).

59. "The reality to which life bears witness must be disclosed in the deep things of all observable phenomena, in their whole context — and in their KRISIS. Only dialectical human thinking can fulfil its purpose, searching out the depth and context and reality of life: only dialectical thought can lead to genuine reflection upon its meaning, and make sense of it." Ibid., 245; original emphasis.

mysticism, new community). Rather, there is a call for us to stand before the Word found there. For Barth, like many others, Rom 1:16-17 is the key passage but, unlike Augustine, Barth reads the text in terms of a human facing the void of life and standing before the faithfulness of God. Only by facing that void in the presence of God's faithfulness can we reflect on true life in this life, and on incorruption in that which is passing to corruption. For Barth, "This is the theme of the Epistle to the Romans."[60]

Rudolf Bultmann: Existence as Eschatology

Not everyone decried the Barthian revolution. Among those who applauded was Rudolf Bultmann (1884-1976), long-time professor at Marburg. Bultmann never wrote a commentary on Romans, but the section on Paul in his *Theology of the New Testament* has strongly impacted readers of Romans for decades.[61]

The background for Bultmann's reading of Paul is complex. Some more obvious considerations would help understand Bultmann's remarkable influence. First was the power of Albert Schweitzer's analysis of Jesus. In 1906, Schweitzer sat down to examine nearly every life of Jesus written on the Continent. When he had finished, the quest for the historical Jesus also was finished.[62] Schweitzer showed that the real Jesus was an apocalyptic fanatic who expected the immediate end of the world — and Jesus was wrong.[63] Granted that Schweitzer took the Synoptic Gospels too literally and that he really intended to replace the time-specific ethic of Jesus with a Kantian categorical imperative, still the impact of his work was enormous. Virtually no one tried to write a life of Jesus for over half-a-century afterwards.

The resolution of Schweitzer's "consequent eschatology" came from several directions, though in each case the intent was the same. Schweitzer's critics argued that he had misunderstood the meaning of eschatology. Some scholars

---

60. Ibid., 42.

61. Rudolf Bultmann, *Theology of the New Testament* (trans. K. Grobel; London: SCM Press, 1952), 190-352.

62. Albert Schweitzer, *The Quest of the Historical Jesus: A Critical Study of Its Progress from Reimarus to Wrede* (trans. W. Montgomery; London: A. & C. Black, 1910); trans. of *Von Reimarus zu Wrede: Eine Geschichte der Leben-Jesu-Forschung* (Tübingen: J. C. B. Mohr, 1906).

63. Albert Schweitzer, *Die Religionsphilosophie Kant's von der Kritik der reinen Vernunft bis zur Religion innerhalb der Grenzen der blossen Vernunft* (Tübingen: Mohr, 1899); "The Conception of the Kingdom of God in the Transformation of Eschatology," in E. N. Mozley, *The Theology of Albert Schweitzer for Christian Inquirers*, 80-108.

with more of a sense of Platonic infinity, especially C. H. Dodd (1884-1973), proposed that Jesus spoke primarily of a realized eschatology, that is, the ultimate now impinges on present history.[64] Jesus' proclamation, "The Kingdom of God has already come near" (ἤγγικεν ἡ βασιλεία τοῦ θεοῦ, Mark 1:15), refers to the present, not the future. Bultmann agreed that Schweitzer had misunderstood eschatology; however, in contrast to Dodd, he believed the end time sharpens and gives meaning to our present life. Bultmann's position gave rise to the famous dictum, *"already, but not yet."*[65] Bultmann's exploration of the dialectical nature of human existence reflects the dialectical theology of Barth, but the language structure reflects more the thinking of the existentialist philosopher, Martin Heidegger. Historicizing and psychologizing have no place in dialectical theology. Bultmann wished

> to make Scripture itself speak as a power, which has something to say to the present, to present-day existence, [not simply] to read the Biblical writing as a compendium of dogmatic pronouncements, or as 'sources' for the reconstruction of a section of past history, or to study a religious phenomenon or the nature of religion in general, or to know the psychological course and theoretical objectivization of religious experiences.[66]

In sharp contrast to nineteenth-century historians, Bultmann gave little credence to the historical Jesus.[67] In contrast to Barth, however, Bultmann's concern was not so much for the divine Word as it was for the human condition. Consequently, Bultmann saw in Romans a description of human existence as it stands between the death of Jesus on the Cross and the resurrection of Christ. Bultmann's analysis of anthropological terms — pairs like flesh and spirit, body and psyche, life and death — stresses the dialectical nature of existence.[68] More than 1:16-17, the real center of Romans is chapter seven because in it Paul describes the constant human condition:

---

64. Kümmel, *Promise and Fulfillment*, 105-40; C. H. Dodd, *The Parables of the Kingdom* (London: Nisbet, 1935).

65. *"Noch nicht, aber doch schon."* See Rudolf Bultmann, *Theology of the New Testament,* Chap. 1, esp. §1.

66. Rudolf Bultmann, "The Problem of Hermeneutics," in *Essays Philosophical and Theological* (trans. C. G. Greig; London: SCM Press, 1955), 258-59.

67. In his *Theology of the New Testament,* Bultmann devotes a mere twenty-nine pages to the topic (3-32).

68. Ibid., 190-269. Cf. Robert Jewett, *Paul's Anthropological Terms: A Study of Their Use in Conflict Settings* (Leiden: Brill, 1971).

For we know that the law is spiritual [ὁ νόμος πνευματικός ἐστιν]; but I am of the flesh, sold into slavery under sin [ἐγὼ δὲ σάρκινός εἰμι πεπραμένος ὑπὸ τὴν ἁμαρτίαν]. I do not understand my own actions. For I do not do what I want, but I do the very thing I hate. . . . I can will what is right, but I cannot do it. . . . So I find it to be a law [Εὑρίσκω ἄρα τὸν νόμον] that when I want to do what is good, evil lies close at hand. For I delight in the law of God in my inmost self, but I see in my members another law at war with the law of my mind, making me captive to the law of sin that dwells in my members. Wretched man that I am! Who will rescue me from this body of death? (Rom 7:14-15, 18b, 21-24)

At the same time the righteousness of God is the eschatological event that counters sin and death with life and obedience.[69]

Bultmann produced many disciples. Arguably the best known would be Ernst Käsemann (1906-1998), who wrote the commentary on Romans never given us by Bultmann.[70] Like Bultmann, Käsemann maintained a time-oriented dialectic. In sharp contrast to many of his nineteenth-century predecessors, and even present-day seekers for the historical Jesus, Käsemann understood apocalypticism, the time dialectic, to be the source for early Christianity.[71] It is Bultmann's individualism that creates the major difference between teacher and student. Käsemann believed Bultmann held too closely to a one-on-one dialectic, like Heidegger's concern for Being rather than society, or Martin Buber's "I-Thou." While there is concern for the individual in Paul's thought, it would be a mistake to reduce justification to the individual person.[72] Paul is concerned about the People of God (Rom 9–11).[73] The resurrection leads all to new life (Rom 5:18).

Because Bultmann focuses on the individual, the crucial element of faith development is to hear the *kerygma*, the proclamation of the death and resurrection of Jesus Christ, present existence and end-time existence. Indeed, Bultmann will judge the New Testament writings according to the centrality of the *kerygma*. For Käsemann the righteousness of God is an eschatological event that alters the course of history. In that sense it is a cosmological event.

69. Bultmann, *Theology of the New Testament*, 270-352.

70. Ernst Käsemann, *Commentary on Romans* (trans. and ed. G. W. Bromiley; Grand Rapids, Mich.: Eerdmans, 1980).

71. Ernst Käsemann, "On the Subject of Primitive Christian Apocalyptic," 108-37 in *New Testament Questions of Today* (trans. W. J. Montague; London: SCM Press, 1969).

72. Ernst Käsemann, "New Testament Questions of Today," in *New Testament Questions of Today*, 14-15.

73. David Way, *The Lordship of Christ: Ernst Käsemann's Interpretation of Paul's Theology* (Oxford: Clarendon Press, 1991).

Anders Nygren: Agapē

Much like Schweitzer, Anders Nygren, Lutheran Bishop of Lund, Sweden, started with the search for a religious *a priori* in Kantian-Schleiermacherian categories.[74] Instead of Schleiermacher's "feeling of absolute dependence," Nygren spoke of "communion with God" as the essence of religion. He sought to define that *motif* which best categorized a religion's perception of the believer's relationship to God.[75]

Nygren differentiated among three kinds of relationship with God: *agapē*, *nomos*, and *erōs*. Communion with God in early Christianity was designated by the Greek word *agapē*, which means "unmotivated love." *Agapē* is indifferent to value, is creative, makes no demands, and is initiated by God.[76] In contrast, Nygren asserted, Jewish fellowship with God was determined by *nomos* or law, and depended on obedience to covenantal law. In the Hellenistic world, the term *erōs* was used to designate communion with God. *Erōs* refers to acquisitive love or the human being's way to the divine, in contrast to *agapē* as God's way to human beings.

Nygren finds *agapē* defined in such parables as the Prodigal Son (Luke 15:11-32) and the Laborers in the Vineyard (Matt 20:1-16). Early Christian theology reached its apex in Paul's *agapē* of the cross, expressed not only in God's action in Jesus Christ (2 Cor 5:18-19), but also as Paul's basic love motif (1 Cor 13). According to Nygren, all three motifs could be found in Christianity after the apostolic period: the *nomos*-type in the Apostolic Fathers (especially the "Two Ways" doctrine) and the Apologists, *erōs* in Gnosticism, and *agapē* in Marcion.[77] Eventually all three were synthesized by Augustine. Theologically speaking, *agapē*, being "voluntary" and "unmotivated," corresponds to the Tübingen school's understanding of divine autonomy. *Nomos*, which demands performance prior to acceptance, presumes heteronomy.

Nygren begins his commentary on Romans by quoting Luther's opinion that it is "the clearest gospel of all."[78] With Luther, Nygren takes 1:16-17 as the

---

74. Anders Nygren, *Dogmatikens vetenskapliga grundläggning med särskild hönsyn till den Kant-Schleiermacherska problemställningen* (*Lunds Universitets Årskrift*, N.F. Avd. 1, Vol. 17, No. 8, 1922), 161-65.

75. Anders Nygren, *Essence of Christianity* (trans. P. Watson; London: Epworth, 1960), 46-47, 56-57; *Agape and Eros* (trans. P. Watson; London: SPCK, 1953), 45, 68, 206-7. See also Bernhard Erling, "Motif Research as a General Historical Method," in *The Philosophy and Theology of Anders Nygren* (ed. C. W. Kegley; *Study of Theological Method in Schleiermacher and Nygren;* Leiden: E. J. Brill, 1964), 91-92.

76. Nygren, *Agape and Eros*, 75-81.

77. Ibid., 253.

78. Anders Nygren, *Commentary on Romans* (trans. Carl Rasmussen; Philadelphia: Muhlenberg, 1949), 1. See Martin Luther's preface to Romans.

center of that "gospel" *(summarium huius epistolae)*. Δικαιοσύνη τοῦ Θεοῦ, as a gift of God, stands over against all human efforts to achieve a relationship with God (δικαιοσύνη ἐκ νόμου or ἐξ ἔργου).[79] For Nygren the gift of δικαιοσύνη is the same as the ἀγάπη τοῦ Θεοῦ (subjective genitive) as seen in the key passage, Rom 5:8.[80] Scandinavian motif research does not make any radical alterations to Luther's reading of Romans but, by building on the Kantian-Schleiermacherian conception of religion as experience, it presents Paul's *agapē* as an experience of God — an idea that has become attractive far beyond Scandinavia and Lutheran circles.[81]

The Romans Debate: A New Perspective

Not unlike the effect of Schweitzer's *Quest for the Historical Jesus* on Jesus research, Barth's dialectical approach to Romans brought a pause in major works on Paul's letter. Recently a new era has begun, characterized by what some have called the "New Perspective."[82] Illustrative of this new approach is the work of E. P. Sanders, who showed that the distance between Judaism and Paul was not as great as New Testament material and later Christian writings would have us believe.[83] The earlier scholarly misinterpretation was caused by two factors: (1) a dependence on the New Testament and other early Christian writings for our picture of Judaism at the time of Paul, and (2) an exposition of Pauline theology that depends on his rejection of "Jewish legalism."[84]

According to the new perspective, the position of the Jews in Rome is almost opposite to that posited by Colenso. The Hellenists, who are the majority among Roman Christians, have the upper hand in the Roman churches and are in danger of ostracizing the Christ-believing Jews.[85] The Hellenistic Christians are the addressees of the letter, and are being asked by Paul to accept the Jews as equals (Rom 11:17-24).

If the "strong" Christians are the Hellenists who enter Christianity without

---

79. Ibid., 79.

80. Ibid., 197.

81. Victor Furnish, *The Love Commandment in the New Testament* (Nashville: Abingdon, 1972).

82. James D. G. Dunn, "The New Perspective on Paul," *Bulletin of the John Rylands Library* 65 (1983): 95-122.

83. E. P. Sanders, *Paul and Palestinian Judaism* (London: SCM Press, 1977).

84. Ibid., 426-27.

85. Mark Reasoner, *The Strong and the Weak: Romans 14:1–15:3 in Context* (Cambridge: Cambridge University Press, 1999).

the "burden" of calendar and food restrictions, then Rom 14:1–15:1 is addressed to the Hellenists and urges them to be considerate of the weaker Christ-believing Jews. Furthermore, the addressees, the Hellenizing Christians, may be in danger of rejecting the Jewish basis of their new faith.[86] The situation was complicated even more by the fact that, while Jews had to alter calendar and food regulations, Gentiles also had to alter their calendar and festivals (Gal 4:8-11).[87]

On the other hand, when Jews are directly addressed (Rom 2:17–3:8), we are to assume they are "on stage" as Paul's dialogue partners to clarify the faith to Christian Hellenists.[88] While keeping clear that God first chose Israel as a people, Paul wants the non-Jews to know they are not superior — even though they have accepted Christ while some obdurate Jews have not.

Some proponents of the "new perspective" consider themselves "enlightened traditionalists." That may be true, but the work of such scholars as E. P. Sanders, James Dunn, William Campbell, and Troels Engberg-Pederson, and Wendy Dabourne[89] have radically altered the Augustinian-Lutheran reading of Romans.[90] Paul the Jew repeats the *Shema* as his basic affirmation of faith: "God is one; and he will justify the circumcised on the ground of faith and the uncircumcised through that same faith" (3:30). God's oneness will be expressed in a oneness of all people, Jew and Gentile. In Rom 9–11, Paul describes how that end-time vision will be accomplished.[91] The bottom line of the new perspective: Paul is a Jew, not an opponent of Judaism.

86. Mark D. Nanos, *The Mystery of Romans: The Jewish Context of Paul's Letter* (Minneapolis: Fortress, 1996), 14.

87. Alan Segal, *Paul the Convert*, 263. Graydon F. Snyder, *Inculturation of the Jesus Tradition: The Impact of Jesus on Jewish and Roman Cultures* (Harrisburg, Pa.: Trinity Press International, 1999), 122-24.

88. Stanley Stowers, *The Diatribe and Paul's Letter to the Romans*, 115-17.

89. For an excellent summary and bibliography see Wendy Dabourne, *Purpose and Cause in Pauline Exegesis: Romans 1.16–4.25 and a New Approach to the Letters* (Cambridge: Cambridge University Press, 1999).

90. E. P. Sanders, *Paul and Palestinian Judaism: A Comparison of Patterns of Religion* (Minneapolis: Augsburg Fortress, 1977, 1983); James D. G. Dunn, *Theology of Paul the Apostle* (Edinburgh: T&T Clark, 1998), 5-6; William S. Campbell, *Paul's Gospel in an Intercultural Context: Jew and Gentile in the Letter to the Romans* (Frankfurt am Main: Lang, 1991), 99-101; Troels Engberg-Pedersen, "Galatians in Romans 5–8 and Paul's Construction of the Identity of the Christ Believers," 477-505 in *Texts and Contexts: Biblical Texts in Their Textual and Situational Contexts* (ed. T. Fornberg and D. Hellholm; Oslo: Scandinavian University Press, 1995).

91. To underscore the Jewishness of Paul several studies have appeared to show Paul's use of Isaiah, particularly in Romans 9–11. For example, J. Ross Wagner, *Heralds of the Good News: Isaiah and Paul "In Concert" in the Letter to the Romans* (Leiden: E. J. Brill, 2002), See also Florian Wilk, *Die Bedeutung des Jesajabuches für Paulus* (Göttingen: Vandenhoeck & Ruprecht, 1998), 304-17.

The worldview of the Western world shifted radically after the Enlightenment. With the demise of Theism, Christians no longer assume the uniqueness of the Christian faith. Understanding and communication among religions are more important than conversion or dogma. The Letter to the Romans speaks to Gentiles, but Paul calls for mutual understanding between the two groups: Jew and Gentile. The "new perspective" has made Jewish-Christian dialogue more likely and more profitable. Works by Alan Segal and Mark Nanos are positive examples of Jewish responses to "new perspective" writers.[92]

Conclusion

James Dunn speaks of Romans as the template for Pauline theology. One might even aver that Romans is the template for the Christian faith. Through the centuries, the importance and centrality of this last of Paul's letters has been undeniable. One can study Romans as a historical document, written by the apostle Paul and transmitted to us with only a modicum of textual variations. While such historical studies are essential, they are not enough. In every generation, from the time of James and Second Peter until today, readers approach Romans with questions of faith. The answers have differed radically, depending on the time in history. Surely there is a time to choose the right way; to recognize that only God can set things right; to say all human community derives from the ἐξουσία of God; to fear theological imperialism. Surely there are times when religious experience must be reaffirmed; when the Word of God must be heard above all other voices; when human existence must be measured by divine reality; when the entire human community must come together. The Letter to the Romans is a powerful writing. It will speak again and again, but always in new ways, to answer present questions.

---

92. E.g., Alan Segal, *Paul the Convert*, 262-64; Mark D. Nanos, *The Mystery of Romans*, 9-16. Cf. Simon J. Gathercole, *Where Is Boasting?: Early Jewish Soteriology and Paul's Response in Romans 1–5* (Grand Rapids, Mich.: Eerdmans, 2002), 266; while approving the direction of the "new perspective," Gathercole doubts that "works" can be eliminated from Judaism and calls for a new vocabulary to avoid the old pitfalls. "Merit" might be more useful.

RHETORICAL APPROACHES TO ROMANS

compiled by Frank W. Hughes

"All God's Beloved in Rome!"
Jewish Roots and Christian Identity

William S. Campbell

Structure and Content in Romans 8:14–11:36

In a previous essay on the structure and style of Romans, I drew attention to the frequency of questions and responses in the diatribe style in certain sections of Romans though this feature is absent in others.[1] I had some difficulty in describing chapter 8 in this approach. In some respects it is similar to the proclamatory style some scholars have noted in 3:21-26 and chapter 5.[2] Yet parts of chapter 8, especially verses 31-39, are very similar to chapter 9. This was awkward for someone like myself who wanted to make a major break at the end of chapter 8, thus dividing the letter into chapters 1–4, 5–8, 9–11, and 12–16. Since the first essay was written, I have become increasingly aware of the strong links between chapter 8 and chapters 9–11 and would emphasize them still more.

A major difficulty with linking chapters 8 and 9 is that the latter is very

---

1. William S. Campbell, "Romans 3 as a Key to the Structure and Thought of the Letter," in *Paul's Gospel in an Intercultural Context: Jew and Gentile in the Letter to the Romans* (*Studien zur interkulturellen Geschichte des Christentums* 69; Frankfurt am Main/New York/etc.: Peter Lang, 1991, repr. 1992); also 251-64 in *The Romans Debate: Revised and Expanded Edition* (ed. Karl P. Donfried; Peabody, Mass.: Hendrickson, 1991).

2. Joachim Jeremias, O. Michel, and others investigated the structural and verbal clues in Romans; for details see William S. Campbell, "Romans 3 as a Key." Rhetorical studies such as Robert Jewett's "Following the Argument of Romans" (in *The Romans Debate*, 265-77), and Neil Elliott's *The Rhetoric of Romans: Argumentative Constraint and Strategy and Paul's Dialogue with Judaism* (*Journal for the Study of the New Testament Supplement Series* 45; Sheffield: JSOT Press, 1990) have greatly assisted our understanding in recent years.

much a discussion of Jewish issues carried out in dialogue with the Old Testament Scriptures, whereas the former usually is read as one of the most explicitly Christian statements in the entire letter.[3] What sort of meaningful links can one discover between chapters of such differing perspectives? Themes in Rom 8 — such as the fulfilment of the law in believers, the witness of the Spirit, the renewal of the creation and above all the secure destiny of those in Christ — have caused chapter 9 and its concern with the Jewish failure to accept Christ to appear as anti-climax to a story which already has reached its conclusion. Chapter 11, with its conclusion advocating the salvation of "all Israel," appears in fact to contradict the neat conclusion already achieved at the end of Rom 8. Small wonder that C. H. Dodd viewed Rom 9–11 as a sermon on the Jewish issue which Paul previously had constructed elsewhere before inserting it rather arbitrarily at this point.[4]

In fact the apparent dissonance between Paul's statements in Rom 8 and 9–11 respectively have individually contributed to two divergent understandings of Pauline theology. One is pronouncedly Christological, representing an evangelical, existential type of theology and stressing radical newness, while the other is *"heilsgeschichtlich,"* stressing continuity with Israel. The former perspective stresses Rom 1–8 and tends to use 9–11 negatively as witness to the disobedience and rejection of Israel, while the latter sees Paul's argument as progressing cumulatively to a positive climax in chapter 11 or 11–16. Even the figure of Abraham is disputed. In his use of the Abraham tradition is Paul simply providing his converts with a fictive-family connection to an individual significant only as a "punctiliar," exemplary believer?[5] Or is he actually relating them to a particular people of God of whom Abraham was the father? Is Paul, in fact, rooting the Gentiles in the ancient stem of Abraham, or is he creating a new people of God?

Recent research on Paul's use of Scripture, and on Scriptural echoes in the New Testament generally, has proved illuminating here.[6] Far from using the

3. Robin Scroggs drew attention to differences within Romans, regarding 1–4 and 9–11 as two homilies diverging greatly from 5–8, "Paul as Rhetorician: Two Homilies in Romans 1–11," in *Jews, Greeks and Barbarians: Religious Cultures in Late Antiquity: Essays in Honour of W. D. Davies* (ed. R. Hamerton-Kelly and R. Scroggs; Leiden: E. J. Brill, 1976), 270-71.

4. C. H. Dodd, *The Epistle to the Romans (Moffatt New Testament Commentary;* London: Hodder & Stoughton, 1932), 148-49.

5. Cf. J. L. Martyn, "Events in Galatia: Modified Covenantal Nomism versus God's Invasion of the Cosmos in the Singular Gospel. A Response to J. D. G. Dunn and B. R. Gaventa," 160-79 in *Pauline Theology,* Vol. 1 (ed. Jouette M. Bassler; Minneapolis: Augsburg Fortress, 1991), esp. 174.

6. Cf. Richard B. Hays, *Echoes of Scripture in the Letters of Paul* (New Haven: Yale University Press, 1989).

Scriptures merely as proof texts or as evidence for his view of the Gospel, Paul has emerged as a serious student of Scripture who not only uses it frequently and explicitly but whose whole thought is permeated with Scriptural nuances and insights. To the careful observer, echoes of the Scriptures are discernible throughout his writings.

In response to Calvin Roetzel in a discussion concerning the origins of Paul's theology, I came to the conclusion that Paul's uniqueness consists not so much in creating absolutely new theological structures as in the creative transformation of his ancestral traditions. Paul both interprets Scripture in relation to contemporary events of his own time, and in turn interprets these events in the light of Scripture. Thus the frequent emphasis on calling (καλέω) in 1 Corinthians reminds us of God's calling of Israel and that "Paul's theologizing takes place within the specific context of ongoing divine activity in relation to a people who are called."[7]

Paul does not suddenly turn to the people of Israel in chapter 9; already beginning with Rom 7:1, and especially from 8:14-39, the story of Israel provides the background to his argument.[8] Sonship, as it is developed in 8:14-15, builds on the consolidation of themes in 6:12–8:11; this is evident particularly in 8:12-17, where the negative formulations that were applied to the Christian life in 6:1-11 (death to sin, release from slavery to sin) are replaced by the positive theme of divine "sonship." The argumentative unit is therefore 6:1–8:13 which is succeeded by a second unit beginning in 8:14 and continuing through to 11:36.[9]

Commentators have noticed the parallels between terms used in chapter 8 and those that recur again in chapter 9 but, in the latter instance, with their primary reference to Israel.[10] "Calling" in various constructions occurs in 8:30; 9:7, 12, 24-26. The first reference to "sons of God" in Romans occurs in 8:14 (cf. 8:19). In Scriptural citations the same or parallel expressions occur in 9:26: "the non-people" become "sons of the living God"; and in 9:27: "though the number of the sons of Israel is as the sand of the sea, a remnant will be saved." Sonship

---

7. William S. Campbell, "The Contribution of Traditions to Paul's Theology," 234-54 in *Pauline Theology*, Vol. 2 (ed. D. Hay; Minneapolis: Augsburg Fortress, 1993).

8. See William S. Campbell, "Divergent Images of Paul and His Mission," 187-211 in *Reading Israel in Romans: Legitimacy and Plausibility of Divergent Interpretations* (ed. Cristina Grenholm and Daniel Patte; vol. 1 of *Romans Through History and Cultures: Receptions and Critical Interpretations*; Harrisburg, Pa.: Trinity Press International, 2000).

9. Cf. Neil Elliott, *The Rhetoric of Romans*, esp. 271-75 on "The Argumentative Coherence of Romans 5–11."

10. Cf. "brethren" (ἀδελφοί) in 8:29 and 9:3. Mark Nanos notes that "Paul regards non-Christian Jews as his 'brethren' throughout this letter," *The Mystery of Romans: The Jewish Context of Paul's Letter* (Minneapolis: Augsburg Fortress, 1996), 110.

occurs first in 8:15, then in 8:23, and again in 9:4 in the sevenfold list of Israel's privileges. "Children of God" occurs in 8:16, 17, 21, and in 9:8. In 8:28 we have reference to those "called according to his purpose" and in 9:11 "the purpose of God in election." "Those whom he foreknew" is found in 8:29 and recurs in 11:2 in connection with "his people." "Glory" occurs throughout Romans but notably in 8:18, 21; 9:4, 23; and 11:36.[11]

Clearly, Paul does not turn to the attributes and privileges of Israel for the first time in Rom 9–11; rather, many of these already had been introduced earlier in the letter in 7:1-2 and in 8:14-39.[12] This enables us to conclude that, firstly, chapters 9–11 are no afterthought and there is no major caesura after 8:39.[13] More significantly, however, another observation is warranted. In 8:1-13 and to a lessening extent as the chapter progresses, the Christological emphases of the Pauline Gospel are present. But surprisingly an increasing ambiguity in terminology emerges so that the new believing community is described in almost similar terms to Israel. Paul uses terms and attributes in chapter 8, and then in 9:4-5 provides a compact list of these referring precisely to Israel (rather than to Gentile Christians), followed by other similar references in chapters 9–11.

This argument from the use of common terms in chapters 8 and 9–11 is greatly strengthened when we take into account not only explicit terms but also Scriptural echoes and implicit allusions. The underlying theme of 8:14-39 is the Exodus narrative as indicated by such terms as "led by the Spirit," "spirit of slavery," and "freedom from fear." More vivid however is the emphasis on "leading" and "sonship," with Israel as the firstborn son and Israel's sonship as derived from the Exodus. Sylvia C. Keesmaat has convincingly argued in a recent study that "Paul echoes the language of the Exodus narrative in a way which is consistent with the prophets, so that the Roman believers have an identity as those who are undertaking a wilderness journey *en route* to the promised land."[14]

---

11. James D. G. Dunn notes many links between Rom 8 and 9 in "Paul's Epistle to the Romans: An Analysis of Structure and Argument," 2842-90 in *Aufstieg und Niedergang der römischen Welt: Geschichte und Kultur Roms im Spiegel der neueren Forschung,* Part 2, *Principat,* 25.4 (ed. Hildegard Temporini and Wolfgang Haase; Berlin & New York: Walter de Gruyter, 1987); and *Romans* (2 vols.; *Word Biblical Commentary* 38A-B; Dallas: Word Books, 1988).

12. The ἐγώ in Rom 7:9 may refer to Israel rather than to Paul, or to Paul as a representative of Israel, which makes good sense in the context. Thus 7:7-25 refers to Israel's struggle with the Law; this view is preferable to a psychological or individualistic interpretation of Paul and prepares for the Exodus allusions in 8:14-39.

13. For an excellent discussion of this and related issues see T. Engbert-Pedersen, "For the Jew First: The Coherence of Literary Structure and Thought in Romans in Conversation with James D. G. Dunn" (paper presented at the annual meeting of the *Studiorum Novi Testamenti Societas,* University of Pretoria, August 1999).

14. Sylvia C. Keesmaat, *Paul and His Story: (Re)Interpreting the Exodus Tradition (Journal*

The content of 8:18-39 also has close parallels to Jeremiah 31 with its emphasis on a new Exodus event, a new covenant, and the assertion that Israel would exist even if the created order were to disappear.[15] From this we discover that faithfulness to the whole of creation and to Israel is the concluding emphasis of chapter 8 and a fitting link to 9–11.[16] From this perspective it is very fitting to describe 8:14–11:36 as "The Heritage of the Children of God."[17] According to Neil Elliott, "connections in vocabulary and themes *across* the artificial boundary at 9:1 constitute the argumentative integration of Rom 8 and 9, and thereby of the larger segments 1–8 and 9–11; . . . the thematic unity of the whole is the hope for the 'glory of the children of God' (8:20-21)."[18]

Although he has transformed the Exodus story by developing the "new Exodus" dimension and applying it to believers in Christ,[19] the intended audience of Paul's address in Rom 8 is no different from that in Rom 9. While the failure of Israel to recognize Jesus as Messiah is stressed and the focus in 9:1-29 (with the exception of 9:24) is Israel, the discussion is nevertheless *about Israel as a third party*. It is not a dialogue with Israel.[20] Thus the eventual import of the argument in chapter 8, and perhaps of the entire letter, despite the allusions to Israel, is in part or in total intended primarily for the Gentile believers more precisely

---

for the Study of the New Testament Supplement 181; Sheffield: JSOT Press, 1999), 153; see also 136-54.

15. Cf. ibid., 153-54. Keesmaat maintains that Paul transforms the tradition, writing as though the new Exodus is now taking place.

16. Cf. ibid., 64: "Paul is concerned with God's faithfulness to all of creation, but in the light of Jeremiah 31, the renewal of creation in Romans 8 is an *affirmation* of God's faithfulness to Israel." Ernst Käsemann and some of his students have been criticized by Karl Kertelge for overemphasizing God's freedom as Creator (in Rom 9), in such a way that faithfulness to Israel is replaced by faithfulness to the creation; cf. Käsemann, "The Righteousness of God in Paul," in *New Testament Questions of Today* (London: SCM Press, 1969), 177-80; Kertelge, *Rechtfertigung bei Paulus* (Münster: Aschendorff, 1967), 308; and Campbell, "The Freedom and Faithfulness of God in Relation to Israel," in *Paul's Gospel in an Intercultural Context*, 43-59; cf. 4-5.

17. When this paper was nearing completion, I was delighted to note that Neil Elliott had thus entitled this section of Romans; see Elliott, *The Rhetoric of Romans*, 253-54.

18. Elliott, *The Rhetoric of Romans*, 257.

19. On this see also W. D. Davies, "Paul and the New Exodus," 443-63 in *The Quest for Context and Meaning: Studies in Biblical Intertextuality in Honour of James A. Sanders* (ed. C. A. Evans & S. Talmon; Leiden: E. J. Brill, 1997).

20. *Contra* J. Christiáán Beker's comment (*Paul, the Apostle: The Triumph of God in Life and Thought* [Philadelphia: Fortress, 1980], 24-25) that "in Romans Paul does not attack Christians for adopting Jewish ways or circumcision but demonstrates instead the way in which Judaism is accounted for in the Gospel. The dialogue with the Jews is at the same time an apology for Israel. . . ." Cf. Campbell, *Paul's Gospel in an Intercultural Context*, 137. Elliott's emphasis on dialogue is rhetorically more sophisticated and avoids the problems which Beker encounters.

addressed in 11:13-14. The goal of the argument is indicated in 11:25. Paul's revelation of a mystery and all that precedes it is to destroy the Gentiles' mistaken and ill-founded boasting, based on an imagined superiority over Jews, "lest you be wise in your own conceits" (ἵνα μὴ ἦτε [παρ'] ἑαυτοῖς φρόνιμοι). We may summarize our thesis here: 8:14–11:36 functions along with 14:1–15:13, to provide support for "the weak in faith" and to humble "the strong in faith."

At this point we are forced to ask the question of Paul's intention in a rhetoric involving the use of similar terms across apparently very dissimilar chapters. It would appear that he is deliberately blurring the distinction between the new believing community and the old.[21] Is he saying firstly that God is faithful in preserving and delivering his own people and secondly that only God knows and determines the boundaries of his elect people? Presumably one or both of these emphases would be relevant to the believers in Rome. We will understand the two possibilities better if we set out their significance. If Paul wishes to blur the lines concerning the description of the elect of God, perhaps it is because some Christians in Rome were in danger of being wrongly excluded from this people, and Paul wants to prevent what he sees as a drastic mistake. This would be more serious if in fact all or even some of the Christ-believers in Rome were meeting in the synagogues and functioning wholly within the larger Jewish community (or communities) in Rome. If Mark Nanos is correct in interpreting "weak in faith" as referring to Jews who as yet are not fully convinced about Jesus as Messiah,[22] then Paul wishes in his argument to be inclusive rather than exclusive to enable such people to get support and encouragement to lead them in the right direction according to his Gospel.

If Paul wishes to oppose Roman Gentile Christians in their mistaken despising of their fellow Jews and Jewish believers in Christ and to prevent their cutting themselves off from the stem of Abraham, then his purpose would be to incorporate them into the story of Abraham and the people of Israel. But this would be done in such a way that they would not be encouraged to "Judaize"

21. D. W. B. Robinson is one of the few exegetes to note this phenomenon. He sees the theme of Rom 8 as being "the liberty of the Jew who has entered his inheritance in Christ and his hope of glory according to promise and election"; Christian experience and the expectation of final glory are set forth deliberately as "the experience of the justified Jew, indeed of Israel itself in the person of the servant and apostle of the Lord" (Robinson, "The Priesthood of Paul in the Gospel of Hope," 231-45 in *Reconciliation and Hope: New Testament Essays on Atonement and Eschatology Presented to Leon Morris on His 60th Birthday* [ed. R. J. Banks; Exeter: Paternoster, 1974], 244-45).

22. Mark D. Nanos, "The Jewish Context of the Gentile Audience Addressed in Paul's Letter to the Romans," *Catholic Biblical Quarterly* 61 (1999): 283-304. For a fuller explanation of his argument see Mark D. Nanos, *The Mystery of Romans* (Minneapolis: Augsburg Fortress, 1996).

(though there was little likelihood of that). Rather, they are encouraged to perceive themselves as Gentile branches in the family tree of Abraham.[23] In this
sense Paul would be encouraging them to see the story of God's elect people as
their story also, and to allow their identity to be reshaped in an "Israelitish" re-
configuration while yet remaining Gentiles.

Jewish versus Christian Identity?

In his recent interesting article on "Jewish versus Christian Identity in the
Church," Bengt Holmberg argues that the conflict in Galatians between Jewish
and Christian identity should be restated as a conflict between Christian identity and Jewish-Christian self-definition.[24] Holmberg concludes that "the common, fundamental Christian identity of the church is more important than inherited ethno-religious self-definitions."[25] Holmberg notes (following Ben
Meyer's insights) that the early church discovered itself and found its own identity by allowing its dynamic missionary work to feed back into its self-
understanding. This meant that previous conceptions about the place and role
of Gentiles had to be drastically revised in the light of the experience of their
participation in the Spirit. Thus it is clear that, "theologically speaking, the
Holy Spirit creates the identity of the church and shows it to her, and the
church's role in this process is to become aware of and obedient to these
experience-based insights."[26] That experience-based insights influenced the
theological development of the church need not be doubted. We are not convinced however that Holmberg's insights setting Jewish identity in antithesis to
Christian identity are valid, especially when applied to Romans.

If our emphasis that Paul has already introduced the theme of Israel in
Rom 8:14-15 is correct, then "it seems clear that one of the things that Paul's
evocation of the Exodus tradition accomplishes is firmly to root and characterize the identity and calling of the Roman believers. As sons of God, redeemed
and called in the climactic new Exodus in Christ, they have a calling to faithful
obedience of the God they serve. As participants in the final Exodus, with its
import for all of creation, their calling has cosmic proportions."[27] In chapters

23. Is Paul's aim in Romans "to show the Gentiles how their hope rests on Israel's Messiah?" Cf. D. W. B. Robinson, "The Priesthood of Paul in the Gospel of Hope," 232.

24. Bengt Holmberg, "Jewish *versus* Christian Identity," *Revue Biblique* 105 (1998):
397-425.

25. Ibid., 424.

26. Ibid., 421.

27. Keesmaat, *Paul and His Story,* 143.

9–11 Paul is seeking to provide the Romans with a revised self-understanding. It would appear that some of them are in the process of, or at least at risk of, developing a new self-understanding that is not only distinct from, but perhaps even in opposition to, their designation as children of Abraham. The conclusion to the main argument in Romans lies in the command to "welcome one another" (14:1; 15:7). This concluding admonition here explicitly is designed to overcome alienation and judging of one another, and thus to encourage mutual acceptance between the various Gentile and Jewish Christian groupings in Rome.[28] What is significant, however, is that it is supported by a *catena* of scriptural citations in 15:9-12; and the emphasis in all four quotations is on the Gentiles confessing and praising Israel's God, *joining with Israel* (μετὰ τοῦ λαοῦ αὐτοῦ).[29] This suggests that Paul saw a need for Gentiles to recognize and relate positively to their Jewish neighbors.

Christian Identity and Negative Self-Definition

Why should there be a reaction against Jewishness when historical evidence demonstrates that Judaism proved very attractive to many Gentiles, some of whom became proselytes despite the physical and social barrier represented by circumcision?[30] The most reasonable hypothesis is that, in some instances, this aversion to Judaism arose as a rejection of former proselyte status and everything associated with it upon entering a Christ-believing community. This would represent, therefore, a turning away from an acquired Jewish identity by former Gentiles.[31] We have in it an example of the phenomenon of a rejection

---

28. Cf. W. A. Meeks, "Judgement and the Brother: Romans 14:1–15:13," in *Tradition and Interpretation in the New Testament: Essays in Honour of E. E. Ellis* (ed. G. P. Hawthorne with Otto Betz; Grand Rapids, Mich.: Eerdmans, 1987), 290-300. Meeks (291) notes that the root κρίν- "becomes a *leitmotif* in our text."

29. Meeks draws attention to this as "one odd thing about this *catena* of texts," "Judgement and the Brother," 291.

30. See Leonard V. Rutgers, *The Hidden Heritage of Diaspora Judaism. Essays on Jewish Cultural Identity in the Roman World* (2nd ed.; Leuven: Peeters, 1998), 33; cf. Tessa Rajak, "The Jewish Community and Its Boundaries," 9-28 in *The Jews Among Pagans and Christians in the Roman Empire* (ed. Judith Lieu, John North & Tessa Rajak; London: Routledge, 1992).

31. Despite the attractiveness of Judaism to many Gentiles, once proselytes became acquainted with the Gentile mission, a new option was then available which had not been open to them earlier; and this may have allowed them to return to the inherent resentment prevalent in Hellenistic society, perhaps encouraged by the very strength and self-confidence of Judaism. See Rutgers, *The Hidden Heritage of Diaspora Judaism*, 37; also J. Barclay, *Jews in the Mediterranean Diaspora: From Alexander to Trajan, 323 B.C.E.–117 C.E.* (Edinburgh: T&T Clark, 1996), 444.

intensified because of high evaluation of the former affiliation. Now they are self-confident and self-aware in their new identity as Gentile Christians, even to the point of despising those Christians, whether of Jewish or Gentile birth, who felt obligated to continue practicing a Jewish life-style.

Their self-estimate is over-inflated for two reasons. First, because they now know that there is no need for Gentile Christ-believers to become Jews; in fact, it is explicitly forbidden by Paul to do so, although it may be that not all the believing proselytes shared this view. Second, they have a new understanding of their own role and status in salvation history in relation to the Jews. "Branches were broken off that I might be grafted in" (11:19) probably indicates traces of group conflict. Whether or not this theological opinion is exactly paralleled by an actual situation in Rome is another highly debated question, but greater consensus now exists concerning the Christ-believing community at Rome, at least with regard to the Roman Gentile believers.[32] We can be reasonably confident that at least some of these believers were using their antipathy toward a Jewish life-style as a means of negative self-definition.

What we seem to have evidence of here is a sectarian type of Gentile Christianity. We are not suggesting that Paul's communities were sectarian, but Paul did not found the church in Rome. A possible explanation for the emergence of this sectarian attitude is that, because their self-definition in Christ was being negatively valued by Jews who did not share their faith, some Christ-believers sought to justify their inclusion by undermining the place and legitimacy of the practice of Jews. While Christianity in its origins may be accurately described as a messianic sect of Judaism,[33] it was not necessarily sectarian in character, and this group in its negative self-definition is an aberration from the norm of the Pauline communities.[34]

How Paul attempts to oppose this self-designation is extremely interesting. His depiction of the Gentiles as branches grafted into the stem of Abraham ✷

---

32. I have argued for this reading of Romans in different articles, some of which are included in my *Paul's Gospel in an Intercultural Context,* but see also more recently "The Rule of Faith in Romans 12:1–15:13," 259-86 in *Pauline Theology,* Vol. 3 (ed. D. M. Hay and E. E. Johnson; Minneapolis: Augsburg Fortress, 1995). Dunn (*Romans,* 2: 801-802) also supports the view that the divide between "the weak" and "the strong" basically was along a Jewish-oriented v. non-Jewish-oriented line — and that Paul is urging the latter to bow to the sensibilities of the former.

33. Cf. Christopher Rowland, who describes Christianity as a messianic sect of Judaism, *Christian Origins: An Account of the Setting and Character of the Most Important Messianic Sect of Judaism* (London: SPCK, 1985; rev. ed., Pilgrim Press, 2002), 109-10 in 1st ed.

34. Contra Francis Watson's thesis that Paul sought to transform a reform movement into a sect (Watson, *Paul, Judaism and the Gentiles: A Sociological Approach* [Cambridge: Cambridge University Press, 1986], 19-20).

demonstrates analogically their dependence on the Jewish foundations of the church. They have no entirely independent identity, whether or not they desire such. If they do not show proper reverence, they too will be broken off; they have no absolute independence or security in and of themselves. They remain branches, which in and of themselves do not constitute a tree. Paul in fact relocates the Gentiles in the family of Abraham. They have to take on the identity or part of the identity of children or seed (σπέρμα) of Abraham. In Romans, as distinct from Galatians, the σπέρμα is comprised of two peoples (4:16).

What is surprising here is that Paul does fully incorporate the Gentiles in the seed of Abraham, but without identifying them as proselytes, despite the connection with circumcision in Genesis 17. That this is the case is demonstrated by the fact that Abraham is described as father both of the circumcised and of those who believe without being circumcised (Rom 4:11-12). The latter are not just "righteous Gentiles" loosely affiliated with Israel; but neither are they Israelites proper, since Paul reserves this title for those who, like himself, are of Jewish ancestry (9:3-4; 11:1-2).[35]

Reports of this aspect of Paul's Gospel may in fact have contributed to confusion concerning Christian identity in Rome.

The status of former proselytes who became believers in Christ is a difficult issue on which to speculate. But that there were such need not be doubted as the reference to Nicolaus, a proselyte of Antioch (Acts 6:5), makes clear. But if among these there were, as we have suggested above, some proselytes who, on joining the Pauline communities, rejected their temporary affiliation to Judaism and its practices, choosing instead to follow a Gentile believer's life-style, this would create a very complex situation for both the Christ-believing communities and for the believing proselytes themselves who for a second time had to decide for or against living a Jewish life.

The proselyte believers most vulnerable would be those who were torn between accompanying their fellow proselytes in their rejection of Jewish practices and a conscience loyal to their previously adopted proselyte faith. In a very real sense, as believers in Christ of Gentile birth and also as proselytes to Judaism, they may not have felt, despite their previous acceptance into the synagogue, entirely at home in either community. They would now literally have been, and also have felt as if they were, in a liminal or even limbo state. Interest-

35. See William S. Campbell, "Israel," 441-46 in *A Dictionary of Paul and His Letters* (ed. Gerald F. Hawthorne, Ralph P. Martin, and Daniel G. Reid; Downers Grove, Ill.: InterVarsity, 1993); cf. J. D. G. Dunn, *The Theology of Paul the Apostle* (Grand Rapids, Mich.: Eerdmans 1998), 525-26, where Dunn suggests that "the identity of Israel as defined by grace and faith included both historic Israel and Gentiles," 526; cf. also T. L. Donaldson, "Proselytes as Righteous Gentiles," *Journal for the Study of the Pseudepigrapha* 7 (1990): 3-27.

ingly, Rom 14–15 makes very good sense if it is read as support for those proselytes who were vulnerable because of the upheaval facing them as a result of their abiding Jewish sensibilities. In conjunction with this, scholars have long disputed the too easy, perhaps simplistic, identification of the weak as Jews and the strong as Gentiles.[36] Recent research has tended to stress the actual orientation of these groups rather than their ethnic origins. A variation on traditional approaches has emerged in Paul Sampley's suggestion of a continuum of commitments along a wide spectrum of Jewish-Gentile stances.[37] The latter viewpoint would find some support and the insights of previous scholars would be respected by positing the existence of an inner group conflict such as I have described.

Moreover it would answer the question posed to me in a discussion by Lloyd Gaston as to how Paul in a letter conciliatory to Judaism, as Romans is, could still describe Jews with conscience scruples as weak. The "weak in faith" are in this proposal Gentile by birth and also Jews by proselytizing. Their weakness is not simply a Jewish conscience but a dilemma caused mainly by others changing and transferring their allegiance. Another strength of this proposal is that Paul's policy of remaining in the state in which one was called (1 Cor 7:17-18) would be welcomed by the "weak in faith."

If a major emphasis in Paul's Letter to the Romans was to promote awareness of the Jewish roots of the new faith and to discourage a separatist Gentile-oriented breakaway group, we may well ask, what effect did his letter actually have on the Roman church, and its subsequent identity? If it was successful, then we would expect a church with harmony between its diverse elements, whether in house churches or in association with a synagogue. We would also anticipate a renewed respect for the scriptures and for the Jewish roots of the faith.

There is, in fact, evidence of a certain Jewishness in the Roman church both in its origins[38] and in its development even towards the end of the first

---

36. Maximilian Rauer investigated this issue many years ago in his *Die "Schwachen" in Korinth und Rom nach den Paulusbriefen* (*The Bible Translator* 120; Freiburg: Herder, 1923). Neil Elliott's *The Rhetoric of Romans* offers a constructive and fresh approach to the topic.

37. J. Paul Sampley, "The Weak and the Strong: Paul's Careful and Crafty Rhetorical Strategy in Romans 14:1–15:13," 40-52 in *The Social World of the First Christians: Studies in Honor of Wayne A. Meeks* (ed. L. M. White and O. L. Yarbrough; Minneapolis: Augsburg Fortress, 1994). Cf. Campbell, "The Rule of Faith," 270-71.

38. Ambrosiaster tells us about Roman Christians: "It is evident then that there were Jews living in Rome . . . in the time of the apostles. Some of these Jews, who had come to believe [in Christ], passed on to the Romans [the tradition] that they should acknowledge Christ and keep the law. . . . One ought not to be angry with the Romans, but praise their faith, because without seeing any signs of miracles and without any of the apostles they came to embrace faith in Christ, though according to a Jewish rite." On this and related issues see J. A. Fitzmyer, *Romans*

century.[39] Perhaps Paul's death in Rome helped to convince some of the believers of the truth of his views and they responded accordingly to make their church(es) inclusive and more harmonious. On the other hand perhaps differing strands of tradition survived side by side, explaining the origin of the Letter to the Hebrews[40] and, possibly, the arrival and relative success of Marcion in Rome in the mid-second century. But in any case, Paul's letter may have helped the church to decide against Marcion's views at a crucial moment in its history, even if the issues raised are still a matter of debate — emerging at the moment around the issue of the basic identity of Christianity. We have, in fact, still not solved the problem faced by Paul so many centuries ago.[41]

That this is still very much a matter of debate is demonstrated by the contrast between Holmberg's view that the issue is one of "Jewish *versus* Christian Identity" and Dunn's claim that the identity of Israel included both historic Israel and the Gentiles. According to Holmberg, "we see both Jews and Gentiles in the Christian movement slowly sliding out of their earlier identities, and becoming something no one had ever been before. This *reciprocal identity displacement,* which is at the same time a *unification process,* started early in the history of the church — actually on Easter morning — even if we do not see it completed in the history of the writings of the New Testament."[42] In my view, this is not an adequate understanding of the complexity and diversity of the process by which Christian identity has been formed.

The issue concerning the true nature of Christian identity is as yet not very clear.[43] One may express it in this way. If we were to follow Holmberg's

(Anchor Bible Commentary 33; New York: Doubleday, 1993), 25-39. Cf. also R. Brändle & E. W. Stegemann, "The Formation of the First 'Christian Congregations' in the Context of the Jewish Congregations," 117-27 in *Judaism and Christianity in First Century Rome* (ed. Karl P. Donfried & Peter Richardson; Grand Rapids, Mich.: Eerdmans, 1998).

39. On this see William L. Lane, "Social Perspectives on Roman Christianity during the Formative Years from Nero to Nerva," 196-244 in *Judaism and Christianity in First Century Rome.*

40. Cf. ibid.

41. Cf. R. K. Soulen, *The God of Israel and Christian Theology* (Minneapolis: Augsburg Fortress, 1996), 25-26, 57-58.

42. Bengt Holmberg, "Jewish *versus* Christian Identity in the Early Church," 422. On the issue of Christianity as a "third race," see William S. Campbell, "Religious Identity and Ethnic Origin in the Earliest Christian Communities," 98-121 in *Paul's Gospel in an Intercultural Context.* My opinion on this issue was greatly influenced by W. Rader's *The Church and Racial Hostility: A History of Interpretation of Ephesians 2:11-22* (Tübingen: Mohr Siebeck, 1978).

43. In a recent article on Jewish-Christian identity ("Who Did Paul Think He Was? A Study of Jewish-Christian Identity," *New Testament Studies* 45 [1999]: 174-93), J. D. G. Dunn concluded that "ambiguity and confusion remain at the heart of Christian identity today" (193). Don Cupitt deplores the fact that today we are absorbed in trying to conserve our separate iden-

reading of Galatians, how then should we read Romans? A certain kind of Christian imperialism has always shown frustration and impatience with Jewish sensibilities. But that same imperialistic spirit is also impatient with the diversity which continues, and which according to Robert Jewett ought to be allowed to continue to exist within Christianity.[44] Käsemann warned us against making our faith the norm for others,[45] an excellent summary of Paul's position in this matter. Ben Meyer attempted to clarify the issue of Christian identity by distinguishing between "identity" and "self-definition."[46] He also acknowledges "that Christian identity was culturally incarnated . . ." and therefore "incarnated diversely."[47] Despite these useful insights, Meyer still tends to operate with a rather static understanding of identity.

Diversity in Christian Identity

It is of considerable relevance to the issue of divergent identities between first-century Jewish and Gentile Christians that modern research demonstrates that identities are neither monolithic nor fixed.[48] This correlates well with recent studies of Diaspora Judaism.[49] While it is true to recognize that, through the ✳ Gospel, Paul to some extent relativizes cultural specificities, yet he does not present the Gospel "as if it carries a whole new cultural package, designed to eradicate and replace all others. It is rather a cluster of values, focused in love which enables the creation of a new community in which variant cultural tradi-

tities ("Identity versus Globalization," 285-91 in *The Future of Jewish-Christian Dialogue* [ed. D. Cohn-Sherbok; Lampeter, UK, and Lewiston, N.Y.: Edwin Mellen, 1999]); Cupitt claims, "In Western society at large, 'the Christian tradition' has become just one more strand in everybody's cultural heritage" (289, 291).

44. Robert Jewett, *Christian Tolerance: God's Message to the Modern Church* (Philadelphia: Westminster, 1982), 35-42.

45. Ernst Käsemann, *Commentary on Romans* (trans. and ed. G. W. Bromiley; Grand Rapids, Mich.: Eerdmans, 1980), 379.

46. Cf. Holmberg, "Jewish *versus* Christian Identity," 422-23.

47. Ben Meyer, "The World Mission and the Emergent Realisation of Christian Identity," 173-94 in *Critical Realism and the New Testament* (*Princeton Theological Monograph Series* 17; Allison Park, Pa.: Pickwick, 1989), 188-89.

48. See, e.g., Daniel Boyarin, *A Radical Jew: Paul and the Politics of Identity* (Berkeley: University of California Press, 1994), 235, 244, and 257. It is possible to have a dual identity — as, e.g., P. Mendes-Flohr has argued for German Jews in the nineteenth and twentieth centuries (*German Jews: A Dual Identity* [New Haven & London: Yale University Press, 1999], *passim*).

49. See J. M. G. Barclay, *Jews in the Mediterranean Diaspora,* 443; also his "'Neither Jew nor Greek': Multiculturalism and the New Perspective on Paul," 197-214 in *Ethnicity and the Bible* (ed. M. G. Brett; Leiden: E. J. Brill, 1996).

tions can be practised."[50] It would seem that for Paul commitment to Christ did not mean installing Christ as the founder of a new culture in opposition to Judaism. Rather this commitment can simultaneously encompass various cultural particularities.

The legacy of F. C. Baur is still visible and influential even in current understandings of Paul's universalism.[51] Paul inevitably appears to be in opposition to particularism, especially that of his own people. Even Boyarin's description of the apostle's subtle "particularist claim to universalism" distorts the variegated vision of Paul in Rom 11.[52] It is only relatively recently that New Testament interpreters have recognized that Paul argues strongly in defense of Jewish-related scruples in Romans 14-15, requiring that each be fully convinced in one's own mind (14:5). Rather than insisting that there is no difference between Jew and Gentile in Christ, Paul is in fact affirming abiding differences between the two, actually recognizing their particular identities, regardless of the way the Gospel relativizes them.

The fallacy in the traditional understanding of Pauline universalism is that the transformative influence of the Gospel is seen as relativizing particular identities to the point that they form one common new identity. But this relativization requires neither the complete obliteration of prior identities nor their complete coalescence into one new identity. One might even ask whether such a conception of a common identity without inherent diversity would allow for the adequate formation of any kind of identity. Jenkins defines social identity as "the ways in which individuals and collectivities are distinguished in their social relations with other individuals and collectivities. It is the systematic establishment and signification, between individuals, and collectivities, of relationships of similarities and difference. Taken — as they can only be — together, similarity and difference are the dynamic principles of identity. . . ."[53] This would suggest the necessity of an "other" in identity-formation.

It would appear that the paradigmatic character of Paul's conversion seems to demand that all Christians ever since should experience a similar religious and cultural transformation to a new identity. Since commitment is necessary for every Christian it is assumed that a similar cultural transformation is also obligatory for all. But as Jenkins notes, there are "primary identities" (such as selfhood, gender and, in Paul's world, kinship and ethnicity) which are established early in a child's experience which are particularly resistant to change,

---

50. Cf. ibid., 211.

51. See F. C. Baur, *Paul the Apostle of Jesus Christ*, Vol. 1 (trans. from the 2nd German edition; ed. E. Zeller; rev. A. Menzies; London: Williams & Norgate, 1876).

52. Boyarin, *A Radical Jew*, 205-8.

53. R. Jenkins, *Social Identity* (London: Routledge, 1996), 4.

whereas transformation of secondary identities can be more easily accomplished.[54]

It is therefore of some significance whether we consider Paul to have received a call to apostleship or to have experienced a conversion to a new religion. Did Paul in fact experience "a resocialisation process in which 'one universe of discourse' or set of shared social meanings was replaced by another"?[55] Should we not rather consider Paul and other Jews as undergoing a process analogous to secondary socialization since their Christian identity was superimposed on a pre-existing Jewish identity? Thus Richard Travisano distinguishes between this, which he terms alternation, and conversion as a radical change of universe of discourse. For him alternation is a less radical form of identity transformation and conversion.[56]

The degree of continuity which we perceive between Paul and his Jewish roots is thus greatly determined by the model of his Damascus road experience which we utilize. Only if we greatly exaggerate the degree of change that was effected in his life are we obligated to consider him as necessarily exchanging a Jewish identity for a Christian one.

If our assessment of Paul's aim in Rom 8:14–11:36 as a continuous argument is correct,[57] it would appear that already in chapter 8 he is beginning the attempt to incorporate Gentile believers in Christ into the story and identity of Abraham's descendants.[58] But this does not mean a common undifferentiated

---

54. Ibid., 20-21. Jenkins' insights are particularly relevant to our hypothesis concerning Gentiles who became proselytes and who later reacted on becoming Christ-believers against their acquired identity.

55. See N. H. Taylor and C. A. Wanamaker, "Paul and the Construction of Christian Identity" (paper presented at the annual meeting of the *Studiorum Novi Testamenti Societas* at the University of Pretoria, August 1999), 3. Cf. N. H. Taylor, "The Social Nature of Conversion in the Early Christian World," 128-36 in *Modeling Early Christianity* (ed. Philip F. Esler; London: Routledge, 1995).

56. Richard V. Travisano, "Alternation and Conversion as Qualitatively Different Transformations," 595-606 in *Social Psychology through Symbolic Interaction* (ed. G. P. Stone and H. A. Farberman; Waltham: Ginn-Blaisdell, 1970).

57. Robert Jewett ("Following the Argument of Romans," 265-77 in *The Romans Debate*, [ed. Karl P. Donfried; Peabody, Mass.: Hendrickson, 1991], esp. 276-77) has argued that we should follow the argument of Romans as a whole to its goal, made explicit in the peroration in chapters 15–16.

58. This means that we should not separate Romans too rigidly into separate subsections that are apparently only slightly related to each other. W. A. Meeks has shown ("Judgement and the Brother," 291-97), with reference to the use of the κρίν- root, that themes may be continuous throughout the letter, whatever its construction. Meeks notes ὁ κρίνων in 2:1 and 14:4, κρίνω in 2:1, 3, 12, 16, 27; 3:4, 6, 7; 14:3, 4, 5, 10, 13, 22; κρίμα in 2:2, 3; 3:8; 5:16; 11:33; 13:2; cf. also διακρινόμενος and κατακέκριται in 14:23.

identity for all. In Paul's understanding, Abraham is the father of us all, i.e., of differing peoples such as Jews and Gentiles. If all were to become Jews or all were to give up their Jewishness, Abraham could not be the father of two different peoples. But whereas the apostle's strategy in Rom 14–15 for those with Jewish-related scruples is to allow them to follow their convictions, in his use of the analogy of the olive tree he seems to be affirming that there is no option for Gentile believers to separate completely from some form of Israelite if not Jewish identity.

However the Gentile believers still are not called Israelites, as this would mean one common, undifferentiated Jewish identity for all. On the other hand, the universalizing of Gentile Christian identity, as has tended to be the norm in the later history of Christianity, simply constitutes another kind of common, undifferentiated identity for all. The complexity of Paul's perspective on diversity, unfortunately lost so quickly in the history of the church,[59] is that although he attaches Gentiles to the stem of Abraham this does not mean their proselytization to Judaism nor the universalizing of their Gentile Christian identity. Thus originally there was no one inclusive term to describe all believers in Christ. There were simply groups of Jewish and Gentile believers distinguished by their differing life-styles.

I trust that this essay is in keeping with the perspectives which Robert Jewett has continued to emphasize in his writings on Romans — such as the individuation of faith, "Not to be super-minded above what one ought to be minded, but to set your mind on being sober-minded, each according to the measuring rod of faith that God has dealt out" — and also that "there are political, ideological, racial, and temperamental components that are legitimately connected with faith. . . ."[60]

---

59. On this see Brigitte Kahl: "Within the framework of Jewish identity Paul thus develops a concept of descent, nation, religion and culture which fundamentally subverts any closed and separatistic group identity. By clothing Paul with a Christian identity in the later sense and after driving the circumcised out of the church we have silenced and buried this highly challenging discourse on identity and difference, which today could be one of the most precious contributions of Paul to the dialogue of religions and cultures, especially to the Jewish-Muslim-Christian encounter" (Kahl, "Gender Trouble in Galatia? Paul and the Rethinking of Difference," 57-73 in *Is There a Future for Feminist Theology?* [ed. Deborah Sawyer and Diane M. Collier; Sheffield: Sheffield Academic Press, 1999], 70-71).

60. Robert Jewett, *Christian Tolerance*, 62, 66.

The Rhetoric of *Persona* in Romans: Re-reading Romans 1:1-12

James D. Hester

Introduction

In 1982, Robert Jewett wrote an article that appeared in the journal *Interpretation*, in which he argued that Romans should be classified as epideictic because it manifests the characteristics of an "ambassadorial speech."[1] He also referred to epistolary handbooks that mention the category "diplomatic letter" (an example of which is found in Philo's *Embassy to Gaius*) and argued that Romans should be understood as such. These claims led to the conclusion that "Romans is a unique fusion of the 'ambassadorial letter' with several other sub-types in

1. Jewett summarizes the conventional solutions to issues of the genre and purpose of Romans as either a "theological treatise or circular letter" or a "situational letter" (Jewett, "Romans as an Ambassadorial Letter," *Interpretation: A Journal of Bible and Theology* 36 [1982]: 5). Neil Elliott also reviews the various proposals that attempt to deal with what some interpreters have called the "double character" of Romans — i.e., Romans is written as an occasional letter to the church announcing Paul's intended visit, or as a theological treatise describing Paul's debate with Judaism (Neil Elliott, *The Rhetoric of Romans: Argumentative Constraint and Strategy and Paul's Dialogue with Judaism* [*Journal for the Study of the New Testament Supplement* 45; Sheffield: Sheffield Academic Press, 1990]). As Elliott notes, other descriptions of the character of Romans are mostly variations on these (ibid., 9-67). Both Jewett and Elliott argue for some synthesis of the two proposals based on a rhetorical analysis of the genre and structure of argumentation. Cf. A. J. M. Wedderburn, "The Purpose and Occasion of Romans Again," *Expository Times* 90 (1978): 137-41.

Editor's note: The present article is a revised version of one originally published on-line in the *Journal for the Study of Rhetorical Criticism of the New Testament* (http://www.rhetjournal.net /Romans.pdf).

the genre: the paranetic letter, the hortatory letter, and the philosophical diatribe." The purpose of the letter was "to advocate on behalf of the 'power of
God' a cooperative mission to evangelize Spain. . . ."[2]

Jewett elaborates his thesis by reference to other places in the Pauline corpus where Paul refers to himself as ambassador, a concept imbedded in the
meaning of "apostle." Jewett also notes that language in the opening greeting of
Romans suggests that Paul wanted to be seen by the Romans as a kind of "imperial representative of Christ Jesus" and that Romans 1:8-12 is "full of diplomatic language."[3] Language and concepts found in the opening verses recur
throughout the rest of the argument of Romans. Paul hopes his diplomacy will
result in the reconciliation between Gentile and Jewish Christians in Rome,
who then would participate in Paul's new missionary enterprise.

Jewett has not been widely followed in his identification of Romans as a
diplomatic or "ambassadorial" letter; but he made several important observations about the rhetorical genre and purpose of the letter that need to be acknowledged.

According to the ancient handbooks, the first part of writing a speech was
invention. It entailed definition of the issue and, based on that, selection of the
genre to be used. Inherent in selection of genre was an understanding of the
"place" for the speech to be delivered (i.e., law court, assembly, or ceremonial
gathering). This was important because "place" helped to define "audience." An
understanding of audience also contributed to the style of argumentation.
Jewett identifies the genre of the letter as "epideictic" or "demonstrative," which
implies that the issue at stake was one of "value." As Chaim Perelman and Lucie
Obrechts-Tyteca have shown, the importance of epideictic lies in its goal of increasing the adherence of the audience to values the speaker advocates. They go
on to say, "Epidictic [*sic*] speeches are prone to appeal to universal order, to a
nature, or a god that would vouch for the unquestioned, and supposedly un-
questionable, values."[4] Jewett's point is that Paul exhorts the Roman house-
church audiences to join his effort to unify the world under the Lordship of Jesus, transforming the world by proclamation of the gospel. Paul's rhetoric appeals to universal values.[5]

Jewett does not address specifically who comprise the audience of
Romans; he mentions only Gentile and Jewish Christians in house-churches in
Rome. He does not argue that the letter was addressed to one or the other of

---

2. Jewett, "Romans as an Ambassadorial Letter," 9.

3. Ibid., 13.

4. Chaim Perelman & Lucie Obrechts-Tyteca, *The New Rhetoric: A Treatise on Argumentation* (Notre Dame: University of Notre Dame Press, 1969), 51.

5. Robert Jewett, "Following the Argument of Romans," *Word and World* 6 (1986): 389.

these groups, but points out that Paul evidenced concern for Jewish Christians in the argumentative structure and style, including numerous citations from Jewish Scriptures and "Hebrew rhetorical series of fives and tens. . . ."[6] Given what he says of Paul's emphasis on "unification through the gospel," it seems Jewett views the whole Christian community in Rome as the audience of the letter.

In this essay I want to revise and elaborate upon Jewett's insights concerning inventional choices Paul made in writing the letter to the Romans. It is unnecessary to classify Romans as an "ambassadorial letter" *per se.* Modern rhetorical-critical theories can demonstrate that Paul wrote this letter in part to provide the Roman Christians with a statement of his understanding of the gospel, his rhetorical vision.[7] Thus Romans *functions rhetorically* as "ambassadorial," even if it might not consistently fit that epistolary model.

The exigency that Paul faced was largely of his own making.[8] He wanted to come to Rome after delivering the collection to Jerusalem (15:22-29) in order to share with the Roman Christians his understanding of the gospel (1:10-11). To be effective in this, Paul had to create a *persona* for the Romans to use in hearing and evaluating his version of the gospel. Because he had little knowledge of the immediate circumstances of the Roman churches, Paul had to create an audience and try to convince them that he and they in fact shared common values. A central ethical issue for Paul was the need for salvation that resulted in the obedience of faith. Thus it was important that the Romans recognize his *persona* as "apostle to the Gentiles." In order to convey to the Romans what that meant, he had to share his Christian *paideia*[9] with them,

---

6. Ibid., 385.

7. See herein page 97, n. 66, for a detailed definition of this term.

Jeffrey A. Crafton ("Paul's Rhetorical Vision and the Purpose of Romans: Toward a New Understanding," *Novum Testamentum* 32 [1990]: 319-20) recognizes Paul's need to explain his rhetorical vision to the Romans, but he bases his case on an understanding of the Roman situation that reads too much into the text. For a critique of that tendency, see J. N. Vorster, "The Context of the Letter to the Romans: A Critique on the Present State of Research," *Neotestamentica* 28 (1994).

8. I am not persuaded by the majority opinion that Paul was writing in part to try to resolve conflicts in the church. As J. N. Vorster points out, there is no scholarly consensus as to who are the parties in such a conflict, and it is difficult to see how Paul would have known about them or their current state if such a conflict had occurred (J. N. Vorster, "The Context of the Letter to the Romans," 130-32, 137-38). Furthermore, the diversity of organization of the community in Rome, which prompted Paul to write to "all God's beloved," makes it likely that the social and religious situation in Rome was so complex that singling out particular groups would have been problematic.

9. The common definition of this word is "education" or "training," but it also implies

both to "strengthen" them (1:11) and to serve as the basis for mutual encouragement (1:12) in the proclamation of the gospel. Presumably that mutuality would result in their sharing in the Spanish mission, although Paul does not ask directly for that support in the letter.[10] First he needs to be accepted into the Roman Christian community on his own terms.

The General Epistolary Structure of Romans

It is self-evident but nonetheless important to note that one of the inventional choices Paul made to communicate with the Romans was to write a letter.[11] It is also apparent that he needed to do more than fulfill the conventional purposes for which letters were used — maintenance of friendly contact over a distance, for example. Paul needed to develop discourse to modify behavior or to prompt action. He had to overcome the distance that separated him from the congregations in Rome (Rom 1:10-11; 15:22-23) and get Roman Christians both to believe as he did and to act on their beliefs.[12] The structure and contents of the letter contribute to that function by conveying Paul's presence narrating a discourse and communicating illocutionary acts.[13]

---

the larger concept of "culture," or teaching that produces a cultured individual. The process of becoming cultured was understood by the Greeks to involve hard work, but the desired outcome — a fully enculturated, virtuous individual — made it worth it. I see Paul's teaching not as a recitation of doctrine but as a system of education that is intended to produce theologically and ethically righteous individuals; thus I characterize the content of his writings as *"paideia."*

10. Nils Alstrup Dahl (*Studies in Paul* [Minneapolis: Augsburg, 1977], 71, 87-88) makes the point that "apostle" and "gospel" are both missionary terms for Paul, and that the theology of Romans is a mission theology. Dahl understands Paul's mention of the collection for Jerusalem as part of the mission strategy in which he wants to involve the Romans (ibid., 77). Jewett takes much the same position in "Romans as an Ambassadorial Letter," 18, and "Following the Argument of Romans," 383, 389.

11. Though apparently mundane, the point is an important one because, presumably, Paul could have written a speech and had it conveyed to the Romans. That, however, would have presupposed a different relationship to the churches and an already established *persona*.

12. Patrizia Violi says that "each letter is written by someone whose emergence in the text is unavoidable," and makes the point that letters are intended to get the recipient to do something (Patrizia Violi, "Letters," 159-62 in *Discourse and Literature* [ed. Tuen A. van Dijk; Amsterdam: John Benjamins, 1985]).

13. An "illocutionary act" is something that someone does as the result of a speaker saying that he or she intends to do something. For example, Paul's promise to visit (1:10) may have illocutionary force if the Romans do something to prepare for that visit. What they do may be guided by what he argues in the letter. Their action is guided by persuasion. In that way, letters have argumentative functions.

The opening greeting in Romans (1:1-7) is more elaborate than any other in the Pauline corpus. It contains far more than the typical identification of the sender and recipients and the grace wish. And, unlike Paul's other letters, it indicates that the recipients are not members of an organization, a "church," but a class of people, "all God's beloved in Rome" (Rom 1:7a). Within this section are found the first elements of the argument to establish Paul's *persona*.[14]

In five of the seven undisputed letters, Paul's opening greeting includes the names of others jointly sending the letter.[15] That does not occur in Romans. Paul alone is identified and, again uncharacteristically, three qualifying phrases are used to elaborate that self-identification: "slave," "called to be an apostle," and "set apart for the gospel."

Only here in the undisputed letters does Paul refer to himself as "slave" or "servant" in the opening greeting.[16] As many commentators have noted, the word "slave" here should not be understood as a spiritual identification with a social class; rather, it expresses a relationship as bond-servant of Christ in service to the gospel and to other Christians.[17] The phrase "slave" or "servant" of God is not new to Judaism.[18] Paul's adaptation of the phrase — "servant of Jesus Christ" — places him squarely in the covenantal tradition of those who stand in the service of Yahweh.[19] Jewett argues that it also alludes to a class of

---

14. This term will be defined on page 98.

15. These are 1 Thessalonians, 1-2 Corinthians, Philippians, and Philemon; in Galatians, Paul mentions "all the brothers and sisters who are with [him]" (Gal 1:2), but does not mention any names. In Romans alone of the seven undisputed letters, Paul mentions no co-senders at the outset of the letter.

During discussions in the Society for Biblical Literature Seminar on Paul in the early 1970s, M. Luther Stirewalt argued that those listed with Paul in the opening greetings were to be understood as the letter-carriers. With the exception of Philippians, this seems to be the case. Whatever the reason for their mention, I reject the contention that they were "co-authors" for reasons that I hope are clear when I explain apostolic *persona* later in this essay. (See the section on "The Rhetoric of *Persona* in Romans 1:1-12," beginning on page 95).

16. However, he does refer to himself and Timothy as "slaves" or "servants" in the opening greeting of Philippians.

17. Joseph A. Fitzmyer, *Romans: A New Translation with Introduction and Commentary* (Anchor Bible 33; New York: Doubleday, 1993), 228, 231; C. E. B. Cranfield, *Introduction and Commentary on Romans I–VIII* (vol. 1 of *A Critical and Exegetical Commentary on the Epistle to the Romans;* Edinburgh: T&T Clark, 1975), 50-51; James D. G. Dunn, *Romans 1–8* (Word Biblical Commentary 38A; Dallas: Word, 1988), 8.

18. It is found, for example, as a designation of David (Ps 36) and Moses (Josh 14:7), in the prophets, and in later traditions.

19. William Sanday and Arthur Headlam, *A Critical and Exegetical Commentary on the Epistle to the Romans* (*International Critical Commentary;* Edinburgh: T&T Clark, 1902), 3; Otto Kuss, *Der Römerbrief übersetzt und erklärt* (Regensburg: Friedrich Pustet, 1957), 3; Otto Michel,

imperial slaves who functioned as "king's officials."[20] So, by the use of this one word Paul is communicating a key aspect of his *persona*.

As in other letters where his apostolic *persona* is integral to the argument (1 Cor 1:1, 2 Cor 1:1, Gal 1:1), Paul also writes in his role as "apostle." However, Paul does not leave that designation unelaborated. As he does in the opening greeting of Galatians, Paul emphasizes his commission. It is not a role he gained by virtue of association with Jesus or his followers, but rather one given by God. Paul's calling was not simply to Christian discipleship but to apostolic ministry.

The next phrase further elaborates the notion of "emissary" or "ambassador" which is integral to the definition of "apostle,"[21] and explicates the nature of Paul's call: he was "set apart" for the Gospel. J. H. Moulton and G. Milligan cite the use of this word in the papyri and other non-literary sources in contexts that suggest the meaning "reserved for" or even "'set apart' as incomparable."[22] Joseph Fitzmyer translates it, "having been divided off from."[23] The phrase echoes Paul's description of his commission in Gal 1:1 and Gal 1:11-12. As will become clear in Rom 11–12, Paul is not implying that somehow he was "set apart" or "divided off" from Judaism and its traditions but rather, as he says in Rom 1:5, that he was designated by God to undertake a particular kind of apostleship.[24] Paul's commission was to preach the gospel of God — and as Rom 1:5 and 11:13 imply, to preach it to the Gentiles.

In Rom 15:14-16a, Paul integrates the two concepts of servant and emissary by saying, "I have written to you rather boldly by way of reminder, because of the grace given to me by God to be a minister of Christ Jesus to the Gentiles in the priestly service of the gospel of God," a clear echo of 1:1-6! Thus his readers could well have understood that Paul's calling and commission were different from those of the other apostles — a further defining of his apostolic *persona*. Standing in the salvation-historical tradition of service to God, he was called and commissioned to undertake a special ministry.[25]

The implication of standing in a salvation-historical relationship to the covenantal tradition is made clearer by the use in 1:3-4 of what most interpret-

---

Der Brief an die Römer (Göttingen: Vandenhoeck & Ruprecht, 1963), 33-35; Ernst Käsemann, *Commentary on Romans* (Grand Rapids, Mich.: Eerdmans, 1980), 5.

20. Jewett, "Romans as an Ambassadorial Letter," 13.

21. Ibid., 10-11; Fitzmyer, *Romans,* 229.

22. J. H. Moulton and G. Milligan, *The Vocabulary of the Greek Testament* (London: Hodder & Stoughton, 1930), 98. As Dunn has pointed out (*Romans 1–8,* 9) it is unlikely that this is a word play on "Pharisee."

23. Fitzmyer, *Romans,* 232.

24. Cranfield, *A Critical and Exegetical Commentary,* 53.

25. Cf. Elliott, *The Rhetoric of Romans,* 72-73.

ers describe as a part of an early Christian confession.[26] Jewett has analyzed the form and structure of the confession, describing Paul's redactional activities in fitting the confession into the topography of the argument here.[27] In its present context, the "confession" functions to undergird Paul's salvation-historical claim and leads the hearer to a further elaboration of his apostolic *persona*. Thus, by the end of verse four Paul has established for his hearers that he is a specially commissioned emissary of Jesus Christ in the service of the gospel of God. In effect, he has re-written the opening greeting of the Galatian letter: "Paul an apostle — sent neither by human commission nor from human authorities, but through Jesus Christ and God the Father, who raised him from the dead" (Gal 1:1). Paul has let the Romans know that he is by no means just another wandering missionary!

The commission Paul received (1:1, 5a) has a pragmatic goal, summarized by the phrase "obedience of faith" (1:5b). That is made clear by the context in which it occurs: "through [Jesus Christ] we have received grace and apostleship to bring about obedience of faith among all the Gentiles for the sake of his name."[28]

A great deal has been written about the meaning of the phrase "obedience of faith" (εἰς ὑπακοὴν πίστεως) and in particular how we are to understand the

26. Commentators often remark that this confession would have been known to some degree by the Romans, although they offer no explanation of why that would have been the case. It seems preferable simply to note that the passage contains portions of an early Christian confessional tradition. Cf. Samuel Byrskog ("Epistolography, Rhetoric, and Letter Prescript: Romans 1.1-7 as a Test Case," *Journal for the Study of the New Testament* 65 [1997]: 41), who makes the point that it is impossible "to be certain that the recipient of the letter knew of this material in [its] pre-Pauline form."

27. Jewett, "The Redaction and Use of an Early Christian Confession in Romans 1:3-4," 99-122 in *The Living Text: Essays in Honor of Ernest W. Saunders* (ed. Robert Jewett and Dennis E. Groh; Washington: University Press of America, 1985). See also James D. G. Dunn, "Jesus — Flesh and Spirit: An Exposition of Romans 1.3-4," *Journal of Theological Studies* 24 (1973): 40-68; George Beasley-Murray, "Romans 1.3f: An Early Confession of Faith in the Lordship of Jesus," *Tyndale Bulletin* 31 (1980): 147-54.

28. Fitzmyer (*Romans*, 237) and Cranfield (*A Critical and Exegetical Commentary*, 65-66) both argue that the phrase "grace and apostleship" should be understood as a *hendiadys*, a figure in which two nouns are connected by "and" to denote one meaning. Fitzmyer translates the figure "grace of apostleship" — but if that translation is used, the figure becomes a *"anthimeria,"* a figure in which one part of speech is used for another. (See Richard A. Lanham, *A Handlist of Rhetorical Terms* [Berkeley: University of California Press, 1991], 13, 82.) It is probably best to understand the phrase as referring to two things: God's saving grace, which even Paul had to experience, and his commission. Cf. L. Ann Jervis, *The Purpose of Romans: A Comparative Letter-Structure Investigation* (*Journal for the Study of the New Testament* Supplement 55; Sheffield: Sheffield Academic Press, 1991), 76.

genitive here.[29] As D. B. Garlington and Mark Nanos, both citing C. E. B. Cranfield, point out, the genitive can be understood as (1) objective: e.g., as obedience to a body of doctrine; (2) subjective: obedience that derives from faith; (3) adjectival: "believing obedience"; and (4) appositive: faith as an act of obedience.[30] Garlington opts for understanding the genitive as expressing "two ideas at the same time: obedience that consists in faith [apposition] and the obedience which is the product of faith."[31] Nanos seems to treat the phrase epexegetically so that in effect the terms are interchangeable. He prefers to see the phrase in context and argues that the clause "obedience of faith *among all the Gentiles,* for His name's sake, among whom you are also called of Jesus Christ,"[32] is a programmatic expression of Paul's missionary work.[33] Daniel Wallace cites the phrase as a possible example of "Genitive of Production/Producer," which would result in its translation as "obedience which is produced by faith."[34] In this he seems to support at least a portion of Garlington's understanding of what Paul is saying.

At least one interpreter comes at the analysis of this enigmatic statement from a different angle. Gerhard Friedrich argues that attempts to understand the nature of the genitive have been misdirected. For example, an epexegetical reading produces a kind of tautology, and an understanding of the genitive as objective results in seeing the content of "faith" as equivalent to the word of faith, or "gospel." So Friedrich tries to resolve the grammatical issue by seeking another translation of the word "obedience" (ὑπακοή). He notes that in the Septuagint version of 2 Sam 22:36 and the apocryphal *Gospel of Peter* 10:42, the word ὑπακοή can be translated as "answer." Friedrich reasons that if the root word includes the idea of responding to someone, this implies an act of hearing, which then makes it possible to render ὑπακοή as "message" or "proclamation."[35]

---

29. For two recent book-length studies, see D. B. Garlington, *The Obedience of Faith: A Pauline Phrase in Historical Context* (*Wissenschaftliche Untersuchungen zum Neuen Testament* 2/35; Tübingen: Mohr Siebeck, 1991), and Glenn N. Davies, *Faith and Obedience in Romans: A Study in Romans 1–4* (*Journal for the Study of the New Testament Supplement* 39; Sheffield: Sheffield Academic Press, 1990).

30. D. B. Garlington, "The Obedience of Faith in the Letter to the Romans: Part I," *Westminster Theological Journal* 52 (1990): 205; Mark Nanos, *The Mystery of Romans* (Minneapolis: Augsburg Fortress, 1996), 224; Cranfield, *A Critical and Exegetical Commentary,* 66.

31. Garlington, "The Obedience of Faith in the Letter to the Romans," 223-24.

32. Rom 1:5-6; his translation and emphasis.

33. Nanos, *The Mystery of Romans,* 224, 237-38.

34. Daniel B. Wallace, *Greek Grammar Beyond the Basics* (Grand Rapids, Mich.: Zondervan, 1996), 104-6.

35. Gerhard Friedrich, "Muß ὑπακοὴν πίστεως Röm 1.5 mit 'Glaubensgehorsam' übersetzt werden?" *Zeitschrift für die neutestamentliche Wissenschaft* 72 (1981): 118-23.

Friedrich's proposal is attractive because it removes the enigma. The phrase then can be read in an almost mundane fashion, "proclamation of faith." The statement as a whole would read "we have received grace and apostleship for [the purpose of] the proclamation of faith among all the Gentiles." The problem with Friedrich's proposal, as Fitzmyer has noted, is that the logic of his argument is "farfetched."[36] However, Friedrich's insight that the concept of "obedience" includes that of "hearing" is in itself a useful one. He has seen that "hearing" is not always passive listening. Active "hearing" can lead to "obedience" (which should not be understood as mere acquiescence); that which is heard is to be acted upon. The phrase "hearing-obedience of faith" implies that faith has pragmatic dimensions.[37]

What conclusions might be drawn concerning the phrase "obedience of faith"? If we view it as epexegetical, it should probably be seen as a circumlocution for "faithfulness," the object of which Paul then outlines in the body of Romans. However, I am drawn to a synthesis of Garlington's and Wallace's positions, taking πίστεως as a "genitive of product." Paul is trying to convey to his Roman hearers that he is commissioned not only to preach the word of salvation but also to help the Gentiles understand the pragmatic aspects of their new status in Christ. His argument, signaled by the thesis in 1:16, is that faith results not merely in acquiescence to the gospel but in morality. Those who hear the gospel are called to be holy![38]

Paul brackets the greeting by use of three references to God's "calling." In verse one he says that he was called to be an apostle; in verses six and seven he says the Romans were called to "belong to Jesus Christ" and to be "holy." The verb "called" should probably be understood to mean "summoned and commissioned."[39] That this is likely in reference to Paul's calling is shown by the argument that unfolds in the rest of the letter. It also is supported by the salvation-historical context provided in 1:3, and its implied foundation in sacred stories that recount earlier acts of God calling other servants.[40] That this is likely in reference to the Romans is shown on the one hand by Paul's reference

---

36. Fitzmyer, *Romans,* 238.

37. Cf. *The Mystery of Romans,* 229-31, *et passim.*

38. In general I support Nanos' thesis about the meaning of "obedience of faith." If the eschatological people of God are to escape the wrath of God and enjoy the fruits of Christ's salvific work, they need to live as morally pure a life as they can in response to grace. This part of Paul's rhetorical vision is not dependent, however, on identification of specific groups in the Christian community in Rome.

39. J. P. Louw and E. A. Nida, *Introduction & Domains* (vol. 1 of *Greek-English Lexicon of the New Testament Based on Semantic Domains;* New York: United Bible Societies, 1988), 424.

40. Sanday and Headlam, *A Critical and Exegetical Commentary,* 4.

to their new status in Christ (they "belong" to Christ and are thus separated out from the rest of the world, a status he will elaborate later in the letter), and on the other by reference to their character (they are to be "holy").

To translate the adjective "holy" as though it were a substantive, "saints," implies an organizational, technical term. Instead, the earlier phrase "obedience of faith" coupled with the description of Christian *paideia* in the body of the letter makes clear that the traditional meaning of the word should be retained. The Romans, like Israel, are God's special people, and are under the same constraints as Israel. They are to be consecrated to God, morally pure, acceptable for the service of God.[41] "Those who have been called by the holy God are holy in virtue of his calling and are thereby claimed for holiness of life."[42] Moreover, Paul's rhetoric in Rom 1:1-7 is also in part an elaboration of the theme of holiness found, e.g., in 1 Thess 3:13; 4:3-7; 1 Cor 6:19 and 2 Cor 7:1. With that in mind, "holiness" is not just a state of being but also a mode of living. Righteousness in not just ontological but also ethical.

Verse 7b contains the typical Pauline "grace" wish.[43] Most interpreters understand the word "grace" to be a substitute for the verb "to greet" that appears as the third element in the opening greeting in the common letter tradition.[44] The second term, "peace," may be understood as a substitute for the so-called "health wish" that usually follows the "greeting" formula and typically has two parts, a statement expressing concern about the recipient's health and another assuring the recipient that the sender is well.[45] As Fitzmyer points out, "peace" seems to reflect the Hebrew notion of *"shalom,"* i.e., Paul's wish that his readers/hearers enjoy "the fullness of God's gracious bounty."[46] The whole is, therefore, formulaic and signals the ending of the opening greeting. Rhetorically it provides a bridge to the thanksgiving.

The greeting is followed by a thanksgiving period.[47] This formal element

---

41. Cf. ibid., 13-15.

42. Cranfield, *A Critical and Exegetical Commentary,* 70.

43. The phrase "grace to you and peace" appears in 1 Cor 1:3, 2 Cor 1:2, Gal 1:3, Phil 1:2, 1 Thess 1:1, 2 Thess 1:2, and Phlm 3.

44. E.g., Dunn, *Romans 1–8,* 20.

45. John L. White, *Light From Ancient Letters* (Philadelphia: Fortress, 1986), 200-2. See also William Doty, *Letters in Primitive Christianity* (Philadelphia: Fortress, 1973), 30.

46. Fitzmyer, *Romans,* 238.

47. The classic study of the Pauline thanksgiving period is Paul Schubert, *The Form and Function of the Pauline Thanksgivings* (*Beihefte zur Zeitschrift für die neutestamentliche Wissenschaft*; Berlin: A. Töpelmann, 1939). See also, Jack T. Sanders, "Transition of the Opening Epistolary Thanksgiving to the Body in the Letters of Paul," *Journal of Biblical Literature* 81 (1962): 348-62. Recently Jeffrey T. Reed ("Are Paul's Thanksgivings 'Epistolary'?" *Journal for the Study of the New Testament* 61 [1996]: 87-99) has argued *contra* P. Arzt ("The 'Epistolary Intro-

in Paul's letters usually includes the topics that will be elaborated in the body of the letter.[48] The thanksgiving in Romans is found in 1:8-12 and contains one major topic, Paul's wish to come to Rome "so that I may share with you some spiritual gift to strengthen you" (1:11b). This goal is related to the statement found in the opening greeting: "we have received grace and apostleship to bring about the obedience of faith among all the Gentiles for the sake of his name, including yourselves who are called to belong to Jesus Christ" (1:5-6). An essential element of that "gift" is an exposition of teachings that can result in obedient living.[49]

It is in the identification of the body opening that I deviate from conventional outlines of the epistolary structure of Romans. Most interpreters see the opening of the letter at 1:16. However, John White has argued that the opening of the letter body can be signaled by some kind of disclosure formula, including statements such as "I want you to know," or "I do not want you to be ignorant."[50] In Romans that convention is found in 1:13, "I want you to know, brothers, that I have often intended to come to you. . . ." There is no reason, based either on epistolographic or rhetorical features, to locate the opening at verse 16. The body of the letter opens at 1:13.[51]

Immediately following the disclosure formula, the argument proceeds with a re-statement of the topic of Paul's desire to visit (recapitulated in the epi-

---

ductory Thanksgiving' in the Papyri and in Paul," *Novum Testamentum* 3 [1994]: 29-46) that, although the subject of the thanksgiving period in Paul does not conform in detail to those found in the familiar papyrus letter, the form, etc., does, and the Pauline variations can be explained by (1) the flexibility of epistolary conventions, and (2) adaptation of conventions to meet the needs of communicating with a given audience.

48. William Baird makes this point ("Romans 1:8-17," *Interpretation* 33 [1979]: 399) but identifies the period as running from 1:8-17. Thus he includes the thesis statement in 1:16-17 among the topics to be elaborated in the body of the letter, rather than understanding that verses 16-17 are included among the elements of the "gift" Paul wanted to share with the Romans.

49. Cf. Nanos, *The Mystery of Romans*, 21-40; also, Mark Nanos, "The Jewish Context of the Gentile Audience Addressed in Paul's Letter to the Romans," *Catholic Biblical Quarterly* 61 (1999): 289-93.

50. White, *Light from Ancient Letters*, 207. White notes three other typical opening formulae: notice of an appended letter, response to information received, and acknowledgment of or compliance with information received. He also notes the presence of amazement formulae, reference to unanswered letters, or expressions of urgency (ibid., 208-9).

51. Elliott (*The Rhetoric of Romans*, 81-84) recognizes the importance of the disclosure formula and also argues that 1:13-17 has to be seen as a unit. However, he places it within what he identifies as the *Exordium* and does not acknowledge its epistolary function. Hence, he fails to recognize the rhetorical function of the epistolary structure and sees the letter through the lenses of a rhetorical handbook.

logue to the letter, 15:22-23), in which he tells them he has been unable to visit (presumably through no fault of his own, 1:13), but wants to so that he can carry on his work. Paul has learned from his experience (1:14) and is eager to build on it (1:15). The presence of the inferential particle "for" in 1:16 indicates the conclusion of a case-result argument begun in 1:14. Since it is the case that Paul has been successful among the Gentiles and has learned from those experiences, the result is that he is not ashamed of the gospel he has preached, nor ashamed to share it with the Christian community in Rome. The argument in the rest of the body of the letter will describe what he wants to share with them.

Recent interpreters have made a strong case that the argument in Romans has to include what has earlier been identified as a section of moral exhortation, 12:1–15:21.[52] That would mean that the body of the letter runs from 1:13 through 15:21. Their argument finds some support in the fact that 15:22-33 contains the "apostolic *parousia*" or "travelogue," that section of a letter where Paul announces an impending visit.[53] The travelogue is usually found between the body of the letter and the section of moral exhortations.[54] In the case of Romans, however, the travelogue follows the paraenetic material and is a kind of recapitulation of the topics of the body of the letter. Furthermore, as Nanos has shown, it plays a role in elaborating the purpose of Paul's apostolic call and motive for writing.[55]

The closing greeting of Romans 16:1-27 is extensively elaborated. It includes a word of recommendation for Phoebe (16:1-2), who probably acted as the letter-carrier; a list of persons in various house-churches to be greeted (16:3-15) and greetings sent by other persons (16:21-23); a conventional exhortation to greet each other with a "holy kiss" (cf. 1 Cor 16:20, 2 Cor 13:12), as well as a statement of greeting from other churches (16:16); instructions to avoid deviant teaching and teachers (16:17-20); and a closing doxology (16:25-27).[56] Jewett argues that, given the diplomatic nature of the letter, this chapter functions to enlist support for Paul's mission to Spain. It is an attractive suggestion because it explains the rhetorical function of this epistolary element.

---

52. E.g., ibid., 58-59.

53. So identified by Robert W. Funk, *Language, Hermeneutic and Word of God* (New York: Harper & Row, 1966), 248, 265, 268-69.

54. E.g., 1 Thess 3:11; Phil 2:19-30.

55. Nanos, *The Mystery of Romans*, 233.

56. The textual history of Rom 16 is notoriously difficult, and it seems likely that verses 17-20 and 25-27 were a later addition to the letter. Fitzmyer (*Romans,* 745) and Cranfield (*A Critical and Exegetical Commentary,* 797) accept verses 17-20 as authentic but not verses 25-27. Jewett ("Following the Argument of Romans," 388) sees both as interpolations that interrupt the rhetorical structure of Chapter 16.

So much for a "re-reading" of the epistolary structure of the letter, and particularly 1:1-12. What is important to keep in mind is that the use of the letter form as the medium of communication is part of the inventional choice of the author, and the letter structure plays a role in structuring the argument itself. The structure, topics and letter formulae are integral to the rhetoric of the letter and, as we have seen, contribute to the task of establishing Paul's *persona* and giving credibility to his *paideia*. It is to the description of the rhetoric of *persona* in 1:1-12 that we now turn.

The Rhetoric of *Persona* in Romans 1:1-12

Recently Samuel Byrskog has argued that interpreters who assume that Paul's letters are substitutes for speeches need to recognize that, although epistolography belonged to a different theoretical system than rhetoric, it is also true that ancient theorists acknowledge the presence of rhetorical elements in letters. Perhaps especially in Romans, epistolary elements have rhetorical functions, and rhetorical elements in the letter helped hearers "fill in the gaps" that occurred when they encountered unexpected features in places like the opening greeting or the postscript.[57] Byrskog's point is important: "The epistolographic approach takes seriously the genre of the text as letter and provides an essential understanding of the basic structure and relational function of the prescript. The rhetorical approach helps significantly in comprehending the features that are strange according to the letter genre and relates them accurately to the rest of the letter."[58] Both are necessary if we are to understand the persuasive strategy of the text.

I want to expand on that insight. Rhetorical criticism of Romans has tended to analyze the argument by use of classical handbook descriptions of rhetorical genre, inventional strategies, figures and style, following the agenda laid out by Hans Dieter Betz and George Kennedy. Jewett and Elliott are cases in point.[59] American rhetorical critics in particular have ignored or avoided modern rhetorical critical theories or, at best, have made partial use of Lloyd Bitzer's early work on the rhetorical situation[60] or Chaim Perelman and Lucie

---

57. Byrskog, "Epistolography, Rhetoric, and Letter Prescript," 44.

58. Ibid., 45.

59. E.g., Hans Dieter Betz, *Galatians: A Commentary on Paul's Letter to the Churches in Galatia* (*Hermeneia*; Philadelphia: Fortress, 1979); George A. Kennedy, *New Testament Interpretation Through Rhetorical Criticism* (Chapel Hill: University of North Carolina Press, 1984). Cf. Jewett, "Following the Argument of Romans"; Elliott, *The Rhetoric of Romans*.

60. Lloyd F. Bitzer, "The Rhetorical Situation," *Philosophy and Rhetoric* 1 (1968): 1-14; also

Obrechts-Tyteca's neo-Aristotelianism.[61] Very few have ventured into the world of modern communications theory, for example. Most of the critical theories they use are based on theories of knowledge that are foundationalist or essentialist. They have made little, if any, use of general theories of rhetoric that derive from dramatistic, functionalistic, or pragmatic perspectives.[62] And, although socio-rhetorical criticism has expanded the analytical tools available to the critic, it is not yet widely used for analyzing Paul's letters.

Symbolic Convergence Theory (SCT)[63] can be a helpful new tool for un-

---

"The Rhetorical Situation," 247-60 in *Rhetoric: A Tradition in Transition* (ed. W. R. Fisher; Ann Arbor: University of Michigan Press, 1974).

61. Chaim Perelman and Lucie Obrechts-Tyteca, *The New Rhetoric: A Treatise on Argumentation* (Notre Dame: University of Notre Dame Press, 1969), 490-503. Elliott does make use of concepts like the "rhetorical situation," first defined by Lloyd Bitzer ("The Rhetorical Situation," *Philosophy and Rhetoric* 1) and then modified by both Bitzer ("The Rhetorical Situation," 247-60 in *Rhetoric: A Tradition in Transition*) and Scott Cosigny ("Rhetoric and Its Situations," *Philosophy and Rhetoric* 7, no. 3 [1974]: 175-86). But Elliott uses the classical concept of *dispositio* or "arrangement" in his analysis of the rhetoric of Romans and, despite the fact that he makes use of their work for other purposes, does not take advantage of Perelman and Obrechts-Tyteca's insight that arguments should be arranged to deal with the successive stages of the audience's response to them. Crafton ("Paul's Rhetorical Vision and the Purpose of Romans") makes effective use of Perelman in discussing the role of audience in argumentation.

62. I am thinking here of the work of Kenneth Burke (e.g., *Rhetoric of Religion: Studies in Logology* [Boston: Beacon Press, 1961] and *A Rhetoric of Motives* [Berkeley: University of California Press, 1969]), the later Bitzer ("Functional Communication: A Situational Perspective," 21-38 in *Rhetoric in Transition* [ed. Eugene White; University Park, Pa.: Penn State University Press, 1980]), and Steven Mailloux (e.g., *Rhetorical Power* [Ithaca: Cornell University Press, 1989]; ed., *Rhetoric, Sophistry, Pragmatism* [Cambridge/New York: Cambridge University Press, 1995]), not to speak of Stephen E. Toulmin (e.g., *The Uses of Argument* [Cambridge: Cambridge University Press, 1958]) or Jürgen Habermas (e.g., *Reason and the Rationalization of Society* [vol. 1 of *The Theory of Communicative Action;* trans. Thomas McCarthy; Boston: Beacon, 1984]; *The Philosophical Discourse of Modernity: Twelve Lectures* [trans. Frederick G. Lawrence; Studies in Contemporary German Social Thought; Cambridge, Mass.: Massachusetts Institute of Technology Press, 1987; repr. 1990], *The Structural Transformation of the Public Sphere: An Inquiry into a Category of Bourgeois Society* [Studies in Contemporary German Social Thought; trans. Thomas Burger with Frederick Lawrence; Cambridge, Mass.: Massachusetts Institute of Technology Press, 1989]; and *Moral Consciousness and Communicative Action* [Studies in Contemporary German Social Thought; trans. Christian Lenhardt and Shierry Weber Nicholson; Cambridge, Mass.: Massachusetts Institute of Technology, 1990]).

63. *Symbolic Convergence Theory* is a general theory of communication that attempts to offer an explanation of the presence of a common consciousness on the part of members of a group. It posits that the sharing of group fantasies and the chaining out of those fantasies are responsible for that consciousness and group cohesiveness. As fantasies are "dramatized," a convergence of symbols on which participants agree occurs, and fantasy themes and fantasy types help the group understand unexpected, confusing, or even chaotic events or experiences. The

derstanding the rhetorical function of Paul's letters. SCT is a general theory of rhetoric that explains the formation of group consciousness through group use of dramatizing messages[64] and sharing of fantasies[65] that converge into a common understanding of the group's social world. I have used SCT in the analysis of 1 Thessalonians, and will make use of it here to analyze the argumentative goal of Romans 1:1-12. The use of SCT does not diminish the importance of recognizing the epistolary and rhetorical elements of the argumentative topography of Romans 1:1-12. Its focus, however, is on the rhetorical vision[66] that un-

---

process of convergence creates social reality for the group until new exigencies cause new fantasies and moments of sharing, which in turn produce new group realities. These realities provide the underlying assumptions used by the group in discursive argumentation.

The chief proponent of the method is its creator Ernest G. Bormann, whose book (*The Force of Fantasy: Restoring the American Dream* [Carbondale: Southern Illinois University Press, 1985]) provides the best overview and application of the theory. See also Ernest G. Bormann, "Symbolic Convergence: Organizational Communication and Culture," 99-122 in *Communication and Organizations: An Interpretive Approach* (ed. L. L. Putnam and M. E. Pacanowsky; Beverly Hills: Sage, 1983); *Small Group Communication: Theory and Practice* (New York: Harper & Row, 1990).

Key terms associated with the Symbolic Convergence Theory are explained in footnotes as they arise in the following discussion.

64. A *Dramatizing Message* (DM) is a story that contains a pun, double entendre, personification, figure of speech, analogy, anecdote, allegory, fable or narrative. The story often deals with past conflict or the potential of future conflict and is thus set in time references of somewhere/sometime rather than the here-and-now. It is based on some original facts. A DM is the basis for group fantasy-sharing. If it is accepted by the group and is chained out in a process of elaboration and other responses, then it becomes a group fantasy. Acceptance may be due to the rhetorical skill of the one conveying the message.

65. *Fantasy* is "the creative and imaginative shared interpretation of events that fulfills a group's psychological and rhetorical need to make sense out of its experience and anticipate its future" (Ernest G. Bormann, *Small Group Communication: Theory and Practice* [New York: Harper and Row, 1990], 104). Fantasies are dramatic re-constructions of past events and experiences that create a social reality for a group and its participants.

Fantasy sharing is a means whereby groups establish identity and set boundary conditions for identifying insiders from outsiders. It is also a way in which group history and traditions are developed, thus enabling the group to think of itself as unique (ibid., 115).

66. A *Rhetorical Vision* (RV) is a unified construction of themes and types that gives those sharing fantasy types and themes a broader view of things. A rhetorical vision may be indexed by a symbolic cue or key word. A number of rhetorical visions can be integrated by means of a master analogy (Sonja K. Foss, ed., *Rhetorical Criticism: Exploration and Practice* [Prospect Heights, Ill.: Waveland Press, 1989], 293). Seven principles apply to all rhetorical visions: novelty, explanatory power, imitation, critical mass, dedication, rededication, and reiteration (Ernest G. Bormann, John F. Cragan, and Donald C. Shields, "An Expansion of the Rhetorical Vision Component of the Symbolic Convergence Theory: The Cold War Paradigm Case," *Communication Monographs* 63 [1996]: 25). It is a rhetorical vision that can attract and help in-

derlies that section — indeed the entire letter — and on identifying such things as fantasy types[67] and fantasy themes[68] suggested by the language of the section. SCT also can suggest at what stage in the life of the community the rhetorical vision might be: consciousness-creating, consciousness-raising, or consciousness-sustaining.

As I indicated above, I view the goal of the opening greeting and thanksgiving as establishing not so much Paul's *ethos* but his *persona*.[69] They are not synonymous although both can be understood as modes of proof. In modern parlance the word *"persona"* can be defined as (a) an individual's social façade that reflects the role in life the individual is playing, or (b) the personality that a person (e.g., an actor or politician) projects in public. In SCT the *persona* is also a representation of a person that has been created by a community, based on fantasy-chaining that has occurred in that community.[70] In the case of an important religious or political figure, for example, the fantasies created by a smaller group — a circle of advisors or a group of disciples — may have been chained out into a larger group to produce a public *persona*. Take the Clinton

---

tegrate larger groups of people into a common symbolic reality (John F. Cragan and Donald C. Shields, *Applied Communication Research: A Dramatistic Approach* [Prospect Heights, Ill.: Waveland Press, 1981], 6).

67. A *Fantasy Type* (fT) is a general scenario that covers several concrete fantasy themes. This scenario may be repeated with similar characters and may take the same form. It can be generalized so that characters become personae who act in predictable fashion. Rhetors simply make use of a familiar type and the audience fills in the particulars. "Fantasy types allow a group to fit new events or experiences into familiar patterns" (Foss, ed., *Rhetorical Criticism: Exploration and Practice*, 292). An example of a fantasy type is "The American Dream," or "Family Values."

68. A *Fantasy Theme* (FT) is a theme that has become part of the group consciousness; it is artistic and organized; and is slanted, ordered, and interpretive. As a result, it provides a way for two or more groups of people to explain an event in different ways. An illustration of an FT is, "Illegal immigrants consume more in social services than they contribute in taxes."

69. Byrskog, using models from classical rhetoric to analyze the letter, identifies 1:1-17 as the *Exordium* and then argues that it functions as it ought, i.e., it establishes a positive relationship with Paul's audience and creates an *ethos* (Byrskog, "Epistolography, Rhetoric, and Letter Prescript," 39).

70. *Fantasy chains* are created when a group member tells about an experience, or event, and others who shared in that experience add their view of it until it becomes the experience of the group.

In SCT *fantasy-chaining* is a form of discourse, the use of language symbols that create social realities for the group. Symbols conveyed by language converge for the group and they agree on certain realities. As Vorster says, "What a social group regards as factual, is factuality by agreement" (J. N. Vorster, "The Context of the Letter to the Romans: A Critique on the Present State of Research," *Neotestamentica* 28 [1994]: 140). Components of this agreement can be used to modify or even create a new rhetorical vision.

impeachment debates, for example. The argument was made that the private person of Bill Clinton had to be held responsible for damage to the public *persona* of the President. Or consider Richard Nixon's visit to China, or George W. Bush's Thanksgiving visit to the troops in Iraq. Private citizens did not make those trips. An individual in the *persona* of the President of the United States did. And that *persona* is largely a rhetorical creation. The same is true for a god *persona* to whom religious groups appeal.[71] Furthermore, it is important to note that a *persona* can function objectively to create discourse and generate more fantasies to be shared without the actual historical person behind the *persona* ever being directly known or encountered.

The problem that Paul faced in writing to the Christian community in Rome is that he had not been directly responsible for the creation of his *persona* for or by that community. Whatever stories they knew about him had been carried there by others, including close co-workers like Prisca and Aquila and the others listed in 16:3-16.[72]

As importantly from Paul's point of view, his lack of participation in fantasy-chaining within the group meant that he was an outsider, one who would not know the details of dramatizing messages and other insider cues that the group would use to make sense of the social world around them. He admits as much in 1:12, when he acknowledges that he has things to learn from them. So, in order to be successful in his implied request to be considered a member of the Roman Christian community (15:24b), he has to make sure they understand and accept his version of his "official" *persona*, his role as apostle to the Gentiles (e.g., 15:14-21). In this *persona* he could expect them to pay serious attention to his *paideia*, the teaching that he has refined from his years of work in the eastern Mediterranean (15:19). The description of his *paideia* in the letter would provide a variety of dramatizing messages that would illustrate his rhetorical vision and provide the foundation for mutual fantasy-chaining when he arrived in Rome.

From the standpoint of SCT, the body of the letter contains expressions of Paul's rhetorical vision, the content of the "spiritual gift" he hoped to impart to Roman Christians. However, it is not the purpose of this essay to analyze the argumentative strategy of the body of the letter using Fantasy Theme Analysis.[73] We must return to a rhetorical analysis of the epistolary elements of the

71. Cf. Ernest G. Bormann, John F. Cragan, and Donald C. Shields, "In Defense of Symbolic Convergence Theory: A Look at the Theory and Its Criticisms After Two Decades," *Communication Theory* 4 (1994): 279; Bormann, *The Force of Fantasy,* 11-12.

72. In that list I count at least eleven persons who might have worked with Paul at one time or other.

73. *Fantasy Theme Analysis* is a method of rhetorical criticism designed to analyze and

opening greeting and thanksgiving to show how Paul attempts to establish his *persona*.

Although an outsider, it is nonetheless clear that Paul understood that he shared much with Roman Christians.[74] The opening greeting is a dramatizing message that reminds the Romans of the history of the promises of God and the conflicts encountered in experiencing their fulfillment — "the gospel of God which he promised beforehand through his prophets" (1:1-2) — and narrates the ancestry and destiny of the Son of God (1:3-5). It contains a series of insider cues that include code words such as "apostle," "gospel," "prophets," "Holy Scriptures," "son of David," "Son of God," "resurrection," and "Lord." Each of these words refers to concepts that were part of the content of the Christian *paideia*, as can be shown by their appearance in other New Testament writings.[75] Their use implies that both Paul and the Romans had been involved in fantasy-sharing that had chained out into the larger group of the "church universal." Paul, therefore, is signaling the Romans that he has something in common with them.[76]

On the other hand, the focus on his apostolic *persona* is signaled by the fact that he does not include the names of any co-workers or letter-carriers in the address, nor indeed mention any other person until chapter 16. The first person plural in the verb "we have received" (1:5) is an example of the "epistolary plural" used when the author is implying a formal statement of authority and is thereby excluding the audience.[77] Paul wants to be the center of attention here in order to establish his definition of both his credentials and his teaching.

As we have seen above, Paul claims to have received a special apostleship. He is apostle to the Gentiles (1:5; 11:13). In terms of SCT, "apostle to the Gentiles" should be seen as a fantasy type. Implicit in that title are the two fantasy themes of "apostle" and "Gentiles." Paul himself had elaborated those themes in Galatians and the Corinthian correspondence.[78] But the combination of the two he had never made quite so explicit. By doing so in 1:5, he invites

---

describe the rhetorical artifacts produced by symbolic convergence, not just in small group communication but also in social movements, political campaigns, etc. Analysis focuses on the content of message and the relationship among message elements.

74. Cf. Elliott, *The Rhetoric of Romans*, 76-77.

75. The phrase "Holy Scriptures" appears only here in the New Testament, but Paul uses the term "writings" in reference to Scripture in several places. See Fitzmyer, *Romans*, 233; or Dunn, *Romans 1–8*, 11.

76. This is illustrated also by his use of a confessional tradition in verses 3-4.

77. Cranfield, *A Critical and Exegetical Commentary*, 65. Wallace, *Greek Grammar Beyond the Basics*, 394-95.

78. E.g., 1 Cor 15:1-11; Gal 1:1, 3:23-29.

the Romans to chain out its meaning among themselves, guided, of course, by what he argues in the body of the letter. In other words, the *persona* of an "apostle" would be part of the shared tradition and might even include, as Jewett suggests, a recognition of the *persona* of an "ambassador."[79] However, the addition of the qualifier "to the Gentiles" elaborates Paul's special commission and would need explanation. As Dunn says, "his apostleship to the Gentiles was absolutely fundamental to Paul's self-understanding," and the Romans needed to know that in order to know Paul's special *persona*.[80]

The statement of the purpose of his apostleship, "for obedience which is the product of faith among the Gentiles," introduces what may be a new fantasy to the Romans. Up to this point Paul used insider cues to refer to fantasy themes that the Romans would have recognized. In describing the purpose of his apostolic mission, Paul is also describing his fantasy, his manner of interpreting his call and his having been "set apart." He makes sense of the revelation of God to him by understanding it as a call to be the Apostle to the Gentiles. Furthermore, he identifies a sanctioning agent;[81] it is "Jesus Christ our Lord" from whom he received "grace and apostleship" for the purpose of "obedience of faith." Christ, then, becomes the source of authority for the rhetorical vision that Paul was to proclaim to all Gentiles, including those in the Roman Christian community. The feature of that vision that he wants to emphasize for the Romans is "obedience."[82] It is a fantasy type that Paul will elaborate for them.

The whole of the opening greeting, one long sentence in Greek, is a carefully constructed rhetorical argument establishing Paul's apostolic *persona* and its authority. It introduces his rhetorical vision by means of a dramatizing message. That vision explains the place of the Gentiles in the economy of salvation, and describes for them the ethical principles involved in living a moral life as part of the eschatological people of God.[83]

The thanksgiving contains an implied invitation to engage in fantasy-chaining with Paul. Despite the fact that, as Paul acknowledges in 1:8, the faith

---

79. Jewett, "Romans as an Ambassadorial Letter," 11.

80. Dunn, *Romans 1–8*, 18.

81. A *sanctioning agent* is "the source which justifies the acceptance and promulgation of a rhetorical drama" (Cragan and Shields, *Applied Communication Research,* 7). Agent can refer to an external source of authority like God or to a dominant feature of a culture or a moment in history, like a war or the Crucifixion.

82. Crafton ("Paul's Rhetorical Vision and the Purpose of Romans," 328) defines the rhetorical vision of Romans as "the divine purpose for nations." I would label that a "fantasy type." The difference may be that Crafton does not seem to know Bormann's method and is therefore using "rhetorical vision" in a more general way.

83. Dunn (*Romans 1-8*, 18) also makes the point that a central theme of the letter is "that the saving purpose of God always had the Gentiles in view. . . ."

of the Romans is well known, he intends to visit in order to "strengthen" them (1:11). Thus, in what Dahl calls "a very polite twist to a conventional epistolary phrase," Paul prays not for the well-being of the letter's recipients, but for his own![84] He needs to avoid trouble, which 15:31 implies he is anticipating, so that the Romans can be benefitted (1:11, 13-15). It is another indication of the importance of his *persona*!

The clause that follows in verse 12 is often understood to "correct" the impression that Paul gives that he is somehow better than the Romans or "above" them.[85] However, as Cranfield points out, it could simply be the statement of a complementary truth.[86] From the perspective of SCT, it also can function as a description of a process whereby Paul's rhetorical vision can be incorporated into theirs. Assuming for the moment that the argument in 1:1-7 is persuasive, then argumentatively the thanksgiving has to establish for the audience that this *persona* has something of value for them to warrant his inclusion into the community. That is, the Romans need to be shown the pragmatic value of Paul's apostolic *persona*. His desire to visit will have some payoff for both parties! That value consists both in the receipt of Paul's gift and the opportunity for mutual fantasy-sharing that grows out of the integration of his *persona* and interaction with his vision, which includes encountering possible new fantasy types and themes.

What Paul is doing in the opening greeting and thanksgiving is establishing the basis for engaging the Romans in a form of rhetorical innovation. He wants to share his rhetorical vision so that it becomes part of the group's consciousness, therefore a part of their social reality, and therefore part of the basis of their discourse. Because his rhetorical vision may contain fantasy themes and types that are not fully familiar to the group or that previously may have been rejected by the group, he is engaged in a form of both consciousness-creating and consciousness-raising, phases in the life-cycle of a rhetorical vision.[87] It is the integration of his rhetorical vision into the group consciousness, with its subsequent effects, that constitutes the gift Paul wants to bring to the community in Rome.

It would take a careful analysis of the body of the letter to show how the communication of his "spiritual gift" functioned both to create and sustain consciousness of group identity and function. At this point it must suffice to

---

84. Dahl, *Studies in Paul,* 76.

85. E.g., Sanday and Headlam, *A Critical and Exegetical Commentary,* 21; Fitzmyer, *Romans,* 248.

86. Cranfield, *A Critical and Exegetical Commentary,* 80.

87. Bormann, Cragan, and Shields, "An Expansion of the Rhetorical Vision Component of the Symbolic Convergence Theory," 2.

point out that consciousness-creating rhetoric tends to be novel, explanatory, and imitative of familiar dramas.[88] While it would be misleading to say that Paul's rhetorical vision in Romans is novel, it is clearly explanatory and imitative. It is his interpretation of the fantasy of the Gospel, the full implications of which Paul is not sure the Romans understand. Thus, what some scholars have identified as theological exposition throughout the letter is intensely pragmatic and situational because it is intended to provide a foundation for fantasy-chaining by the Romans that will lead them to a new rhetorical vision and social worldview.

Consciousness-raising rhetoric depends on the presence of a group that has found a pragmatic rhetorical vision, one that helps them make sense of the world around them. The group seeks to propagate the vision, looking for new converts. That means that they take some kind of public action to testify to the utility of the vision.[89] In Romans that goal is clear from beginning to end, and it has direct, situational expression in Paul's closing explanation for writing (15:14-21) and report of his upcoming travel (15:22-29). Assuming that he is successful in creating a new group consciousness, Paul can turn to the ethical value of faith. Jewett makes the point succinctly:

> [T]he proofs of the earlier chapters are seen to have a practical purpose announced in the introduction and developed with powerful emotional appeals at the end of the discourse. This purpose was to elicit the cooperation of the Roman house churches in Paul's missionary activities, thus serving the ultimate purpose of divine righteousness in regaining control of a lost and disobedient world. . . . Salvation is inextricably joined here with world transformation, theology with ethics.[90]

Conclusion

As Ann Jervis has summarized it, there are "three main proposals as to [Paul's] purpose for writing" the letter to the Romans: (1) theological; (2) evangelical; and (3) pastoral.[91] Paul wants to describe his gospel; or he wants to lay a foun-

---

88. Ibid., 3.

89. Bormann, Cragan, and Shields, "An Expansion of the Rhetorical Vision Component," 10-11.

90. Jewett, "Following the Argument of Romans," 389.

91. L. Ann Jervis, *The Purpose of Romans: A Comparative Letter Structure Investigation* (*Journal for the Study of the New Testament Supplement* 55; Sheffield: Sheffield Academic Press, 1991), 14.

dation for the extension of his missionary work into Spain; or he wants to dispute errors or correct deviant behavior in Rome.

I have argued above that a pastoral purpose for the letter is the least likely of the three scenarios. The controversies he addresses are by no means unique to the experience of the Roman Christian community. Correct behavior as a means to escape the wrath of God is found in the Thessalonian correspondence. Eschatology is discussed both in 1 Thessalonians and 1 Corinthians, as is dying and rising with Christ. The role of the law is discussed in Galatians. The problem of the "strong and weak" is addressed in 1 Cor 8. The role of Abraham and Israel in the economy of salvation is covered in Gal 3–4.

That is not to say, however, that Romans is entirely derivative and contains no new perspectives. One has only to think of chapters 9–11 to recognize discourse not undertaken elsewhere in Paul's writings, or the particulars of the paraenetic teaching in 13:1-7 to see problems addressed that appear to be peculiar to the Roman audience. The point is that the reason for most of the discourse in Romans need not lie exclusively in the Roman situation. Even the argument in chapters 9–11 could have been triggered by reflection on his upcoming visit to Jerusalem (15:30-32), and the issues concerning secular authority could have arisen from a variety of historical circumstances.[92]

I think it is more useful to view the purpose of this letter as a combination of (1) and (2). These two purposes are brought together out of (a) the struggle Paul had during his eastern-Mediterranean ministry that caused him to formulate his *paideia;* and (b) his desire to see an end to that ministry and the beginning of another in a new territory, perhaps with the help of the Romans (15:17-29). In order to fulfill the latter he had to establish his apostolic *persona* with the Romans. And in order to do that, he had to describe the gift of the gospel he had been given and wanted to pass on to the Romans for their edification. This is the answer to the question as to why Paul wrote the letter. In the descriptive language I have chosen: Paul had to establish his *persona* with the Romans in order effectively to share his *paideia* with them, the rhetorical vision that he hoped would create and then raise a different group consciousness for the Romans, a consciousness that might include support for his missionary ventures.

It would appear, then, that rhetorical analysis of the epistolary elements of the opening greeting and the thanksgiving supports the general concept that Romans was intended to function as a "diplomatic letter" and that Paul wanted the Romans to regard him as more than simply an "apostle." While epistolary

---

92. Jan Botha, *Reading Romans 13: Aspects of the Ethics of Interpretation in a Controversial Text* (Stellenbosch, South Africa: Stellenbosch University Press, 1991), 144-46.

theorists may argue against Jewett's conclusion on the grounds of genre criticism, clearly the rhetorical function of the beginning of the letter is to create and support Paul's *persona* as that of an "ambassador for Christ" (2 Cor 5:20) whose special commission was to be apostle to the Gentiles wherever they may be found.[93]

93. I want to thank Mark Nanos and David Hester-Amador for offering suggestions for improvement on a earlier draft of this paper. Their criticisms were extremely useful. They cannot, however, be held responsible for any weaknesses that might remain.

Reading Romans in Context

Wilhelm Wuellner

Introduction

Reading as mental activity with the material medium of written texts will be analyzed as dependent on, and determined by, three areas of contextuality:

1. The duality of the actual and implied contexts of the text *producer:* the contexts for the *real* author's, and thereby also the *implied* author's, thinking and interacting by writing; the contexts for generating "written" texts over time and in time.
2. The duality of the actual and implied contexts of the text as *product:* the very materiality of written texts, whether cheirographic, typographic, or other forms of the technical, material aspects of the product (for both author/producer, and reader/consumer), and the distribution or "marketing" of the text as product over time. The text as product has its contexts in church or synagogue; in Bible societies or the world of commercial publishers; in educational institutions or scientific, scholarly societies, etc.
3. The duality of the actual and implied contexts of the text *user:* the contexts for the real reader's and the implied reader's thinking; the contexts for generating read texts over time and in time.

Editor's note: We are grateful that Prof. Wuellner was able to contribute this article to our collection. Its value is heightened by the knowledge that, because of his unexpected death on February 15, 2004, as this book was in production, this essay is perhaps his last contribution to New Testament scholarship.

The text for consideration is Romans 1–6.[1] It is a religious text, and part of a larger text generated religiously, that is, within or out of a symbolic universe; materially produced, preserved, and distributed by communities adhering to this symbolic universe. Reading Rom 1–6 in context means reading it as "performative literature."

The text is meant to be used religiously; from its very beginning it is meant to be read or "performed" religiously in the context of other religious texts. First it is performed in the context known as the "Canon" of the Jewish Bible; then it is performed in the context of the emerging Christian Canon with its intermittent stages of (1) the formation of the Pauline *corpus*,[2] and (2) the linking of Luke's Acts with the emerging Pauline *corpus* as its preface and with Romans acquiring the role of being first in the collected letters.[3] The context for reading varied: Jewish- and Gentile-Christian, orthodox and heretical audiences; public worship and corporate or private edification; general literary or artistic culture[4] and distinctively religious culture; first and third world; capitalist and socialist ideologies; racist/sexist societies and non-racist/non-sexist societies, etc.

The methods by which to analyze the contextual determination of the reading of texts are drawn from two distinct areas of scholarly discourse (with other distinct areas of critical discourse, such as social anthropology, implied or presupposed):

1. The theory of argumentation as pioneered by Chaim Perelman (and others) in reconceptualizing traditional rhetoric in terms of a theory of practical reasoning.[5] This approach will help us come to terms with two claims: first, George Kennedy's claim that "all religious systems are rhetorical."[6] And then there is the claim explored in this paper that the *con-*

---

1. The text selection was proposed by the leadership of the *Studiorum Novi Testamenti Societas* Seminar Group on "The Role of the Reader in the Interpretation of the New Testament" for its annual meeting in 1987 in Göttingen.

2. For an example, see C. Lecompte, *De korporatieve lezing. Een nieuw methode van tekstbenadering toegespast op 1 Thessalonicenzen* (Th.D. diss., Protestant Theological Faculty, Brussels, 1981).

3. For a discussion of the issues involved, see Bruce M. Metzger, *The Canon of the New Testament: Its Origin, Development, and Significance* (Oxford: Oxford University Press, 1987).

4. As in Northrup Frye, *The Great Code: The Bible and Literature* (New York and London: Harcourt Harvest, 1983, 2002).

5. Chaim Perelman, "The New Rhetoric: A Theory of Practical Reasoning," 1-42 in *The New Rhetoric and the Humanities: Essays on Rhetoric and Its Application* (*Synthese Library* 140; trans. W. Klubach; Dordrecht, Boston, and London: Reidel, 1979).

6. George A. Kennedy, *New Testament Interpretation through Rhetorical Criticism* (Cha-

textual components of *religious* texts — comparable to, but distinctive
from, contextual components of *any* text — are essential for the pragmatic, communally, culturally responsive reading. Reading religious texts,
like praying or loving, can always and only be done "without ceasing"
(ἀδιαλείπτος — 1 Thess 5:17; Rom 12:12). All reading (ἀναγινώσκων) determined by contextual factors is re-minding (ἐπαναμιμνῄσκων; Rom
15:15, the *recapitulatio* for reading Romans).

2. The theory of intentionality[7] and its relation to a theory of action.[8]

In linking intentionality and action, and in re-connecting philosophy and
rhetoric (or better still, re-conceiving philosophy *as* rhetoric), this approach
will help us come to terms with intra-textual features in Romans which show
author and reader in relation to inter-textual and contextual components.
Three features demand our special attention as readers/exegetes (the more so as
they consistently are ignored):

1. The modal expressions (modality) which "modify the reality, the certainty or the importance of the data."[9]
2. The indexical expressions (modality) which direct the reading process
   "by means of indicating relations in which the object referred to stands to
   the utterance of the expression itself"[10] — such as personal deixis
   ("I/you/we"; but also "everyone" and "all," a deixis so crucial to Romans),
   spatial deixis (here/there; but also "coming/going"; e.g., Is Paul coming or
   going to Rome?), or "temporal deixis" ("now/then" and the deictic use of
   tenses).
3. The use of proper names as a means of focusing the writer's and reader's
   intentionality "in some way."[11] In Romans we find Jew/Greek, Jew/Gen-
   tile, Abraham, David, Adam, Moses, Rome, Jerusalem, Spain, etc.

---

pel Hill and London: University of North Carolina Press, 1984), 158. But no less rhetorical are
other "systems," even philosophy!

7. John R. Searle, *Intentionality: An Essay in the Philosophy of Mind* (Cambridge, London,
and New York: Cambridge University Press, 1983), esp. chap. 1 and 6 on its relation to "speech
acts" in the philosophy of language; see also H. C. White, ed., *Speech Act Theory and Biblical
Criticism* (*Semeia* 41; Decatur, Ga.: Scholars Press, 1988).

8. John R. Searle, *Minds, Brains, and Science* (Cambridge, Mass.: Harvard University
Press, 1984), 57-70.

9. Chaim Perelman and Lucie Obrechts-Tyteca, *The New Rhetoric: A Treatise on Argumentation* (Notre Dame and London: University of Notre Dame Press, 1969), 154-63; Searle,
Intentionality, 255-58.

10. Searle, *Intentionality*, 218-30.

11. Ibid., 231-61. For narratives, see T. Docherty, *Reading (Absent) Character: Towards a
Theory of Characterization in Fiction* (New York & Oxford: Clarendon Press, 1983), 43-86.

The World of the Text and Reading
in the Light of Modern Rhetoric

How does rhetoric, re-conceptualized as theory of argumentation, or as theory of practical reasoning, help us in coming to terms with both aspects of the world of the text and its reader/audience: the intra-textual and the inter-textual (or contextual)? We are focusing in our discussion primarily on the latter: the contextual or inter-textual aspects.

But we must be aware all along that intra- and inter-textual aspects are inseparable; they are two sides of the same coin. This inseparable unity is equally true whether it concerns (a) the text producer/speaker/author, the genetic part of a text; (b) the finished product, i.e., its structure and genre; or (c) the user/audience/reader, i.e., the text's usage.

"Text and context are complementary,"[12] as sense and reference, intentionality and action are complementary. According to John Lyons, "the context of an utterance includes, not only the surrounding co-text (if there is any), but also the relevant features of the situation of utterance . . . what is sometimes referred to as the context of situation."[13] The rhetorician will speak here of the rhetorical situation(s). Propositional content, whether that of Paul's theology or that of his readers, gets modified by "social and expressive meaning [which] is conveyed at all levels of language structure; and it is very heterogeneous."[14]

The Theory of Argumentation

The *framework of argumentation* or the presuppositions for argumentation as practical reasoning are twofold but complementary: The will, the desire of the author to write *for* someone, and the disposition of readers to read what is written for them. The product has to be accessible.

One of the presuppositions for Perelman is "the contact of minds," "the existence of an intellectual contact,"[15] or "a meeting of minds."[16] It is "a preliminary agreement arising from the norms set by social life."[17] Every society has

12. John Lyons, *Language, Meaning and Context* (*Fontana Linguistics*; Bungay, Suffolk: Chaucer, 1981), 200.

13. Ibid., 206.

14. Ibid., 211.

15. Perelman and Obrechts-Tyteca, *The New Rhetoric*, 14-17.

16. Chaim Perelman, *The New Rhetoric and the Humanities*, 11.

17. Perelman and Obrechts-Tyteca, *The New Rhetoric*, 15.

evolved both customs or habits, and detailed rules for achieving the conditions for establishing this contact of minds, such as "membership in the same social class, exchange of visits, and other social relations."[18] "Every argument presupposes a meeting of minds — a meeting which social and political institutions can facilitate or prevent,"[19] as can be seen from house, synagogue, temple conventions in Israel, or from house school or academy, secular or religious "volunteer associations," and civic forum conventions in Rome. In current theories of intentionality the same issue is being discussed under the prerequisites of "directions of fit."[20]

An extension of this "meeting of minds" as presupposition or part of the framework of argumentation is the relation between author and reader.[21] What constitutes an author's readership, or a letter writer's recipient, is not necessarily just the person addressed by name.[22] To paraphrase Perelman, readers of epistles (or gospels) are "the ensemble of those whom [the author] wishes to influence by his argumentation."[23] The purpose of the writing and influence on the reader are then but two sides of the same coin.

The "implied reader" has been studied in terms of its psychological and sociological components.[24] It is here that we encounter a very important "contextual" component. Behind the traditional classification of readers/audiences in terms of the three types of roles that they were expected or known to perform (the rhetorical genres of deliberative, forensic, and epideictic speech) lie "the social functions exercised [by the readers]."[25] As we will see, in Romans the readers are addressed as ones assumed or known to be in social relations with people everywhere (Jews and Gentiles).

This, then, is the ensemble Paul wishes to influence by his writing. The persuasive or convincing rationale in a given writing is determined by "the

---

18. Perelman and Obrechts-Tyteca, *The New Rhetoric*, 17; Perelman, *The New Rhetoric and the Humanities*, 11.

19. Chaim Perelman, *The Realm of Rhetoric* (Notre Dame and London: University of Notre Dame Press, 1982), 11.

20. See herein, pages 123-33.

21. Perelman and Obrechts-Tyteca, *The New Rhetoric*, 17-45; Perelman, *The New Rhetoric and the Humanities*, 14; *The Realm of Rhetoric*, 13-20.

22. As Lars Hartman has recently shown applying also to construction of the writer (Lars Hartman, "On Reading Others' Letters," 137-46 in *Christians Among Jews and Gentiles: Essays in Honor of Krister Stendahl* [ed. George W. E. Nicklesburg and George W. MacRae; Philadelphia: Fortress, 1986]).

23. Perelman and Obrechts-Tyteca, *The New Rhetoric*, 19; Perelman, *The Realm of Rhetoric*, 14.

24. Perelman and Obrechts-Tyteca, *The New Rhetoric*, 9-23.

25. Ibid., *passim*.

quality of the audience at which it is aimed" or by the "beliefs accepted by the audience."[26] Whether the "implied reader" is addressed indirectly in third person singular or plural (he/they) or directly in second person singular or plural (you), or expresses itself in first person singular or plural (I/we), the crucial presupposition for argumentation is that this "implied reader" is "reasonable."

Closely related to "implied reader" and "rhetorical situation" is rhetoric's traditionally keen interest in *topos* choice underlying argumentation.[27] The classification of topics into those related to persons or agents and those related to actions foreshadows the distinction between philosophy of the mind and its focus on intentionality, and philosophy of action.[28] What is important for our discussion of the *con*-textual factors of "the world of the text" is rhetoric's keen interest in the topics as "the special circumstances impinging on the rhetorical act, . . . a logic of social inferences generally similar to but specifically different from the propositional logic of dialectic." This "material perspective [on the nature and function of 'invention' or *topos* choice] places the topics in closer contact with actual situations and calls attention to the circumstantial character of rhetorical inference" as part of "the framework" and not just "the techniques" of argumentation.[29]

This is the "universal" or "ideal" reader.[30] In Perelman's words, "the appeal to reason is conceived as an appeal to an ideal audience — which I call the universal audience — whether embodied in God, in all reasonable and competent men [*sic*], in the man [*sic*] deliberating or in an elite."[31] Perelman is quite aware of the fact that a rational argumentation (like that in Romans) "depends on the historically grounded conception of the universal audience."[32] Perelman even goes a step further when he maintains that "each individual, each culture

26. Perelman, *The New Rhetoric and the Humanities,* 14. On "beliefs," see Radu J. Bogdan, ed., *Belief: Form, Contents, and Function* (Oxford: Oxford University Press, 1986).

27. Michael C. Leff, "The Topics of Argumentative Invention in Latin Rhetorical Theory from Cicero to Boethius," *Rhetorica* 1 (1983): 23-44.

28. This will be explained more fully on pages 123-38.

29. Leff, "The Topics of Argumentative Invention," 41-42.

30. Perelman and Obrechts-Tyteca, *The New Rhetoric,* 31-35; on Habermas' *"ideale Sprechsituation,"* see Helga Gripp, *Jürgen Habermas* (Paderborn, Munich, Vienna, Zürich: Schöningh, 1984), 46-55.

31. Perelman, *The New Rhetoric and the Humanities,* 14.

32. Ibid. For Bakhtin the term is "superaddressee." "In various ages and with various understandings of the world, this superaddressee and his ideally responsive understanding assumes various ideological expressions (God, absolute truth, the court of dispassionate human conscience, the people, the court of history, science, and so forth)" (Mikhail M. Bakhtin, *Speech Genres and Other Late Essays* [*University of Texas Press Slavic* 8; Austin: University of Texas Press, 1986], 126).

has . . . its own conception of the universal audience."[33] But Perelman never openly acknowledges that the social, cultural component of reasonableness for Western, Mediterranean, and Biblical minds tends to be restricted to "men" (Paul's "brethren" address) and all that means for the "implied reader."[34] Petersen will be speaking here of Paul's "narrative world" and "symbolic universe"[35] and Patte of "system of convictions."[36]

The traditional distinction between convincing and persuasive writing has been redefined by Perelman as follows: argumentation is *persuasive* if it "only claims validity for a particular audience"; *convincing* if it "presumes to gain the adherence of every rational being."[37] Giving this schema, Romans appears in large parts convincing and only in a few parts persuasive. For even the "address to the imaginary interlocutor" in Romans,[38] as well as those portions in Romans where Paul "deliberates with himself," are never "more than floating incarnations of [the] universal audience."[39] The "striking result of [Kennedy's] study . . . [namely the] recognition of the extent to which forms of logical argument are used in the New Testament,"[40] is another tribute to the importance of the universal audience. This, in turn, is important for the text's context, the world outside the text, or better, presupposed by the text as argumentation, "the social grounds of knowledge" involved in every argumentation.[41]

Universal audience and elite audience get distinguished in modern rhetoric.[42] When Paul identifies himself as "called to be an apostle, set apart . . ." (Rom 1:1) and his readers as "called to be saints," the elite audience will appear to some as "no more than a particular audience"[43] (which is said

33. Perelman and Obrechts-Tyteca, *The New Rhetoric.*

34. See Genevieve Lloyd, *The Man of Reason: 'Male' and 'Female' in Western Philosophy* (London: Methuen, 1984).

35. Norman R. Petersen, *Rediscovering Paul: Philemon and the Sociology of Paul's Narrative World* (Philadelphia: Fortress, 1985), 1-42.

36. Daniel Patte, *Paul's Faith and the Power of the Gospel: A Structural Introduction to the Pauline Letters* (Philadelphia: Fortress, 1983), 1-30.

37. Perelman and Obrechts-Tyteca, *The New Rhetoric,* 28.

38. Stanley K. Stowers, *The Diatribe and Paul's Letter to the Romans* (*Society for Biblical Literature Dissertation* 57; Chico, Calif.: Scholars Press, 1981), 79-100.

39. Perelman and Obrechts-Tyteca, *The New Rhetoric,* 31.

40. George A. Kennedy, *New Testament Interpretation Through Rhetorical Criticism* (Chapel Hill and London: University of North Carolina Press, 1984), 159.

41. Charles A. Willard, *Argumentation and the Social Grounds of Knowledge* (Birmingham: University of Alabama Press, 1983).

42. Perelman and Obrechts-Tyteca, *The New Rhetoric,* 33-34; Perelman, *The Realm of Rhetoric,* 16-17.

43. Perelman and Obrechts-Tyteca, *The New Rhetoric,* 34.

to match the allegedly sectarian character of early Christianity).[44] But rhetoric is not part of sociology, though rhetoric has its own profound commitment to social and cultural factors, especially when it comes to the *con*-text so essential to all argumentation.

For Perelman "the elite audience [can be] regarded as a model to which [persons or groups] should conform in order to be worthy of the name: in other words, the elite audience sets the norm for everybody. In this case, the elite is the vanguard all will follow and conform to . . . [it] embodies the universal audience only for those who acknowledge this role of vanguard and model."[45] This perception may aid us — if only in avoiding the wrong kind of contextualization promoted by advocates of "sociological exegesis" who are solely interested in exegesis served by, and serving, social description. What we find as presupposition of Paul's argumentation in Romans may become clearer to us when we approach Romans with these two observations. On the one hand, "particular concrete audiences are capable of validating a concept of the universal audience which characterizes them. On the other hand, . . . the undefined universal audience [can be] invoked to pass judgment on what is the concept of the universal audience appropriate to such a concrete audience. . . . [A]udiences pass judgment on one another."[46] We learn more of these audiences by analyzing the rhetorical situation in which they are addressed.

One of the most essential elements in the analysis of what constitutes the framework of argumentation is the recognition of the importance of "the rhetorical situation," by which is meant that specific condition or situation which invites utterance. Each of the major rhetorical genres has its appropriate rhetorical situation. With Romans identified as belonging to the epideictic genre,[47] what would that mean in terms of its rhetorical situation? In Perelman's terms, epideictic's intentionality is to strengthen adherence to values already affirmed for the purpose of paving the way or bringing about the necessary "action." This action is defined by Mark Jordan for the protreptic genre as "wanting the hearer's whole self for an ongoing pedagogy."[48] For Perelman the action pre-

44. Wayne A. Meeks, *The First Urban Christians: The Social World of the Apostle Paul* (New Haven and London: Yale University Press, 1983), 74-100.

45. Perelman and Obrechts-Tyteca, *The New Rhetoric*, 34.

46. Ibid., 35.

47. Wilhelm Wuellner, "Paul's Rhetoric of Argumentation in Romans: An Alternative to the Donfried-Karris Debate over Romans," *Catholic Biblical Quarterly* 38 (1976): 330-51; = 152-74 in *The Romans Debate* (ed. Karl P. Donfried; Minneapolis: Augsburg, 1977).

48. Mark D. Jordan, "Ancient Philosophical Protreptic and the Problem of Persuasive Genres," *Rhetorica* 4 (1986): 332-33.

pared by any of the rhetorical genres is *commitment* to the intentional content of the argumentation.

On the one hand, the rhetorician points out that there is "a close connection between argumentative thought and the action [for which] it paves the way . . . or [that it] brings about." On the other hand — and here is where context re-asserts itself — the rhetorician must acknowledge and fully account for the fact that argumentation develops "in a situation that is socially and psychologically determined."[49]

The premises of argumentation[50] — the basis of agreement, or what is supposed to be accepted by the readers — contain important clues to a text's context.

Besides the familiar list of *loci* or topics,[51] there are the less familiar but equally important enumerations of the agreed upon "facts and truths" along with "values" (both abstract and concrete) and "hierarchies" (e.g., Jew/Gentile; male/female; master/slave; believer/unbeliever). The technique of question and answer, or the related one of rhetorical questions, sets the premises used in argumentation "on firm ground."[52] What premises are chosen and adapted for argumentation may be as indicative of a text's context as the mode of presentation of those premises. In the latter case we have the consideration of the choice of modality and indexicality which will be important also to our following discussion of intentionality and action theories.

The more familiar terrain of rhetoric appears in discussions of "techniques of argumentation,"[53] "the structure of argument," or "the argumentative process."[54] These techniques, or this process or structure, fall for Perelman into two types: the argumentative processes of association or liaison and of dissociation.

Argumentative association reveals context in each of the three categories employed by Perelman:

---

49. Perelman and Obrechts-Tyteca, *The New Rhetoric,* 59. This crucial point receives, however, only sporadic and somewhat minimal attention (ibid., 59-62) The same can be said of the briefest of treatments that modality and indexicality in argumentation receive in Perelman's work, as in most studies of the nature of argumentation, ancient or modern.

50. Perelman and Obrechts-Tyteca, *The New Rhetoric,* 65-114; Perelman, *The New Rhetoric and the Humanities,* 15-17; Perelman, *The Realm of Rhetoric,* 21-32.

51. Wilhelm Wuellner, "Toposforschung und Torahinterpretation bei Paulus und Jesus," *New Testament Studies* 24 (1978): 463-83. The reader is reminded of the discussion earlier in this paper on topics as part of the "framework" (see page 111).

52. Perelman, *The New Rhetoric and the Humanities,* 16; Wuellner, "Paul as Pastor," 63-65.

53. Perelman, *The New Rhetoric and the Humanities,* 185-508; *The Realm of Rhetoric,* 48-137.

54. Perelman, *The New Rhetoric and the Humanities,* 18-25.

1. Quasi-logical arguments which reveal what the reader accepts as logical/illogical, serious/ridiculous, compatible/incompatible, wholes/parts, and others;[55]
2. Arguments based on the structure of reality which reveal what the reader accepts as causal link; as ends and means; as authority (e.g., ambassadors/apostles; Holy Scriptures, etc.), or symbolic reality;[56]
3. Arguments acceptable for "establishing the structure of reality," such as examples, illustration, models, analogies, metaphors, and occasionally irony.[57]

Argumentative dissociation — an area of study largely neglected by the rhetorical tradition — reveals context in what is judged as misleading, merely partial appearance in contrast to the full reality (e.g., the fleshly Israel v. the true Israel). "The dissociation results in a depreciation of what had until then been an accepted value and in its replacement by another conception to which is accorded the original value."[58] The dissociation of outward/inward, fleshly/spiritual, and γράμμα/πνεῦμα in Paul's argument about "the advantages of being Jewish" in Rom 2–3 is one example.

The order and interaction of arguments are "dictated by adaptation to the audience and the argumentative situation . . . [they are] functional.[59] In the rhetorical approach to texts, "context" lies in both the "adaptation to the audience" and the "argumentative situation."[60] The different order in the "transitions" from the thanksgiving section of the letter opening to the letter body, as highlighted by Roberts,[61] is due to "function" — which is another word for "adaptation to audience" and "rhetorical situation." ("Transition" is a technical term in rhetoric for the move from the *exordium* to the main point of the argu-

---

55. Perelman and Obrechts-Tyteca, *The New Rhetoric,* 193-260; Perelman, *The New Rhetoric and the Humanities,* 19-21; *The Realm of Rhetoric,* 53-80.

56. Perelman and Obrechts-Tyteca, *The New Rhetoric,* 261-349; Perelman, *The New Rhetoric and the Humanities,* 21-22; *The Realm of Rhetoric,* 81-105.

57. Perelman and Obrechts-Tyteca, *The New Rhetoric,* 350-410; Perelman, *The New Rhetoric and the Humanities,* 22-23; *The Realm of Rhetoric,* 106-25.

58. Perelman, *The New Rhetoric and the Humanities,* 24; see also Perelman and Obrechts-Tyteca, *The New Rhetoric,* 411-59; Perelman, *The Realm of Rhetoric,* 126-37.

59. Perelman and Obrechts-Tyteca, *The New Rhetoric,* 501; see ibid., 460-508; Perelman, *The New Rhetoric and the Humanities,* 24-25; *The Realm of Rhetoric,* 138-52.

60. Cf. our previous discussion on pages 109-11.

61. J. H. Roberts, "Transitional Techniques to the Letter Body in the Corpus Paulinum," 187-201 in *A South African Perspective on the New Testament: Essays by South African New Testament Scholars Presented to Bruce Manning Metzger during His Visit to South Africa in 1985* (ed. J. H. Peterzer and P. J Hartin; Leiden: E. J. Brill, 1986).

ment.) Order and interaction of arguments determine the meaning of the *paraenesis* in Paul's letters.[62] What does it say about the text's context that Rom 12:1–15:13 is the climax of the *whole* argumentative structure and interaction beginning in 1:18 and ending with 15:13? The pedantic application of epistolary genre conventions is helpful only up to a certain point.[63]

To say that function determines "the essential core of the argument" is to say that context is determinative.[64] And context in rhetorical perspective always means "adaptation to audience" which means "exigence"; it is closer to form criticism's crucial concept of *Sitz im Leben* which, in its generic or typical interest, is more related to "mood" or "intentionality" than the specificity of a historical situation.[65]

Application of Rhetorical to Text/Context Reading of Rom 1–6

The meeting of minds is a basic presupposition for a rhetorical reading of Romans. Biblical exegesis, along with literary scholarship in general, can be chided with Bakhtin's charge that "the complex event of encountering and interacting with another's word has been almost completely ignored. . . . The real object of study is the interrelation and interaction of 'spirits.'"[66] This interaction of spirits is contextually presupposed in the commonality of the writer Paul and the Roman readers sharing outwardly a common mission (proclaiming one's faith/the faith in all the world), and the mutual benefaction each side experiences when being host to the other, both indebted to the one divine benefactor.[67] Writing and reading are both understood as means of re-minding, under divine grace (15:15). The pending visit is part of a network of visits by Paul and others with numerous benefactors all over the Empire. The meeting of minds is thus both conditioned and presupposed by this social, cultural institution. It provides a context which is both very concrete and symbolic. The bene-

---

62. For Galatians, see Steven J. Kraftchick, *Ethos and Pathos in Galatians Five and Six: A Rhetorical Analysis* (Ph.D. diss., Emory University, 1985). For 1 Thessalonians, see Bruce C. Johanson, *To All the Brethren: A Text-Linguistic and Rhetorical Approach to 1 Thessalonians* (*Coniectanea Biblica, New Testament* 16; Stockholm: Almquist & Wiksell, 1987).

63. It is no more helpful than analysis of rhetorical genre patterns. See the critical reflections on the protreptic genre by Mark D. Jordan ("Ancient Philosophical Protreptic and the Problem of Persuasive Genres," 309-33).

64. Roberts, "Transitional Techniques," 197.

65. Kennedy, *New Testament Interpretation Through Rhetorical Criticism*, 34-36.

66. Bakhtin, *Speech Genres and Other Late Essays*, 144.

67. Frederick W. Danker, *Benefactor: Epigraphic Study of a Graeco-Roman and New Testament Semantic Field* (St. Louis: Clayton, 1982).

factor is part of Paul's and the readers' "narrative world" or "symbolic universe"; it is a system which nourishes and supports, thus enabling, satisfying, and empowering both benefactor and beneficiary. Letter-writing and reading (as distinct from having a letter read to you) are integral parts of this system.

Another system supporting the notion of "bringing obedience to the faith for the sake of [God's] name among all the nations" (Rom 1:5), which motivates the faith-spreading activities of both writer and readers and motivates their writing their writing and reading, is Israel's "narrative world" anchored in the Biblical stories ("the oracles of God entrusted to Jews," Rom 3:2) and in the tradition of the sages down to the days of Paul and his readers. It is a basis for "boasting of your relation to God" (2:17).[68]

The assumed/implied reader is one who approves that the readers' faith is proclaimed in all the world (1:8), one who understands the symbolic universe of the Holy Scriptures, one whose narrative world begins with Adam, develops with the elect (elite) character of Abraham and Israel in opposition to the Gentiles, progresses *via* Moses and David and Christ to the sonship for all who believe, and climaxes with the realization and hope of being heirs of God. The implied author shares theses premises with the reader.

This assumed reader is a construction of the writer. This implied reader is as self-assured of its faith and faith mission as the implied author in Paul is of its faith. The *exordium* contains all the ingredients which resurface at the beginning of the peroration, following the main body of Paul's argument (1:18–15:13), when the readers are presumed to be "full of goodness, filled with all knowledge, and able to instruct one another" (15:14). This is sufficient reason for a thanksgiving to God "for all of [the readers]" (1:8). The acknowledged capability of the readers for instructing one another, let alone instructing all the nations, presumes an ongoing divine activity that is manifest "through faith for faith" (1:17) — which accounts also for the presumed appreciation for mutual encouragement by each other's faith (writer and readers). This too is a context which is both very concrete and symbolic.

There is, of course, a concrete and particular reader — historically the real readers in Rome, the Roman Christians, and, throughout history, presumably beginning with Paul's very first letter,[69] also the real readers of fellow Christians everywhere who, then as now, read Paul's letters "as if they were addressed to themselves rather than to their original recipients."[70] But in address-

---

68. Personal deixis and its content/context reference will be discussed more fully beginning on page 127.

69. See 1 Thess 5:27, "read to *all* of [the brothers and sisters]."

70. Hartman, "On Reading Others' Letters," 137.

ing real and as such always particular readers, Paul addresses a variety of other readers. The real readers may not be a construction of the writer, but these other readers in the text and its context are. Whether speaking of the original Romans or any of the subsequent readers, as "real readers" of Paul's letter as argument (or argument as letter) they/we are held "capable of validating a concept of the universal audience which characterizes [every real reader]."[71]

On the other hand, Paul's argument invokes "the undefined universal audience" for a dual purpose. First of all, "to pass judgment on what is the concept of the universal audience appropriate to such a concrete audience [as that of the Roman community, made up of Jews and Gentiles, Greeks and barbarians, etc.; in other words: a concrete audience very mixed, anything but homogeneous] . . ."; and secondly, "to examine, simultaneously, [both] the manner in which it was composed, [and also] which are the individuals [and groups!] who comprise it. . . ."[72]

In three explicit ways the ideal reader (Perelman's "universal audience") can be discerned in Romans 1-6:[73]

1. In the arguments presupposing assent by the general reader:
   a. Sentences with third person singular or plural subject (impersonal speaker/impersonal audience): 1:1-4b (as part of 1:1-7); 1:17 part of the *exordium* "transition"; 1:18-32 the first argument; 2:6–16:26; 2:28–3:4; 3:10-18 (Old Testament quotes), 20-26; 4:2-8, 10-25; 5:12-21; 6:23
   b. Sentences with impersonal speaker/You-plural addressee: 1:6-7 (as part of 1:1-7, with God as "third party" as speaker); 2:24 (Old Testament quote); [2:25]; 6:3 ("do you not know . . ."); 6:11-14, 16-22
2. In arguments expressing a single interlocutor/reader.[74] The rhetorical figure of *apostrophe,* changing to a single reader, is found in Rom 2:1; 2:3-5; 2:17-23.[75]

71. Perelman and Obrechts-Tyteca, *The New Rhetoric,* 35.

72. Ibid.

73. Passages from Romans 1–6 cited below without any brackets mark the texts which invoke the universal audience. The citations in parentheses mark those texts which state a particular audience's view without its universal audience component, or with a concept of universal audience judged to be inappropriate. Square brackets mark those texts which combine two aspects — taking a particular (e.g., Jewish, Gentile, or Christian) concrete reader position and showing by argumentation how, and to what effect, the universal audience can be invoked as "the incarnation of a particular audience" (Perelman and Obrechts-Tyteca, *The New Rhetoric,* 39).

74. They have been examined by Stowers, *The Diatribe and Paul's Letter to the Romans.*

75. These are *all* the examples to be found in Rom 1–6; Stowers (*The Diatribe and Paul's Letter to the Romans,* 213, n. 1) offers some others from Romans, but not all, "only those which are most important in the argumentation of the letter."

3. In arguments where the writer argues with himself: in sentences with first person singular or plural subject, but no addressee:[76]
   a. "I" (as self-deliberating individual): The expressions of prayer in 1:8-10 and of desire in 1:11-13 make these "transition" sections self-deliberating, along with 1:14-15 (Paul's mental state) and 1:16 a credal statement;[77] [3:7]
   b. "We" (as self-deliberating collective or "elite"): 1:4c-5 (as part of 1:1-7); 2:2 ("we know . . ."); [3:5-6]; [3:8-9]; 3:19 ("we know . . ."); [3:27–4:1]; [4:9]; 5:1-11; [6:1-12]; 6:4-10; [6:15]

The universal audience is invoked for each of the *particular* readers: for me/us/you/them Jews and Gentiles in Rom 1:18–4:25 (as again in Rom 9–11), and also for me/us/you/them Christians in Rom 5–6 (and, of course 7–8, and again 12-16) in my/our/their particularity — convictionally, and not just ethnically, culturally. Why, or for what purpose is it done? To aid real readers in passing judgment on the appropriateness of their respective claims of "concrete universality." For our discussion of the context factor in reading, we need to appreciate the paradox of "concrete universality" where "context" is marked by the social, cultural concreteness of (1) the self-deliberating writer/speaker (as individual or group); and of (2) the single interlocutor as dialogue partner;[78] and (3) the convincing and persuading parts of the remaining bulk of the letter. In each of the three cases derived from Perelman we can see instances of what Bakhtin calls "the responsive nature of contextual meaning."[79]

"Convincing" and "persuading" forms of argumentation need to be distinguished. Persuading argumentation makes its appeal to special, particular readers; convincing argumentation appeals to the ideal reader or universal audience. Whereas one might anticipate a preponderance of persuasive argumentation in Paul's letters, for Romans the opposite is the case. Rom 1:1a and 1:7a is the only appeal (and an epistolary convention at that) to the real readers in all of Rom 1–6 (indeed till Rom 11!); the second time the writer makes a persuasive appeal is Rom 12:1 where the first real persuasion takes place! All the rest of Rom 1–11 shows Paul arguing by seeking to convince.

---

76. On "the case of the diary," see Walter J. Ong, "The Writer's Audience Is Always a Fiction," *Publications of the Modern Language Association* 90 (1975): 9-21; repr. in *Twentieth Century Literary Theory: An Introductory Anthology* (ed. Vassilis Lambropoulos and David Neal Miller; Albany: State University of New York Press, 1987), 419.

77. Roberts, "Transitional Techniques," 193.

78. This includes potentially *all the apostrophe* sections in Paul's collectively addressed letters.

79. Bahktin, *Speech Genres and Other Late Essays*, 145.

This startling observation has consequences for our discussion of the context of reading. This shows Paul's intention of addressing himself, "by way of reminder," to *every* believer; Paul intends to be convincing, "that is, acceptable in principle to all the members of the universal audience"[80] — regardless whether the reference is to Jews, Gentiles, or Christians. The context, then, for convincing argumentation in Rom 1–6 is *not* speculative abstraction, but "boldness" in acting/writing "as a 'philosophical' or religious-ethical teacher"[81] — which is the same context for the rabbinic sages in Israel as for the protreptic philosophers in Rome. Paul already *does* in his writing what he *intends* to do when visiting Rome: to elaborate and deepen, to confirm and strengthen what is experientially and cognitively known, hence already "relevant," for "every one who has faith," whether Jew, or Greek, or Christian. The context is not that of either missionary or polemicist, but of educator or pastor whose "school" or "parish" is the world.[82]

The audience context for Romans is significant. Paul uses elite audiences to embody the universal audience. On the surface of Romans, the context appears to point to three distinct elite audiences as three particular types of readers, and hence three distinct social, cultural, linguistic contexts: the Jewish elite (called/chosen/God's son descended from David/etc.), the Gentile elite (knowing God's decree/God's law written on hearts/etc.), and the Christian elite (called/set apart/Holy Spirit given/etc.). But Paul uses each of the three elite audiences to bring about, for each individually and for all collectively, adherence to the universal audience: the ideal reader who knows what he is doing and who practices what he knows and preaches.

The representational context for this implied reader is, besides God, God's Son, Holy Scriptures (γραφαῖς ἁγίαις), and other "authorities." These other authorities, equal in convictional value, include the model life of Paul (or other apostles besides or before him, as individuals or groups of "fellow workers"), of "the saints in Jerusalem" and, not least, of "God's beloved in Rome [whose] faith is proclaimed in all the world."[83]

Paul's argumentative premises and the *topoi* in Rom 1–6 provide rich information for the context of the letter.

There is a cultural context evident in the use of such familiar "hierarchies" as Jew/Gentile, Greek/barbarian or, as in all cultures, wise/foolish.

---

80. Perelman, *The Realm of Rhetoric*, 18.

81. Stowers, *The Diatribe and Paul's Letter to the Romans*, 180.

82. On the difference between reading (literacy) and hearing (orality), see Ong, "The Writer's Audience Is Always a Fiction," 404, 418.

83. See Patte (*Paul's Faith and the Power of the Gospel*, 9-27) on Paul's "system of convictions" (Paul's convictional logic as distinct from his argumentative logic).

Within the Jewish tradition there is the accepted superiority of patriarchy (Abraham as father of us all) over matriarchy (Sarah as secondary).

In the letter *topos* of "desire to see you" the whole benefactor system can be seen to be operative in the opening "transition" from thanksgiving to body of the letter.

Denunciation of social evils (covetousness, murder, etc., in 1:29) and the "justness" of punishment ("they deserve to die" in 1:32) are as topical in Romans as in Jewish society. Rhetorical questions evoke social or cultural value responses, such as 2:3 with affirmation from Jews and non-Jews alike; or 2:21-23 with affirmations evoked from Jewish culture.[84] Rom 4:4 presumes the value of workers' rights for due wages, but 2:6 presumes the value of workers' obligation. In 6:16 the social practice of "offering oneself to another person as obedient slave/servant" is taken for granted, whereas in 1:1 and 1:6-7 the servant status is considered subject to someone's call or appointment. In 6:3 all believers are expected to affirm the symbolic reality established by baptism, etc.

The choice of the quality-*topos*,[85] which here in Romans is the emphasis on "all" or "everyone" as over against "some" or "few,"[86] carries in its inclusiveness a special value which as *topos* choice[87] was familiar to Jew and Gentile alike.[88]

Besides the selection of premises for his argumentation, which are indicative of the social, cultural values the readers are expected to approve, there is also the presentation of the premises to be considered for the implied context encountered in reading. One major feature of the presentation of the premises already has been mentioned: the interrogative mode. But one should also look for the use of imperatives, i.e. what is presumed to be an acceptable deontic mode (in its negative form, the "don'ts" in the list of wrath-evoking vices). Also the use of the contingency mode: what "might" be right or proper. Values also are reflected in such chosen indexicalities as Gentiles, the ungodly (in contrast to the advantage of the Jew), and in such time deixis choices of then/now as equal to the contrast between inferior or even bad and the superior or good. There may even be value connotations in whether one "comes" or "goes" to Jerusalem or Rome.

Analysis of Paul's techniques of argumentation in Romans uncovers sig-

---

84. Note the mix of one positive and several affirmations.

85. Perelman and Obrechts-Tyteca, *The New Rhetoric*, 89-93.

86. "Personal deixis" is discussed more fully beginning on page 127 in the present essay.

87. The reader will remember the discussion of "topics" on page 111.

88. Wuellner, "Toposforschung und Torahinterpretation bei Paulus und Jesus," 476-79; Jouette M. Bassler, *Divine Impartiality: Paul and a Theological Axiom* (*Society for Biblical Literature Dissertation* 59; Chico, Calif.: Scholars Press, 1982).

nificant context factors that should be taken into account in a rhetorical analysis of the letter.

The technique of *associative argumentation* brings up a variety of contextual factors in each of the three categories advocated by Perelman.[89] There are the causal links between evil actions and punishment; the very existence of a symbolic universe associated with one or the other religious or philosophical tradition; the existence of authority figures or institutions, such as sacred codes (Holy Scriptures in Rom 1:2; see also 3:2). To read Romans contextually, the importance of figures of speech (e.g., metaphors, comparisons, and ironies), and also the power of both individual and corporate role-models need to be considered.

The technique of *dissociative argumentation* relies on important contextual factors, as in the dissociation of a Jew who is (allegedly) only outwardly one v. one who is inwardly; when that dissociation of the true Jew from the superficial Jew is elaborated further in terms of dissociations of spirit from flesh, or spirit from letter, then, as history has shown, false contextual inferences can be drawn from the use of this argumentative technique. The dissociation of the believer's present status of grace[90] from the fullness of the future status[91] embodies values familiar to the universal audience, the implied reader of first-century Mediterranean cultures, i.e., all the values which dissociate the priority of reality (truth) from mere secondary appearances (phenomena). This, in turn, sets the context for logical, or at least quasi-logical, techniques of argumentation (such as "if X, then Y") which get used more in Rom 5–6. Dissociation, however, is not to be confused with spatial and temporal deixis.[92]

The order, sequence, and interaction of arguments in Rom 1–6 provide important clues for understanding both the text and its context.

The "theme" or "thesis" for the whole of Romans, as stated in 1:16-17, presents three interrelated issues, each with a polarity or dialectic of its own which, in turn, determines both the sequence and interaction of the unfolding arguments in Rom 1:18–15:13.[93]

1. The power of God for salvation for everyone who has faith, involving not only Jews and Greeks, but "Jews first and also Greeks." Rom 1–9 elaborates this dialectic, especially in 1–4 and in 9–11.
2. The disclosure of divine righteousness, involving not just faith, but a dia-

89. As previously outlined on pages 114-15.
90. E.g., "having obtained access to this grace in which we stand" (Rom 5:2).
91. E.g., "our hope of sharing the glory of God" (Rom 5:2).
92. See page 126.
93. Which I take to be the body of the main argument.

lectic spelled out cryptically as "through faith for faith." Rom 5–8 elaborates this dialectic, especially for Christians.

3. The traditional faith-righteousness with emphasis on its equally traditional dialectic component of the possibility or necessity of practicing it: "shall live" as not an expression of tense, but of modality. Rom 12:1–15:13 elaborates that part.

Only as a whole and sustained argumentation (with Rom 1–6 only a part of the whole) does the context for both producing (i.e., writing) and using (i.e., reading) the text of Romans come into focus.[94] Context, then, serves as another term for "the rhetorical or argumentative situation" or "exigency" which has to be met the first time and every time the text gets used. The history of interpretation of Romans proves otherwise: exegetes imposed the exigencies of their respective situations (e.g., Romans as "polemical" for sixteenth-century Reformers and Counter-Reformers). In Sternberg's terms, Romans became largely over-read or under-read respectively. Modern historical criticism has compounded the problem by focusing exclusively on the historical reader and the historical situation. What Jordan has to say about the readers in Graeco-Roman protreptic literature applies also to Paul's epistles: the protreptic, like the letters, "do not agree on the hearer's condition or how to approach it; but they agree in wanting the [readers'] whole self for an ongoing pedagogy."[95] In Romans it is the ongoing development ἐκ πίστεως εἰς πίστιν.

The World of the Text and Reading in the Light of the Theory of Intentionality and Theory of Action

The Theoretical Framework

Intentionality is basic to the mental activity of reading. The term "intentionality" covers the whole range of mental states on the sides of both author and reader — such states as the beliefs or convictions relating to cognition on both sides, and the desires relating to volition on both sides. These mental states have their propositional content and their appropriate action, whether as intention *preceding* the action (e.g., Paul's desire to visit Rome and to be sped on to Spain), or *in* the action (e.g., God's rendering to all human beings according to their actions, in Rom 2:6).

---

94. On the second order of complexity in intentionality, see page 133.

95. Jordan, "Ancient Philosophical Protreptic and the Problem of Persuasive Genres," 332-33.

Then there is the matter of the complexity of intentionality: is it first or second order; fixed or open? The author, no less than the reader, can be subject to degrees of complexity. The intention of a specific act (e.g. for Paul to visit Rome or to go to Spain; or to write a given letter) is less complex (first order) than the intention of a whole set or series of actions (e.g. reaching out "to all the world"). By analogy, the intention in the production of any *one* of the argumentative units in Romans, whether the *exordium,* or the portion of the "body" of the argument which we chose to analyze (Rom 1–6), is less complex than the (second order) interactive argument of Romans as a whole.[96]

With the author or the reader there may be a fixed or an open intention. As regards the author, Paul has an intention that is "fixed" as far as his visit to Rome (and beyond to Spain) is concerned. He is fixed also in his intention that his outreach to the rest of the Gentiles should involve both Greeks and barbarians, i.e. the culturally privileged and unprivileged. But he is "open" in his intention when consciously accommodating phenomena of intrusion, as in roadblocks made explicit in Rom 15:25-32. As regards the reader, the fixed intention of coming to share the glory of God, based on the sure knowledge or belief that "God's love has been poured out into our hearts through the Holy Spirit which has been given to us" (5:2, 5), becomes an "open" intention when accommodated to the intrusive phenomena of suffering (5:3-4). In the case of both author and reader, the intrusions which modified fixed intentions into open ones were related to the intentions of a third party: God and God's will or intention (1:10; 15:32 for Paul, the writer; see Rom 8:17, 27-39 for the reader).

But why is intentionality even brought into our discussion about reading and context? For Searle, intentionality (on Paul's side, or on the side of any of the readers of his letter) is always part of an "entire holistic network (of subsidiary intentions)" which are said to shade off into "the background"[97] which others call "context."[98] Not only the historical author and the historical reader have such a context; likewise the text does. Nor does the text of Romans have *merely* a historical context. There also is a context, a background, an entire holistic network of subsidiary intentions to be recognized on the part of (a) the *co-author* of every *bona fide* religious author, namely God, or the Spirit of God, and (b) the co-texts both preceding Romans in the form of (Jewish) γραφαῖς ἁγίαις and following Romans — whether in the form of the Paulinist writings,

96. See herein, pages 115 and 123.

97. Searle, *Intentionality,* 141-59.

98. Dan Sperber and Deirdre Wilson, *Relevance: Communication and Cognition* (Cambridge, Mass.: Harvard University Press, 1986), 118-71.

supremely in the form of Ephesians as summary of the Pauline corpus, or in the form of the emerging *Christian* canon of γραφαῖς ἁγίαις. Not once, not even at its very first reading, has Romans been read without background or context — nor could it be. But different times and cultures could, and have, generated backgrounds or contexts other than the one prevailing at the time the text was first produced. And every time the text is re-generated in reading, the contextual dimension of the intentionality of "fixed" author/text on the one hand and "open" reader on the other does change.[99]

Modalities affect the reading of texts by "modify[ing] the reality, the certainty, or the importance" of what an argumentation is all about; hence the importance attributed to the argumentative role they play.[100] In order to make the controlling role of modalities in argumentation more explicit, we have to specify the particular modal systems, not only as operative in the structure of the text's intentionality (including presumably the author's), but also as operative in the reader or user. Modalities in argumentation can be shown to correspond to general (logical) modalities.[101] They operate jointly; every human action — e.g., whether that of writing or reading — is determined by:

1. Natural possibilities (the author's/reader's ability, skill, competence to write/read);
2. Deontic norms (e.g. Paul's obligation or "commitment" in Rom 1:14; or the laborer's due reward or wage in Rom 4:4);
3. Social or individual values (desires), such as the benefactor's desire to import "some gift" in Rom 1:11; or the sower's/workman's hopes of reaping "some harvest" (1:13); the contingency in a given society for "hardly (sacrificing oneself) for a righteous person, though perhaps for a good person someone may dare even to die" (5:7);
4. The writer's/reader's knowledge and beliefs (e.g. God's "will," "wrath," and "judgment," but also God's "kindness/forbearance/patience," etc.)[102]

---

99. Exegetes need to be alerted to the liabilities known as the "intentional fallacy" and the "encoded reader fallacy." Here the concerns of feminist criticism need to be registered. See Mary Field Belenky, et al., *Women's Ways of Knowing: The Development of Self, Voice, and Mind* (New York: Basic Books, 1986).

100. Perelman and Obrechts-Tyteca, *The New Rhetoric*, 154; F. R. Palmer, *Mood and Modality* (Cambridge and New York: Cambridge University Press, 1986).

101. Ivan Darrault, "Modalités logique, linguistique, sémiotique," in *Langages* (Paris) 43 (1976): 3-124.

102. See Patte, *Paul's Faith and the Power of the Gospel*, on Paul's and his reader's "system of convictions."

In his essay on "modality and textual structuration," Edward Costello suggests that modalities in a given text can be taken as "the realization of what [the text] contains within itself as its own potential."[103] In line with our three-fold emphasis (author, text, reader), we need to see also the implied reader's modality to which the real reader is expected to "conform," especially if reading is taken as an "action," as mental activity, which is inter-acting with the author's/text's "mood," and this interaction is dependent upon, if not determined by, context.[104]

Context, like text, has two components:

1. Its propositional or intentional "content" or reference. This has been the almost exclusive focus in our exegetical studies, exemplified by the Kittel-Friedrich *Theological Dictionary of the New Testament* and all forms of Biblical Theology, concerns with Scriptural Semantics, and the still-current vogue of Redaction Criticism.
2. Given "the fact that language [both as speaking/writing, and as hearing/reading 'activity'] is essentially a *social* phenomenon and that the forms of intentionality [including modality] underlying language are *social* forms,"[105] the context "provides a set of enabling conditions that make it possible for particular forms of intentionality [like modality and deixis] to function."[106]

The same is true of the role of indexical expressions of deixis in argumentation (or narration).

"Deixis" refers to the orientation of the content of a sentence in relation to time, place, and personal participants. The spatial, temporal, and interpersonal orientation of a sentence is expressed by deictic indicators (here/there; come/go; then/now; I/you; we/they; etc.).[107] Moreover, deictic and interpersonal features of language are used, in narrative no less than in argumentation, to construct

---

103. Edward T. Costello, "Modality and Textual Structuration," in *Poetics and the Theory of Literature: A Journal for Descriptive Poetics and Theory of Literature* 4 (1979): 308; Darrault, "Modalités logique, linguistique, sémiotique," 3-124.

104. Patte expresses the demand for "refining our understanding of the role of 'modalities'" (Patte, *The Gospel According to Matthew* [Philadelphia: Fortress, 1987], 14, n. 7).

105. Searle, *Intentionality*, viii; emphasis mine.

106. Ibid., 157; see Hans Sluga's critique of Searle in Hans Sluga, "On Writing" (unpublished manuscript, Department of Philosophy, University of California at Berkeley, Berkeley, Calif., 1987). The present article provides a brief sketch of Sluga's critique, beginning on page 132.

107. Roger Fowler, *Linguistic Criticism* (Oxford and New York: Oxford University Press, 1986), 57, 69.

contexts of utterance and of reference.[108] A text's deictic features relate both what is said and the reader of what is written "to a context of culture, a social and historical context in which people interact through language which reflects their social roles and statuses."[109] "The basic function of deixis is to relate the entities and situations to which reference is made in [a text] to the spatio-temporal . . . here-and-now of the context of utterance"[110] which, in the *reading* of utterance, is the context of reading, not of writing; the context of use, not of production.

The examples selected from Romans which illustrate the contextual component of indexical expressions will be discussed below.[111] Here are only a few samples: The *personal deixis,* which includes the use of personal and demonstrative pronouns and, of course, also the use of personal names, appears in these instances:

1. The author/writer Paul speaks of "my God" (1:8) and "my gospel" (2:16), in distinction from "our Lord" or "our Father" (1:4, 7); and the respective inclusive "we" as either "we believers" or "we Jews" (3:9).
2. The readership is addressed as *individual* "you" for the first time in 2:1; 2:11 has as its content or context humanity at large; the context is generic (as perceived by the standards of contemporary Hellenistic culture which has its own ways of transcending "Greek and barbarian").

This index of all-inclusiveness is heavily emphasized in the indexical use of "all" and "every."[112] But in 2:17, the individual "you" gets "named" by the content/context reference as "Jew" which refers to the ethnic, cultural context by which "Jews" know/believe and desire/will to be different from "Greeks."[113] This distinction is analogous to indexical distinction between "Jews and Gentiles" to be found in 1:5, 13; 2:14, 24 (Old Testament quote); 3:29; 4:17-18, and then not again till Rom 9–11, and 15–16.

The readers *collectively* are addressed in the emphatic and inclusive "all" as mentioned above in 1:7, 8 and in 1:16 as part of the actual addresses which are

108. Ibid., 90.

109. Ibid., 96.

110. John Lyons, "Deixis and subjectivity: *loquor, ergo sum?*" 101-24 in *Place and Action* (ed. R. J. Jarvella and W. Klein; New York: Wiley, 1984), 28.

111. See pages 133-38, below.

112. Understanding "all" as inclusive of the addressees in 1:7, 8; as distinct from "all/every" concerning the subject matter under discussion, e.g. 1:5, 16; 2:1, 6, 9, 10; 3:4, 9, [12, Old Testament quote], 19-20, 22, 23; 4:11, 16; 5:12, 18.

113. This "name" gets used in distinction from the name "Jews" in 1:16; 2:9-10; 3:9; and only once more in 10:12.

still indexed as such in 1:8-13, 15 as part of the conventional thanksgiving and the equally conventional "transition" sections. But a different collective "you" is indexed when the reference is to the "universal audience."[114]

It is significant that this shift in address to the collective "you," following the conventional use in Rom 1:1-15, does not take place until 6:11, but then it is very emphatic ("So indeed you [or: you yourselves] also must") and extends into 7:4, and after that resumes again not until 8:9.[115]

In the choice of the personal pronoun "his" to index the context/content of a given reference as "divine" rather than human,[116] the reader experiences an intentionality with an entire network of subsidiary intentions. But enough of *personal* deixis. What about some *other* indexical expressions?

Deixis by intonation is clearly involved in the "O!" (as distinct from "oh!") exclamations in Rom 2:1, 3 (also 9:20; 11:33) and conventionally is employed "to express emotion, either of a lesser (e.g., Rom 2:1, 3) or greater degree."[117] But why, and to what ends, intonate so emotionally at this point of the argument? Stanley Stowers offers some helpful comments as to "the function,"[118] but we also need to recognize — and not merely in addition, but primarily — the intended *Ideologiekritik:* the social, cultural context of deserved and celebrated "praise" or "boasting," equally prevalent among cultured ("wise") Greeks as among "righteous" Jews, which gets evoked emotionally in the indictment of this cultural norm which affected Christians as well.[119] That is the whole point of Bakhtin's interest in "expressive intonation" as part of the expressive (modal and deictic) aspects of literature which concern "the speaker's evaluative attitude toward the referentially semantic element in the utterance."[120]

Spatial deixis is clearly involved in Paul's declared intention of visiting the addresses (1:10, 13). But does he intend to "go" or to "come" to Rome? A *topos* of another kind is involved in the phrase slanderously attributed to "us" according to which the action of "doing evil things" has the intentionality of "good things coming/going" as cause/means (3:8).

---

114. See page 120 on three elite audiences as embodiments of the universal.

115. See page 112 on the difference between persuading and convincing argumentation.

116. Prophets 1:2; Son 1:3, 9; 5:10; kindness 2:4; glory 3:7; presence 3:20; grace 3:24; forbearance 3:25; being righteous 3:26; life 5:10.

117. Robert Funk, *A Greek Grammar of the New Testament and Other Early Christian Literature* (Chicago: University of Chicago Press, 1961), 81.

118. Stowers, *The Diatribe and Paul's Letter to the Romans,* 110-12.

119. Christopher Forbes, "Comparison, Self-Praise and Irony: Paul's Boasting and the Conventions of Hellenistic Rhetoric," *New Testament Studies* 32 (1986): 1-30.

120. Bakhtin, *Speech Genres and Other Late Essays,* 90.

Temporal deixis, "then/now" (3:21; 5:9; 6:19-22), serves to distinguish, if not to separate, what is believed, known, valued in its intentional content, its context, to be old/new, pseudo/true, etc., thereby clearly highlighting social and cultural norms in conflict. This is different in form and function from the dissociative argumentation discussed earlier.[121]

The use of *proper names* in argumentation serves a more significant function than simply that of referring to persons[122] or places.[123] Searle suggests that it also "serve[s] to focus the [author's] and [reader's] intentionality in some way."[124] As elite groups can be presented as embodiments of the universal audience,[125] so also can named individuals be presented as embodiment of a named group.[126] In this case a name encountered in reading acquires, or even presupposes, "some intentional content associated with [it]."[127] A name "represents someone or something. This representational content consists, like all intentional states, of two components: (1) some propositional content,[128] and (2) what Searle calls some "psychological mode"[129] or world-to-mind direction of fit as in success/failure or fulfilled/unfulfilled when it comes to volitional modality of desire, intention, or the like. Thus the name "Abraham" fits the personal and social reality of "the father of Israel" or Israel's first patriarch, but the success or failure of this named reality is subject to intentional states and their background or context. Feminist criticism has shown that this "psychological mode" and its notion of "fit" are heavily determined contextually.

A philosophy of action and reading provides a theoretical framework for considering contextual factors in reading Romans. The ensuing discussion is based on the following preliminary considerations:

1. Reading is a form of human behavior; it is more than a mental activity, though, of course, it is that too. It is, like all forms of human behavior of action, subject to the following distinctions:

---

121. See pages 115 and 122.

122. Paul; Jesus Christ; David; Abraham/Sarah; Adam; Moses; see numerous names again in the peroration (Rom 16:1-23); also groups (Gentiles/Jews; barbarians/Greeks).

123. Rome; see numerous place names in the peroration, Rom 15:19–16:5.

124. Searle, *Intentionality,* 231-61, esp. 231-32.

125. See page 120, above.

126. Perelman and Obrechts-Tyteca, *The New Rhetoric,* 321-27.

127. Searle, *Intentionality,* 260.

128. Which determines what speech-act theory calls "conditions of satisfaction," which is to say, it meets a known definition in some linguistic or social "dictionary."

129. Which determines what speech act theory calls "the direction of fit" as either mind-to-world direction of fit as true or false (as in modality of belief, statement, and the like.

a. Reading as individual behavior as distinct from reading as social behavior;

b. Reading as collective social behavior as distinct from individual behavior within a social collective;

c. The activity of reading as something engaged in for the sake of something else as distinct from reading for its own sake.

2. Reading, like all action (consider here also the nature of narrative and narration; the nature of story), requires space and time to execute it.[130]

3. To *reflect* on reading as part of the theory of action with its concern for "the structure of action"[131] makes us realize that "the principles by which we identify and explain action are themselves part of the actions, that is, they are partly *constitutive* of actions."[132]

Reading brings us face-to-face with not one but two contexts: the contexts from within and out of which the original writer once wrote, and the cultural and technological changes affecting the text's materiality.

The contexts from within and out of which the original writer (Paul *and* his scribe, Tertius) once wrote include the contexts of the materiality of the produced text for the user/reader: the manuscript text of the individual scroll or codex delivered to, and circulated in, a specific community of believers. This is the context of the original text production, the context of a text's genesis and, with it, its structure.

But even at this first level we must ask, "What kind of reader do the [letter's] tone, rhetorical tactics, stock of imagery, armory of assumptions imply?"[133] To avoid falling victim to "the encoded reader fallacy,"[134] we need to be reminded that reading is not a "dialogic relationship with an object." Exegesis as a form of reading is more than "explanation" which has "only one consciousness, one subject"; it is "comprehension" which has "two consciousnesses and two subjects."[135] It deals with not one but two intentionalities;[136] with not one but two relevances.[137]

---

130. Searle, *Minds, Brains and Science,* 61-62.

131. Ibid., 57-70.

132. Ibid., 59.

133. Terry Eagleton, *Literary Theory* (Minneapolis: University of Minnesota Press, 1983), 120.

134. Wilhelm Wuellner, "Is There an Encoded Reader Fallacy?" (paper presented to the Reader Criticism Seminar of the *Studiorum Novi Testamenti Societas,* Atlanta, 1986).

135. Bakhtin, *Speech Genres and Other Late Essays,* 111.

136. Searle's principle of intentionality.

137. Sperber and Wilson's principle of relevance.

Even at this first level we have reading conceived as "dialogic relation" with a text as "a unit of speech communication that has not mere formal definition, but *contextual meaning* (that is, integrated meaning that relates to value — to truth, beauty, and so forth — and requires a *responsive* understanding, one that includes evaluation)."[138]

Even at this first level of contextual reading we need to be mindful of the misleading tendency (not only in the exegesis of Pauline letters, but in literary criticism generally) of thinking of "a writer as dealing with an 'audience,' even though certain considerations[139] may at times oblige us to think this way. . . . [A] writer does not quite 'address' [readers], . . . he writes to or for them. . . . '[R]eadership' is not a collective noun. It is an abstraction in a way that 'audience' is not."[140] Reading a material letter, a letter as literature, is more than, and is other than, hearing Paul speak. In a letter, the reader is "set . . . in a relationship to the writer [that is] different from that of non-chirographic personal contact";[141] "a literary work is not actually a 'living' dialogue or monologue."[142]

The second level for considering context deals with the cultural and technological changes affecting the text's materiality; at first the development of the cheirographic "industry" associated with institutions other than a local church, such as diocesan "schools" or academies (Alexandria, Antioch, Caesarea, etc.), or the imperial court beginning with Constantine's fateful era. I am thinking of the contextual factors ranging from the deictic dimensions of giving literary documents "names" or titles, to the introduction of first punctuation marks and paragraphing, then chapter and verse markings, also marginal notes and comments, to finally the inclusion of script ornamentation and iconographic "signs."

All of this is conceivable even if, as is progressively unlikely, we were to look at any document like the letter to the Romans as an individual, isolated, material text. When its materiality gets preserved in a sacred canon, it acquires a contextuality that goes beyond the inter-textuality indigenous to every linguistic entity. Sanders' and Childs' differing notions of what constitutes canon are but two sides of one and the same coin.

New contexts are generated by the technology of print, let alone the latest electronic technologies, each one in its own ways materially/technically em-

---

138. Bakhtin, *Speech Genres and Other Late Essays*, 125.

139. E.g., Michael Bünker, *Briefformular und rhetorische Disposition im 1. Korintherbrief* (*Göttingen Theological Arbeiten* 28; Göttingen: Vandenhoeck & Ruprecht, 1984), 11: "die Verwandtschaft zwischen Brief, Rede, und Gesprach."

140. Ong, "The Writer's Audience Is Always a Fiction," 404.

141. Ibid., 418.

142. Eagleton, *Literary Theory*, 119.

bodying what Bakhtin calls "contextual meaning" inviting reader, viewer, user to interaction as "*responsive* understanding."

This emphasis on the materiality of texts (and their changing technologies of production, distribution, and use) as *constitutive* for reading as an intentional act leads me to support Hans Sluga in his critique of Searle's theories of intentionality and action which reduce all mental states and structures of action to the materiality of biological bodies on the one hand, and his critique of those (similar to exegetes infatuated with sociological exegesis) who reduce all materiality of texts and contexts, and their respective intentionalities, to economics and sociology.[143] Studying the problem of reading/understanding texts in the context of a theory of action and theory of intentionality is *not* merely another "attempt to define the study of literature in terms of either its method or its object," but is an attempt, based on "the re-invention of rhetoric," which starts "from what we want to *do*, and then seeing which methods and theories will help us to achieve these ends."[144]

"What we want to do" when we read a material text arises "not merely from causal relations between material things [a material text and a flesh-and-blood reader], but [from] what [Sluga calls] formal or logical relations" which are themselves the product of processes of material human culture. All reading, which like all other intentional acts merits the distinction between intention and action, is based on background, or context meaning, which though internalized in terms of its intentional elements, as in the cognitive and volitional modalities, is "a late product of external processes [namely those of human material culture] that have become internalized."[145] Sluga does in critiquing Searle what Bakhtin, Eagleton, Jameson and others do in critiquing the dominant mode of literary criticism whose hegemony has extended over Biblical exegesis (Jewish and Christian alike) for centuries. The conviction that "literature . . . *is* an ideology," and that the theory and practice of reading literature is, willy nilly, an exercise in "political criticism,"[146] fits with Sluga's conviction that the wider context for dealing critically with the dilemma of reading texts is the understanding of human culture. Here Sluga echoes some of the same concerns voiced earlier in Wayne Booth's *Critical Understanding* which pointed out both "the powers and limits of pluralism."[147] Once more the contributions of feminist criticism need to be fully acknowledged.

143. Sluga, "On Writing."

144. Eagleton, *Literary Theory*, 210.

145. Sluga, "On Writing."

146. Eagleton, *Literary Theory*, 22, 194-214.

147. Wayne C. Booth, *Critical Understanding: The Powers and Limits of Pluralism* (Chicago and London: University of Chicago Press, 1979).

The Application of Intentionality and Action Theories to Reading Romans in Context

We have seen above that intentionality, whether on the side of the text's implied author, or its implied reader, is determined by an entire network of subsidiary intentions, and that means context. Paul's intention in both writing and visiting "fits" the intention on the part of his addressees when (or whenever) they either read Paul or visit with Paul. Both writer and reader have a meeting of minds and, whether in writing/reading or in visiting, both are led to act: whether in terms of "mutual encouragement" which is always "from faith to faith,"[148] or whether in terms of intensifying their respective living as those knowing, believing, being committed to a belief, to a system of convictions shared by Jews and Greeks alike, namely that (1) divine power exists for the purpose, or has the intentionality, of saving and of vindicating (or *thereby* vindicating) the righteous quality of *divine* intentionality; and (2) the righteous quality of *human* intentionality is vindicated by its appropriate "fit," namely by demonstration of living the appropriate life, by behavior or action (Rom 1:16-17). The *con*-text of such writing and reading intentionality is the "background" which is familiar to Jews and Gentiles alike, indeed is forcefully evoked in the first series of rhetorical questions in Rom 2:1-9 as a background which is *universally* acknowledged/acknowledgeable, namely that *human* intention (whether cognitional or volitional) and *human* action tend to separate instead of unite. Christians face the same distinction-becoming-dichotomy between intentionality and action, as Rom 5–6 and the subsequent chapters in Paul's argumentation and our reading experience of it "boldly" remind us of (Rom 15:15) both convincingly and persuasively.

The levels of complexity — from the less complex intentions of specific or individual intentional acts to the more and more complex levels of intentions which involve a semantic universe — reveal another context which is also shared by Jews and Christians alike, namely the conviction that "the various elements of human experience are interrelated in a necessary way."[149] This confirms what was said and shown earlier about the "order and interaction of arguments":[150] the levels of complexity in the coherence of the argumentation and its structure, chiefly the complementarity of *exordium* (Rom 1:1-17) and peroration (Rom 15:14–16:24) and the semantic and pragmatic coherence of the

---

148. Rom 1:12, 16; see its recapitulation in 15:14 as the activation of the ability to instruct one another.

149. Patte, *Paul's Faith and the Power of the Gospel*, 21-25.

150. See pages 115-16 and 122, above.

body of the argument (1:18–15:13). This makes a case for the coherence of "letter body" and argumentation (Rom 1:18–11:36 climaxing, "fitting" with 12:1–15:13).[151] But such paraenetic climax or "fit" — whether in Romans or Galatians (or any of the other letters of Paul) — does *not* give us reason to speak of these letters as generically hortatory: whether as part of the deliberative genre of rhetorical theory (as Kennedy argues about Galatians) or as part of the protreptic genre as a literary convention (as Malherbe argues about 1 Thessalonians).

Where Hendrickus Boers says "what gives *coherence* to Paul's thought is *contradiction* at its most fundamental level,"[152] I am saying that what gives coherence to Paul's thought *and* life, as well as coherence *in the reading* (Bakhtin's "responsive understanding") of Paul's letters as literature, is the distinction at the most fundamental level between intentionality and action. Boers' student H. Wayne Merritt comes closer to what I am saying when focusing on the collocation "word and deed."[153] Likewise Perelman's insistence on the relation between argumentation and commitment, or argumentation and action, provides a better account of the coherent and cohesive center of Paul's writing (and not just of Paul's thought or theology) than Beker's dialectic of coherency and contingency.[154]

An analysis of the key modals in Paul's argumentation in Romans helps to explicate these relationships. The two major modals in Paul's argumentation in Romans are the cognitional and volitional modals. For the specific forms of intentionality (which specific modals are) to function in the act of reading, "the act of responsive understanding," there must be "a set of enabling conditions."[155] That "set" is provided by the background or context.

On the level of *cognitional* modality in Paul's argumentation we have the conviction, the belief of a status, an appointment, a call, shared by writer and reader: having received grace and apostleship. The *exordium* of the argument

151. What is being shown here for Romans also has been shown by Steven J. Kraftchick for Galatians *(Ethos and Pathos in Galatians Five and Six)* and by Bruce C. Johanson for 1 Thessalonians *(To All the Brethren)*.

152. Hendrickus Boers, "The Foundations of Paul's Thought: A Methodological Investigation" (paper presented at the annual meeting of the Society of Biblical Literature, Atlanta, November 1986).

153. H. Wayne. Merritt, *In Word and Deed: Moral Integrity in Paul (Emory Studies in Early Christianity* 1; New York: Peter Lang, 1993).

154. Robert Detweiler's analysis of the intention and act of *Reading Religiously* (New York: Ktav, 1987) and Lewis R. Donelson's analysis of the logic of the ethical argument in the Pauline Pastorals *(Pseudepigraphy and Ethical Argument in the Pastoral Epistles* [Tübingen: Mohr Siebeck, 1986]) are getting at the same issue.

155. Searle, *Intentionality,* 157.

makes it clear, by the semantic choices of its propositional content (God's prophets, Holy Scriptures, Davidic sonship, Spirit of holiness, and Messiahship), that the context is exclusively Jewish, and patriarchal in its "code." This "set of enabling conditions" would not function for non-Jews or non-Jewish Christians. Only later in Paul's argumentation do we encounter convictions and social norms which are shared by non-Jews. The example mentioned earlier is Rom 4:4, according to which the wages of workers are not reckoned as gift or benefaction, but as their due (ὀφείλημα). One does not have to be Jewish to come to a responsive understanding of that.

On the level of *volitional* modality, however, Paul's argument is perhaps more even-handed in the use of Jewish and non-Jewish "codes." God's promises and God's will fit existing codes in both cultures. The declared intention of the divine "call" to reach every human soul, the "whole world," may also be rated as functional for both types of readers. So too were the desires and expectations associated with the system of benefaction in New Testament times when it was equally familiar to Jews and Greeks.[156] The generosity and impartiality of benefactors extends, as a set of enabling conditions, from the social action of Paul and his readers to the symbolic action of God and Christ. Social and economic conditions are the context for "responsive understanding" of expectations concerning the reaping of "some harvest"; but more political and ideological conditions are in the set of enabling conditions for the wish, or daring, to die for some righteous vs. good cause embodied in a given person (5:7). The whole complex of modals associated with "impartiality"[157] — divine *and* human — is culturally coded to maximize the reader's own responsive understanding by promoting and consolidating both the intentional content and the resulting behavior appropriate to impartiality. Perelman defines impartiality in argumentation (intentionality) as that "balance of forces, maximum attention to the interests at issue, but with this attention equally divided among the different points of view."[158] In Romans this impartiality volitional modal is used to bring Jews and Gentiles, Greeks and barbarians, wise and foolish to live in peace, to live in grace. Likewise, but later on in the argument (12:1–15:13), Christians face the appeal to be impartial and to live impartially in much the same way that Rom 5–6 with its appeal to Christians follows logically right after 1:18–4:25, and as 12–15 follows right after 1–11.

Analysis of deictic argumentation in Romans provides even more clues to its "context."

156. Danker, *Benefactor*.
157. Jouette M. Bassler, *Divine Impartiality*.
158. Perelman and Obrechts-Tyteca, *The New Rhetoric*, 60.

The use of personal deixis[159] has led us to the realization that the whole portion 1:16–6:10 has a different addressee focus from the part preceding it (1:1-15), which contains the conventional letter address and the identification of the writer, but also from the part following (6:11–7:4), in which the Christian reader is again addressed directly. The same switch occurs in the sequence of arguments that follow: 7:5–8:8 is at the same level as 1:16–6:10, but with 8:9 we resume addressing the Christian reader directly. The indirect argument — whether in the third person singular or plural, or addressing the universal audience by either universal appeal to humanity at large (1:18–2:11), or by appeal to an elite audience, the Jews (2:12–4:25) as embodiment of the universal audience — provides the convictional basis, in terms of convincing arguments, for the subsequent direct appeal to the collective Christian reader. The particularity of Jews and Gentiles is employed respectively to convince the reader of the "concrete universality," or the truth of the intentional content (its propositions and its values), before the appeal is made to the Christian reader to affirm, confirm, or otherwise "act" (e.g., by intensifying, deepening the adherence to the proposed "content" of the argument). It is the external "set of enabling conditions" in the social and cultural environment inhabited by the reader that makes these personal deixis uses functional.

The use of intonation in 2:1 and 3 made apparent that the expressive quality and purpose was determined by the cultural, ideological context of status and reputation based on demonstrated, and thus discerned or judged, reputation or boasting. But that determinative context is employed to make reference to standards of higher discernment or judgment by way of the use of argumentation which seeks to be rhetorically *convincing*, before making the argument rhetorically *persuasive* beginning with 5:1.

The context for the use of spatial deixis is apparent in the different perspective coming to expression depending on whether Paul's expressed long-standing intention of visiting Rome was one of "coming" or "going" to Rome. There is certainly a personal or psychological mode involved when someone says, and means to say, that she is "going" to visit you (the addressee) or "coming" to visit you. I leave it as a mere suggestion that the benefactor social system was implied in the hosting of traveling *symbolic* benefactors (apostles, teachers) by resident *real* benefactors. If that "set of enabling conditions" were operating here, as it may well be, then the ambiguity may be deliberate. A similar ambiguity may be involved in the spatial deixis in 3:8: if doing evil is believed (or said) to be a *cause* for good, then "good may *come*"; if it is said to be a *means* for good, then "good may go forth" in the intentionality expressed.

159. See page 127.

In the choice of such deictic temporal contrasts as "then" vs. "now" a contrast is generated, both in the convincing portion of the argumentation (3:21; 5:9) and in the persuasive appeal (6:19-22), which the social, cultural context makes function, in the reading, as contrasts to existing cultural norms ("*now . . . apart* from the law"; "*now . . .* in *his* blood"). In 6:19-22 the contrast relies for its proper functioning on the cultural code of qualitatively contrasting Jews and Gentiles, the latter coded as going from bad to worse, the former coded as going from good to better. But this deep-rooted cultural cliché is applied to believers to appeal for intensifying allegiance to life against death — an appeal presumably appealing to everyone.

The deictic quality of the use of names is perhaps most apparent in the use of "Jew" (2:17), or even, with personal deixis, "we Jews" (3:9), and the most prominent use of Abraham (Rom 4:1-23) as model for a "concrete universality." It is significant that not until Rom 16 do we get any indication of the significance in the former near absence (Mother Sarah is nearly eclipsed by Father Abraham) but then prominent presence of the names of women along with names of men. The volitional modal associated with the same Abraham must remind us, however, that the argumentative dissociation of the fleshly Abraham from the spiritual Abraham (as model of faith) is arguing for the success v. failure, not for the truth v. falsehood, of the propositional content under discussion. Everyone and anyone who, like Abraham, "has faith" before, or aside from, "circumcision," is under the volitional modal benefits associated with God: fulfillment of promises, life out of death, etc.

Intentionality and action in Romans are as intimately related to each other, when analyzed in terms of the philosophy of mind and philosophy of action,[160] as argumentation and commitment are intimately related to each other when analyzed in terms of (Perelman's) theory of argumentation.

We stressed earlier[161] the importance of the rhetorical situation for a "responsive understanding" of such argumentative literature as the epideictic, demonstrative, educational genre, of which Romans is a part,[162] as are also the numerous and varied documents that belong to the ancient philosophic protreptic genre.[163] The "situational analysis" proposed by Jordan, based on the full recognition of the "exigency" factor in argumentation, brings into focus "not the content or consequences of the intended effect, but [the intended effect's] intensity."[164]

160. See page 129, above.

161. See the discussion beginning on page 113.

162. Wuellner, "Paul's Rhetoric of Argumentation in Romans."

163. Jordan, "Ancient Philosophical Protreptic and the Problem of Persuasive Genres," 309-33.

164. Ibid., 331.

The same can now be seen as applying to Romans. The situation which "socially and psychologically" determines Paul's argumentation in Romans is the same for Paul as it is for the reader: both share not only adherence to a certain convictional system; they also share a commitment to a lifestyle, to behavior and to actions presumed to be familiar to each other. The action for which Paul appeals in his unfolding argumentation and in the reader's "responsive understanding" of it is the same which Jordan sees as the action sought in the philosophic protreptic: intensifying the commitment, or "wanting the [reader's] whole self for an ongoing pedagogy . . . grounded . . . in a tacit agreement about the situation of radical choice."[165] This assessment will be supported by earlier and other observations, such as those about the order and interaction of arguments[166] and about the complementarity of intentionality and action[167] as a better key to the solution of the problem of the coherence of the thought and of the life of Paul.

Conclusion

In reading Paul, and in the study of the theories of reader criticism applied to Pauline literature, we have — I trust convincingly if not persuasively — argued that, just as intentionality and action are complementary, so also are argumentation and commitment, and lastly, so are text and context complementary. The two factors which modify the character of this complementarity are: the inclusion of Romans into a larger text, or rather collection or canon of texts; and the changes in the materiality of the text's technical transmission from cheirographic to typographic to electrographic technologies, each with a new clientèle of producers and distributors and, not least, a new type of consumer with changing institutional settings (educational institutions, commercial institutions like "clubs" for books, audio- and videocassettes; cultural institutions like the film and television industries; along with the changing social institutions of family homes and of religious institutions). Arthur Miller observes in his autobiography *Timebends* that the power film has had on our culture is "an immense pressure on the way we write, tell stories, even think. The methodology of movie storytelling reflects dreams. It's gotten deep into the way we write. And it's perfectly admissible."[168]

The pluralism of interpretive communities — of which the scientific,

---

165. Ibid., 333.
166. See pages 115-16 and 122, above.
167. See page 129.
168. Arthur Miller, *Timebends: A Life* (London: Methuen, 1987).

scholarly community is no longer just one among other interpretive communities; the once monolithic interpretive community of scientific Biblical exegesis has fragmented — leaves modern readers of Romans, whether as individuals or as members of a collective, to struggle with "the powers and limits of pluralism,"[169] now irreversibly all-pervasive in all of the existing interpretive communities. Never before has it been more true than today that text and context are complementary. The value of text (including its implied or encoded reader) is determined by the context. As they say in the real estate market: the value of your home is determined by its location.

169. Booth, *Critical Understanding.*

SOCIAL-HISTORICAL APPROACHES TO ROMANS

compiled by Robert Atkins

Paths of Early Christian Mission into Rome: Judaeo-Christians in the Households of Pagan Masters

Peter Lampe

Translated by Margaret Birdsong Lampe

Christianity became established in Rome in the 40s of the first century, initially in one or more of the synagogues. The Christian message kindled unrest among the Roman Jews, causing Claudius to expel from the city the main propagators of this internal Jewish quarrel.[1]

The paths that led Christianity into the Roman synagogues have not yet been discovered. However, piecing together the mosaic stones of different sources reveals a model for finding a solution.

First Clement (63.3; 65.1) mentions a Roman Christian named Valerius Biton. The elderly man was part of the Roman delegation that carried the *First Letter of Clement* to Corinth, thus endorsing the letter with his personal presence. Described as an old man in the 90s of the first century, Valerius Biton must have been born in the 30s or 40s. He experienced the beginnings of Christianity in Rome as a child. His name identifies him as a freedman or the son of a freedman of the *gens Valeria*.

A pagan Latin epigraph from Rome in the first century C.E. provides us with the second piece of the mosaic.[2] This grave inscription lists freedpersons of the *gens Valeria*, including a Valeria Maria. In this case, "Maria" is clearly a

---

1. Acts 18:2; Gaius Suetonius Tranquillus, *On the Lives of the Caesars: Claudius* 25.4; Orosius, *History Against the Pagans* 7.6.15-16; cf. Cassius Dio Cocceianus, *Roman History* 60.6.6-7; cf., e.g., Peter Lampe, *Die stadtrömischen Christen* in *den ersten beiden Jahrhunderten* (Tübingen: Mohr Siebeck, 1989), 4-8. The discussion of "Claudius' edict" does not need to be re-examined here.

2. *Corpus inscriptionum latinarum* [*CIL*], Vol. 6 (ed. G. Henzen, et al.; Berlin/New York: Walter de Gruyter, 2000), 27948.

cognomen, not a *gentilicium.*[3] The use of the cognomen "Maria" seldom occurs in *Corpus inscriptionum latinarum* VI. Usually "Maria," like "Marius," indicates the *gens Maria* in the Latin inscriptions of the city of Rome. The *cognomen* "Maria" can be found only seven times in *CIL* VI.[4] However, it clearly represents the Semitic name, so that in all probability our Valeria Maria of the first century C.E. was Jewish or Jewish-Christian.

The inscription identifies Valeria Maria as a freedwoman of a certain Lucius Valerius Diogenes.[5] Diogenes was the heir of a Lucius Valerius Hiero, and Hiero in turn was the heir of a Lucius Valerius Papia. If Valeria Maria died in the 90s of the first century C.E. at the latest, then the dates of death for Diogenes, for Hiero and for Papia can be extrapolated at the latest for the 80s, 50s, and 20s respectively. This shows that, in any case, Lucius Valerius Papia was born in the first century B.C.E.

A first-century B.C.E. Senator Lucius Valerius, who was friendly to the Jews, is described by Flavius Josephus in *Antiquities* 14.8.5. In 47 B.C.E., the *praetor urbanus* Lucius Valerius, son of a Lucius Valerius, moved to renew the friendship and alliance with the Jewish people while leading a Senate meeting. He also moved to send letters to "the free cities and kings" within the realm of Roman influence in order to secure unhindered access for the Jews to harbors and other public areas. Prior to this, Lucius Valerius had received a three-member Jewish delegation asking for these privileges. The Senate approved Lucius Valerius' motion.[6]

3. Editor's note: According to ancient Roman naming conventions, men's names "typically contain three proper nouns which are classified as *praenomen* (or given name), *nomen* (or Gens name [= *gentilicium*]) and *cognomen.*" The praenomen is used for friendly, informal address; the *nomen gentilicium* is one's clan name; the third name, one's *cognomen,* typically inherited from father to son, was used "to distinguish a family within a *Gens.* Often the cognomen was chosen based on some physical or personality trait." (Jimmy Wales and Larry Sanger, founders, "Wikipedia: The Free Encyclopedia," n.p. [cited 15 December 2003]. Online: http://en2.wikipedia.org/wiki/Roman_naming_convention.

4. *CIL* VI:14025; 27948; 12907; probably also 11175; 19039; 13717; 10881. In contrast, the *gentilicium* "Maria" occurs about 108 times in *CIL* VI.

5. The epigraph presents two groups of freedpersons who were given a burial place by their patrons. Both of these patrons, Lucius Valerius Amphion and Lucius Valerius Diogenes, had inherited the place from a man named Lucius Valerius Hiero (probably their father). In the epigraph, Amphion is named first before Diogenes. Therefore, one can assume that the first group of freedpersons was dependent on Amphion, while the second, which included our Maria, was dependent on Diogenes. Significantly, in the second group, one of the freedmen again carried the name Diogenes.

6. It is possible to connect this *Senatus consultum* with 1 Maccabees (15:15-24; 12:16-17; 14:22-24) and, contrary to Josephus, to date it in the 130s B.C.E. (See, e.g., T. R. S. Broughton, *The Magistrates of the Roman Republic,* Vol. 1 [New York: Oxford University Press, 1951], 491-92.) But much debate surrounds this issue. According to both texts, a golden shield was brought by the

It is plausible that there is some connection between the Senator Lucius Valerius, who demonstrated a friendly attitude toward the Jews, and the *familia* of the Jewish Maria, who was a freed slave of a Lucius Valerius Diogenes. However, new epigraphical material would be necessary before we could determine the nature of this connection. In any case, our Jewish Maria and the Senator Lucius, friendly to the Jews, belonged to the same *gens* or "clan."

The Roman rhetorician, Marcus Valerius Messalla Corvinus, is another probable patron of Valerian Jewish freed slaves. The son of a consul, Valerius Messalla was born circa 64 B.C.E. After residing in Greece, Macedonia, Asia Minor and Alexandria,[7] he put in a good word in Rome for Herod the Great in the year 40 B.C.E.[8] Valerius Messalla became governor of Syria around 28 B.C.E. There, he disbanded a gang of gladiators outside of Antioch.[9] Together with Marcus Agrippa, Valerius Messalla received the house of Mark Anthony on the Palatine as a gift of honor in 29 B.C.E.[10]

Like Valerius Messalla, Marcus Agrippa was politically active in the eastern Empire; he was general governor of the eastern provinces toward the end of the 20s B.C.E. In 17 B.C.E., he again set off for the east. A close friend of Herod the Great, he is described as friendly toward the Jews.[11] Marcus Agrippa's household in the city of Rome included Jewish slaves and freedpersons. In the first century C.E., they formed the Synagogue of the *Agrippesioi,* for which we have epigraphical evidence.[12] There is no other patron in sight for this Jewish synagogue besides Marcus Agrippa himself.

Jewish delegation. Both texts mention renewed friendship and the writing of letters of protection. In both cases, a Numenius, son of Antiochus, was part of the Jewish delegation, and a senator Lucius set the tone. And in both cases, a "son of Jason" was the second delegate, although he was named Antipater in 1 Maccabees while Josephus names him Alexander. (Josephus also differs from 1 Maccabees in that he knows the name of a third delegate.) If, according to the context of 1 Macc 15, Josephus' *Senatus consultum* were to be dated in the 130s B.C.E., and if Josephus consequently made a mistake in the dating of his source material, then our senator Lucius Valerius was identical with the consul of the year 131 B.C.E., Lucius Valerius Flaccus. The latter became consul as *flamen Martialis* and probably belonged to the circle around the Gracchi (cf. Alan E. Astin, *Scipio Aemilianus* [Oxford: Clarendon, 1967], 192, n. 3). Consequently, our Lucius Valerius who was friendly to the Jews would not have been from the first century B.C.E. but even earlier, from the second half of the second century B.C.E.

7. Cf. Cicero, *Letters to Atticus* 12, 32.2; Appian, *Civil Wars* 4.159-160; Cassius Dio Cocceianus, *Roman History* 47.33.1-2; Plutarch, *Brutus* 40.41; Velleius Paterculus 2.71.1.

8. Flavius Josephus, *Antiquities* 14.14.4; *Jewish Wars* 1.284; see also 1.243.

9. Cassius Dio Cocceianus, *Roman History* 51.7.7; Albius Tibullus, *Elegies* 1.3.1.

10. Cassius Dio Cocceianus, *Roman History* 53.27.5.

11. Josephus, *Antiquities* 14.14.4; *Jewish Wars* 1.284; see also 1.243.

12. *Corpus inscriptionum graecarum* [*CIG*] 9907; *Corpus inscriptionum judaicarum* [*CIJ*] I:503; 425; 365.

"Volumnius" was the *nomen gentile* of a Roman legate who resided in Syria in 8 B.C.E. and whose friendship was enjoyed by Herod the Great.[13] This Volumnius is the most probable patron of the Jewish slaves and freedpersons who founded the Synagogue of the *Volumnenses* (first century C.E.) in the city of Rome.[14]

From these data we can conclude that at least two, if not three, Roman patrons can be named who lived for some time in the eastern Empire, including Syria, maintained friendly relations with Herod the Great, and included Jewish freedpersons and slaves in their households in Rome. In at least two cases it can be proven that these *liberti* and *servi* formed their own respective synagogues and had no compunction about naming them after their pagan patrons (*"Agrippesioi," "Volumnenses"*).

After all this material, it is no surprise that a Synagogue of the *(He)rodioi* also can be verified in the city of Rome.[15] Even if this inscription does not come from the first century C.E., considering its name, we cannot exclude the possibility that this Jewish congregation originated in the time of Augustus. Here we have at least the possibility that Jewish slaves and freedpersons of the Herodian royal household also had a synagogue of their own in Rome.

In the first century C.E., freedpersons of the imperial household formed the Synagogue of the *Augustesioi* in Rome.[16]

Contemporaneously, there was the Synagogue of the Vernaculi in the city of Rome.[17] The meaning of this name, however, is ambiguous: either "house slaves, slaves born in the house" gathered together in this synagogue; or "native, Roman" Jews (as opposed to Jewish immigrants) met here.

Not only Jewish freedpersons and slaves of pagan households formed their own synagogues; also Christian *liberti* and *servi* of non-Christian masters organized house congregations of their own. In Romans 16, Paul sent greetings to various congregations in Rome, among others to:

- "Those who are part of Aristobulus' domestic staff" (16:10);
- "Those in the Lord who are part of Narcissus' domestic staff" (16:10);
- The house church of Prisca and Aquila (16:3-5);

13. Josephus, *Jewish Wars* 1.27.1-3 (535-536, 538, 542); *Antiquities* 16.9.1-3 (277ff); 16.10.7 (332); 16.10.8 (335ff); 16.10.9 (351, 354).

14. *CIL* VI:29756; *CIJ* I:343; 402; 417; 523.

15. *CIJ* I:173.

16. *CIL* VI:29757; *CIG* 9902-3; *CIJ* I:284; 301; 338; 368; 416; 496. Phil 4:22 shows that there were Christians within the imperial household in the middle of the first century C.E., at least in the east.

17. *CIJ* I:318; 383; 398; 494.

- The Christians who were together with Asyncritus, Phlegon, Patrobas and Hermes (16:14); and
- The saints who were with Philologus, Julia, Nereus and his sister, and Olympas (16:15).

If we assume that the fourteen other persons greeted in the chapter did not belong to any of the five crystallization points mentioned — and they hardly belonged to only one further group — then it follows that, in the 50s of the first century c.e., at least seven different Christian islands existed in the capital of the Empire. There are no signs of a central meeting place for the Christian circles scattered throughout the city, neither at this time nor in the later decades of the first two centuries c.e.[18] Each group must have celebrated its own worship services somewhere in an apartment, workshop, or private house. Thus, these circles can be called house churches.

Two points are clear for the two Christian circles in the households of Aristobulus and of Narcissus: (a) Neither patron was a Christian himself, otherwise Paul would have included him in the greeting; and (b) Not all freedpersons and slaves in the two households were Christian, otherwise Paul would have formulated the greeting more simply to "Aristobulus' domestic staff" and to "Narcissus' domestic staff."

Aristobulus' name was not common in Rome.[19] He had probably immigrated to Rome from the east (together with his Christian slaves?). Another possibility is that he himself actually lived in the east, and kept only part of his household in Rome. The name "Aristobulus" was favored by the Herodian family, which fits with the above data but is not in itself conclusive.

Not only Jewish or Christian slaves and/or freedpersons but also pagan servants of a household could form an independent religious unity within their *oikos*. In pagan houses and estates, *collegia* of slaves administered the cult of the Lares or the cult of the genius of their master. The slaves themselves held the honorary and priestly positions in these cult communities.[20] Cornelius Tacitus knew of Roman households in which the servants practiced a religion different from that of their masters.[21] At the beginning of the fourth century, pagan slaves were worshiping their own idols, even in the homes of Christian masters.[22]

---

18. Cf. Lampe, *Die stadtrömischen Christen*, 301-45.

19. The masculine form occurs only twice in *CIL* VI, in 17577 and 29104.

20. See Lampe, *Die stadtrömischen Christen*, 319.

21. Cornelius Tacitus, *Annals* 14.44.3.

22. Canon 41 of the Synod of Elvira. For a pagan slave in a Christian home, see Onesimus. In the first century c.e., he followed paganism until his conversion by Paul (Phlm 10-11). It is not clear, however, in which form he practiced his pagan religion — whether together with other

The material gathered here demonstrates at least four points:

1. Synagogal and Christian congregations could sometimes define themselves within the limits of the *oikos* in which their members lived and
   worked as slaves or freedpersons. The primary scene of work and living
   and the place of religious activity were two concentric circles.

2. The women or men who were patrons of the households in question
   practiced a religion different from that of their servants.[23] In these cases,
   the synagogal and Christian house communities were organized by the
   initiative of the house servants but were tolerated by the pagan masters
   and mistresses of the household.

3. The fragmentary evidence names some owners and patrons of Jewish-
   Christian slaves and freedpersons in the city of Rome. Some of these pa-
   trons had worked for a while in the Syrian east and kept up contact with
   Herod (Agrippa, Volumnius, cf. Valerius). In two other cases (the
   Herodioi and Aristobulus' people), a proximity to the Herodian royal
   household appears at least possible.

4. A co-existence of Jewish and Christian slaves and freedpersons can be
   proven at least in the *gens Valeria* and in the Emperor's household.

It is very tempting to assume that the Christian Valerius Biton, already elderly at the end of the first century c.e. (*1 Clement* 63.3; 65.1), came into contact
with the Christian proclamation through Valerian Jewish-Christian
freedpersons. Perhaps the Jewish or Jewish-Christian Valeria Maria was even
his mother or another close relative. New epigraphical material would be
needed, however, to be able to substantiate such a hypothesis. Nevertheless, we
can cautiously formulate at least one generalization: it was through the aforementioned Roman households — in particular, through their Jewish *servi* and
liberti and their descendants — that Jewish-Christianity found one of its ways
into the city of Rome from the Syrian-Palestinian east in the 40s of the first century c.e.

---

pagan slaves in Philemon's house or outside of it. For Christian slaves in pagan houses see also
1 Tim 6:1; Tit 2:9-10; Origen, *Against Celsus* 3.55.

23. This is true for nearly all households mentioned by name in the foregoing discussion.
The *Herodioi* comprise the only exception.

Romans "Down the Pike": Glimpses from Later Years

Carolyn Osiek

The focus of this essay in honor of Bob Jewett, who has devoted so much time and energy to Paul's Letter to the Romans, is to see what we can learn about the first-century Roman context from later Christian texts. To do this, we will have to make some carefully nuanced assumptions that what is true at a slightly later date was probably true earlier as well. Some things seem to have changed, but "plus ça change, plus c'est la même chose."

In a previous article I suggested three characteristics of the Roman church that endured through its first centuries: considerable cultural and theological diversity; a strong Jewish component; and a tendency to choose moderate rather than extreme positions.[1] To these three, I would also add a lack of centralized organization even when the evidence suggests that other churches are moving definitely in that direction. In Paul's Letter to the Romans, we already see three of these characteristics emerging. The one that is not clear there is the third, the choice of moderate rather than extreme positions. Certainly one could say that Paul's advice with regard to the "weak" and the "strong" in chapters 14–15 represents a moderate position over against an extreme of disdain and separation between the two parties or positions, whatever they may be. We will see that later on, the extreme position did exist in the Roman church. One could also argue that Rom 13:1-7 is a moderate if not conciliatory stance toward the question of submission to civil authority, especially when contrasted with something like Revelation. But these are *Paul's* positions, and

---

1. Carolyn Osiek, "The Second Century through the Eyes of Hermas: Continuity and Change," *Biblical Theology Bulletin* 20, no. 3 (1990): 116-22.

did he know?

Jew?
Gentile?

there is not enough information in the letter about what attitudes the Roman Christians were taking at that time, though one could certainly assume with confidence that "weak" and "strong" were having some problems relating to each other. If not, Paul would not have spent so much time giving them advice. This tendency to moderation on the part of the Roman church comes clear only later, in its rejection of Valentinus, Marcion, and Montanus in the second century, and of Novatian and Cyprian on re-baptism in the third.

Here, I would like to consider the other three characteristics, cultural and theological diversity, the Jewish component, and the lack of centralized organization, all from the perspective of how slightly later information may be able to inform or confirm our understanding of earlier years.

Cultural and Theological Diversity

Much has already been said in description of the diversity of early Roman Christianity within the larger urban context. The very cosmopolitan and commercial nature of the city necessitated the intermingling of people of many different types, especially at the lower levels of the social system, where most Jews and Christians were to be found. Continuing social investigation of the evidence suggests large numbers of both groups and combinations of the two resident in the *Transtiberium (Trastevere)* and *Porta Capena* areas of the city, to the southwest and south respectively. These were heavily commercial areas in which any evidence for luxurious housing is slim. Warehouse and dock workers, brick and tile factory laborers, and leather workers are representative of the kinds of occupations prevalent there.

The social levels of first-century Roman Christians have also been studied, especially by Peter Lampe.[2] The prosopography of early Christian Rome suggests overwhelmingly that the church was composed of persons of humble ancestry, often Greek, with many probable freedmen/women, some perhaps connected to aristocratic or imperial families, such as Claudius Ephebos and Valerius Vito (*1 Clem.* 65.1). With the exception of the doubtful Pomponia Graecina,[3] only the names of Titus Flavius Clemens, Flavia Domitilla, and

2. Peter Lampe, *Die stadtrömischen Christen in den ersten beiden Jahrhunderten: Untersuchungen zur Sozialgeschichte* (Tübingen: J. C. B. Mohr, 1987; rev. and expd. ed., Mohr Siebeck, 1989), 38; idem, *From Paul to Valentinus: Christians at Rome in the First Two Centuries* (Minneapolis: Fortress, 2003).

3. The wife of Aulus Plautius was accused of *superstitio externa* (foreign cult practices) in about 57 B.C.E., tried in the traditional way (by her husband and before the household), and acquitted (Tacitus, *Annals* 13.32). On the basis of a reconstruction of two Greek inscriptional frag-

Manlius Acilius Glabrio surface from the first century as possible aristocrats associated with Christianity through the charge of adopting Jewish practices, and they some years later, at the end of the reign of Domitian (ca. C.E. 96). Here the archaeological evidence at the burial area today called the Catacomb of Domitilla supports a very early connection between her family and Christian burials, so that Eusebius' report[4] of Domitilla's connection with Christianity could be substantially correct.[5] Eusebius further reports that, by the reign of Commodus late in the second century (C.E. 180-192), many Romans of wealth and high birth became Christian.[6] This development represented a new kind of diversity that would take the Roman church further into property ownership and status.

Theological diversity was not wanting from the earliest years. The first manifestations seem to have been over the question of Law observance and Jewish practices, quite understandable given the mixed Jew-Gentile component of the community, to be discussed further below. This is the controversy to which Paul attempts to respond from his own experience in the letter — he being one of the major figures who began the controversy!

Later in the second century, we know of a number of theologically controversial teachers who came to Rome, functioned within the Christian groups for a long period of time, and were eventually cut off from communion as "heretics," including Valentinus, Marcion, Marcella, and Hippolytus.

Another key figure who came to Rome early in that process, sometime before the middle of the second century, was Justin Martyr. Born in Neapolis of Samaria in Palestine, he taught philosophy as a Christian for a while in Ephesus before moving his school to Rome. He too contributed to the theological diversity of the community and became an influential teacher there for some years before meeting the fate of execution along with six companions about C.E. 165. Though his *Dialogue with Trypho* is set in Ephesus, it is thought to have been composed during his teaching years in Rome.[7] The two *Apologies* attributed to him were surely written in Rome. The *Acts of Justin and Companions* are considered to be authentic reports of his trial and execution. Justin represents the first serious Christian attempt to bring Christian belief into interaction with

---

ments in the catacomb of Callistus, several modern scholars have assumed that her devotion was to Christianity, but there is no convincing evidence of this.

4. Eusebius of Caesarea, *Church History* 3.18.4.

5. Further discussion in Osiek, *Rich and Poor in the Shepherd of Hermas*, 93-95; Lampe, *From Paul to Valentinus*, 198-205. If this Domitilla did not have Christian sympathies, a descendant of the same family in the third century did.

6. Eusebius, *Church History* 5.21.1.

7. Eusebius, *Ch. Hist.* 4.18.6.

the philosophical tradition. Thus his unique Christology and Scriptural exegesis were a major contribution to the theological diversity of the Roman community.

Justin laments that the name of Christian is borne by some with whom he would not agree, or with whom he is ashamed to share the name. He admits that some Christians are convicted of crimes and should be punished for those crimes, not punished as Christians.[8] Others in other ways do not live up to the name they bear.[9] But some who even blaspheme the creator of the world (surely a reference either to Gnostics or Marcionites) are called Christians, even though the likes of Justin do not agree with them.[10] Many embarrassing figures like Simon, Helena, and Marcion are called Christian, so that the name embraces a wide group of persons and theological and philosophical positions, just as the name "philosopher" includes a wide variety of types of people and beliefs.[11]

By the second century, accusations of social and moral depravity (*flagitia*) were commonly leveled at Christians. The stock elements that reoccur with regularity concern a secret nocturnal meeting in which both sexes and all social statuses mingle indiscriminately. The meal is in some way outrageous, usually eating the flesh of a baby. At some point in the festivities the lamp is overturned by a dog, the group is thrown into darkness, and sexual promiscuity ensues. These accusations are already reflected in the famous letter of the Roman aristocrat Pliny the Younger, governor of Bithynia and Pontus in north-central Asia Minor about C.E. 110, to the Emperor Trajan. Pliny inquires of his superior whether it is the mere name of Christian that should be punished, or rather the *flagitia* associated with the name.[12] When he makes further inquiry of some who claim to have given up Christianity, he learns only of early morning meetings consisting of hymns and oaths *not* to commit crimes (he sounds surprised at this, having expected the opposite), and a later daytime meal with ordinary, harmless food.

Justin too, a few years later in Rome, knows of these accusations (upset lamp, promiscuous sexual contact, and cannibalism), and leaves open the suggestion that others, including heterodox Christians, might engage in them with impunity and without intervention by the authorities.[13] Later in the century, the North African Minucius Felix, in a dialogue with a pagan friend set at Ostia

8. Justin, *1 Apology* 7.
9. Ibid., 16.
10. Justin, *Dial.* 35.5.
11. Ibid., 26.
12. Pliny, *Epistles to Trajan 10*, 96.2.
13. Justin, *1 Apol.* 26.

on a brief vacation down the Tiber from the law courts of Rome, discusses the accusations in some detail.[14] His contemporary Tertullian, in his usual sarcastic way, claims that inquiry should be made of Christians, how many babies each has eaten, who cooked them, and which dogs cooperated.[15] These passages indicate good evidence that the slanderous and scandalous portrait of Christian atrocities was circulating early in both Rome and North Africa.

While there is no clear suggestion in Paul's Letter to the Romans that such accusations were already active in the middle of the first century, it has frequently been suggested that the reason for the somewhat defensive display of civic loyalty in Rom 13:1-7, unprecedented in any other Pauline letter, is concern for the public image of Christians at the heart of the Empire, especially perhaps in the face of some concrete situation that they were dealing with in Rome. It is then pointed out that there is no evidence of persecution of Christians in Rome before Nero. True, in the most public and obvious sense. But commentators often neglect the point that "persecution" need not be by magistrates and with mortal danger, but can also be perpetrated by friends and neighbors with gossip that threatens honor and reputation. Rom 12:14-21 is filled with careful warnings against hatred and vengeance: "Bless those who persecute you.[16] . . . Do not repay evil for evil. . . . Live in peace with everyone as far as possible. . . . Do not take vengeance. . . . Do not be conquered by evil, but conquer evil with good." These admonitions could be seen as a continuation of ordinary paraenesis following from the beginning of chapter 12. Yet placed in the context of what follows in 13:1-7, Rom 12:14-21 would speak eloquently against reaction to slanderous talk already circulating, and reinforce the need to present to others a loyal and innocent face.

Continuing Jewish Influence

There is general consensus among scholars that the Roman Christian community from its inception and for at least the first two centuries of its history was characterized by large Jewish membership and continuing influence. The Hellenistic Jewish character of such texts as *1 Clement* and the *Shepherd of Hermas*, from the period covering the end of the first and beginning of the second century, is well known.[17] Less well-analyzed is the information given by Justin,

---

14. Minucius Felix, *Octavius* 8.3-4; 28.1–29.1; 30, 31.
15. Tertullian, *Apology* 2.5; 7.1.
16. Τοὺς διώκοντας, the usual word for persecutors.
17. For *1 Clement*, the argument was first and most thoroughly put forth by Wilhelm

himself an uncircumcised Gentile,[18] about the different positions with regard to the Mosaic law given in his writings. Because of his long and final association with Rome, it can be assumed that these positions are also represented in his mid-second century Roman community. If this is the case, Christian life in Rome was complicated not only by the mingling of Jews and Gentiles, but also by the mingling of Law-observant and non-observant persons on both sides. Life surrounding these issues after Paul seems not to have become more simplified, but rather more complex.

Eight different positions with regard to Christian Law observance can be gleaned from Justin's comments, five of them from Chapter 47 of the *Dialogue with Trypho*. It is to be assumed that each position represents a set of people, though not necessarily in socially distinct groups. The first position presented is the simple one of Christian Jews who keep the Law by choice. Justin has no objection to them, and declares that they will be saved, but his comments are revelatory of the fact that a century after Paul, there were still members of the community who took this stance.

The second position builds on the first. These are Christian Jews who not only keep the Law but try to persuade Gentiles to do so as well, trying to convince them that they will not be saved unless they do. Here Justin cannot go along, but considers their salvation to be in peril. Yet a third group are those Gentiles who *are* persuaded by Christian Jews to keep the Law. Grudgingly, Justin concedes that they too will probably be saved. A fourth group, whether Jewish or Gentile is not specified, does distance itself from Jews who keep the Law (the first group), thinking they cannot be saved, and refuses to receive them in hospitality or communicate with them in any way. Justin disapproves of these and presents a fifth position, his own: those who do not keep the Law but nevertheless welcome those who do. Finally, there is the case of Christian Jews who revert to Judaism after having once professed Christ. For them, he concludes, there can be no salvation.

Beyond the subject of full Law observance, there is the old vexing question of meat sacrificed to idols, a question closely related to that of Law observance, a major topic in Paul's First Letter to the Corinthians (1 Cor 8 and 10), a condition for the central agreement on admission of Gentiles at the Council of Jerusalem

---

Wrede, *Untersuchungen zum ersten Klemensbrief* (Göttingen: Vandenhoeck & Ruprecht, 1891); for *Hermas*, see Robert Joly, "Le milieu complexe du 'Pasteur' d'Hermas," in *Aufstieg und Niedergang der römischen Welt: Geschichte und Kultur Roms im Spiegel der neueren Forschung*, Part 2, *Principat*, 27.1 (ed. Hildegard Temporini and Wolfgang Haase; Berlin & New York: Walter de Gruyter, 1993), 524-51; also Erik Peterson, "Beiträge zur Interpretation der Visionem im 'Pastor Hermae,'" *Frühkirche, Judentum, und Gnosis* (Freiburg: Herder, 1959), 271-84.

    18. Justin, *Dial.* 28; 122.5.

(Acts 15:20, 29), a point of boundary establishment for the author of Revelation (Rev 2:14, 20), and a major issue of cultural accommodation in the early church. The usual interpretation of Paul's position, that he counseled banning such eating only if and when it gave scandal to a weaker person (1 Cor 10:25-29),[19] pits his thinking directly against that of Acts and John the author of Revelation, thus creating an interesting study of different approaches to cultural accommodation and religious purity within the New Testament period. The controversial question is probably a subject of discussion in Romans 14-15 along with the larger question of Law observance (e.g., Rom 14:1, 20-21). A century later, this was still a point of controversy. Justin presents it as the normative position that no Christians eat such meat. While Justin is not a Law-observer, he is observant on the question of meat offered to idols. Yet his imaginary dialogue partner, the Jewish philosopher Trypho, says that he knows Christians who do eat this meat.[20] Justin does not deny that claim, but counters that it is all the more motive to make the rest of believers faithful, against heresy and false prophecy. In other words, this practice is anathema to him, yet he cannot deny that it takes place.

In those brief comments in two parts of the *Dialogue*, Justin tells us worlds about the disputes still going on in the middle of the second century over the transition from Jewish to Gentile Christianity, left as Paul's legacy. Despite the optimism of another writer in the Pauline tradition about how the divisions were neatly overcome in unity (Eph 2:11-22), on the contrary the divisions continued, were magnified, and certainly became more complex, even as Christianity moved inexorably toward Gentile identity. We see in Justin's remarks, moreover, that it was not only a matter of theological differences, but sometimes of social divisions. Some Christians refused to extend hospitality to those who observed the Law. Are we to assume the refusers of hospitality were Gentiles convinced that they needed nothing from Israel, perhaps Christians of Marcionite persuasions? Or were they believers of Jewish origin who so thoroughly repudiated their past identity as to withhold communion from those of their own background who clung more firmly to that identity?

Justin does not say. He holds for full communion among believers, no matter what their positions. At a time when we can assume that the social organization of the Roman church was still in some kind of subgroups (more on that below), withholding hospitality does not simply mean social snubbing but

---

19. A case could be made, however, that the insidious way Paul presents the argument — with the *excursus* in 1 Cor 9 on all the rights he could make use of but does not — leads to his intended conclusion that only an arrogant, selfish person would insist on eating what is offered to idols. Even the positive statements to eat what is offered (1 Cor 10:25, 27) could be understood as sarcastic: "Go ahead, eat, and see if I care!"

20. Justin, *Dial.* 34-35.

refusal to be in full communion with believers in another worshiping group (the kind of thing that was happening elsewhere and earlier in 3 John 9-10). Yet there is a limit to Justin's tolerance. He has nothing good to say about Christian Jews who have renounced Christ and returned to Judaism. Along with the Jews themselves, especially those who curse Christ in the synagogues, they cannot be saved. His criterion for salvation is faith in Christ.

Even this eighth group, Jewish Christians who renounce their Christian faith and return to Jewish practices exclusively, must represent persons known by Justin to have done just this. Such conversions and retroversions could only be possible if two factors are still present in the Christian community of mid-second century Rome. First, there are still conversions from Judaism to Christianity happening. This presumes that the two communities know each other well enough and there is no strict banning of interaction between them. Second, the ties between Jewish and Christian Jewish families are still close, with mixed marriages and mixed family composition occurring with some frequency. It is the rare independent thinker, a Justin or an Augustine, who searches through various religious and philosophical systems as an intellectual pilgrim until he finds the truth. In most cases of changing religious allegiance, family and friendship pressures must have been the determining factor.

We can thus conclude that while Jews and Christians were fairly distinct by the time of Justin with regard to their religious identity, the lines continued to be blurred for those of Jewish origin who embraced the Christian faith, with relative fluidity of movement between the two groups. Some writings like the earlier 1 *Clement* seem to indicate clearly established boundaries, with Christians freely drawing on the Hebrew Scriptures and the traditions of the Hellenistic synagogue with their own by now distinctive interpretations.[21] The apologetic Christian literary genre "Against the Jews," in which budding theologians sharpened their rhetorical teeth by attacking the religious claims and institutions of Judaism, developed soon after. Justin's own *Dialogue with Trypho* was his own less vitriolic version. But Justin suggests that the social reality was not so clearly distinguished, and that there was actually a great deal of social interaction not only between the two groups as different entities, but also a great deal of mixed identity and mutual attractiveness. Since forward movement led inevitably toward separation, what seems evident for a later time must also be assumed to be true earlier, even in the time of 1 *Clement*.

---

21. James C. Walters, "Romans, Jews, and Christians: The Impact of the Romans on Jewish/Christian Relations in First-Century Rome," 175-95 in *Judaism and Christianity in First-Century Rome* (ed. Karl P. Donfried and Peter Richardson; Grand Rapids, Mich.: Eerdmans, 1998), 193-94.

Loose Organizational Style

The third characteristic of the Roman church that can be seen already in Paul's Letter to the Romans and continues to be reflected in later Roman texts is the lack of clearly centralized organization in the first two Christian centuries. In one way, this should not be surprising. Everywhere in the Mediterranean world, local Christian churches operated with relative independence, in collegial relationships and networks with other churches. We know of some of these early networks: the Pauline communities of a given region, the seven churches of Revelation, the churches of the Presbyter, Gaius, and Demetrius with their problematic brother Diotrephes (3 John), etc. About sixty years later, we see another network operating in western Asia Minor in the set of churches with which Ignatius makes contact on his way as a prisoner to Rome: Ephesus, Magnesia, Tralles, Philadelphia, and Smyrna, a list that partially overlaps with the churches of Revelation.

Scholars have also puzzled over the fact that, when Paul addresses the Roman congregation, he does not address them as a "church" (ἐκκλησία), quite contrary to his usual custom. Of the other Pauline letters, whether judged authentic or not, that are intended for groups rather than individuals, only Philippians, Ephesians, and Colossians do not call the recipients a church in the opening greeting. Care must be taken not to make too much of this omission.[22] However, if it is significant, some explanations have been put forth suggesting that the reason has to do with the Roman assemblies' particular form of organization, or lack thereof.

For several reasons it is often expected that the Roman church would have organized itself centrally at an early date: the Roman gift for governmental organization; the evidence of *1 Clement* that is often interpreted in that direction; the second-century testimony of Papias that he acquired the list of Roman bishops going back to Peter;[23] and later (third century and beyond) evidence for strong centralization. Yet George LaPiana argued convincingly some time ago that the Roman church did not come under a central authority until the end of the second century under the leadership of Victor.[24]

---

22. Colossians and Ephesians have their own distinctive theology of church which cannot be discussed here. The omission of the term in the greeting of Philippians may indicate that, in both there and in Romans, there is no purpose other than variation. Phil 4:15 proves that Paul certainly did think of the Philippian community as an ἐκκλησία, and so no complex reason for the omission need be supposed there.

23. Eusebius, *Ch. Hist.* 4.22.3.

24. George LaPiana, "The Roman Church at the End of the Second Century," *Harvard Theological Review* 18 (1925): 201-77.

We know from the letter of Ignatius of Antioch to the Roman church and from later tradition that Ignatius was brought under guard as a condemned prisoner to Rome and executed there in the arena by wild animals[25] in the first or second decade of the second century. But as Ignatius visited with communities along the way and then wrote letters to them, he had an agenda besides his coming death. He believed firmly in the necessity of strong central organization under the leadership of a single "bishop" (ἐπίσκοπος) who governed with a group of presbyters and was assisted by deacons. In his letters back to churches that apparently had adopted this form of government, he advocates the strong exercise of authority on the part of the bishop and submission of everyone else to his authority and that of the presbyters.[26] When Ignatius writes ahead to the Romans, however, anticipating his arrival as a prisoner, he has no mention of a bishop or any in positions of leadership.

The principal message in Ignatius' letter to the Romans is his desire that they not buy his freedom, but allow him to die as a martyr. Did he later have time when in Rome to propound his model of church leadership to them? The *First Letter of Clement* is usually dated before the arrival of Ignatius, but could come at any time during the turn of the first to the second century, possibly even after Ignatius.[27] While Clement frequently uses titles of office, he does not do so in the direct way in which Ignatius does.[28] Clement speaks of the leadership function as "overseeing" (ἐπισκοπή, *1 Clem.* 44.4) but never calls any living person a "bishop" (ἐπίσκοπος). Rather, the leaders of the church of Corinth to whom he writes seem to be a group of presbyters governing collegially, the same kind of government that was common elsewhere.[29] In short, the author of *1 Clement*, for all his rhetoric about the reception of the Gospel from the apostles — who received it from Jesus who received it from God[30] — says nothing about a central church organization, neither in Rome nor in Corinth.

The same collegial, presbyteral government is witnessed in the *Shepherd of Hermas*, which probably was written in Rome over a long period of years, from

---

25. The capital sentence *condemnatio ad bestias.*

26. E.g., Ignatius, *To the Ephesians* 2, 4-6; *To the Magnesians* 3-4, 6-7, 13, 15; *To the Trallians* 2-3, 7; *To the Philadelphians*, Preface, 1, 3, 7; *To the Smyrnaeans* 8-9.

27. Larry Welborn has shown ("On the Date of First Clement," *Biblical Research* 29 [1984]: 35-54) that the traditional date in the 90s of the first century rests on very tenuous arguments.

28. Clement will use such terms as "bishops and deacons" (ἐπίσκοποι καὶ διάκονοι, *1 Clem.* 42.4), but in a less general way than does Phil 1:1, and in dependence on a misquote of Isa 60:17, which really speaks in the LXX of "rulers and overseers" (ἄρχοντες and ἐπίσκοποι).

29. *1 Clem.* 47.6; 54.2; 57.1).

30. *1 Clem.* 42.4, a text often taken as the origin of the idea of "apostolic succession."

the end of the first century into several decades at the beginning of the second.[31] Like *First Clement, Hermas* speaks of leaders under the traditional titles of "overseers" (ἐπίσκοποι) and "ministers" (διάκονοι), as well as apostles and teachers,[32] but always in a general way, usually as past leaders. His one clear reference to titles in present leadership structures is to a group of presbyters who preside over the church, with whom he is to proclaim the revelation that he has received.[33] Elsewhere in *Hermas* there are two allusions to church leaders in more general terms. In *Vis.* 2.2.6, the woman revealer who is the church, in her initial public revelation, warns the whole congregation of the need for conversion, but addresses a warning specifically to the "leaders" of the church (προηγούμενοι τῆς ἐκκλησίας) that they need to change their ways. Later in *Vis.* 3.9.7, a similar message is directed to the same προηγούμενοι as also those who take the front seats, or preside (πρωτοκαθεδρίται) We can assume on the basis of *Vis.* 2.4.3 that the collegial leaders of the church were at times called elders or presbyters, but at times by other names, and so that the language for their function was fluid.

Some years later, Justin speaks only of a presider at liturgy (ὁ προΐστως), assisted by deacons, and not of the ways in which such leaders might guide wider aspects of the church, nor what their titles might be (*1 Apol.* 65, 67). By the time of Hippolytus in the early third century, the classic threefold ministry is in place: one presiding bishop[34] with deacons and presbyters.[35]

Did Ignatius leave any trace in the thinking of the Roman church? It would seem not, and perhaps there was even a conscious rejection of his organizational model, all the while he was venerated as a martyr. If any trace of his influence remained behind in Rome, it is perhaps the odd occurrences in *1 Clement* and *Hermas,* as discussed above, of these titles "bishops" and "deacons" for what would later be called church office. Perhaps the language, if not the form, is the legacy of Ignatius' brief and final passage through Rome.

Robert Jewett in an unpublished paper, "Addressing the House and Tenement Churches in Rome," has argued that the omission of the term "church"

---

31. Carolyn Osiek, "The Oral World of Early Christianity in Rome: The Case of Hermas," in *Judaism and Christianity in First-Century Rome* (ed. Karl P. Donfried and Peter Richardson; Grand Rapids, Mich.: Eerdmans, 1998), 151-72; idem, *The Shepherd of Hermas,* 9-10.

32. Shepherd of Hermas, *Vision* 3.5.1; *Similitude* 9.15.4; 16.5; 17.1; 25.2.

33. Shepherd of Hermas, *Vis.* 2.4.3. Some would see a further reference to presbyters at *Vis.* 3.1.8, where the woman "church" invites Hermas to sit by her on a couch, and he demurs, saying that the "elders" (πρεσβύτεροι) should sit first. But there is no further mention of presbyters in the passage, so it is improbable that the term "elder" (πρεσβύτερος) is being used in a technical sense; most likely the statement simply means "elders first."

34. Hippolytus, *Apostolic Tradition* 20-31 *et passim.*

35. Ibid., 24.

(ἐκκλησία) in the address of Paul's Letter to the Romans is a deliberate one because Paul attached this word only to assemblies that met in private homes, of which there was only one instance in Rome at the time, the house church of Prisca and Aquila, about which this term *is* used (Rom 16:3-5). The rest of the meeting groups, according to Jewett's argument, were not hosted in private homes, and so met in apartment or tenement houses, thus unable in Paul's thinking to be called by the term "church" (ἐκκλησία). He therefore avoided using the term because of the vast differences in organization and thinking among the various Christian groups.

An analysis of the list of persons addressed in Romans 16 yields the conclusion that there are five groups and several "floating" individuals, though the individuals could also belong to the previous group named:

1. Those who worship in the house church of Prisca and Aquila (16:3-5);
2. Those "belonging to Aristobulus" (16:10), slaves and freedpersons of the household of a distinguished person who was not himself Christian;
3. Those "belonging to Narcissus," another similar group (16:11);
4. A group of "brothers" under the leadership of four men, Asyncritus, Phlegon, Hermes, and Patrobus, all very likely slaves or freedmen (16:14);
5. Another group headed by five persons whose names most likely indicate servile origin, Philologus and Julia (probably either husband and wife or brother and sister), Nereus and his unnamed sister, and Olympas "and all the holy ones with them" (16:15).

But Epaenetus, Maria, Andronicus and Junia, Ampliatus, Urbanus, Stachys, and Apelles (16:5b-10a) could belong to the house church of Prisca and Aquila; Herodion to the Aristobulus group (v. 11a); and Tryphaena and Tryphosa (probably sisters), Persis, and Rufus and his mother to the Narcissus group (16:12-13). The fact that Paul seems to know so many more people in the house church of Prisca and Aquila may be indicative of his reception of hospitality in their house previously in Ephesus and his expectation of the same reception in Rome. Even if this were not the only house church in Rome, his expectation of hospitality there would not be surprising given his past associations with this couple and their household.

The absence of tight organization in the middle of the first century seems to have continued into later years, as evidenced by *1 Clement,* the Shepherd of Hermas, and Justin. By the time of *1 Clement,* the term "church" (ἐκκλησία) was in use to refer to the entirety of Christians in Rome, as with Ignatius,[36] in the

---

36. *1 Clement,* prescript; Ignatius, *To the Romans,* prescript.

same way that Paul had used the term much earlier of the Corinthians or Philippians (1 Cor 1:2; Phil 4:15) and others. By the time of the writing of *1 Clement*, the Roman Christians were an ἐκκλησία, but still not a centrally organized one. Thus Jewett's insights about the organization of the first-century Roman community play out in what we know of its slow pace of later development.

Conclusion

These brief glimpses of what life was like in the second-century Christian community of Rome may help to illuminate the earlier period about which we have less information. The later evidence points to a loosely organized network of worship groups with strong and continuing Jewish connections and characteristics. But because of the widely diverse cultural and ethnic population of the capital, these Christian gatherings were also characterized by a degree of cultural and ethnic diversity unparalleled in other Christian networks throughout the Empire. The beginnings of these characteristics were already present in the groupings that Paul attempted to address from a distance in anticipation of his first-time visit. How he was received is the question whose answer we would most like to know.

FEMINIST APPROACHES TO ROMANS

compiled by Sheila E. McGinn

Feminist Approaches to Paul's Letter to the Romans

Sheila E. McGinn

Feminist Approaches to Paul

Paul of Tarsus, alternatively glorified or vilified as a "founding father" of Christianity, left one of the most influential legacies among early Christian authors. Feminist exegetes, relative new-comers to the field of biblical hermeneutics, are increasingly more influential interpreters of early Christian writers. Paul and feminists, however, have not always been seen as the most amicable of "bedfellows."

Feminist interpreters of the Bible were quick to latch on to the Jesus material. Even before the rise of the historical-critical method, women looked to Jesus as a model of women's empowerment. Over a century ago, Elizabeth Cady Stanton commented with approbation upon several sayings and actions of Jesus in her counter-cultural reappraisal of the Bible.[1] In the last quarter-century or more, feminist scholars have mined the sayings of Jesus and the gospel stories about him, and have found there a liberative vision of full personhood for both women and men.[2]

---

1. Elizabeth Cady Stanton, *The Woman's Bible* (New York: European Publishing, 1895; repr. Salem, N.H.: Ayer, 1988).

2. To be sure, this is not all they have found in the gospels. I do not mean to suggest that the gospels are "feminist" writings, nor to deny the androcentric and even misogynist elements of some of the gospel materials. But the basic point remains: feminists, even non-Christian ones, have been looking to the Jesus material and have found there elements of a liberative vision. E.g., Rosemary Radford Ruether and Eleanor McLaughlin (eds.), *Women of Spirit: Female Leadership in the Jewish and Christian Traditions* (New York: Simon & Schuster, 1979), 16-70;

The move toward Paul has been somewhat more tentative. A few feminist scholars such as Elisabeth Schüssler Fiorenza, Mary Ann Getty, Carolyn Osiek, and Antoinette Wire have published book-length studies on Pauline material.[3] Many others have begun to contribute short commentaries or essays on portions of the Pauline corpus.[4] Of these works, many have been what one might call "remedial" in aim, promoting a critical reappraisal of the text-critical and translation issues, and suggesting a revisionist interpretation of Paul.[5] Nevertheless, feminist exegetes continue to show a certain amount of ambivalence to the Pauline corpus.

When one looks at the broad spectrum of feminist writings on the Pauline material, one finds a curious fact. Whereas the four longer letters or *"hauptbriefe"* to the Romans, Galatians, and Corinthians have taken center stage in the malestream history of exegesis of Paul, feminist exegetes have tended to focus on the shorter letters of Paul, and have taken a rather piecemeal approach to the others. Among these studies, certain portions of the Pauline corpus have taken center stage, most notably Gal 3, 1 Cor 11, and Rom 16.[6]

For example, on the Romans passage, we find recent contributions from Reta Finger ("Was Julia a Racist?"), Wendy Cotter ("Women's Authority Roles in Paul's Churches"), Caroline Whelan ("*Amica Pauli:* The Role of Phoebe in the Early Church"), Elisabeth Schüssler Fiorenza ("The 'Quilting' of Women's History: Phoebe of Cenchraea," and "Missionaries, Apostles, Coworkers: Rom

---

Letty M. Russell, *Household of Freedom: Authority in Feminist Theology* (Philadelphia: Westminster, 1987), esp. chapters 2 and 4; Sheila E. McGinn, "Women in the Priesthood: God Forbid?" (unpublished essay; Evanston, Ill.: Northwestern University, 1977).

3. Elisabeth Schüssler Fiorenza, *In Memory of Her* (New York: Crossroad, 1983), parts 2-3; Mary Ann Getty, *Philippians and Philemon* (*New Testament Message* 14; Wilmington, Del.: Michael Glazier, 1980); Carolyn Osiek, *Galatians* (*New Testament Message* 12; Wilmington, Del.: Michael Glazier, 1980); Antoinette Wire, *Corinthian Women Prophets: A Reconstruction through Paul's Rhetoric* (Minneapolis: Augsburg Fortress, 1990).

4. E.g., those in *Searching the Scripture*, Vol. 2: *A Feminist Commentary* (ed. Elisabeth Schüssler Fiorenza; New York: Crossroad, 1994) and *The Women's Bible Commentary* (ed. Carol A. Newsom and Sharon H. Ringe; Louisville: Westminster John Knox; London: SPCK, 1992).

5. I do not intend "remedial" to be construed in a pejorative sense. I would include much of my own work thus far in this category.

6. Sheila E. McGinn, "'Εχουσίαν ἔχειν ἐπὶ τῆς κεφαλῆς: 1 Cor 11:10 and the Ecclesial Authority of Women," *Listening, Journal of Religion and Culture: The Social World of Saint Paul* (Lewis University, Romeoville, Ill; 1996): 91-104; "Galatians 3:26-29 and the Politics of the Spirit," *Proceedings: Eastern Great Lakes and Midwest Biblical Societies* (1993): 89-101; Luise Schottroff, "Die Schreckensherrschaft der Sünde und die Befreiung durch Christus nach dem Römerbrief des Paulus," 57-72 in eadem, *Befreiungserfahrungen: Studien zur Sozialgeschichte des Neuen Testaments* (Munich: Kaiser, 1990).

16 and the Reconstruction of Women's Early Christian History"), and Isabelle Houen ("Les femmes et l'apostolat").[7]

In addition, some men who identify with feminist interests have taken up the baton. For example, Ray Schulz ("A Case for 'President' Phoebe in Rom 16:2"), John Thorley ("Junia, a Woman Apostle") and Marco Zappella ("A propositio di Febe *prostatis* [Rom 16:2]").[8]

Taking a broader swath, Wilhelm Linss ("St. Paul and Women") argues — on the basis of Gal 3 combined with 1 Cor 7 and 11 — that Paul was an advocate of women's liberation and equality with men before God. And William Klassen makes a similar argument in his article "Musonius Rufus, Jesus, and Paul: Three First-Century Feminists."[9] In these articles, they echo arguments made by Robert Jewett in such essays as "The Sexual Liberation of the Apostle Paul" and "The Conflict over Sexual Roles in Pauline Churches."[10]

---

7. Reta Halteman Finger, "Was Julia a Racist? Cultural Diversity in the Book of Romans," *Daughters of Sarah* 19 (Summer 1993): 36-39; Wendy Cotter, "Women's Authority Roles in Paul's Churches: Countercultural or Conventional?" *Novum Testamentum* 36 (Oct 1994): 350-72; Caroline F. Whelan, "*Amica Pauli*: The Role of Phoebe in the Early Church," *Journal for the Study of the New Testament* 49 (Mar 1993): 67-85; Isabelle Houen, "Les femmes et l'apostolat," 187-94 in *La Politique de la mystique: hommage à Mgr Maxime Charles* (ed. J.-L. Marion, et al.; Limoges: Criterion, 1984); Bernadette J. Brooten, "Women and the Churches in Early Christianity," *Ecumenical Trends* 14, no. 4 (1985): 51-54; Sister Philsy, "Diakonia of Women in the New Testament," *Indian Journal of Theology* 32, no. 1 (1983): 110-18; Elisabeth Schüssler Fiorenza, "The 'Quilting' of Women's History: Phoebe of Cenchraea," 35-49 in *Embodied Love: Sensuality and Relationship as Feminist Values* (ed. P. Cooey, S. Farmer, M. Ross; San Francisco: Harper Collins, 1987); and idem, "Missionaries, Apostles, Coworkers: Rom 16 and the Reconstruction of Women's Early Christian History," *Word and World* 6, no. 4 (1986): 420-33.

8. Ray Schulz, "A Case for 'President' Phoebe in Rom 16:2," *Lutheran Theological Journal* 24 (Dec 1990): 124-27, and "Romans 16:7: Junia or Junias?" *Expository Times* 98 (Jan 1987): 108-10; John Thorley, "Junia, A Woman Apostle," *Novum Testamentum* 38 (Jan 1996): 18-29; Marco Zappella, "A propositio di Febe *prostatis* (Rom 16:2)," *Rivista Biblica* 37 (Apr-June 1989): 167-71; Gerhard Lohfink, "Weibliche Diakone im Neuen Testament," 320-38 in *Die Frau im Urchristentum* (ed. G. Dautzenberg, H. Merklein, K. Müller; Freiburg im Breisgau: Herder, 1983).

9. Wilhelm C. Linss, "St. Paul and Women," *Dialog* 24 (Wint 1985): 26-40; also rejoinder to reply of M. P. Pauli, *Dialog* 24 (Winter 1985): 226-28; William Klassen, "Musonius Rufus, Jesus, and Paul: Three First-Century Feminists," 185-206 in *From Jesus to Paul: Studies in Honour of Francis Wright Beare* (ed. P. Richardson and J. Hurd; Waterloo, Ont.: Wilfrid Laurier University Press, 1984); cf. R. J. Raja, "Pauline Women: A Probe into Women's Ministry (a Study of Romans 16)," 213-20 in *Ministries in the Church in India: Research Seminar and Pastoral Consultation* (ed. D. S. Amalorpavadass; New Delhi: Bangalore, 1976).

10. Robert Jewett, "The Sexual Liberation of the Apostle Paul," *Journal of the American Academy of Religion Supplement* 47 (1979): 55-87; "The Conflict over Sexual Roles in Pauline Churches," 151-60 in *Wesleyan Theology Today: A Bicentennial Theological Consultation* (ed. Theodore Runyon; Nashville: Kingswood, 1986).

Even for those feminist exegetes who have begun to show interest in the *hauptbriefe,* the letter to the Romans remains anomalous. This last of the authentic letters — and arguably the most significant of Paul's letters for the development of Christian doctrine — has received very little attention from feminist scholars. And, as we saw above, what little attention feminist exegetes thus far have given to Romans (perhaps not surprisingly) tends to focus almost exclusively upon chapter sixteen — or other passages which explicitly mention women or sexual matters.[11]

This curiosity is easily explained, however, when one looks at the approach that feminist exegetes have taken. Since a revisionist or remedial approach "attempts to rediscover all the information about women that still can be found in the biblical writings,"[12] its utility presumes explicit mention of women in the text. Romans may be the most influential of Paul's letters for the history of interpretation but, excepting its relatively independent last chapter, the letter lacks the kind of obvious references to women which a revisionist approach requires. The two feminist commentaries on Romans which have appeared to date serve rather to illustrate this fact than to controvert it.

Feminist Studies of Romans

Beverly Roberts Gaventa wrote an eight-page commentary on Romans for *The Women's Bible Commentary,* edited by Carol Newsome and Sharon Ringe.[13] Gaventa spends fully half of her article on introductory matters, which she divides into three categories: Contents, Occasion and Purpose, and Theological Significance. In the portion on Theological Significance, she outlines four central themes, each of which she connects to "women's issues" in her theological application. In the remaining commentary portion of the essay, Gaventa takes a basically revisionist approach, and addresses her comments to seven specific portions of the letter which she sees as having particular pertinence for women. Perhaps not surprisingly, four of these sections discuss sexual operations, sexual relationships or involve sexual metaphors (Rom 1:18-32; 2:25-29; 7:1-6;

---

11. Elsa Tamez is one of the exceptions to this trend. See, e.g., "God's Election, Exclusion and Mercy: A Bible Study of Romans 9–11," *International Review of Mission* 82, no. 325 (1993): 29-37.

12. Elisabeth Schüssler Fiorenza, "Charting the Field of Feminist Biblical Interpretation," *But She Said: Feminist Practices of Biblical Interpretation* (Boston: Beacon, 1992), 22.

13. Beverly Roberts Gaventa, "Romans," 313-20 in *The Women's Bible Commentary* (ed. Carol A. Newsom and Sharon H. Ringe; Louisville: Westminster John Knox; London: SPCK, 1992).

8:18-25). Of the last three of these seven sections, Gaventa uses the first to focus on the question of to what extent women are included in a discussion which is inclusive in the original text but which has been made explicitly androcentric in the translations (5:12-21); the next to discuss ethnic tolerance (14:1–15:13); and the last to highlight the list of women in Rom 16 and describe their roles.

Surely these prior studies have made significant contributions to Pauline scholarship, especially because analysis of such issues as women's roles and sexual metaphors has been important in recovering the history of women in early Christianity. For example, the list of Pauline church leaders in Rom 16, because it includes several women, has been of value to feminists for developing the broad outlines of ministry in the Pauline churches. This is a tremendous advance over the previous consensus, of hardly more than a quarter-century ago, that there simply were no women leaders in the early Christian congregations.

However, limiting analysis of the Pauline corpus to those passages which explicitly mention women or sexual roles creates an unnecessary dead end for feminist exegesis of Paul. For example, its dubious connection with the foregoing chapters prevents any analysis of Rom 16 from furthering our understanding of the letter as a whole. If we are to look at only those passages which explicitly mention "women's concerns," vast sections of the Pauline corpus simply will be omitted from consideration. And this includes the vast majority of Paul's letter to the Romans. The letter to the Romans has been too significant for Christian history to justify this decision of feminist exegetes to leave it on the sidelines. It is imperative that feminist scholars begin to address the content of Rom 1–15, and not just the letter's appendix.

Elizabeth Castelli produced the second "commentary" on Romans, this one twenty-eight pages long, for the *Searching the Scriptures* collection edited by Schüssler Fiorenza.[14] Castelli, unlike Gaventa, begins with a discussion of the feminist method she will use in this essay, including a critique of the commentary genre itself.[15] She concludes that "[a] feminist commentary, in this instance, will critically gloss the text by examining the ways in which language, ideology, and imagery underwrite certain relationships of power while rendering others impossible or unthinkable."[16] Castelli then moves into a discussion of how to recover the history of early Christian women, using Rom 16 to present as an example of such historical reconstruction.[17] From that point, she moves into a process of what she calls "using women to think with" — an ex-

14. Elizabeth A. Castelli, "Romans," 272-300 in *Searching the Scriptures*, Vol. 2: *A Feminist Commentary* (ed. Elizabeth Schüssler Fiorenza; New York: Crossroad, 1994).

15. Ibid., 272-76.

16. Ibid., 276.

17. Ibid., 276-80.

pression which she borrows from Karen King.[18] Beginning with the passages in Rom 1:18-32 and 7:1-6 which explicitly mention women, Castelli moves to the *meta* level of discourse analysis, focusing on Paul's treatment of Adam and the law, ethnicity, slavery and imperialism. In the end, Castelli produces a sort of anti-commentary, rather than simply adopting the commentary form as it traditionally is found.

Elizabeth Castelli's critique of both the commentary form and the contents of Paul's last letter are signals of where feminist exegetes must go next if they are to engage the Pauline correspondence. The approach of "using women to think with" — and particularly the strategy of discourse analysis — shows more promise for looking at texts in which women figure less prominently, or perhaps are not mentioned explicitly at all. As Castelli has shown, to break open the letter to the Romans for feminist exegesis, we need to break out to a new approach, one which requires a deeper engagement with the text, its author, and its history. Otherwise feminist Biblical scholars must resign themselves to relegating such "theological" letters as Romans to the periphery, and restrict themselves to "rehabilitating" the sections of Paul's letters which explicitly mention women or "women's concerns."

Romans has been too significant for Christian history to justify such a decision to leave it on the sidelines. To do so would be to "ghettoize" feminist exegesis when one of the main objectives of feminist hermeneutics has been to press the significance of women's experience in interpreting all of reality, not just "women's concerns." The letter to the Romans has been the single most influential of Paul's letters in the history of interpretation of the Pauline corpus, and in the historical development of dogma in the Christian churches. Until now, feminist exegetes have largely capitulated to the traditional malestream interpretation of Romans. By leaving the majority of the letter unexamined, we have allowed other exegetical models and hermeneutical agendas to dominate this tradition by default. It is imperative that feminist scholars begin to take a voice in interpreting the letter that culminated Paul's entire evangelistic career — and that means undertaking a thoroughgoing analysis of *all* of the letter. It is time we address a feminist hermeneutic to the body of the letter, Rom 1–15, and not just the letter's appendix.

The three essays in the present section attempt to do just that. Each author has selected a section of the body of the letter to the Romans and used a feminist hermeneutic to provide a new analysis of this key text. Each essay illus-

---

18. The process seems to be a hybrid of strategies four through eight outlined by Elisabeth Schüssler Fiorenza in "Charting the Field of Feminist Biblical Interpretation," *But She Said: Feminist Practices of Biblical Interpretation* (Boston: Beacon, 1992), 20-50.

trates a somewhat different approach to feminist hermeneutics, but all three authors take the significance of women's experience and the immeasurable value of human life, female and male, as the starting points for their investigations.

Elsa Tamez, a Central American feminist and Biblical theologian, has chosen the doctrine of "justification" in Rom 1–8 as the focus of her present essay. The traditional understanding of this doctrine provides the basis for her exploration of what this fundamental Pauline notion of the δικαιοσύνη τοῦ Θεοῦ means for women, especially those in the "two-thirds world" and those who are marginalized in "first world" societies. It should hardly be surprising that her analysis of Paul's term, δικαιοσύνη τοῦ Θεοῦ, gives rise to a significantly different understanding than the traditional "consensus" view.

In essays such as the one in this collection and her prior one on "God's Election, Exclusion and Mercy: A Bible Study of Romans 9–11,"[19] Tamez illustrates an approach somewhat similar to Castelli. Both Castelli and Tamez create a conversation between the world of the text and the world of today, with Castelli putting a somewhat greater emphasis on the former and Tamez on the latter. Tamez' liberation theology approach is less focused on specific details of the text than are traditional commentaries; she emphasizes key theological themes in the text and develops how those apply in contemporary culture, especially when read from the viewpoint of Christians of marginalized groups (e.g., women in her own Latin American context). In her previous essay on Rom 9–11, Tamez did not specifically address the impact of these themes upon women. Her essay in this volume, on Rom 1–8, advances the discussion by dealing directly with this issue, providing a sustained examination of how women have heard — and need to hear (or to stop hearing) — one of the most fundamental doctrines in this foundational Pauline letter.

Pamela Thimmes, like Castelli, takes a more detailed look at the text in her analysis here of Rom 7:1-4. The actual arguments within the text and the socio-historical situation in which it was produced receive considerably more attention than in Tamez. Like Castelli, Thimmes engages in a certain amount of discourse analysis, especially honing in on Paul's use of the marriage/adultery analogy in his discussion of the role of the Law in Christian life. Does Paul, consciously or unconsciously, re-inscribe a gender hierarchy through his use of this analogy? If so, how might that have been heard by Paul's initial audience? In

19. Cf. Elsa Tamez, "Justification by Faith," in *Dictionary of Feminist Theologies* (ed. Letty M. Russell & L. Shannon Clarkson; Louisville: Westminster John Knox, 1996); "Der Brief an die Gemeinde in Rom: Eine feministische Lektüre," 557-73 in *Kompendium Feministische Bibelauslegung* (ed. Luise Schottroff and Marie-Theres Wacher; Gütersloh: Gütersloher Verlagshaus, 1998); and *The Amnesty of Grace* (Nashville: Abingdon, 1992).

particular, how did the women in the Roman audience construe his use of this analogy? And what are women in a contemporary audience to make of it? Here the strategy of "using women to think with" leads to a challenging interpretation of this often-overlooked section in Rom 7.

Several themes and features of the letter to the Romans hold promise for further probing by feminist exegetes. Key among these themes is that of relationships: between Jew and Gentile (in Rom 9–11), and between Christian believers and non-Christian authorities (in Rom 13). In addition, one of the most interesting features of Romans is Paul's mode of argumentation in his exposition of the love-ethic (in Rom 12–15). Investigation of these areas from the vantage point of feminist hermeneutics holds promise both for advancing our understanding of the Pauline corpus, and for further developing a specifically feminist methodology.

Women Reading Romans 9–11

In the remainder of this discussion, I will utilize a strategy similar to Castelli's in my analysis of what many recent Pauline scholars have judged to be the heart of the letter to the Romans, chapters 9–11.

The culminating section of his argument in the letter (the "proof" section), Rom 9–11 is where Paul deals explicitly with the relationships between Jewish and Gentile believers, and between believers (of both ethnic backgrounds) and non-Christian Jews. Not surprisingly, Paul's primary focus is the former relationship, which he re-conceptualizes in two ways. First, the identity of Jewish v. Gentile believers may appear to be a question of race or ethnicity, but in fact it is a question of Israel "according to the flesh" v. Israel "according to the promise." Secondly, while the promise might be understood as restricted to those who have inherited the promise to Abraham by entering into the Mosaic covenant through circumcision, in fact the promise is given to all those who have the Spirit of Jesus. This twofold re-conceptualization is key to the dynamic and power of Paul's discourse, so I will focus my remaining comments on the strategy and substance of Paul's rhetoric here.

Paul begins this section with an appeal to *ethos*. In 9:2-3 he testifies to his solidarity with his kinfolk, mentioning his "anguish for the sake of my own people." This expression of Paul's *pathos* is designed to get the attention of the Jewish believers in Rome. Paul's "own people" are "the sons of Israel," "Israel according to the flesh," those who belong to the Mosaic covenant of circumcision, by birthright or conversion. While the Jewish believers in Rome have not yet met Paul, they hear of his tremendous concern for the Jewish people and are invited to trust him, believing that he has their best interests at heart.

However, this very appeal risks alienating the Gentile members of his audience unless they can sympathize with the *pathos* to which Paul attests. So, hard on the heels of this assertion, Paul shifts from his language about the sons of Israel (his brothers κατὰ σάρκα) to language concerning the children of the promise (τὰ τέκνα τῆς ἐπαγγελίας) — among whom his Gentile hearers can be expected to number themselves. And to ensure that this promise is taken seriously by his audience, Paul mentions it repeatedly, giving a synopsis of what one might call its historical development, and then amplifying the notion with a variety of parallel ideas.

Rom 9:2-3	"anguish . . . for the sake of my own brothers of my people according to the flesh," τῶν ἀδελφῶν μου τῶν συγγενῶν μου κατὰ σάρκα)
vv. 6-7	not all those who are of Israel [according to the flesh] are truly Israelites (οὐ γὰρ πάντες οἱ ἐξ Ἰσραὴλ οὗτοι Ἰσραήλ)
v. 8	it is not the children of the flesh (τὰ τέκνα τῆς σαρκὸς) who are the children of God (τέκνα τοῦ Θεοῦ), but the children of the promise (τὰ τέκνα τῆς ἐπαγγελίας) who are counted as descendants
v. 16	So [election] depends not on human will or exertion, but on God who shows mercy
v. 18	God has mercy on whomever God chooses
v. 25	As indeed [God] says in Hosea, "Those who were not my people I will call 'my people' (Καλέσω . . . λαόν μου), and she who was not beloved I will call 'beloved.'"
v. 26	". . . they shall be called children [lit., 'sons'] of the living God" (υἱοὶ Θεοῦ ζῶντος).
vv. 30-33	Righteousness comes from faith, not law. Law is linked with creation — it is part of the order of nature — but righteousness is linked with faith — it is part of the order of grace. Therefore, the Gentiles and Israel both are made righteous by faith.

If righteousness comes from belonging to the Mosaic covenant by circumcision and adherence to the Law, by definition it excludes the salvation of Gentiles, who are uncircumcised.[20] But Paul already has given his most heated

20. This goes for both Gentile men and women, all of whom are uncircumcised, although there is no clear evidence that Paul has Gentile women in mind. Given that circumcision

argument in Gal 3–4 as to why it cannot possibly be the case that the righteousness of God (δικαιοσύνη τοῦ Θεοῦ) derives from Law-observance. The Law is linked with nature and, in fact, embodies the order of creation, so in itself the Law is good. However, God's mercy goes even beyond this initial revelation. The Christ event has opened the creation to a reality beyond nature, the reality of grace where God rules alone, above the Law. The righteousness that comes by the faith of Jesus Christ participates in this reality of grace which transcends the natural order.

Hence, even the uncircumcised can be made righteous by the faith of Jesus Christ; and this fact of right relationship is made visible in their faith: for God "has mercy on whoever are chosen" (9:18). The faith of the Gentiles (men and women?) demonstrates that God's mercy has been poured out upon them, uncircumcised though they be, for God alone is the source of faith. The logical conclusion that Paul does not make explicit is that, likewise, the faith of women — whatever their ethnic origin — shows that God has chosen them for vessels of mercy, regardless of their exclusion from the covenant of circumcision.

One could continue with a further analysis of how Paul amplifies this case in Rom 10–11, but this review of chapter nine illustrates the major thrust of Paul's argument. Flesh is not the source of salvation, but rather its recipient. And the circumcised have no advantage over the uncircumcised in the covenant of the promise made manifest in Christ Jesus.

Paul concludes this section with a prayer praising the inscrutability of God's wisdom in overturning the traditional relations of power inherent in what some have called "the order of nature" or "the order of creation." From the mouth of a circumcised man, this is a fine appeal to *ethos* for the Gentile men in the audience.

Less noticeable, perhaps, is that the appeal functions in precisely the same way for the Christian women in Paul's audience. Paul's emphasis on the gracious act of God in "right-wising" believers, regardless of circumcision, could have been heard by the Roman women believers as validating their own faith-filled relationship in Christ as one of ultimate, salvific significance. Paul says nothing to dispute this conclusion; on the contrary, intentionally or not, he provides ample supporting evidence.

Still, one might wish that Paul had taken his argument to its logical conclusion. If he had, the argument would have looked something like this:

---

is exclusively a male rite, it is unlikely women are in Paul's range of vision at this point. If they were, he might have pointed out that, logically speaking, if righteousness is received by Law-observance and circumcision, this excludes the salvation even of Jewish women, who can no more be circumcised than their Gentile sisters — but Paul does not draw this conclusion.

v. 8	it is not the children of the flesh (τὰ τέκνα τῆς σαρκὸς) who are the children of God (τέκνα τοῦ Θεοῦ), but the children of the promise (τὰ τέκνα τῆς ἐπαγγελίας) who are counted as descendants
v. 16	So [election] depends not on human will or exertion, but on God who shows mercy
v. 18	God has mercy on whomever God chooses
v. 25	As indeed [God] says in Hosea, "Those who were not my people I will call 'my people' (Καλέσω . . . λαόν μου), and she who was not beloved I will call 'beloved.'"
v. 26	". . . they shall be called children of the living God" (υἱοὶ Θεοῦ ζῶντος).
vv. 30-33	Righteousness comes from faith, not law.
Therefore	Circumcision matters nothing. Whereas under the covenant of circumcision women could be saved only by affiliation with circumcised men, under the promise all women of faith are saved by grace through the faith of Christ. Regardless of their affiliation with a man, circumcised or not, women are saved AS WOMEN.

For a community with so many women church leaders, the implications of Paul's argument are of tremendous significance.

Just how are the Roman Christians to act on this reality of the transformation of nature by divine grace? Paul spells out these details in the final chapters of his letter. A look at the "opening gambit" in Rom 12:1-2 gives enough for his audience — whether ancient or contemporary — to work on for quite a while.

> I appeal to you therefore, brothers [and sisters], by the mercies of God, to present your bodies [whether circumcised or uncircumcised, branded or not, white or black, male or female] as a living sacrifice, holy and acceptable to God, which is your spiritual worship. Do not be conformed to this world, but be transformed by the renewing of your minds, so that you may discern what is the will of God — what is good and acceptable and perfect.

If one reads the ἀδελφοί in Rom 12:1 as exclusive ("brothers"), this is Paul's plea that the Roman men will sacrifice their whole lives to God, letting go of the worldly traditions and assumptions they held before coming to Christ —

including traditions of male privilege and the belief in male superiority — and putting on "the mind of Christ," who provided the ultimate example of humility (Phil 2:5-8).

If ἀδελφοί is read as inclusive ("brothers and sisters"), we hear a plea to the Roman women and men to take on the priestly role, offering their very selves — their *embodied* selves (τὰ σώματα ὑμῶν) as women and men — entirely to God. In the process, God will transform their minds, setting aside their past assumptions and leading them into true wisdom.

Whichever way one reads it, here is a vision of humanity transformed by divine grace that overcomes racial, class, and yes, even gender boundaries. Small wonder that Paul named it *euangelion.*

Justification as Good News for Women: A Re-reading of Romans 1–8

Elsa Tamez

Translated by Sheila E. McGinn

Traditionally justification by faith or the justice of God has been understood as pardon of sins and remission of guilt. If this affirmation is not situated in the concrete context of history, it makes no sense; and, if one does not use the necessary care concerning precisely *what* is the sin which God pardons, it easily may lead to an irresponsible position. For the sin which kills today is very tangible, as tangible as are the victims of sin. What one hopes for today is the manifestation of God's justice rather than God's forgiveness of the guilty. If we read the traditional, and I would argue, false understanding of justification from a feminist point of view, the result is even more problematic.

When one speaks of liberation from guilt, we typically understand this guilt to correspond to a real, criminal act. But this does not work with women. If we were to preach to them about justification as liberation from guilt, we should ask ourselves, for what are we blaming women? Of not wanting to be the woman that society defines? Of wanting to be persons with their own identities?

As we can see, women have been gratuitously condemned by society. They have not earned this condemnation, nor does it derive from any acts of in-

The foundations of the reflections in this article can be found in Elsa Tamez, "Justification by Faith," in *Dictionary of Feminist Theologies* (ed. Letty M. Russell & L. Shannon Clarkson; Louisville: Westminster John Knox, 1996); "Der Brief an die Gemeinde in Rom: Eine feministische Lektüre," 557-73 in *Kompendium Feministiche Bibelauslegung* (ed. Luise Schottroff and Marie-Theres Wacher; Gütersloh: Gütersloher Verlagshaus, 1998); and *The Amnesty of Grace* (Nashville: Abingdon, 1992).

justice on their part; it comes simply from the fact of being born a woman in a patriarchal society. The greatest injustice of society is to brand the innocent as guilty.

If we view justification from the perspective of liberation from sin and guilt, then we must admit that truly the "sin" characteristic of women is that of not transgressing their socially defined role as women. They have committed the "crime" of abdicating from the choice to be their own persons. So if woman is a "sinner" like the rest of humanity, *her* sin consists in not transgressing the second-class status assigned to her by society.

It is impossible, therefore, to speak of liberation from guilt and forgiveness of the sinner without analyzing this concrete reality. Justification by faith has to be understood in a deeper way that is grounded in an analysis of the sinful relationships of society.

Injustice and Sin

In Paul's theology of sin (ἁμαρτία) and the justice/righteousness of God (δικαιοσύνη τοῦ Θεοῦ, Rom 1–3), he does not explicitly mention the Roman Empire. He speaks of the impiety and injustice of people who hem in the truth with injustice (ἀδικία, Rom 1:18), and asserts that no one has been born with the capacity to do justice. But a study of the Roman situation from the perspective of those who are excluded immediately reveals the link between the power of sin and the socio-economic situation, as well as the contrast between the justice of God and the justice of the Empire; between divine grace which grants justice as a gift (in the face of the practical, human impossibility of realizing it) and the merit of status, riches and power that imbues Roman Imperial law.

It seems that Paul sees in the Roman imperial system an economic, political, and military power structure that is impossible to confront. This system of power therefore becomes a structure of sin that leads to death. Paul sees it as a system that presents itself in the guise of "protector" and "peacemaker" in the provinces, but which actually uses these appearances to cloak its practices of injustice. For Paul, this is pure idolatry, the absence or denial of God.

It is noteworthy that Paul uses the word "sin" (ἁμαρτία) in chapter three of Romans but not before then. In Rom 1–2 he speaks only of injustice (ἀδικία). For Paul, the practice of injustice by everyone has distorted the true understanding of God. This means even truth is hedged by injustice (1:18). Sin is the mark of a perverted society in which everyone is an accomplice, even if they do not wish to be. In Rom 1:18-32, Paul outlines the process of societal inversion in three movements: first, God makes himself known to humanity (1:19, 20); next, human beings distort that revelation (1:21, 23, 25); and finally, human beings act in ways which are totally inappropriate (1:21, 22, 24, 26, 27, 29-31).[1]

This lack of justice, the absence of the true God, leads Paul to a theology of sin as originating with Adam. The Roman Empire was neither the first nor the only experience of the domination of nations. For Paul, there must be something deeper, something intrinsic to humanity that ineluctably makes people responsible for the injustices which ensnare them. For, at any given moment, injustice gains autonomy and generates structures of social relations that are sinful, uncontrollable, and enslaving of all human beings.[2]

Paul does not perceive, in his own age, any justice that carries the stamp of truth. The Jews thought that by fulfilling the Law they were fulfilling true justice. Paul proves the contrary: Jews seek the justice demanded by the Law and the result is injustice (2:21-23). Sin even swallows up the Law which was graciously given by God (7:7-13).

Structural Sin of Patriarchal Society

Violence against women is the dark mark that delineates the perverse structure of a racist, patrikiriarchal society like the Roman Empire of the first century.[3] Likewise, violence against women is one of the most shameful realities of contemporary civilization. There is not one country, rich or poor, where one cannot find daily denunciations of physical, psychological, and sexual aggression against women of every age, race, and social class, but especially the poorest ones. Violence is systematic; it occurs at work, in school, in the street, and in the home. All women know the fear of being physically and sexually victimized in any of these circumstances. The deceptive division between private and public merely hides or relativizes this reality.

From women's testimonies we know that this physical, psychological and sexual aggression mars a woman's self-image and affects her profoundly, diminishing her humanity and self-esteem. Systematic violence against women

---

1. Unfortunately, Paul uses homosexuality — a common Jewish complaint against Gentiles — as an illustration of the inversion of society. In this he follows the traditional Jewish understanding of heterosexuality as normative.

2. Cf. Luise Schottroff, "Die Schreckensherrschaft der Sünde und die Befreiung durch Christus nach dem Römerbrief des Paulus," *Evangelische Theologie* 39 (1979): 496.

3. The term "patrikiriarchal" was coined by Elisabeth Schüssler Fiorenza in "Ties That Bind: Domestic Violence Against Women," *Voices From the Third World* 18, no. 1 (1995): 122-67; repr. in *Women Resisting Violence: Spirituality for Life* (ed. Mary-John Mananzan, et al.; Maryknoll: Orbis, 1996; see 44 in the latter.

frequently provokes an impotent fury which can be vented only on their children, who are even more fragile than they are. This spiral of violence, which turns the stronger against the weaker, manifests the monstrosity of the patriarchal system.

Structural sin permeates all of society and even the cosmos. In Paul's list in Rom 1:29-31, the emphasis is on evil as "the violation of proper relationships with others."[4] If violence is an expression of relationships of domination, this is most visible in the relationships between men and women, and in the violent ways that humans treat nature. Systematic violence is expressed in militarism, in domestic relations and in commercial structures. A detailed analysis of each one of these areas clearly reveals that women and girls are the primary victims. Given the realities of the feminization of poverty, the fight for survival, consumerism, and competition, violence deepens, ranging from its most sophisticated forms to the blatant murder of women and girls.

In this situation, neither the male aggressors, nor the women victims, nor society as a whole can reflect full humanity, since the victimizer himself is a victim of his own violence. And all of society is complicit in this sin precisely by refusing to recognize it and name it as sin.

What is needed to be free from this sin is a radical transformation of patriarchal, racist and sexist society. Salvation does not come from the enforcement of juridical legislation, even though this sometimes may prove to be helpful. We may recognize the advances of society in this respect yet, on the other hand, one must also acknowledge the increase in violence. Laws are manipulated to benefit those who have power and money. What is necessary is a radical conversion, which includes becoming conscious of sin itself and of our complicity in it as structurally-related individuals. One must have faith in the distinctly different logic of the inter-human male-female relationship, and must make a concrete commitment to live by the re-creative power of the Spirit. The pre-Pauline baptismal formula that appears in Gal 3:28 is a fundamental affirmation of the faith to live the new creation. "To believe whole-heartedly in justice and to confess with our mouth that Jesus reigns" (Rom 10:9-10) implies that both women and men confess, from the depths of our hearts, that in Christ there is no longer male nor female, master nor slave, Jew nor Greek nor barbarian (Gal 3:28; Col 3:11). Violence against girls and women of all ages is a manifestation of a sick society that is in need of divine healing, for "no one is just, not even one" (Rom 3:10); no human has the capacity to eliminate this structural sin.

4. Rosemary Radford Ruether, *Gaia y Dios. Una teología ecofeminista para la recuperatión de la tierra* (México: DEMAC, 1993), 139; trans. of *Gaia & God. An Ecofeminist Theology of Earth Healing* (San Francisco: HarperCollins, 1992).

The Justice of God v. the Justice of Patriarchal Society

The term "righteousness of God" (δικαιοσύνη τοῦ Θεοῦ) carries distinct connotations. It can be seen as forensic justice, as the manner in which God's justice has always acted in history, and as the justice which human beings are expected to practice. Despite these distinct connotations, all of them point toward the differences between this ideal of justice and the justice that first-century Christians actually experienced, whether in the realm of forensic or social justice. The reality of forensic justice was discrimination (e.g., penalties for a crime were different depending upon whether the accused was poor or rich). "Social justice" — equity among human persons — simply did not exist; human social relations were founded on the assumption of inequities and injustice.

According to Paul, there is neither an objective nor subjective possibility of doing true justice on one's own power in an unjust world dominated by sin (Rom 3:9-10). Thus, the proclamation of God's justice appears as great news (Rom 3:21).

Paul concludes that, given the precariousness of life and human inability to overcome the injustice of which it is a victim and for which it is responsible, the justice of God dignifies human beings and enables them to be makers of true justice. Jesus was the first just man and, through him, all have access to this grace, even the victimizers, if they are able to believe in the God who raises the dead — even dead women (cf. 4:24a). This faith in the impossible (cf. 4:19) fortifies them in the struggles and dangers of daily life (cf. 1 Cor 15:31a).

The actualization of God's justice in a patriarchal society consists in the egalitarian proposal of justification by faith rather than by fulfilling the demands of traditional patriarchal culture. It is a free gift, bestowed by grace, in a society which knows nothing of grace but rather uses merit alone to determine whether or not a person has value. The logic of merit is the natural way our hierarchical, patriarchal society functions. It is society's way of judging, the "justice" proper to it.

Women's testimonies show that they strive to be loved and, therefore, they try to fulfill all of the obligations that society imposes upon them. Despite these efforts, however, they are not loved. A woman experiences insatiable demands to make herself worthy: she is overworked in domestic labor, overtaxed in the bed, over-exploited at work, besides the demand of caring for herself in order to be acceptable to others. Through the mass media, she imbibes excessive demands to consume, to fulfill herself as a woman, a modern housewife. If she does not comply with these societal demands, she meets with punishment, recriminations, and even physical and psychological violence. Hence women are not free persons, nor do they feel free.

The justice of God is diametrically opposed to all this. First of all, it follows the logic of grace. Women do not resort to "bargaining for their humanity," accumulating economic, cultural, or social merit in order to be seen as persons. Through grace, all are seen as equal persons who deserve respect amid all their differences. Women are loved by God "just because," nothing more, as a gift that is offered time and time again, without exception. No one is excluded from the justice of God which manifests itself in mercy for crucified women, as it is seen in the passion of Jesus Christ and in his vindication through the resurrection. In the justice of God, there is no demand for useless sacrifices by women. The good news is that the Crucified One is risen. The justice of God is verified in this act of the resurrection.

When one acknowledges the structural sin of patriarchal society, women are freed of false guilt and feel challenged to face daily, social life in accord with the wisdom of grace rather than according to the slave identity that society assigns to them.

From the Christian canon, Christian women see the justice of God revealed in history in the Jew, Jesus Messiah, who lived a life of faith according to the logic of grace in favor of all those who suffer discrimination. The liberation gained in Jesus Christ is the freedom to live according to this grace, in opposition to the slavery of which women are victims through the very laws of patriarchal society.

When women accept themselves as free persons, because the justice of God accepts them precisely as women, they become responsible for their own consciences. They are then capable of transgressing any law that diminishes their lives, for they realize that they have been justified by their attitude of faith, like that of Jesus, and not by following the strictures of a patriarchal society.

Since the justice of God is for all people, not only for women, men also can acknowledge this justice and be guided by a logic contrary to the violence generated by patriarchal society. Justification is a gift meant for all, not just for women. The justice of God is a firm guarantee that the sinful logic of misogynist patriarchal structures is overthrown by divine grace.

Traditionally Christians have believed that one is justified by faith in Jesus Christ (διὰ πίστεως ᾽Ιησοῦ Χρίστου, 3:22) through his death on the cross. Another possible translation is that one is justified by the faith of Jesus Christ — that is to say, his life of faith as manifested in his works of justice in Palestine. Jesus himself was not guided by blind obedience to the law — which one might call an imperialism of the law — when it harmed the life of human persons. Regardless of the law, Jesus followed the way that led him to actualize the message of the Kingdom of God impregnated with grace.

God justified Jesus because of his ministry of justice. That Jesus was raised is evidence that he was justified by God, confuting the judicial system which condemned him in accordance with Roman and Jewish law.

Paul, in Rom 5:12-21, contrasts Adam and Jesus Christ as the two protagonists who inaugurated distinct eras. They are the prototypes of the old and the new humanity. While it is true that they were both male, Paul at least does not make this an opportunity to reinforce the common thought of patriarchal society that Eve was responsible for introducing sin into the world because she induced Adam to eat of the forbidden fruit. Paul's concern in this text is to show the superiority of the new era inaugurated by Jesus Christ, the second Adam. The first Adam (of whom all humanity is part) leads to death, condemnation and sin; the second Adam (of whom all humanity also is part, by grace) leads to life, grace, justice. For women who struggle to confute the ideology of patriarchal society, ensconced as it is in ancient tradition, it is fundamental to stress what a *kairos* this is, the "newness" of this time when interpersonal relations can take place within the sphere of justice and grace.[5]

From Sacrificial Theology to the Theology of Praxis and Grace

In recent years feminist and liberation theologies have argued against a sacrificial theology.[6] In Christian tradition, the most noticeable values of this sacrificial theology are similar to the ones that patriarchal society requires of women: sacrifice, suffering, abnegation, and willing acceptance of hardships. Moreover, to speak of God as one who sends his innocent son to die on the cross has a parallel in the abuse of paternal authority in regard to sons and daughters. Clearly the sacrificial metaphor concerning God the Father and the sacrifice of the Son is elaborated within the patterns which characterize patriarchal society.

A reading of the theological tradition from the perspective of grace as outlined in Romans also excludes the theory of penal satisfaction (developed by Anselm of Canterbury) which maintains that, in order to satisfy divine justice and obtain pardon for sins, it was necessary for God to violently sacrifice his Son. In such a view, the crucifixion was the necessary work of redemption in

---

5. See Letty Russell, *Household of Freedom: Authority in Feminist Theology* (Philadelphia: Westminster, 1987), 18, on her "appeal to the future."

6. Cf. Joanne Carlson Brown and Carol R. Bohn, eds., *Christianity, Patriarchy and Abuse: A Feminist Critique* (New York: Pilgrim, 1989); Hugo Assmann, ed., *Sobre ídolos y sacrificios, René Girard con teólogos de la liberación* (San Jose: DEI, 1991). [Editor's note: Cf. also Robert Jewett's work on this topic, esp. his book with John Shelton Lawrence, *The Myth of the American Superhero* (Grand Rapids, Mich.: Eerdmans, 2002).]

order to pay off a debt that humanity owed to God because of its sinful offenses. In Romans, however, justification has its roots in the gracious solidarity of the Triune God with the outcasts of history. Therefore, God cannot at the same time demand the shedding of the blood of the Outcast *par excellence,* "the stone which the builders rejected" (1 Pet 2:7), to reconcile the world both with God and with itself. The tradition has placed such an overemphasis on the sacrifice of Christ, his shedding of blood on the cross, that this later reading has totally subsumed the actual facts of the historical event of Jesus' condemnation on the Cross by the Roman Empire.

The epistle uses some pre-Pauline formulas that mention Jesus' bloody death. However, Paul does not stop there but conjoins justification with the resurrection. In 4:25 we read "he was handed over for our sins [pre-Pauline formula], *and raised for our justification* [Pauline redaction]."

Romans 3:24-26a is a pre-Pauline, cultic fragment, possibly known in the primitive communities, which recalls the liberating function of Christ and the pardon of sins.[7] This fragment annuls the saving character of the Jewish Law. Perhaps this was a soteriological tradition which originated among the Hellenists at Antioch who proclaimed Jesus as reconciler, holding in mind not only the tradition of Lev 16 but also the annual celebration of the Day of Atonement in the Temple at Jerusalem. Jesus is presented as ἱλαστήριον — a difficult and extensively-debated term — both place of sacrifice and sacrificial victim at the same time, God himself expiating, once and forever, the sins of all humanity. In this way, the expiatory function of the Temple priests is annulled, and with it the ritual law. Salvation extends to all the nations. Paul uses ἱλαστήριον simply as a sacrificial image without specific reference to the life and work of Jesus the Messiah. It is a parable.

The Paschal faith sees in the death and resurrection of Jesus the end of ritual sacrifices required by the Mosaic Law for pardon of sins. It invalidates the sacrifices, the Law which requires them, and the centrality of the Temple with its system of priests as mediators who administer pardon. With the world and humanity described in this way as a dead end, the Good News of the justice of God is not that God pardons sinners through the blood of his Son, but rather that God offers the opportunity to transform this upside-down world — which excludes those who are discriminated against because of their gender, race or class — by raising up the One who was condemned for his practice of justice. The ultimate intention of God's justice is not to pardon sin, but rather to remake human creatures into worthy subjects capable of transforming a world

---

7. Cf. Peter Stuhlmacher, "Zur neueren Exegese von Rom 3.24-26," 117-35 in *Versöhnung, Gesetz und Gerechtigkeit* (Göttingen: Vandenhoeck & Ruprecht, 1981), 134.

inverted by sin. Therefore, God "does not count their sins against them." (This fact also is good news since "the wages of sin is death," 6:23.) In this way God manifests divine mercy and patience. The cultic-sacrificial key to reading the letter to the Romans is not a viable option for feminist theology.

Women reject the notion of sacrificial love and self-abnegation because these values are imposed upon them by the ideology of the dominant society. These duties are laws from which women seek liberation without any feelings of guilt. Therefore, to speak to them of the grace of God is a liberating message for women. In the first case, grace opposes any laws that require a person to earn human rights or dignity. Secondly, for those persons transformed by the justice of God, the praxis of justice is not required as if it were another enslaving law. Rather, since such a praxis follows the logic of grace, it erupts spontaneously, not out of obligation but from consciousness and from the heart, which seek to demonstrate "the love of God [which] is shed abroad out in our hearts by the Holy Spirit" (5:5). Finally, grace offers a space for the freedom to live together and share concrete, daily life with its celebrations. The old concern for efficacy or the practice of justice by being a "superwoman" no longer predominates in the arena of grace. One recognizes one's limitations as a human being, heir to the corrupt nature of Adam, but one also holds on to the faith conviction that "where sin abounds, grace abounds even more."

Women Faced with the Logic of Law and the Logic of Faith in the Context of Exclusion

Both Paul's letter to the Romans and the one to the Galatians specify that God makes men and women just by faith and not by the works of the law. In this way and others, Paul makes a radical critique of the Mosaic Law and circumcision. This critique, and other statements directed against the Jews in the gospels, has generated and legitimated anti-Jewish attitudes throughout history, to totally irrational ends. For this reason, and because of advances in the study of rhetoric and of our knowledge of first-century Judaism, exegesis of the "Second Testament," for many years now, has been very careful in its affirmations concerning the Jews — and rightly so.

We cannot deny that Paul criticizes the Law and those who seek to impose it, attaching to it a salvific character. However, Paul is a Jew and he is making a self-critique of blind obedience to the Law. He does not reject the Law out of hand, but rather relativizes it as a real option for transforming the world of sin in which "truth has been imprisoned by injustice." He considers himself obliged to seek and demonstrate a much stronger force which is able to make possible the realization of justice on earth. This force is grace, faith manifested in Jesus the Messiah and actualized in human beings who are re-created to fashion new relationships: among humans, with the cosmos, and with God. What interests Paul, a Jew, is to achieve reconciliation between the Jewish and non-Jewish worlds. He puts them on the same level: both are sinners, and both have access to grace. All men and women are sons and daughters of Abraham and Sarah, not only the descendants of Sarah and Abraham according to the flesh. Faith, not law, is what allows the possibility of a break with inequalities. Law, on the contrary, does not guarantee equality; it marks off distances, and it is always open to manipulation.

This affirmation of transformation extends as well to male-female relations. The Jewish Law, including circumcision and other regulations, marks differences between men and women — just like the ones that occur in Roman Law when it refers to women and their social status. These precepts of both worlds make the structures of exclusion in patriarchal society function. The dimension of faith, on the other hand, transcends the conditioning factors of the law and makes possible the full inclusion of those in the community who, by law, are excluded (Gal 3:28). Faith encompasses a way of looking at the world where discernment on behalf of life takes priority over mere law and tradition.

The rite of baptism symbolizes the new creation (Rom 6:11), and it does not include circumcision (a physical mark that is exclusively masculine) as an obligation. In the new creation all women and men, persons, communities and cultures share the same rights. Baptism symbolizes death to the sin of patriarchal society unto the new life manifested in new inter-personal relations, according to the will of God, Who is the woman-friend who reconciles us to Herself and all creation. She is the one who unites us as sisters and brothers by manifesting herself as mother of all. The terms "mother" and "woman-friend," used here for God, are correlatives to the terms "father" and "man-friend" which are used by Paul.

Discrimination has no place in the arena of faith. If Paul is critical of the "Judaizers" who wish to impose the law and the Jewish practice of circumcision on those of other cultures, he is likewise very critical of Gentile Christians who discriminate against those of other cultures — like Jews (Rom 11:16-24; 14:1–15:13). All this throws into relief the problem of law itself as something that excludes other peoples and individuals.

Still, Paul goes even further. By contrasting law with faith and grace, Paul finds in all types of law, whether judicial or "invisible" — like the law or logic of tradition, institutions, culture, and dogma — a very harmful regimen because it interferes with the exercise of discernment.[8] It regulates itself and imposes it-

---

8. Cf. the critique of the law in Franz Hinkelammert in *La fe de Abraham y el Edipo Occidental* (San José: DEI, 1989).

self on the lives of individuals, without leaving any room for grace. Paul criticizes this law, and contrasts it with "the law of the Spirit," a different logic of grace and faith. Paul does not reject the Mosaic Law; he considers it just, good, and holy in its intentions (Rom 7:12). Rather, he criticizes the mechanism of any law, including the Mosaic Law, which insists on governing all by itself. In modern terms, he is talking about imperialism of law. The Mosaic Law, just like any other law, is vulnerable to being all too easily absorbed into the service of structural sin (7:8). The problem is not with the law itself, but with sin that manifests itself through the regimen of law which, leaving no room for human discernment, produces death.

The tendency of sin is death, and the tendency of grace or faith is life (Rom 8:6). The Mosaic Law could be influenced either by sin or for grace. When one is oriented toward grace, it becomes the "law" of God, "the Law of the Spirit." Faith, says Paul, does not invalidate the law, but rather frees it. Regardless of restraints that might be put upon the law, when it is absorbed by sin the law itself is transformed into something that can manifest the sin that leads to death.

For feminist theology, the patriarchal paradigm consists in the fulfillment of the law that "only provides knowledge of sin" (Rom 3:20), that makes possible the living reality of sin (7:8-9). More specifically, it is the fulfillment of a traditional and macho culture when every institution functions according to the patriarchal-juridical ideology.

To receive the gift of "justification by faith and not by the law" implies adhering to a paradigm different from that of the "patriarchal" law of sin and death. The good news for justified men and women who embrace faith as a new way of life, just like the faith of Jesus Christ, is a new awareness of being free women and men, and the realization that in faith it is possible to transform society where sin reigns in the structures opposed to woman. By faith we affirm that, although we live in a world riddled with sinfulness and impregnated with sexism, this reality does not dominate those who are guided by the logic of grace: "you are no longer under law, but under grace" (6:14).

Faith in the Resurrection of the Body

Abraham is an exemplary friend of God because of his faith that God "can create life out of death and call into being things that do not yet exist" (Rom 4:17). Our ancestors in the faith, Abraham — and also Sarah — believed that out of Abraham's impotent body and Sarah's sterile and worn-out bosom could emerge a new life. Abraham and Sarah were justified because they believed what was impossible according to human logic and laws, but not according to the logic of God.

To have faith means to believe that God raised up the body of the innocent, crucified victim, condemned by the law that makes patriarchal society function. The body of the Crucified is actualized today in the bodies of women who are beaten, violated, tortured. It is not actualized in order to legitimize such victimization, but rather to create solidarity with victimized women and to resuscitate them. According to feminist theology, it is crucial to stress "the resurrection of the body" in order to vanquish the evil, patriarchal dualism which despises matter and emotion (identified with woman) and privileges the soul and intellect (identified with man).

It may be that Paul contrasts Spirit and flesh because of some influence from the dualistic anthropology of Platonic tradition.[9] But the significance of this Spirit/flesh contrast for Paul is not at all connected with a dualism which deprecates the body. Spirit (πνεῦμα) is the arena and the power where life and peace abound; men and women can act within this dynamic space. Flesh (σάρξ) is the arena and force which tends toward sin and death, which God rejects. This is where men and women can conduct themselves according to the logic of the flesh. But, thanks to the Spirit which abides in each woman and man, the bodies of women and men are clothed and vivified. Women and men guided by the Spirit are converted into sisters and brothers through divine adoption (8:14-17). Paul here is proclaiming a new kind of interpersonal relations permeated with solidarity. In this new humanity there is no gender which can be considered inferior.

Even now, according to Paul, one lives this experience in faith, since the new creation, although inaugurated with Jesus Christ, is yet to come in its fullness. The dimension of grace is present but sin remains, manifested in and through patriarchal society. As a result, systematic violence and discrimination continue. The difference is that now one believes with faith and hope in the real possibility of a new creation, including humanity and the entire cosmos. This faith in the resurrection of the body is the power which helps to resist present sufferings and to struggle for "the revelation of the sons and daughters of God" (Rom 8:18). The entire creation, says Paul, wails as a woman with labor pains, hoping anxiously for liberation. Paul also applies this figure of the woman in labor to himself in Gal 4:19. Our own groaning (στενάζομεν) and the groaning (στεναγμοῖς) of the Spirit are united to the groaning (συστενάζει) of the creation in a concerted prayer to God for the resurrection of the body.

Here, then, new interpersonal relations between men and women,

9. Esperanza Bautista, *La mujer en la Iglisia primitiva* (Madrid: Verbo divino, 1993), 138.

women and women, men and men are proclaimed, if we avail ourselves of the gift of faith through our own faith and praxis. We must believe that the violence against the bodies of women and girls of all ages will end. But this is possible not simply because we vehemently affirm it but because we commit ourselves henceforth to announce the good news of the liberation of woman, to practice new interpersonal relations in a daily life oriented toward grace, and to affirm with faith the revival of the suffering bodies of women. This means that "we make our members weapons of justice for the service of God, like dead women raised back to life" (cf. 6:13). To this end, we women proclaim ourselves opposed to all condemnation (Rom 8:34-39).

"She Will Be Called an Adulteress . . .":
Marriage and Adultery Analogies in Romans 7:1-4

Pamela Thimmes

[7:1] *Do you not know, brothers and sisters — for I am speaking to those who know the law — that the law is binding on a person only during that person's lifetime?* [2] *Thus a married woman is bound by the law to her husband as long as he lives; but if her husband dies, she is discharged from the law concerning the husband.* [3] *Accordingly, she will be called an adulteress if she lives with another man while her husband is alive. But if her husband dies, she is free from that law, and if she marries another man, she is not an adulteress.* [4] *In the same way, my friends, you have died to the law through the body of Christ, so that you may belong to another, to him who has been raised from the dead in order that we may bear fruit for God.*

Several years ago Robert Jewett set out, explicitly, to read Paul through the lenses of North American culture.[1] This might seem an obvious task for an American scholar, but why was it necessary for Jewett to be explicit about his social location? The answer, as he demonstrates, is just as obvious: the majority of Pauline scholarship has advanced a Eurocentric reading of Paul (and I would add, a *male* Eurocentric reading), providing a history of scholarship that reads Paul as an "Apostle to the Europeans."[2]

One of the readings Jewett offers in *Paul the Apostle to America* is of

---

1. Robert Jewett, *Paul the Apostle to America: Cultural Trends and Pauline Scholarship* (Louisville: Westminster John Knox, 1994).
2. Ibid., x.

Romans 7:5-8, where he finds that the heart of Paul's argument about the law can be related to the conformity issues (including conformity to non-conformity) that hold contemporary Americans captive.[3] And, as he sees it, such conformity is illustrated in covetousness (Paul's term in 7:8) as manifested in expressions of aggression, control, and rituals of consumption, all of which indicate self-centeredness.[4]

Jewett's reading of Romans 7 does put a different interpretive strategy into play. Reading Paul within a framework of an explicitly American praxis adds a new dimension to the standard readings of this chapter. On the other hand, a history of interpretation of Romans 7 according to traditional interpretive models yields scores of monographs and hundreds of articles mostly concerned (and consumed) with specific (and often unanswerable) questions of *Law*.[5] Clearly, Romans 6:15 onward begs for clarification of what law means to Paul, which law is meant, and the role of law in the Christian life. However, most of these "law" readings ignore the contemporary implications of the analogies Paul uses to speak of his understanding of law.

This essay is concerned only with Romans 7:1-4, the marriage and adultery analogy that launches Paul into a later, long discussion of the law. Here, the interest is on the analogy, what Paul's use of this analogy tells us about him and his audience, and the implications of this analogy for contemporary readers and preachers.

The adage, "what you see depends on where you stand," is as appropriate to methodological issues as it is to the act of writing, reading strategies and interpretation. I agree with Jewett, social location is important and, to that end, my reading of this text comes from a specific social-political framework. As a single, North American woman, an academic, active and struggling in particular communities of faith, I am concerned about the ways the Bible has been used and continues to be used to silence, marginalize, (mis)represent, and stereotype women. So, this text raises a number of questions: about Paul's audience, about the choice and use of the marriage/adultery analogy in his rhetorical scheme, and about how contemporary readers hear and understand this text. Pursuant to these questions, I will examine the following areas: a brief history of interpretation of the text, analogies and their use, marriage and adultery as subjects of an analogy, implications this text might have had for women in the community at Rome, and the significance of this passage for contemporary communities of faith.

---

3. Ibid., "Discharged from the Law of Consumerism," 87-97.

4. Ibid., 91-93.

5. For a recent survey of Paul and the Law see Calvin J. Roetzel, "Paul and the Law: Whence and Whither?" *Currents in Research: Biblical Studies* 3 (1995): 249-75.

History of Interpretation

Except for a few studies, Romans 7:1-4 has generally been ignored or glossed by commentators, although the remainder of the chapter has been the subject of immense scrutiny. Those who do linger on the first few verses expend great effort making sense (or trying to make sense) of Paul's analogy and some, wittingly or unwittingly, turn the analogy into an allegory. Interpretive problems arise because in 7:1-3 Paul lays out an analogy with what appears to be direct, one-to-one correspondences (law is to husband; adulteress is to law-breaker) and *quid pro quo* applications of marriage laws (dead husband yields married woman freed from commitment; free woman who marries yields a wife under the law [and her husband]). In 7:4, though, Paul attempts to introduce the example of the Christian believer into the analogy about marriage and adultery laws, offering a practical application for the analogy in 7:1-3, but rupturing the earlier analogy introduced in Rom 1–3: according to Paul, Christians have died to the law and now belong to Christ, explicitly through the death of Christ. Paul's point in 7:1-2 is that the law is binding on humans only during their lifetime, so when a husband dies, the woman is released from the law that bound her to her husband. How can the dead husband, who seemingly was equated to the bounds of the law in 7:2, also be equated with the believer who has died to the law in 7:4? Paul's analogy breaks down in what seems an awkward attempt to equate the believer (who does not literally "die") with the husband (who does die), and whose death frees the woman from marriage laws. In addition, the analogy does not work on the applied level because the believer is not the one who controls and arbitrates the law to which he/she dies, as the husband controls his wife through the marriage laws.

For interpreters from John Chrysostom, to John Calvin, to contemporary scholars, Paul's tortured or inept analogy has proven an exercise in close reading and creative interpretation. The majority of commentators read Paul's analogy in terms of a one-to-one correspondence: the *law dies* just as the *husband dies*. These readings persist even though Paul never says the law *dies*. Instead, Paul speaks about the husband's death and the believer's death *through the body of Christ*, but even here, there is no actual correspondence between dead husband and metaphorically dead believer.

At the end of the nineteenth century, William Sanday and A. C. Headlam offered a quasi-psychological interpretation, reading the wife as the believer's "self" while the husband represented the pre-conversion "self," whose death in/with the crucified Christ was death to the old "self."[6] Käsemann and others

---

6. John D. Earnshaw, "Reconsidering Paul's Marriage Analogy in Romans 7:1-4," *New*

also have offered psychologizing interpretations of Romans 7, taking their lead from the opening analogy, but utilizing these readings to draw sharp (I would add, imagined and flawed) distinctions between Judaism and the Law as the antithesis of Christianity and faith.[7]

Unique interpretations also abound, like that of R. C. R. Lenski who finds no confusion in Paul's analogy.[8] Rather, he finds Paul's articulation useful, purposeful, and the best example he could use to illustrate his point, suggesting that Paul's choice reflects the spiritual reality that he wants to highlight.[9] John Paul Heil offers a reader-response interpretation of Romans but never considers which literary device Paul uses (analogy? allegory? illustration?). Instead, Heil is interested in supporting Paul's use of topic — laws governing marriage as illustrative of the law under whose domination Christians no longer labor.[10]

Heikki Räisänen, C. H. Dodd, and Nils Dahl, on the other hand, suggest that Paul's analogy simply does not work and that efforts to rehabilitate it are impossible because of its incoherence, confusing articulation, and internal contradictions.[11] Luke Timothy Johnson succinctly comments that the analogy "limps, because Paul gets the relations confused."[12] C. E. B. Cranfield sees such negative interpretations as an affront to Paul's intellectual and rhetorical abilities. He uses a philological and textual argument to suggest that reading these verses as an analogy or an allegory is a misunderstanding of Paul's attempt to provide instead an *example* or an *instance* to the community.[13] Joseph Fitzmyer, attempting to comment on form (analogy) but concentrate on subject (law), sees 7:1-4 as an example of two arguments: the first argument (7:1, 4a) posits that the law binds only the living,

---

Testament Studies 40 (1994): 69; Earnshaw is summarizing the work of William Sanday and A. C. Headlam, from their commentary *The Epistle to the Romans* (*International Critical Commentary;* New York: Charles Scribner's Sons, 1896), 171-73.

7. See Stowers' discussion of this in Stanley K. Stowers, *Rereading of Romans: Justice, Jews & Gentiles* (New Haven: Yale University Press, 1994), 258; and Ernst Käsemann, *Commentary on Romans* (trans. G. W. Bromiley; Grand Rapids, Mich.: Eerdmans, 1980), 195.

8. R. C. R. Lenski, *The Interpretation of St. Paul's Epistle to the Romans* (Columbus: Wartburg, 1945), 743-44.

9. Cited in Andrzej Gieniusz, "Rom 7.1-6: Lack of Imagination? Function of the Passage in the Argumentation of Rom 6.1–7.6," *Biblica* 74, no. 3 (1993): 389.

10. John Paul Heil, *Paul's Letter to the Romans: A Reader-Response Commentary* (New York: Paulist, 1987), 73.

11. See the discussion of these positions in Earnshaw, "Reconsidering," 69.

12. Luke Timothy Johnson, *Reading Romans: A Literary and Theological Commentary* (New York: Crossroad, 1997), 106.

13. C. E. B. Cranfield, *The Epistle to the Romans,* Vol. 1 (*International Critical Commentary;* Edinburgh: T & T Clark, 1975), 334-35.

and the second argument (7:2, 3, 4b) "is only an illustration of the first, and not a perfect one at that."[14]

Over the last two decades, three scholars have provided longer studies of Paul's analogy, and each offers a reading that attempts to "save the analogy as analogy" (or in one case, the *exemplum*), while at the same time defending Paul's rhetorical skills. In the first study, Joyce Little notes that Paul frequently used analogies in his letters, and although 7:1-6 is an example of an analogy, she acknowledges it is not one of his clearer ones.[15] However, she suggests that Paul frequently uses *sequential* rather than *integrative* thought in his arguments,[16] and the analogy in 7:1-6 is an example of Paul's sequential thinking in an analogical framework of three parts: the role of the law prior to the coming of Christ, the role that death plays in changing one's relationship to the law, and the role that death to the law plays in the new life of the Spirit.[17] Her argument is a specific response to Dodd's assertion that Paul "lacks the gift for sustained illustration of ideas through concrete images. . . . It is probably a defect of imagination."[18] Instead, Little suggests that the analogy is difficult to understand because Paul suffers "if anything, an excess of imagination which propels him through the above-noted succession of ideas so rapidly that he has neither the time nor the opportunity to bring his images to completion."[19] Little wants to have it both ways (ironically, she accuses Paul of the same thing).[20] She wants to read 7:1-6 as an analogy but at the same time say it does not work as such.

The second study by Andrzej Gieniusz[21] gives attention to the "surface of the text"[22] or Paul's rhetorical design, while asking if 7:1-6 can be linked to Paul's argument beginning in Romans 6:1. Noting that Paul uses other analogies that seem odd or awkward (e.g., the olive tree in Rom 11:17-24), Gieniusz suggests that Romans 7:1-6 displays all of the characteristics of the *peroratio* (epilogue) of the *dispositio rhetorica*, which would systematically and schemati-

---

14. Joseph Fitzmyer, *Romans: A New Translation with Introduction and Commentary* (Anchor Bible 33; New York: Doubleday, 1993), 455.

15. Joyce A. Little, "Paul's Use of Analogy: A Structural Analysis of Romans 7:1-6," *Catholic Biblical Quarterly* 46, no. 1 (1984): 82-90.

16. Ibid., 88.

17. Little, "Paul's Use of Analogy," 90.

18. C. H. Dodd, *The Epistle of Paul to the Romans* (New York: Harper, 1932), 103.

19. Ibid., 90.

20. "[H]e wishes to employ the analogy in two directions at once, both backward in relation to v. 1 and forward in relation to the rest of the pericope. To put the matter analogically, he is trying to burn the candle at both ends simultaneously, and it is by no means clear that such a procedure can be carried out in a neat and tidy fashion." Ibid., 90.

21. Gieniusz, "Rom 7.1-6," 389-400.

22. Ibid., 389.

cally "recapitulate the themes dealt with in the preceding argumentation (ἀνακεφαλαίωσις) in order to attract both the consent and emotional involvement of the listeners."[23] He suggests that the form of Paul's argument, using the marriage/spousal image, is an *exemplum* (παράδειγμα) that represents for the Christian both past and present, consequences and obligations. In the end though, Gieniusz has to admit that even as *exemplum* it is incompatible with the announcement in 7:1.

> [T]he Apostle can permit this incongruity because freedom from the law is not the point of his demonstration and he cannot avoid it because of the absolute and paradoxical novelty of the Christian experience which contradicts any comparison and escapes any illustration. In this sense the partial bankruptcy of the *exemplum* could be an invitation addressed to the reader to become also a sharer in the fascination of the *kainotês*. . . .[24]

Gieniusz' conclusion is flawed in two respects: (1) freedom from the law is the central point of not only the analogy but also of Romans 7:1c, "that the law is binding on a person only during that person's lifetime"; and (2) the claim that Christian experience is incapable of being illustrated (regardless of the device used: analogy, allegory or *exemplum,* etc.) undercuts Gieniusz' argument about Paul's rhetorical scheme, and calls into question a good deal of Paul's technique used throughout his letters. How does any writer, preacher or teacher call individuals to a new experience or a new understanding without using examples and comparisons based in the hearer's experience?

At the outset of the third study, John Earnshaw[25] indicates the perplexing nature of 7:1-4, and illustrates such with comments from Stephen Westerholm that Paul's analogy "is not the most perspicuous in the literature,"[26] and A. T. Robinson's statement that the details of the analogy become "more difficult the more you inspect them."[27]

Arguing that 7:1-4 is an analogy, and that the "law" discussed is the Mosaic Law, Earnshaw is primarily interested in the theological application of the analogy. Simply put, his thesis is "that Paul's marriage analogy is properly understood only when *the wife's first marriage is viewed as illustrating the believer's*

---

23. Ibid., 400.

24. Ibid., 400.

25. Earnshaw, "Reconsidering," 68.

26. Ibid., 68; quoting Stephen Westerholm, *Israel's Law and the Church's Faith* (Grand Rapids, Mich.: Eerdmans, 1988), 206.

27. Ibid.; quoting A. T. Robinson, *Wrestling with Romans* (Philadelphia: Westminster, 1979), 77.

union with Christ in his death and her second marriage is viewed as illustrating the believer's union with Christ in his resurrection."[28] Through the use of ten interlocking points of correspondence,[29] Earnshaw argues that the only way to understand these verses and to see them as a functioning analogy is to understand that Paul has constructed his analogy based on the premise of a "participationist soteriology," in which the wife's marriages (first and second) correspond to the believer's union with Christ first in death and second in resurrection.[30]

In order to reach this conclusion Earnshaw spends most of the article illustrating his understanding of the correspondence of the marriage law with the Mosaic Law (*contra* most commentators who read a correspondence between the first husband and the law). His argument, though wide-ranging, deals principally with an understanding of ὕπανδρος as meaning, simply, "married." He suggests that the traditional translations of the term ("under a man," "to be or come under a man," "being legally bound") have been the pivotal point of misunderstanding and misinterpreting the analogy, because "it has caused interpreters to view the first husband as being in a role of authority over his wife, making the correspondence between the first husband and the Mosaic law irresistible. Once this first step is made, however, no amount of ingenuity can rescue the analogy."[31]

Earnshaw's careful alignment of "appropriate" correspondences does allow 7:1-4 to function as an analogy. However, his discussion of ὕπανδρος raises more questions than it answers. Ὕπανδρος is not a value-neutral term, as he pretends. His careful lexical study does not deal successfully with either the sociological underpinnings or the implications of the term for the community to whom Paul writes. Instead, Earnshaw seems intent on two outcomes: to read the text as an analogy and to imply that terms like marriage (and I add, adultery) are value-neutral, and if read "properly" serve to allow Paul's analogy to function as such. In practice, terms concerned with relationships (personal, social, political, religious) are not value-neutral. Instead, they frequently are connected with boundary control and group values.[32]

---

28. Ibid., 72.

29. Ibid., 72-73.

30. Ibid., 88.

31. Ibid., 78.

32. For example, B. Bernstein, "Social Class, Language and Socialization," in *Language and Social Context: Selected Readings* (ed. P. Giglioli; Hammondsworth: Penguin Books, 1972), 158-71.

Analogies

Commentators on Romans acknowledge that Paul uses analogies, sometimes clearly and effectively, other times not. Students in the Greco-Roman world were schooled in the use of literary devices, the persuasive capacity of language, the order inherent in a well-crafted text/oration, and the aesthetic pleasure provided by a melodious phrase. Rhetoric and literature were accountable to basic, critical requirements: to educate, to entertain, and to please.[33] How one used the language determined whether the critical requirements were fulfilled and whether the speech was successful.

Within this rhetorical and literary framework, the analogy is a common literary device and works only when the hearers/readers find some degree of similarity between one thing or process and another that is said to compare, correspond or share equivalency or proportion. The term *analogy* comes from the Greek phrase ἀνὰ λόγον, meaning "according to a ratio." Terms and phrases like "proportional relationship," "equivalency," "similarity," "likeness of relations," or "functional equivalency" are commonly used to explain how an analogy works.

Analogies build idea-bridges and transfer connections from a familiar concept to an unfamiliar one that was not apparent before the connection was made. In other words, the analogy is a reasoning strategy that allows the alignment of new and related elements. To be effective, the subject of the analogy and its object must share common properties, a structure that coheres and corresponds, and provide new information or specific information that allows immediate connections to be made. In fact, effective analogies not only allow comparisons and parallels to be seen in a new light, but also they can be a source of inspiration, allowing the hearer/reader to move beyond the corresponding elements and observe the same or different equivalencies in other new ways. However, as the history of interpretation of Romans 7:1-4 demonstrates, if the analogy is not clear — if the elements are not aligned in such a way that the hearer/reader immediately connects the appropriate elements — it breaks down, fails to build the idea-bridge, hindering communication and creating the possibility of misunderstanding.

Language and linguistic devices, then, are more than non-material tools. Both require a closer look at social context and social systems because language

---

33. Aristotle, *Poetics,* 47-66 in *Critical Theory Since Plato* (ed. H. Adams; New York: Harcourt Brace Jovanovich, 1971); *The 'Art' of Rhetoric* (trans. J. H. Freese; *Loeb Classical Library* 22; Cambridge, Mass.: Harvard University Press, 1982); Longinus, "On the Sublime," 76-92 in *Critical Theory Since Plato.*

is a function of social arrangements. Keys to understanding both social context and social systems are carried and transmitted in and by the linguistic codes, the communicative conventions used. Language socializes individuals and communities into particular symbolic and metaphoric worlds within which meaning is made, worlds are created, and boundaries erected and maintained. Lexical choice and speech forms, then, are indicators of self-definition, social and cultural values and prescribed (and inscribed) social arrangements. In this sense Clifford Geertz' theory of *culture as text* is read back as *text as culture*, and the circle is constantly repeated.[34]

Barnes and Duncan argue "writing is constitutive, not simply reflective; new worlds are made out of old texts, and old worlds are the basis of new texts."[35] Paul's analogies in Romans may be seen as both the use of a linguistic device or communicative convention, and as a window into his culture, through which he reveals as much about himself as he does the world he represents.

Marriage and Adultery

As noted earlier, most studies have bounded past Romans 7:1-4 in an attempt to get to the "meat" of Paul's argument, the section regarding the law. Of those who have paused over these verses, few have examined marriage and adultery as analogical elements, or commented on the implications of using these examples. Certainly marriage is a common, even ordinary experience in every culture. In fact, sociologists frequently note that the consequence of marriage, the family, represents the culture in microcosm. In this way, marriage is a familiar image that could represent and reflect a host of cultural and political connections like interpersonal relationships, obligations, commitments, monogamy, legal affairs, children, and family.

What makes Paul's analogous use of marriage interesting is that in 1 Corinthians 7:1-7 he deals almost exclusively with the relationship/obligation/monogamy elements that define marriage partners and ignores the procreation, children and family components. This is quite different from discussions of marriage in the Greco-Roman world where the primary purpose of marriage was procreation and the symbol of family predominated and

---

34. Clifford Geertz, *The Interpretation of Cultures* (New York: Basic Books, 1973).

35. Trevor J. Barnes and James S. Duncan, "Introduction: Writing Worlds," in *Writing Worlds: Discourse, Text and Metaphor in the Representation of Landscape* (ed. T. J. Barnes and J. S. Duncan; New York: Routledge, 1992), 3.

flourished as ideal and as metaphor, evoking images of patriarchy, hierarchy, power, and stability.[36]

At the same time, it must be noted, Paul uses familial or kinship terms when referring to members of his communities, even to himself: he calls himself "father" (πατήρ),[37] and he refers to community members as "children" (τέκνα, υἱός), "brother(s)" (ἀδελφός/ἀδελφοί),[38] and rarely, "sister(s)" (ἀδελφή/ἀδελφαί).[39] Paul's communities appear to be structured using a combination of both household and "brotherhood" structures; the language of kinship (τέκνα, υἱός, ἀδελφός, ἀδελφή) is used to demarcate community relationships and structures and provide a theological model and praxis for how these communities regarded and presented themselves.[40] This household-brotherhood construction is focused on the authority structures of the community as well as on internal community relations regarding the ways power is gained and used, and in whose interests. The ongoing tension between these elements shapes the message Paul delivers and can be seen in the ongoing conflicts that arise between him and within his communities.

Paul saw himself as *paterfamilias,* the male ascendent with both theological and familial authority *(potestas),* whose apostleship established him as a broker on behalf of Christ.[41] In the Roman model, the *paterfamilias* negotiated relationships between family members and the culture. These relationships had economic, religious, and political implications inside and outside the group.[42] At the same time, his contractual negotiations for marriages also orchestrated internal relationships that had implications regarding gender, sexuality and reproduction in the family. As I will argue below, Paul's use of the marriage/adul-

---

36. Eva Marie Lassen, "The Roman Family: Ideal and Metaphor," in *Constructing Early Christian Families: Family as Social Reality and Metaphor* (ed. H. Moxnes; New York: Routledge, 1997), 114.

37. Phil 2:22; 1 Thess 2:11.

38. For example, 1 Cor 4:14; 2 Cor 6:13; 12:14; Gal 4:6, 19, 28, 31; 1 Thess 2:11.

39. Rom 16:1; 1 Cor 7:15; Phlm 2.

40. For a discussion of this see Karl Olav Sandnes, "Equality within Patriarchal Structures: Some New Testament Perspectives on the Christian Fellowship as a Brother- or Sisterhood and a Family," in *Constructing Early Christian Families,* 150-51.

Contra Elisabeth Schüssler Fiorenza and Klaus Schäfer, Sandnes argues that old and new structures (household and brotherhood) converge in the New Testament, and that Pauline communities were not egalitarian fellowships devoid of patriarchal elements.

41. Stephan J. Joubert, "Managing the Household: Paul as *paterfamilias* of the Christian Household Group in Corinth," in *Modeling Early Christianity: Social-Scientific Studies of the New Testament in Its Context* (ed. Philip F. Esler; New York: Routledge, 1995), 216.

42. Whereas Jews practiced *endogamy* (marriage within the kinship group), Greeks and Romans practiced *exogamy* (marriage within the kinship group was prohibited).

tery analogy portrays him as a *paterfamilias* who negotiates relationships within the community.

So, it is within a household-brotherhood community context that Paul introduces an analogy that unites two elements familiar to the Roman community — marriage and law. What makes this association interesting is that Paul's analogy — regardless of whether it is a tortured analogy, confusing allegory, or simple *exemplum* — appears in a letter to a community he did not found, had not visited, nor even knew personally. Possibly this is why he used general categories as tacit and conventional symbols to make his point.

Perhaps for Paul, an unmarried itinerant, marriage served as a generalized marker for a narrow range of implied relationships, but for those in the Roman world, marriage was a complex, yet expected obligation. The Christian community at Rome would have represented a complicated mix of individuals bringing diverse experiences, expectations and traditions to bear on the topics of marriage and adultery. Paul's linkage of marriage and adultery laws in Judaism and the "law" (Mosaic law?) would need to be immediately understandable to his audience; otherwise his analogy would be dead on arrival. It must be assumed, then, that the Roman community was conversant with Jewish marriage and adultery laws and customs.

Jewish marriage involved a series of social and legal contracts that, once negotiated, established a system of relations. It meant that a woman was seen only in relation to her husband, that she was the property of her husband. In Jewish law there was no such thing as an autonomous woman. In fact, the law is interested in women only in times of transition — marriage, widowhood, divorce — times that bind her and transfer her ownership from one man to another. The bride-price was a compensation "for the loss of the daughter's virginity which was treated as an economic asset."[43] Accordingly, when Paul uses marriage laws as an analogy to the Christian's relationship to the law, he is speaking of Jewish marriage laws where a woman is understood solely in terms of her husband; as Wegner argues, she is a "chattel," one who lacks power, rights or duty under the law.[44] Beneath Paul's example is an understanding of marriage as both religious and cultural construct, with implicit group values and

---

43. According to Exod 22:16-17 and Deut 22:28-29 the father was entitled to collect a bride-price from the man who married his daughter, from the man who seduced her, or from one who raped her. For more on this see Judith Romney Wegner, *Chattel or Person? The Status of Women in the Mishnah* (New York: Oxford University Press, 1988), 13. Cf. Rebecca Alpert, "Challenging Male/Female Complementarity: Jewish Lesbians and the Jewish Tradition," in *People of the Body: Jews and Judaism from an Embodied Perspective* (ed. H. Eilberg-Schwartz; Albany: SUNY Press, 1992), 364-65.

44. Wegner, *Chattel*, 6.

social codes. Even though Paul, in 1 Corinthians 7:1-7, seems to stress the egalitarian aspects of the marital relationship, this emphasis is missing in Romans 7:1-4. In fairness to Paul, Romans is not a teaching on marriage, it is an analogy. Still, Paul's choice of marriage as example does have implications and consequences. I would argue that Paul sees and uses marriage as an example of boundary control — a boundary (binding) that evaporates only when the husband dies. Also, the use of marriage as the subject-comparison in the analogy reminds the reader of prophetic uses of marriage as emblematic of the community's relationship (healthy or fractured) with YHWH. Both Paul and the prophets use spousal relationships to speak about relationships with God/Christ and this is dangerous territory. However, in his discussion about freedom from the law and its boundaries, Paul uses only women as players: a married woman, faithful to a husband until death brings her freedom; a married woman living with another man and, therefore, an adulteress. In this case it becomes clear that an analogy is a simplistic device that works effectively playing on generalities and stereotypes.

Paul sees marriage as a simple example that illustrates his point about Christians' freedom and the law. Women, though, might read the example in a quite different way. Underlying Paul's analogy are issues of possession and freedom, and as Castelli notes, "sexuality, while not the topic of discussion per se, nevertheless is bound up in this passage."[45] Contrary to Earnshaw's argument,[46] ὕπανδρος, in common parlance, does mean "under a man" and "legally bound to a man." There is no parallel Greek construction to ἡ ὕπανδρος γυνή, nor does the phrase ὁ ὑπογυναικὸς ἀνήρ appear in Greek literature.[47] Marriage linguistically does not simply imply ownership of a wife by her husband, it legally enforces it. Paul, by using marriage as the subject of his analogy, makes his point regarding the law using an example that reinscribes gender hierarchy in the community. In this way, Paul's teaching insured that marriage (and gender) would remain a boundary issue in Christian communities. Boundaries are erected to exert control, to establish status, and marriage was an example of ultimate control: women's dress, public role, biology (menstrual taboos), and legal status were all governed through marriage. Eilberg-Schwartz argues that

> Status assignation has a critical impact on shaping individuals' experiences of social life, and those experiences are expressed in symbolic processes.

45. Elizabeth A. Castelli, "Romans," in *Searching the Scriptures: A Feminist Commentary* (Vol. 2 of *Searching the Scriptures*; ed. Elisabeth Schüssler Fiorenza; New York: Crossroad, 1994), 281.

46. Earnshaw, "Reconsidering," 74-77.

47. Castelli, "Romans," 283.

The more ascription plays a role in defining status, the less control individuals have in determining who they ultimately are or will be.[48]

Further, Eilberg-Schwartz sees "a probative connection between the way in which status is assigned to individuals in a social system and the symbolic distinctions that govern the system of impurity."[49] For women, status and purity issues go hand-in-hand. A woman's status was determined purely by gender; regardless of her "freedom" (the legally emancipated daughter who has outgrown her father's jurisdiction, the divorcée, the widow whose husband left an heir)[50] or "dependency" (minor daughter at home, wife, levirate widow),[51] she was ultimately under the control of men and labeled as either pure or "contaminated" (e.g., adulterous).

Paul's assertion about the adultery law for a woman who lives with a man while she is still married to another is not followed by a claim about the husband's obligation to faithfulness. Nor is the husband ever termed an adulterer,[52] because in the Biblical tradition and Roman law adultery is a violation of property rights and therefore can only be committed by a wife against her husband, not by a husband against his wife.[53] Instead, in a world governed by honor and shame, a man's honor was judged according to factors of purity and possession: the purity of the women (daughters, wife) to whom he was related, and an honorable marriage (including the expectation of female sexual purity) in which he exercised exclusive possession of his wife's sexual and reproductive potential. Failure to protect his women's sexual purity was considered a humiliating failure and challenge to his masculinity.[54]

In his article on Romans 7:5-8 Jewett writes convincingly about Americans' problems with consumption (property, ownership), and to that end I see a connection with 7:1-4. In affirming the traditional role of the husband as *paterfamilias,* negotiating and governing relationships for and with the women in his life, most notably his wife, Paul's teaching using the analogy of

---

48. Howard Eilberg-Schwartz, "The Status of Impurity: Descent, Social Experience, and Plausibility," in *The Savage in Judaism* (Bloomington: Indiana University Press, 1990), 197.

49. Ibid., 196.

50. Wegner, *Chattel*, 14.

51. Ibid.

52. Beverly Roberts Gaventa, "Romans," in *The Women's Bible Commentary, expanded ed. with Apocrypha* (ed. Carol A. Newsom and Sharon H. Ringe; Louisville: Westminster John Knox, 1998), 408.

53. Wegner, *Chattel*, 53.

54. David Cohen, "The Augustan Law on Adultery: The Social and Cultural Context," in *The Family in Italy from Antiquity to the Present* (ed. D. K. Kertzer and R. P. Saller; New Haven: Yale University Press, 1991), 112.

marriage and adultery is embedded in the language of property and owner-ship/possession.

Regardless, it is worthwhile to speculate how real women in the Roman community might have heard Paul's analogy. Did the freedom to which Paul calls them in later verses obviate the realities or legalities of marriage implied in Paul's example? Did raising issues of status, sexual purity, and women as prop-erty cause dissensions in the community among those who had differing un-derstandings of "freedom" in Christ? How did the Roman community under-stand freedom from the law given the cultural and legal constraints of marriage and other social customs? And finally, how did single women in the community respond to Paul's analogy? These are compelling questions given the fact that membership in the Pauline communities was not determined by descent (Rom 1:16; 2:9), nor by social, political or economic status; rather, the community supplied a new set of relationships for its members where beliefs and behavior mattered.[55] Since Paul's letter was a one-way communication, we will never know the answers to these questions. It is striking to note, though, the develop-ment of Christianity after Paul attempted to rein in the role of women, reinscribing traditional roles in hierarchical models like the *Haustafeln*.

In today's world it is easy to say "talk is cheap" when we constantly are bombarded by television, videos, talk radio, magazines and the Internet. "Talk" (language) envelops us so much that we do not even notice it. But our experi-ence of "talk" is no different from that of our ancestors in that language still creates worlds and has implications for how we see ourselves, our world, and how we should interact with others. Contemporary communities of faith might hear Paul's marriage/adultery analogy in a very different way from the ancient Roman community, but communities today still must come to grips with ways they "innocently" inscribe public prayer, teaching, doctrine, and mission with concepts that free some at the expense of others.

---

55. Eilberg-Schwartz, "Status," 200-201.

ROMANS IN DIALOGUE
WITH CONTEMPORARY LIFE

compiled by Keith Augustus Burton

"Regarding Henry" and the Discovery of Grace

Keith Augustus Burton

> *But now, apart from the law, the righteousness of God has been disclosed,*
> *and is attested to by the law and the prophets, the righteousness of God*
> *through faith in Jesus Christ for all who believe. For there is no distinction,*
> *since all have sinned and fall short of the glory of God; they are now justified*
> *by his grace as a gift, through the redemption that is in Christ Jesus.*

ROMANS 3:21-24

"Regarding Henry" is a film about a successful New York corporate lawyer who
is miraculously transformed after being shot in a robbery.[1] Before the tragedy,
Henry Turner (Harrison Ford) was a callous, materialistic, insensitive individ-
ual who appeared to be in full control of his career and family. After the tragedy,
Henry regains the innocence of a child and helps to redeem those he has hurt.
In the words of critic Marc Savlov, the movie portrays the transformation of
"Henry the Ruthless Lawyer" into "Henry the Reborn."[2] The metaphor of re-

---

1. "Regarding Henry" was directed by Mike Nichols, with a screenplay by Jeffrey
Abrahams, and produced by Scott Rudin and Mike Nichols. It was released by Paramount Pic-
tures in 1991.

2. Marc Savlov, "Regarding Henry," *Austin Chronicle* (July 12, 1991). The "reborn" metaphor is also used by Jack Matthews, "Rebirth, Redemption, 'Regarding Henry,'" *Newsday* (July
10, 1991): 46; Edward Guthmann, "Little Regard for 'Henry,'" *The San Francisco Chronicle* (July
10, 1991): E1; Vincent Canby, "The Attitude Adjustment of a Bullet in the Brain," *The New York
Times* (July 10, 1991): C13; and Ellen Goodman, "Do We Have to Shoot Henry to Save Him?"
Newsday (July 16, 1991): 84.

birth conjures images in the minds of Christians, who see Nicodemus coming to Jesus in the thickness of night and being told that he must be "reborn" (John 3:1-5). Indeed, like Nicodemus, it is night when Henry undergoes his rebirth experience. Reflecting on the religious imagery, Roger Ebert proposes that the aim of the movie is to demonstrate "how Henry becomes more lovable and human as a result of his injury — how his *soul is healed* and his family *saved* by the experience."[3]

What does all this have to do with Romans? Plenty. A major segment of the audience of Romans included people like the first Henry: people who were under the illusion that their inherited identity automatically made them righteous (4:1-12); who tended to look down on others because they had something the others did not (3:1-2; 9a); who presumed that their privileged status placed them in a position where they could judge but never be judged (2:17-20). The original recipients of the letter also included some who resembled the second Henry. They were people who realized that all humans have equal access to God's righteousness (3:28-30); who rejoiced that they now shared in the blessings that originally were reserved for one segment of humanity (4:13-25); and who acknowledged that no human being is so filled with grace as to make it impossible to sin (3:9b). Though separated by almost two millennia, Paul's letter to the Romans definitely provides an opportunity for meaningful dialogue with the movie.

Entering into dialogue with Romans and "Regarding Henry" also provides an opportunity to see what lessons can be learned by the twenty-first-century citizen. As Robert Jewett recognizes, there may be some who find it hard to accept the marriage of the sacred and secular in experiments like this.[4] How can a

---

3. Roger Ebert, "Regarding Henry," *Chicago Sun-Times* (July 10, 1991), http://www.suntimes.com/ebert/ebert_reviews/1991/07/659178.html; my emphasis. The metaphors of "salvation" and "redemption of the soul" are also used by Goodman, "Do We Have to Shoot Henry to Save Him?" 84; Janet Maslin, "In the 90's, the 80's Turn to Junk," *The New York Times* (July 14, 1991): Sec. 2, 9; and David Ansen, "You Need This Movie Like," *Newsweek* (July 15, 1991): 56. Frank Rizzo, "Regarding Mike Nichols," *The Hartford Courant* (July 10, 1991): B1, includes the following quote from a press conference with director and executive producer Mike Nichols: "What interested me about [the story of 'Regarding Henry'] was that it was about redemption."

4. Robert Jewett, *Saint Paul at the Movies: The Apostle's Dialogue with American Culture* (Louisville: Westminster John Knox, 1993), 4, lists religious and scholarly objections: "But should being 'all things to all people' really include taking in the movies? They are secular forms of entertainment, produced for profit, conveying cultural ideals and norms that are far from those of religious communities. And in the minds of the highly trained scholars, oriented more to books than to films, there is a cultural abyss between the realms of theological analysis and historical research on the one hand and popular culture on the other."

movie with "a fair amount of profanity and a discreet sex scene"[5] be used to illuminate theological truth? While I object to hedonistic excesses in movies, many movies can be interpreted as parables that, when viewed through theological lenses, provide a deeper understanding of the timeless truths contained in scripture.[6] In this age of Biblical illiteracy, the parabolic, theological interpretation of movies helps to reawaken the timeless relevance of inspired writ.[7] "Regarding Henry" is a powerful parable that not only speaks to those of us who claim to be religious but, in a national sense, it is especially relevant to those who are afflicted by the "Captain America Complex"[8] and are still bemused over the tragic events of September 11, 2001. In light of recent events, Henry can be seen as a personification of America, Mr. Matthews as a debtor nation, Henry's associates as America's western allies, and Rachel as the youth of America. However, since I wish for the reader to analyze the movie as a parable, I will try to avoid commentary and allow you to draw the relevant application.[9]

When analyzed from the vantage point of biblical exegesis, the movie is not as simplistic as Ebert charges.[10] What he dismisses as "a soap opera subplot" and Henry's insignificant confrontation of the "dishonesty in his old law firm" are the very issues that make the movie theologically meaningful. As we investigate "Regarding Henry" through the lense of Paul's letter to the Romans, we see the emergence of themes that speak to us individually and collectively. The illusive world of the gentry is exposed. The innermost thoughts of the soul are unveiled. The *karma* of our actions is analyzed. But most importantly, those who are unconscionable perpetrators are provided with the opportunity to discover the joy of indiscriminating grace.

5. Chris Hicks, "Regarding Ford's Portrayal of Disabled Man's Struggle in 'Henry' — It's convincing, maybe Oscar material," *Deseret News* (July 12, 1991): W3.

6. In Matthew Gilbert, "Still the Czar of *Zeitgeist* in Hollywood," *The Boston Globe* (July 7, 1991): "Arts and Film," 41, we learn that, while Nichols does not claim to be writing theology, "he likes to shape a movie around a moral center." Nichols comments: "I like to have a reason for telling the story. And it should have some application to our lives."

7. See Jewett, *St. Paul at the Movies*, 5.

8. For an explanation of this concept see Robert Jewett, *The Captain America Complex: The Dilemma of Zealous Nationalism*, 2nd ed. (Santa Fe: Bear and Company, 1984).

9. Analyzing the movie as social commentary, Craig MacInnis, " 'Regarding Henry': A Grown-up 'Graduate,'" *The Toronto Star* (July 10, 1991): F1, remarks: "In its own way, 'Regarding Henry' couldn't be tougher on New York's rich professional class, or the faulty social systems that allegedly keep America running."

10. Ebert, "Regarding Henry."

The Illusion of Worth

What then? Are we any better off? No, not at all; for we have already charged that all, both Jews and Greeks, are under the power of sin.

(ROM 3:9)

The movie opens with a scene of a New York courthouse on a snowy day in the holiday season. The viewer is gently ushered into the main door and quickly rushed to the courtroom where an important case is being tried. As attorney Henry Turner presents his summation, the camera scopes the courtroom. The drab view through the window contrasts only slightly with the dismal splendor of the courtroom. Engraved on the wall behind the judge's bench is the American motto, "In God We Trust" — a phrase that is probably meaningful only to Mr. Matthews (the plaintiff) and his wife, as they will soon be thrust into a period where they will be forced to exercise Job-like patience in the face of adversity.

The camera moves to Turner as he skillfully plays on the jurors' collective sympathy. Whom are they going to believe, an alcoholic who recently attempted suicide, or a respectable hospital? He even pretends to understand Mr. Matthews, "You desperately want to blame someone else. We understand that; it's natural." However, this is one time when Matthews will have to pay for his own sins. He cannot use the East Shore Hospital as a scapegoat here. He is a proven sinner — an alcoholic, a self-murderer — and now he has demonstrated his ability to lie. Decent people cannot condone these despicable acts, no matter how pitiful the plaintiff looks. He has suffered irreparable medical damage because he did not tell the care-givers that he was a diabetic, and now he must live with the results of his inexcusable negligence.

After such a compelling speech, the verdict is so predictable that the screen writer does not even think it is necessary for the plaintiff's lawyer to speak. When it is all over, Henry takes a quick glance at the table where the defeated Matthews and his family sit in bemusement. They make hasty, uncomfortable eye contact, and he rushes out of the courtroom as if he wishes to avoid confronting them "off stage."

At the celebration party, Henry proposes a toast, "To Mr. Matthews." Look who raise their glasses — a room full of lawyers in designer clothing, drinking champagne bought with money that had been extorted from the potential coffers of the penniless Matthews. There is no remorse in this room; no sense of guilt; no reasoning that, even if Matthews had not disclosed his medical condition, those in a position of privilege may still have a moral responsibility. As far as they were concerned, they had used the law to achieve their purpose. The means justified the end. Even if they had suppressed some relevant facts — as we discover later — they were legally righteous.

The illusion of worth is a theme that runs throughout the movie. Simply by virtue of their positions in society, Henry and his companions believed they were worth more than ordinary folk. They only valued people who operated in their sphere of influence. Henry apparently had both inherited and earned his worth. During the celebration party, senior partner Charlie Cameron congratulates him with the accolade, "Like father, like son." Henry obviously had followed in the footsteps of his father. He had a name to protect. Later, during the recovery period when his daughter Rachel reveals to Henry who he used to be, we learn something about his upbringing: "Your father used to make you mow the lawn and take out the garbage and walk the dog and wash the car, and then you learned to appreciate the work ethic."[11] Henry is confused by the term "work ethic." "What's that?" he asks. "I don't know," Rachel replies. But in his former life, Henry knew very well what the work ethic was. He had learned his part on the stage of life and played it well. After returning home from the rehabilitation facility, Henry asks the maid, "Rosella, what do I do when I'm home?" Rosella replies, "You're working all the time."

Henry's sense of worth is juxtaposed to the supposed worthlessness of others. While he awaits the jury verdict, Henry chides the interior decorator for ordering the wrong table for his home and orders her to make it right by the end of the week. Jessica, his secretary, scurries behind him like a disenfranchised slave who jumps at his every command. Even his daughter stares blankly into his face as he lectures her about her thoughtlessness. Then there's poor Eddie, the doorman. After returning home from a dinner party, the faceless chauffeur drops the Turners in front of their exclusive apartment complex. Rushing to open the door first, Eddie greets Mrs. Turner, who responds, "Hi, Eddie." Then Eddie says good evening to Henry. Henry keeps walking as if Eddie's words had been quieted by the stillness of the night. For Henry, Eddie does not even exist. Even his last encounter before the tragic shooting exposes his elitist attitude. Henry walks into the store where he is to be shot and demands a pack of cigarettes. No greeting to the storekeeper. No vain niceties. No attempt to establish a relationship. As far as he was concerned, the storekeeper existed in this life for one purpose only: to provide him with cigarettes.

Sarah Turner is also driven by the illusion of worth. She was a legal secre-

---

11. Kenneth Turan, "Disregarding 'Henry,'" *Los Angeles Times* (June 10, 1991): F1, notices that the new Henry "discards his work ethic." See also a sarcastic comment in Ansen, "You Need This Movie Like," 56: "No more nasty striving for our Henry, who fortunately seems to have a limitless supply of money so that he can renounce the work ethic in high style."

tary when she first met Henry and was impressed by the confidence this young attorney displayed. On the very day she met him, she went home and told her roommate that she had met the man she was going to marry. The ambitious Sarah married the man of her plans, and tried hard to keep up appearances with and for him. In providing a rationale for Rachel's attendance at the exclusive Huntington school, Sarah says, "That school only takes thirty kids a year, and Rachel's one of them. . . . It's a great opportunity for her *and for us.*"

After Henry is shot, Sarah sees it as her duty to continue keeping up appearances. She even attempts to shelter their daughter, Rachel, from the truth. Rachel is not given the opportunity to see her father until months after his accident, when he has been partially rehabilitated. When he is still comatose and Rachel inquires about his well-being, Sarah answers, "He wants to get better before you see him." Sarah is very careful to maintain the illusion of success and security, even when their financial irresponsibility begins to catch up with them. During a house-shopping trip, her friend, Phyllis, convinces her to tell the truth about their financial status. When Sarah discloses the true picture of their near-bankrupt state, Phyllis responds, "Can I give you a little advice? Do not tell anyone what you just told me." Phyllis knows that this information could be damaging for Sarah, who would be seen as one of "them" by her socialite companions. Sarah is so careful to protect their true financial status that even when Charlie, a long-time family friend, offers to help, she retorts, "We're in wonderful shape; no problems, really." She is too embarrassed to expose the true situation, especially after Charlie says, "I knew I could count on Henry."

Rachel Turner still has most of her innocence and initially appears in the movie as an emotionless *tabula rasa*. She reacts neither positively nor negatively when her father chastises her for soiling "his" piano. There is no negotiation or temper tantrum when she is grounded. When she receives an apology in the form of a philosophical explanation for her father's unilateral verdict, her nonresponse leads her father to conclude in Latin, "*qui tacet consentere videtur* — he who is silent is understood to consent." But Rachel is still trying to figure things out. When her mother gives the impression that her father does not want to see Rachel in his debilitated state, she requests, "Can we get a puppy?" as if asking for one object to replace another object. But, even in her innocence, Rachel notices something about self-worth. When Henry is still comatose, Sarah gives him an update on Rachel's preparation to go to her new school. She tells him, "Rachel got her school uniform. It's the most adorable thing. She put it on and she said, 'Mom, I don't *feel* smart.'" Rachel understood something that Henry will not discover until the end of the movie, when he tells Sarah that he does not like his clothes: uniforms are superficial. True worth is not determined by external manifestations of affluence. Rachel even tries to escape her prescribed destiny when she pleads with her father not to send her to the exclusive Huntington School. "I can go to school around here," she says.

The reborn Henry is very willing to grant Rachel's wishes. He cannot understand why he and his daughter should be separated. But it is not up to him. It's Sarah's decision, and she has not yet had her rebirth experience. So, Rachel is shipped off to Huntington where she is to be molded in a superficial image. She has gone to be plated in illusory gold. The final scene of the movie provides a peek into the process that produces these pretenders. The young girls are sitting in the assembly hall at Huntington as an administrator addresses them and reminds them why they have come. Assuming the role of self-help guru she preaches, "And you are all learning what that means when you ask yourself, why do I push myself? Why do I strive to be a harder worker? A better listener? Look around you. There are the answers to those questions. Competition. Everyone close your eyes. Repeat to yourself silently. 'I will work harder. I will listen better.'" Rachel is about to learn all about the "work ethic." Poor Rachel.

The Tragedy of Hypocrisy

> *Therefore you have no excuse, whoever you are, when you judge others; for in passing judgment on another you condemn yourself, because you, the judge, are doing the very same things.*
>
> (ROM 2:1)

Those who have been beguiled by a false sense of value often are blinded to their own weaknesses. Although the audience is not enlightened until the end of the movie, the opening scene depicts evil in its worst form. Henry would make a great case study for a chapter in M. Scott Peck's *People of the Lie*.[12] Here in the courthouse, where justice is supposed to reign unshackled, this supposedly respectable attorney intentionally suppresses a vital piece of evidence that would have vindicated Mr. Matthews. Instead, Henry's only concern is to bring victory to his powerful client. His face betrays an element of guilt when his eyes meet Mrs. Matthews' after the verdict is given. He knows he has done wrong. He knows he has violated the law. Yet, as we visit the celebration party once more and hear him propose a toast, "To Mr. Matthews," he feels he has performed his job competently. Although he suppressed vital evidence, he has been justified by his works. His conscience is quickly quieted.

12. M. Scott Peck, *People of the Lie: The Hope for Healing Human Evil* (New York: Simon & Schuster, 1983).

In the first encounter Henry has with his daughter, Rachel, he trades the role of defense attorney for that of prosecutor and judge. As he stands at her bedroom door while she sits on her bed, he lets her know that he would accept no explanation for her transgression. She must learn to respect other people's "things." The crime? She spilled juice on his piano. Imagine, this same man who deliberately broke the law earlier that day becomes judge and executioner for his very own daughter.[13] If only he could have heard what Paul had to say:

> But if you call yourself a Jew and rely on the law and boast of your relation to God and know his will and determine what is best because you are instructed in the law, and if you are sure that you are a guide to the blind, a light to those who are in darkness, a corrector of the foolish, a teacher of children, having in the law the embodiment of knowledge and truth, you, then, that teach others, will you not teach yourself? . . . You that boast in the law, do you dishonor God by breaking the law? (Rom 2:17-21a, 23)

Henry is not the only one in the movie whose hypocrisy is exposed. Sarah also has been trapped in the treacherous snare. Her hypocritical behavior appears to be a direct consequence of her yearning for status. During a conversation with Henry on the night he is shot, she informs him with a satisfied grin, "Frances says Carol's daughter was not accepted at Huntington. They were dying when they found out that Rachel got in." Henry spices the poisonous moment with his interjection, "Carol's daughter is a virtual idiot." Sarah is very amused at his comment and laughs heartily. There appears to be nowhere in her soul for sympathy. The real tragedy is the fact that Carol is probably in their circle of worthies.

But in a superficial world, you had better believe that those who talk about others also are being talked about. Sarah has to face this when she has a conversation with Rachel while Henry is recovering. Rachel asks in her dispassionate monotone, "Are we going to be poor now?" Then she proceeds to inform her mother of what Jennifer Lerner's mother is saying about her extravagant spending habits. Sarah is infuriated. "You can tell Jennifer Lerner that her mother doesn't know what she's talking about, and if she has anything to tell me she can pick up the phone and say it herself. Who the hell does she think she is?" This would have been a good time for Sarah to look in the mirror — "You then that teach others, will you not teach yourself?" (Rom 2:21a).

---

13. Turan, "Disregarding 'Henry,'" F1, accuses Henry of "badgering his young daughter like a reluctant witness to a capital crime."

Another exposed hypocrite in the movie is Bruce. Bruce is Henry's partner in law, and partner in crime. They seem to have had an almost brotherly relationship before the shooting. When Henry is shot, it is Bruce and Charlie, among the male partners, who rush to the hospital to show concern and to comfort Sarah. Bruce is also the only colleague who is seen visiting Henry's domicile and giving him gifts when he returns home after treatment.[14] While eating lunch with Bruce and Linda, Henry discloses that he has been reviewing the Matthews v. East Shore files and has discovered that Mr. Matthews told the truth — he did inform the nurse about his diabetes. Bruce tries to brush it off and the reborn Henry proclaims, "What we did was wrong." In the spirit of the old Henry, Bruce responds, "What we did is paying for our lunch." Mind you, this is the same Bruce who, just a few days before, when visiting Henry's home, remarked of the person who shot him, "If they found the son of a bitch, I would have brought the death penalty back to New York singlehandedly." For Bruce, justice really means "just us." Only the privileged deserve to have the law work in their favor.

Phyllis is also exposed. Like Bruce, Phyllis appears to be a close family friend. She is one of the two women supporters at the hospital on the night of the shooting. She is also the one who acts as Sarah's confidante when Sarah tries to hold together the fragile family finances. Surely Phyllis is a genuine friend. Even when she sees Sarah and Henry in a down-scale section of town showing overly public displays of affection like love-sick teenagers, she overlooks the inappropriateness of their behavior and invites them to her house opening. Surely Phyllis is a friend. But, in the tragic world of hypocrisy, what goes around often comes around. While Henry and Sarah work the room at Phyllis' party, Phyllis and three other socialites make light of their "friends'" tragic plight. Fueled by the belittling statements, Phyllis' partner remarks, "One minute you're an attorney, and the next you're an imbecile." As gut-wrenching laughter is evoked among them, the camera slowly turns and exposes two unsuspecting spectators to the ad-hoc show. Henry is in a state of shock as Sarah calmly announces their departure and they go home to brood. If only they could have recalled the earlier scene in the movie when Sarah laughed with equal heartiness at her husband's statement, "Carol's daughter is a virtual idiot." Paul could very well have appended to his list of *exempla* in Rom 2:21-22: "You who abhor being belittled, do you belittle?"

---

14. We later discover that Bruce's exuberant behavior probably results from the guilt he feels about his brief affair with Sarah before the tragedy.

Keith Augustus Burton

The Inevitability of Judgment

Do you imagine, whoever you are, that when you judge those who do such things and yet you do them yourself, you will escape the judgment of God?

(ROM 2:3)

"Regarding Henry" reminds us that judgment follows works. Before we really know what is going on in the movie, those of us who are appalled by the rampant recklessness of renegade litigators may have seen Matthews as another ambulance chaser. It may be true that he was injured during the operation but, if he had not been an irresponsible drunk, the staff at the hospital would have known that he was a diabetic. Why should he be rewarded at the expense of decent citizens whose insurance premiums would help to fund his medical lottery award? Why should his act of greed have a negative financial impact on the very doctors who tried to save his life?[15] While the sensitive viewer may have wished for the afflicted Matthews to receive grace in that courtroom, based on the skewed evidence that was heard in Henry's summation, it did appear as if justice was accomplished. The absence of Matthews or even any reference to him for the next hour in the movie gives the impression that his is a closed case.

Unlike that of Matthews, Henry's judgment will take place outside of the courtroom. The audience is first provided with the opportunity of casting judgment on Henry. Within the first few minutes of the movie, the viewer is forced to form an impression about Henry. This smooth-talking lawyer, who at first appeared to be concerned with the affairs of both the defendant and the plaintiff, is quickly exposed as a callous megalomaniac who has lost touch with his feelings. He is riding on a very high horse and you can almost anticipate his fall. Nobody would have expected Henry's day of judgment to come as quickly and unexpectedly as it did. As he makes a late night call for some cigarettes at the local mini-market, he interrupts a robbery in progress and is the recipient of two bullets. One pierces his chest close to his heart, and the other penetrates the frontal lobe of his brain. This heartless, quick-witted lawyer who has, in essence, robbed Matthews of his compensation is now the victim of negative judgment. Henry did not live by the rules, and now he receives a lawless judgment. "All who have sinned apart from the law will also perish apart from the law . . ." (Rom 2:12a).

Judgment day also comes for Sarah and Bruce. Remember Bruce, the family friend who seems so awkwardly devoted to Henry after the accident?

---

15. See the impact that malpractice suits have on the medical profession in Mary Brophy Narcus, "Healthcare's 'Perfect Storm,'" *U.S. News & World Report* (July 1, 2002): 39-40.

From the time he visits Henry at home and holds a semi-cordial conversation with him, you are forced to wonder what his story is.[16] It soon becomes evident that Bruce is living under the heavy yoke of guilt. Although Henry has no idea that Bruce has wronged him, Bruce believes that, by giving gifts, he may somehow win Henry's favor. Bruce is trying to atone for his sins by good works. Did he not know that "'no human being will be justified in his sight' by deeds prescribed in the law" (Rom 3:20)? Ironically, it was his dubious deeds that exposed him. Henry was the only one home when Bruce's housewarming gift was delivered. As he opened the handwritten note that Bruce had thoughtfully included, he noticed that the stationery was the same as some he had seen neatly hidden in a box in one of Sarah's drawers. Henry rushes to the drawer and retrieves the letters. He opens one and reads aloud, "Sarah, I need you now. Feel you against me. Call me tonight. Bruce." When Sarah arrives home, she finds Henry sitting silently and then notices the letters in his hands. He refuses to listen to her explanation and storms out of the house amidst her pleas for forgiveness. His encounter with Bruce takes place behind closed doors. When Henry emerges, Bruce follows behind him expressing his deepest apologies. Bruce wants to experience grace. Sarah wants to experience grace. But Henry is not prepared to give it. "All who have sinned under the law will be judged by the law" (Rom 2:12b).

The Discovery of Grace[17]

All have sinned and fall short of the glory of God; they are now justified by his grace as a gift, through the redemption that is in Christ Jesus.

(ROM 3:23-24)

Although naive, "Henry the Newborn" is not totally innocent. He had undergone a born-again experience, but the previous actions of "Henry the Ruthless Lawyer" could not be erased easily. Even in his state of righteousness, Henry has to learn that "*all* have sinned and fall short of the glory of God" (Rom 3:23). Notice that "fall" is rendered in the present continuous. Paul does not say that all "have fallen" from God's glory. Even those who have sinned only once in life

---

16. MacInnis, "'Regarding Henry': A Grown-up 'Graduate,'" F1, describes him as "suitably off-putting."

17. The understanding of grace here is similar to that of Robert Jewett, *Saint Paul Returns to the Movies: Triumph over Shame* (Grand Rapids, Mich.: Eerdmans, 1999), 6: "As in the Pauline letters, grace . . . takes the form not of forgiveness of individual sins but of overcoming dishonorable status."

have missed the glorious mark. Only God's grace can compensate for the short-fall (Rom 3:24).

The one who taught Henry about grace was one of "them" — Bradley, a sex-crazed Black man who served as Henry's physical therapist at the rehabili-tation center. In his former life, Henry would probably have been disgusted at his crude demeanor and objectification of females. But Bradley had more than a job, he had a ministry.[18] Going above and beyond the call of duty, Bradley se-cretly mixes cayenne pepper and tabasco sauce into Henry's eggs and forces him to talk again.[19] He cajoles him to walk and rejoices with his success. So at-tached do they become that Henry does not want to leave the rehabilitation center without him. When Henry falls into a state of depression after discover-ing the hypocrisy of his "friends," Sarah calls for Bradley. Bradley had been suc-cessful in the initial remaking of Henry, and Henry trusts him.[20]

Henry confides, "I thought I could go back to my life, but I don't like the way I was. Bradley, I don't fit in." Henry had experienced conversion. Henry's "old self was crucified . . . that the body of sin might be destroyed" (Rom 6:6). Bradley smiles as he testifies to Henry that he, too, had to undergo conversion. He was on top of his game in college football when a knee injury made it im-possible for him to play again. When he reflects on his experience, he con-cludes, "It was a test. I had to find a life. . . . The therapist who helped me walk again — he was so cool, I said, that's what I want to do. . . . I don't mind having bad knees." Bradley was a wounded healer.[21] Someone had helped Bradley to find life and, in return, he devoted his life to helping others find life.[22] His final advice to Henry: "Don't listen to nobody trying to tell you who you are. It might take a while but you'll figure yourself out."

It did not take too long for Henry to figure himself out. In fact, he had been figuring himself out ever since Bradley forced him to say his first word: "Ritz." Bradley assumes Henry likes Ritz crackers and, for the rest of the movie, the Ritz emblem intermittently looms in the background. On the last day of his

---

18. Desson Howe, *Washington Post* (July 12, 1991), recognizes that Bradley (Bill Nunn) "plays a significant helpmate in Ford's spiritual recovery. . . ."

19. Ebert, "Regarding Henry," is unimpressed by Bradley's "Pavlovian" techniques.

20. Henry's dependence on Bradley leads some critics to detect a father-son relationship. See Matthews, "Rebirth, Redemption, 'Regarding Henry,'" 46; Goodman, "Do We Have to Shoot Henry to Save Him?" 84.

21. For the concept of the wounded healer see Henri J. N. Nouwen, *The Wounded Healer: Ministry in Contemporary Society* (New York: Doubleday, 1972).

22. Matthews, "Rebirth, Redemption, 'Regarding Henry,'" 46, notices his effectiveness: "Nunn . . . is so full of life and its affirmatives you may want to erase your own brain and start over with him."

stay in the rehabilitation center, Henry finishes an oil painting of a "Ritz Crackers" box. This painting is the last item that is packed in the back of the taxi that takes him home with his family. When Bruce visits Henry to welcome him back, the painting is accusingly positioned on the floor behind the chair where Bruce sits. During his first post-injury staff meeting at the office, while his law-partner Linda briefs her colleagues, the camera turns to Henry and Charlie who sit together on a sofa. On the wall behind the sofa hangs the Ritz portrait. The painting eventually finds its way to Henry's office, where it remains unhung behind his chair.

On the day Henry learns about Sarah's infidelity, the Ritz secret is revealed. After he withholds grace from Sarah and Bruce, Henry walks frantically down the street with his portfolio. His journey takes him past the Ritz Carlton hotel. Slowing down, he looks at the sign: Ritz Carlton. "Ritz"; this is where he is supposed to be. This is where he will figure himself out. This has to be a place of significance. Henry checks into a room where he can savor a period of solitude while he tries to make sense of his life. While he sits on the bed, there is a knock on the door. Careful observers already know who it will be: it is Linda. She revealed a lot in the way she looked at Henry on his first day back at the office. She appeared to be more than a friend. The bewildered Henry is surprised to see her. How dare she invade his privacy! This is wrong. Then comes the moment of truth. Linda laments, "You are not the only one who lost in this. I lost, too. I lost the one man I ever loved. . . . It's hard to see you every day in the office and you don't know me. This is our hotel. Every Tuesday and Thursday at the Ritz. . . . You were going to leave Sarah for me, and now it's gone, it's all gone." With this revelation, Henry looks as if he has just been shot again. As Linda sits temptingly on the bed, he rushes out of the room as if preemptively extinguishing any potential flame. "You that forbid adultery, do you commit adultery?" (Rom 2:22a).

Having been confronted with his sin, Henry runs to the bay by the river. As he paces the pavement, the flowing water evokes the notion of a cleansing. Symbolically, Henry is being reminded of his bullet "baptism." Henry has been given a second chance. Paul explains the mystery of baptism in Romans 6:4: "Therefore we have been buried with him by baptism into death, so that, just as Christ was raised from the dead by the glory of the Father, so we too might walk in the newness of life." Henry decides that he cannot return to his old life, and he is determined to sever all ties. His first stop is the Matthews' apartment. Mrs. Matthews opens the door and, upon recognizing Henry, asks, "What are *you* doing here?" With the sincerity of an infant, Henry replies, "I came to apologize." He hands her a file with exonerating information and admits, "Your husband did tell the nurse that he was a diabetic. It's all in there. I'm sorry." Almost dumbfounded by the gesture, Mrs. Matthews asks, "Why?" With a sheepish grin, Henry declares, "I changed." "I guess!" she affirms, as her countenance is illuminated with rays of hope.

Not satisfied with his first act of grace, Henry returns to the office to tie up loose ends. He walks past Charlie's secretary and interrupts a high-powered meeting that Charlie is conducting with important clients. After Henry gives voice to his resignation, Charlie feigns a desire to have Henry stay on at the firm. Henry will not relent and, as he prepares to leave, Charlie's secretary answers the phone and informs Charlie that the attorney for the Matthews is on the phone. A sly, satisfied grin creeps over Henry's face as he exits. On his way out, he stops by Jessica's desk and informs her of his decision. "Mr. Turner, what happened?" she asks. Harking back to an earlier scene in the movie, when she almost poured too much milk in his coffee, Henry replies, "I had enough, so I said, 'When.'"[23] "Good for you," she affirms, as a contagious smile plasters her face. Henry has one more stop to make. He opens the door to a colleague's office and says, "Bye, Linda." There was a lot in that "Bye." It was the kind of "bye" that Donnie McKlurkin sings about in his "Carribean Medley."[24]

Goodbye world, I'll stay no longer with you,
Goodbye pleasure of sin, I'll stay no longer with you,
I've made up my mind to go God's way the rest of my life.
I've made up my mind to go God's way the rest of my life.

Feeling the intensity of the farewell, Linda looks hurt and lost. But this is goodbye. No Ritz painting dominates this scene.

In the following scene, Henry knocks on a familiar door. When Sarah answers, he reminisces, "I know this great blowfish place. . . ." "I'm sorry," she blurts out. "No, I'm sorry," Henry equalizes. "You were right; things were different." As they embrace he reveals, "I have something I need to tell you." Is this his confession? Not quite, but close enough. "I don't like my clothes. Maybe they used to be my favorite, but I don't feel comfortable in them anymore." Here Henry resonates with Rachel's earlier discovery: clothes do not make a person.[25] In fact,

---

23. Susan Wloszczyna, "'Regarding Henry': A flimsy flip-flop," *USA Today* (July 10, 1991): 4D, believes that the coffee-pouring incident was too obvious. She jokes, "you know this loaded line is going to reappear. But you'll say 'when' long before that."

24. Donnie McKlurkin, "Carribean Medley," in the video "Live in London and More" (Zomba Recording Corporation, Verity label: 2000).

25. Critic Michael Upchurch, "Maudlin 'Henry' has going for it . . . Harrison Ford," *The Seattle Times* (July 10, 1991): E7, refers to some of the supporting characters as "a procession of evil, business-suited mannequins. . . ."

uniforms give only an illusion of worth. Henry realizes that he is more than his clothes. He is more than his career. His legalistic life is a thing of the past. "I hate being a lawyer," he declares. "I quit and I told Charlie goodbye. I want us to be a family for as long as we can, Sarah, for as long as we can."

At this point, the family needs Rachel to be complete. The next scene takes us to Huntington where Rachel and her peers are being indoctrinated in the ways of capitalist individualism. The brainwashing assembly is interrupted by Rachel's parents and puppy, as if they are rescuing her from a predestined fate. As Buddy, the puppy, finds his mistress, Rachel abandons protocol and shrieks in delight. Henry approaches the podium and informs the administrator, "I missed her first eleven years, and I don't want to miss any more." The family meshes together as they exit the building. They walk away from the white-steepled chapel and all that it signifies. Why perpetuate the emptiness of a legalistic lifestyle? Why sentence Rachel to a graceless existence? Henry has discovered grace. Sarah has discovered grace.[26] And together, they will help Rachel to discover grace.

---

26. MacInnis, "'Regarding Henry': A Grown-up 'Graduate,'" F1, notices: "Bening's [Sarah] transformation — from chilly society matron to human being — runs parallel to Henry's own journey out of darkness."

Getting Along When We Don't Agree:
Using Simulation and Controversy to Help
Students and Lay Persons Interpret Romans

Lareta Halteman Finger

Compared to some of the other essays in this volume, this one takes a more pedagogical and hermeneutical slant. However, since Robert Jewett's strenuous exegetical efforts were regularly combined with creative contemporary application, I trust that these words will not be out of place in this *Festschrift* dedicated to his scholarship on Romans.

In the fall of 1987 I began a master's degree at Garrett-Evangelical Theological Seminary, planning to continue in their joint Ph.D. program with Northwestern University. My area of interest was New Testament, particularly the Pauline letters, so I was excited about studying with Robert Jewett. Having been editor of the Christian feminist magazine *Daughters of Sarah* for a number of years, I gradually was picking up feminist biblical analysis, as well as a bit of social-scientific criticism. I found both of these emphases far more stimulating than the theological or apologetic approaches from my college days in the early 1960s.

Registering for the fall term, I saw that Dr. Jewett was offering a course in Romans. I was disappointed. All I knew about Romans at that point was that it was abstract and theological and told people how to get saved by faith. Thirsting for more social background, I assumed Romans did not have much. Thus my first class was a shock. Jewett read from a paper he had written on "Paul, Phoebe, and the Spanish Mission."[1] Spain? I was not aware that a con-

---

1. Robert Jewett, "Paul, Phoebe, and the Spanish Mission," 142-61 in *The Social World of Formative Judaism and Christianity: Essays in Tribute to Howard Clark Kee* (ed. J. Neusner, et al.; Philadelphia: Fortress, 1988).

temporary country like Spain was even mentioned in the New Testament. Phoebe? It was just a name from lists that always were ignored in Sunday School lessons or any of my previous Bible studies. Now I was learning about Phoebe's critical role, not only as a mail carrier but as the interpreter of Paul's letter, and about Paul's hope for mission work in Spain after his journey to Jerusalem with the collection (Rom 15:22-29).

From that first class, through the days and weeks of intense study that followed, I felt like the top of my head was being taken off and all my gray cells rearranged. We read the first edition of *The Romans Debate*,[2] which traced some of the developments in thinking about Romans since 1938. We debated some of the arguments presented on topics like why Paul ever wrote this letter in the first place, whether he mostly had Rome or Jerusalem in mind, whether chapters 15–16 were part of the original letter, and what rhetorical style Paul used and why he used it.

Unknown to the class, Peter Lampe's brilliant dissertation on Roman house-churches in the first two centuries just had been made available in German earlier that year.[3] One afternoon Bob was feeding us juicy tidbits from it about the names in Romans 16 and what social, economic and theological light they might shed on the nature of the early Roman house-churches. Finally one stunned student asked where he was getting all this material. With a gleam in his eye like someone just discovering a vein of gold in a coal mine, Bob told us about Lampe's book. I heaved an internal sign of relief. It was not that I had been totally ignorant of Romans scholarship; this was new information not even accessible in English.

It became clearer and clearer to me throughout the course that the new rhetorical and social-scientific tools I was being given for interpreting Paul's letter to the Roman believers were changing its meaning. No longer was the overall thrust, "how can I as a sinner get right with God?" It concerned rather the struggle among Jewish and Gentile Christians and the nature of Yahweh's original covenant with the Hebrews. Paul was far more positive about his Jewish theological roots than I had ever imagined.[4]

---

2. Karl P. Donfried, ed., *The Romans Debate* (Minneapolis: Augsburg, 1977; rev. and expanded ed.; Peabody, Mass.: Hendrickson, 1991).

3. Peter Lampe, *Die stadtrömischen Christen in dem ersten beiden Jahrhunderten: Untersuchen zur Sozialgeschichte* (Tübingen: J. C. B. Mohr, 1987; rev. and expd. ed., 1989); henceforth, *Die stadtrömischen Christen.*

4. Cf. E. P. Sanders, *Paul and Palestinian Judaism* (London: SCM Press, 1977), and James D. G. Dunn, "The New Perspective on Paul," *Bulletin of the John Rylands Library* 65 (1983): 95-122.

Aids to Conducting a Simulation of Roman House-Church Dynamics

I. Inductive Preparation for Role-playing House-Churches
Hearing Romans 1:1-17 and 15:14—16:23 *

- The salutation and greetings in Romans 1:1-7 are longer than in any other letter of Paul's. Underline any words or phrases that you think would especially appeal to the Jewish members of the Roman house-churches. CIRCLE the words or phrases that would especially appeal to the non-Jews. Draw a *wavy line* under the words Paul uses to describe himself.
- In 1:8-15, underline why Paul thanks God for the Roman Christians. Underline any reasons Paul gives for why he wants to visit these churches in Rome. Is Paul acting authoritative or diplomatic in this paragraph?
- In Romans 1, CIRCLE the thesis statement for Paul's entire argument. Underline "the obedience of faith" in 1:5 and 16:26. Is this a contradiction in terms?
- In 15:14-21, underline phrases or sentences that show that Paul thinks he is especially commissioned to proclaim the gospel to non-Jews. Underline the part that tells you that Paul is NOT coming to Rome to preach the gospel there.
- In 15:22-29, underline the reason why Paul cannot come to Rome now and the reason he wants to come later. Draw a *wavy line* under the part that shows Paul is worried about his trip to Jerusalem.
- In 16:1-16, underline the references to five house-churches or cell groups. Star the one you are in! CIRCLE the names of people who are especially commended by Paul.
- In 16:17-27, CIRCLE the names of people in Corinth who are sending their greetings to the Roman believers.

*Each student should have an inexpensive paperback version of the New Testament to underline and annotate.

How Can I Preach This Gospel?

As someone more experienced in religious journalism than scholarly research, the questions recurring over and over in my head throughout that course were, "Why didn't I learn this in Sunday School? Why didn't anybody teach me this before?" And more importantly: "How can this material be made accessible in church school education and to lay Christians in general?"

Because the new methods of Romans study highlighted the huge culture gap between the first-century Jesus movement and contemporary Western society, it seemed important that such a gap be acknowledged and bridged. Gradually an idea formed in my mind. If the original historical situation can be reconstructed to some degree, why not devise an interactive simulation? A class of students could re-create as much as possible one or more Roman house-churches, with each member playing a different role as Jew or Gentile, slave or free, male or female, poor or not-so-poor. Then "Phoebe" could read segments of text aloud (as would have happened in a mostly illiterate group with no access to extra copies of the letter), and the "Romans" could discuss among themselves what they thought about Paul's ideas and whether or not they agreed with him. Finally, they would end the simulation and discuss what the text may mean today in a changed situation.

With Jewett's encouragement and with enthusiastic, practical assistance from Garrett's Christian education professor, Linda Vogel, this curriculum became my master's thesis, and eventually the book *Paul and the Roman House Churches*.[5]

Jewett's course on Romans turned out to be an academic watershed in my life. In a few short weeks I had to comprehend an entirely new paradigm for understanding this Pauline letter, and also learn how to use new methods for broader biblical study. I compare it to a cross-cultural experience, where one is plunged into a foreign environment and forced to adapt or leave. If one adapts and embraces it, new worlds begin to open up.

During the past decade, I have taught the book of Romans many times and adapted this simulation to classes in church school, college, and seminary. The ideal teaching situation is a three- or four-week course that meets every day for several hours. This keeps students more immersed in their roles in the house-church, providing larger blocks of time for a sustained simulation and discussion of contemporary application. However, conditions are usually not

---

5. The "Aids to Conducting a Simulation of Roman House-Church Dynamics" included in this essay are excerpted from *Paul and the Roman House Churches,* (Scottsdale, Pa.: Herald, 1993), esp. 69-70.

Aids to Conducting a Simulation of Roman House-Church Dynamics

2. Creating Individual Characters for Role Play:
Questions to Ask Yourself

- What is your name and your house-church? Are you a slave, a freedperson, or freeborn?
- What is your occupation? How many hours a day do you work? Where do you work? With whom?
- Where do you live? What are your living quarters like? With whom do you live? Do they also attend your house-church?
- How important to you is your participation in your house-church?
- Are you educated? Intelligent? (Uneducated persons may be intelligent, and vice-versa!)

If you are Jewish:
- Did you leave Rome because of Claudius' edict? Or were you a slave, or too poor, or did you pretend to be a Gentile? If you left Rome in C.E. 49, how did you fare economically or socially?
- Why did you join a Christian house-church? Because you disliked all the rules and regulations in Judaism? Because all your friends and family joined? Because you think the Christians understand Judaism correctly?
- Do you still participate in a Jewish synagogue in Rome?
- Do you have family or friends in Palestine?

If you are Gentile:
- Why did you join the Christian house-church? Because you were attracted to Judaism and this group of Jewish folks accepted uncircumcised Gentiles? Because you were attracted to the stories of their leader Jesus? Because you think the Christian philosophy is better than other philosophies? Because it gave you a group to belong to, and your friends also joined? Because you were attracted to Jewish law and a high standard of ethics?
- What were your religious beliefs before joining the Christian house-church? How have they changed?
- Do you still participate in other religions in Rome?

---

ideal, and the material must be adapted to shorter and/or fewer classes. This can range from a one-session class on Romans 14 to a three-session "highlights of Romans" study to a one-month, twice-a-week book study in my first year "Introduction to Biblical Studies" college course.

In addition to providing historical and cultural background and using material from the beginning and end of Romans to suggest reasons why Paul wrote this letter, I provide profiles of each of the five house-churches or cell groups mentioned in Romans 16.[6] Because of their varied ethnic and economic composition, these groups may not have been getting along very well.

When house-church members have developed their character sketches, they introduce themselves to everyone else in their group, and then the various house-churches introduce themselves to each other. Only then can we begin reading and discussing the text of Romans. For oral reading, I try to find a good public reader to take Phoebe's role, or I do it myself.

The Challenge of Reaching Consensus

My first experience teaching Romans (after a trial run during Sunday School in my home church) was with a small class of eight at Eastern Mennonite Seminary, Harrisonburg, Virginia, during the month-long January 1990 term.[7] With so few people, we developed only one house-church — that of Prisca and Aquila, mentioned in Romans 16:3-5. As would have been typical for a single household, we assumed that members were socially, economically, and ethnically diverse. This allowed for lively conversation.

Initially, some students were skeptical. For the first two days, Kurt (a mediocre student, I was warned ahead of time) sat slouched over in a position of boredom. But the weekend intervened, and by Monday Kurt was leaning forward, enthusiastically immersed in the conversation. When I commented on the difference, he admitted that he finally started reading the material over the weekend and got turned on. As the most liberal (or licentious) Gentile in our group, someone who was "continu[ing] in sin in order that grace may abound" (Rom 6:1b), we needed Kurt's antinomian remarks and accounts of his questionable behavior on trading journeys for his master.

---

6. For evidence supporting the five-church theory see Peter Lampe, "The Roman Christians of Romans 16," in Donfried, *The Romans Debate*, 2nd ed., 216-30.

See Finger, *Paul and the Roman House Churches*, 31-43, for descriptions of the house-churches, along with suggested names for characters. Chapter 6 includes several specific characters for each house-church along with possible backgrounds of their lives in Rome (63-71).

7. Students' names have been changed to protect their anonymity.

Aids to Conducting a Simulation of Roman House-Church Dynamics

3. Sample Roles From One House-Church:
The Brothers and Sisters (Rom 16:14)

Most of the Brothers and Sisters are cobblers who live in small rooms in an *insula,* or tenement house, in *Porta Capena.* This is a noisy, crowded slum on the outskirts of Rome; the Appian Way, a major Roman road, runs through it. The cobblers work together in a shop on the first floor of the *insula.* Most are freedpersons who live at a subsistence level. *Hermes* and *Patrobas* are shoe salesmen who travel from door-to-door or sit in the marketplace with their wares.

Phlegon and *Dorea* are in charge of the shop. They both were freed five years ago but still owe deference to their former owner, who lives six blocks away. They must visit him each morning and, in exchange, he finds some customers to buy their shoes. Phlegon and Dorea became Christians in their master's household, where they had worked as slaves alongside a Christian Jew. They were attracted to monotheism and Jewish ethics, and now are learning to read the Psalms from the Septuagint. *Suria,* their teenage daughter, takes care of the young children of the shoemakers.

Hermas is a young slave-apprentice of Phlegon who is learning the cobbler's trade. *Irene* works as a doctor-midwife. She is a freedwoman who learned medicine as a slave and who now works mostly with lower-class people. She is the wife of *Asyncritus* and the daughter of Greek slaves, but she knows nothing about her parents because she was sold away from them as a young child. Before becoming believers, Hermas followed the Eleusinian mysteries and Irene those of Isis.

Persis and her husband Stephanus were once co-leaders of this group with Phlegon and Dorea. Because of their ties with a nearby Jewish synagogue, they were expelled from Rome in AD 49, traveled east, and met Paul in Corinth, where Stephanus died. Now Persis has returned to rejoin both the shoemaker's trade and the cell group. Persis is a warm and loving older woman and a natural leader — Paul calls her "the beloved" — yet the group is nervous about her return. They want to avoid any political trouble or the loss of their shop. Life is precarious as it is. Some of them worry about Paul's influence on Persis. The conservatives among them think Paul is too liberal, and the liberals think he is too conservative. With the arrival of Paul's letter, tension has increased.

More difficult to manage was Nicky, a member of the Foursquare Gospel Church, who was preparing to be a pastor. Nicky's story brought home to me and to the rest of our class how dangerous it can be to even discuss some contemporary implications of Romans.

Nicky was a good speaker, so I asked her to be Phoebe and read each section of Romans for the group, in addition to playing another role within the house-church. But by the end of the first week, she was ready to drop out. She previously had taken a course on Romans using the traditional paradigm at some other school, and this new approach aroused her suspicions. It was simply too human. "I don't believe the New Testament Christians experienced such conflict with each other. That's not the way Christians behave. When you get to know the Lord, you all agree and get along with each other. That's what happened to me." I talked her into staying with the course, especially since it would hardly be appropriate to lose Phoebe!

Nicky managed to do so until the last Wednesday, when we discussed Romans 13 — the passage on paying taxes and obeying the government. As we moved into a discussion of contemporary implications of this text, denominational proclivities emerged. "If Paul asks us to pay our taxes, what do we do about war taxes?" asked Luke, a Mennonite pastor taking courses during his year's sabbatical. "If Paul tells us to feed our enemies instead of killing them (12:14-15), how can we pay taxes that support war?"[8] Another student who had seen the Nicaraguan oppression first-hand also struggled with the tax issue.

Nicky was appalled that anyone would question the Republican administration's foreign policy. "We have to support democracy against Communism. It can't be helped if some people get themselves killed in the process. We must obey the government, just like Paul says," Nicky declared. "On the other hand, I'll pay your war taxes if you pay my taxes for welfare," she added. "I think it's wrong to give money to people who don't work for a living."

The discussion moved towards abortion, since many Mennonites link their ethics of abortion to their general position on nonviolence. Here Nicky was adamant. Abortion was always wrong because it killed human life. Alice, one of the most astute students in the class, asked Nicky what she would do if she lived in China, where abortion was mandatory in the event of a second pregnancy. "Would you obey the government in this instance?"

---

8. This was around the time American involvement in Central America dominated the news, such as the murders and other terrible human rights abuses in El Salvador that had connections to the School of the Americas in Georgia; and United States destabilization of the Sandinista government in Nicaragua, including the Iran-Contra scandal.

Aids to Conducting a Simulation of Roman House-Church Dynamics

4. Suggestions for Role-playing House-Churches Hearing Rom 13:1-7

For the House-Church of Prisca and Aquila (Rom 16:3-5):

Epaenetus, a Jewish-Christian formerly expelled from Rome, is bitter about having lost so much of his property and having to flee his city as a refugee. Now he is back but still has little. He is considering joining other returning Jews, including those in the synagogue, to protest oppressive taxes and the general discrimination against Jews in Rome. What can this house-church do for Epaenetus?

For the Christian slaves working and living in the households of Aristobulus or Narcissus (Rom 16:10-11):

Neither the house-churches of the Saints (16:15) nor the Brothers and Sisters (16:14) can pay the high taxes that they owe the government. Some of them are considering joining in a tax revolt that includes other Jews from the synagogues, as well as foreigners who are pagans and too poor to pay what the government demands.

Would you consider helping either of these house-churches financially if they asked you for help to pay their taxes? It may mean you will have to share some of the hard-earned cash you were saving to buy your freedom.

On the other hand, since you work for a master who is high up in the government, you do not want any Jew or Jewish-Christian to make political trouble. It may affect your house-church and you might lose your status and perhaps be beaten, crucified, or at least sold away from Rome.

For those in the house-churches of the Brothers and Sisters (Rom 16:14) and the Saints (Rom 16:15):

Your house-church is too poor to pay your taxes, but you know you will get into big trouble and lose your business if you do not pay. Some of the more militant Jews in your house-church want to join the tax revolt that includes other Jews from the synagogues as well as poor, foreign pagans living in Rome. But this will call attention to your house-church and may make it illegal to meet as a church. You know the churches that meet in the households of Aristobulus and Narcissus are wealthier than you. Would you consider asking them for money?

"I certainly would not!" she maintained. "I would *never* have an abortion!"

"But then you'd be disobeying the government," insisted Alice. "How is that consistent with your view of Romans 13?"

Nicky was trapped and silenced. Even though I internally sided with the majority in this conversation, I felt uncomfortable about Nicky's isolation, since I knew no one else agreed with her views on foreign policy. "I can't wait until tomorrow," I thought. That is when we deal with Romans 14 and how to get along with each other even when we do not agree.

When we reconvened after our last break of the day, Nicky was absent. I worried about this, as did the other students, afraid they had been too hard on her. I was more concerned the next day when she did not come at all. My hopes were dashed; so much for putting into practice "strenuous tolerance"[9] with Christians who did not agree with each other! Of all people, Nicky, who declared that when people love the Lord they all get along together, needed to understand the message of Romans 14. Instead, Nicky's absence provided a powerful, negative lesson for the rest of the class on the importance of accepting others when we do not agree with them — and how hard it is to practice this acceptance. I hope none of those students ever forget Paul's instructions to welcome others — "but not for the purpose of quarreling over opinions" (14:1); I never will.

When Nicky did not come the following day, our last day of class, it became clear that she would not finish the course. I phoned her to find out what happened. "I couldn't come back," she said. "I was so upset by our conversation on Wednesday and that Christian people can actually relativize abortion. I could have never gone back." The implications were that the rest of us were heretics with whom she could not associate, at least not in a class on Romans.

"However," she said, "my husband and I are moving soon anyhow. We want to attend Pat Robertson's new seminary in eastern Virginia. I think we'll be a lot more comfortable there."

"I'm sure you will be," I thought, knowing I had failed to reach this student with Paul's message of strenuous tolerance. Figuring out the contemporary implications of Romans certainly can be risky!

---

9. Jewett coins this phrase in his discussion of Romans 14 in Robert Jewett, "Strenuous Tolerance Flowing from Vital Faith," chap. 1 in *Christian Tolerance: Paul's Message to the Modern Church* (*Biblical Perspectives on Current Issues*; Louisville: Westminster John Knox, 1982), 13-42.

Keeping It Real

My most enthusiastic Romans class came a few years later, also at Eastern Mennonite Seminary. It was another January term, but this time I had nearly thirty-five students, enough for five house-churches. Some of the students had remarkable acting skills, and our "Phoebe" was a woman who was an experienced reader and always performed in costume. In addition, the class was enormously enriched by the fact that nearly a third of the students were from "other" cultures — either international students or persons of color from urban backgrounds in the United States. The ethnic diversity of Romans delighted them. "That liberal/conservative struggle among Jews and Gentiles in Romans is the same sort of thing that's happening in my church back home," said one Ethiopian man.

Another church leader from El Salvador connected the attitudes of scorning and passing judgment among the Roman Christians with paternalistic attitudes of white, American, Mennonite church administrators toward native leaders in his country. A Japanese woman drew diagrams of Paul's theology from Romans 1–4 and the particular message it had for her church back home in Japan. A Chinese pastor wrote her paper on the women of Romans 16, thrilled that she could find strong evidence for women's leadership in first-century Roman churches. Planning to return to China in a year or two, she was arming herself with Biblical evidence that women can — and should — be pastors.

In his reflection paper at the end of the course, I was touched by one Puerto Rican man who told how skeptical he was at the beginning of the course. "I thought role-play was just for children," he wrote, "but within a few days I found out that I really WAS Vitalis, a humble cobbler in the house-church of the Saints (16:15). I could learn better about Paul's letter from Vitalis' perspective."[10]

Perhaps this diversity also sharpened students' awareness of economic and class issues in the Roman churches. They took seriously the fact that at least

10. For the use of role play as a teaching tool, see Donald E. Miller and Graydon F. Snyder, *Using Biblical Simulations* (Valley Forge, Pa.: Judson, 1975); Robert Axelrod, *The Complexity of Cooperation: Agent-Based Models of Competition and Collaboration* (Princeton: Princeton University Press, 1997); Steven L. Lamy, et al., *Teaching Global Awareness with Simulations and Games: Grades 6-12* (Denver: University of Denver Center for Teaching International Relations, 1984, 1994); Farren Webb, et al., *Conflict Activity Cards: Grades 9-12* (Denver: University of Denver Center for Teaching International Relations, 1995); and Karen Isaacson, *Playing the Market: Students Learn Important Math Concepts While Engaged in a Stock Market Investment Simulation* (Arata, Calif.: Real Day Educational Publications, 1995).

a third of them were slaves with no human rights, and that most of them lived at a subsistence level.[11] For instance, the slave Theotekna attended the house-church of Prisca and Aquila, though she came from another household where her master regularly beat and abused her. Theotekna had heard of the gospel through her brother Aurelius, a slave in Prisca and Aquila's household. Despite his lowly position, Aurelius brought Theotekna's plight to the whole group and pleaded with them for help, finding support in Paul's vision of the equality of Jew and Gentile. The house-church decided to save money to buy Theotekna from her master. By the end of the course, they had succeeded in doing so. They were thrilled, and the rest of us celebrated with them.

I also was pleased at the ingenuity of the poverty-stricken house-church of the Saints living in the slums of *Trastevere*.[12] Discussing the ethics of hospitality and the command to "contribute to the needs of the saints" in 12:13, this house-church pondered how they would keep from starving if they paid their taxes as instructed in 13:1-7. Visiting another house-church at the time, I looked up to see the entire group of Saints marching over to the Narcissus cell group, who were supposedly economically better off as upwardly mobile slaves in an imperial household. "Can you share some of your food?" they begged. "We had to pay our taxes and now we're starving!" The *Narcissiani* were startled by the request — and sheepish because they had to say they did not have any food at the time. However, at the next day's simulation they produced pretzels and cookies and ceremoniously presented them to the Saints!

Today I teach on the college level, and spend a month on a Romans study with first-year students. With less knowledge or experience in multi-cultural situations, these students naturally exhibit less maturity and theological understanding. Sometimes house-church discussions on the earlier chapters of Romans get repetitive when students do not prepare adequately ahead of time and end up arguing the same issue of law-observance versus non-law-observance for several consecutive class periods. However, "dear diary" requirements for each class have helped alleviate that. A liberal, Gentile man will occasionally boast of sexual indiscretions or flirting with orgiastic religions, shocking his more conservative Jewish counterparts. One very creative Prisca

---

11. For a discussion of slavery in ancient Rome see Peter Garnsey & Richard P. Saller, *The Roman Empire: Economy, Society, and Culture* (Berkeley: University of California Press, 1987); Thomas E. J. Wiedemann, *Greek and Roman Slavery* (Baltimore: Johns Hopkins, 1981); Moses I. Finley, *Ancient Slavery and Modern Ideology* (New York: Viking, 1980); and Keith Hopkins, *Conquerors and Slaves* (Cambridge: Cambridge University Press, 1978).

12. Editor's note: known in the Roman period as the *Transtiberium*, it was a largely manufacturing sector of the city on the opposite side of the Tiber River. It is reputed to have had a large Jewish population in Paul's time.

suggested to her surprised house-church that she was pregnant and would need to buy the abused slave Theotekna for the baby's nurse! Several times I have had a bright, articulate Epaenetus (16:5) play the role of a returning Jewish butcher who insists on preparing meat for the household and persuading everyone else to eat kosher, to the annoyance of the Gentile household manager.

The reality of ancient slavery is difficult for today's American youth to comprehend. They rarely see it as degrading and brutal as slavery was in our own country 1700-1800 years later.[13] When those playing slave roles write up their character sketches, they usually have considerate masters who teach them how to read and write, and who promise to free them when they become adults so they can get married and have a house and children. I often require them to do further research and rewrite their character sketches in order to get some sense of what it would be like to live with no human rights, not even the right to one's own body, and to realize one is not likely to be manumitted until one is old or sick. This introduction to ancient slavery also provides me with the opportunity to introduce today's horrific reality of slavery: the international trade in sex slavery; the virtual slavery of millions of children forced to work long hours in sweatshops; and government-forced labor in Sudan as one side of the brutal civil war in that country.[14]

Teaching Romans to an upper-level college class of Bible and Christian Ministry majors and minors provides more excitement and versatility than the first-year general education class. Recently a vocal and articulate house-church called "the Brothers and Sisters" deadlocked over conservative v. liberal lifestyles and beliefs that pervaded every conversation throughout simulations on Romans 1–11. Their intense arguments would distract the neighbors living only a few feet away. But by the time we reached the ethical admonitions of Romans 12, something changed. I was sitting with another house-church when I looked up to see the most legalistic, loud-mouthed Jewish Brother embracing each of his fellow brothers and sisters. He had at last "seen the light," come to understand Paul's message of a law-free gospel, and was becoming reconciled with his cell group!

---

13. For a comparison of slavery in ancient Rome and the United States see Allen Dwight Callahan, Richard A. Horsley, and Abraham Smith, "Introduction: The Slavery of New Testament Studies," 1-15 in *Slavery in Text and Interpretation* (*Semeia* 83/84; 1998); Richard Horsley, "The Slave Systems of Classical Antiquity and Their Reluctant Recognition by Modern Scholars," ibid., 19-66.

14. For a discussion on slavery in the Sudan, see Madut Jok, *War and Slavery in Sudan* (Philadelphia: University of Pennsylvania Press, 2001); Marc Lacey, "Panel Led by U.S. Criticizes Sudan's Government Slavery," *New York Times* (May 23, 2002): A17; and Nicholas D. Kristof, "A Slave's Journey in Sudan," *New York Times* (April 23, 2002): A23.

Aids to Conducting a Simulation of Roman House-Church Dynamics

5. Sample Page from Romans "Diary"
  (*Student role-playing Aurelia, from the church in the house of Prisca and Aquila*)

Dear Diary,

Today was an unusual day — a day I had been looking forward to all week. Ever since Phoebe of Cenchreae arrived, we had heard that one of the Christian missionaries, Paul of Tarsus, had written a letter just for the believers in Rome. Phoebe, of course, is Paul's co-worker and patron down near Corinth.

Well, today we finally heard the beginning of the letter — and Paul's greetings at the end. We could not get any farther because everyone wanted to talk about what Paul had said, even his opening lines! Our worship services are usually pretty lively, but this time *everybody* had something to say. Prisca, who led the meeting, could hardly get people to wait in line!

Some of our people think Paul is great because they met him back East and heard him preach. But Epaenetus is pretty wary. He is more conservative than Paul, and now he is afraid he is going to lose his battle with Felicia about eating only kosher meat. We have not heard yet if Paul said anything in his letter about keeping the food laws; maybe that is coming later. But Olympios is nervous about Paul's letter for the opposite reason. That old pagan thinks the whole Jewish law should be dumped! (I know I shouldn't call him "pagan," but I do it just to tease him.)

Well, I am just a slave, so I did not say much at first. But I heard Paul say that *he* was a slave, too — a slave of Jesus Christ. At first, I thought he was kidding. This guy is free to go wherever he wants; he is even a citizen of the Empire, just like my masters, Prisca and Aquila. But Aquila reminded me that Paul really does feel especially called by God to preach the gospel to the Gentiles, and he has been through more hardships than probably many slaves in this huge city.

So what did I think about Paul's opening greeting, after the "slave" part? I think he is trying really hard to get on our good side. He talked about Jesus "descended from David according to the flesh," so that made the Jews among us feel good. You know how they can lord it over the rest of us sometimes because they are the *real* Chosen People. But then right away Paul moved to our common belief in Jesus' resurrection from the dead, and how *that* is where Paul's power comes from, not so much that he was a Jew. Actually, I thought he was pretty inclusive, all things considered. I just wonder if he will be able to hold the attention of all the diverse people in our house-church. Phoebe's visit sure will be exciting!

We conclude each course with a Roman meal, inviting all the house-churches to participate. I usually prompt Prisca and Aquila to issue the invitation, assuming they are the only ones wealthy enough to have a house. Because of the deep symbolism of commensality in this culture, bringing the squabbling house-churches together is a momentous occasion. Still in their roles, they can mix with each other and tell stories from their own house-church experiences. The Lord's Supper ritual is also shared, using the Mediterranean meal custom of bread-breaking before the meal and the drinking ritual at the end.

I arrange a Roman meal with the college dining services for my first-year students, but we have a potluck instead if participants can prepare their own meals. My book includes lists of appropriate foods and a number of recipes.[15] Group members are restricted to bringing only those items that are appropriate to their religious or socio-economic stations in life — e.g., no meat from poor people, and probably none from the "weak" conservatives (Rom 14:2). I make sure some of the wealthier, more liberal Gentiles bring pork or ham so the food laws can be observed or flouted, depending on one's character. Some conscientious, role-playing, observant Jews will watch what they eat with great care.

Can simulated agape meals and Holy Communion have real spiritual meaning for the participants? While it does not always happen among the less mature college students, others react differently. Two years ago I led a Romans simulation for Mennonite Ministers' Week in Toronto, Canada. We concluded with a ritual of hand-washing and sharing bread and grape juice in separate house-churches. The leader of one house-church told me afterward that he had been concerned about whether this ritual would have appropriate spiritual impact within a simulation. In fact he found it deeply meaningful for himself, and looking around his group he saw tears in many eyes. It was a time for unity after many heated debates.

Teaching Through Controversy and Conflict

There are challenges when using a simulation to teach Romans. It is true that this method does not allow material to be presented as systematically as I would like it to be. My tension also mounts when house-churches get stuck on repetitive conflicts, mostly because they have not done enough homework. I think about how much more thoroughly the theological details would be covered if I

---

15. See Finger, *Paul and the Roman House Churches,* 154-63.

Aids to Conducting a Simulation of Roman House-Church Dynamics

6. Debriefing and Applying: Sample Entry from Romans Reflection Journal*

At first I felt a little awkward about role-playing Aurelia. I am not used to it. And never having been a slave, I have a hard time imagining what that would have been like. I am not used to listening so carefully either; I worked hard to keep my mind from wandering. But as people in our house-church talked, it got easier and more fun. I really want to get into my character and show the rest of my house-church how well a mere slave can understand Paul's letter. I'll prove to some of those free Jews that an illiterate slave can also be intelligent!

I never knew before that Romans had anything to do with Jews and Gentiles getting along together and how hard that might have been. I think today we usually hang around with people who are like us and who believe the same things we do. Even coming to college this year was a big adjustment because I am living around people who come from different backgrounds and sometimes believe different things from me. Some of my teachers really have different views. It is hard to believe some people are even Christians if they disagree on something as important as [baptism, pacifism, alcohol or drug use, predestination, gifts of the Spirit, women's roles, abortion, homosexuality, music, politics; fill in the blank]. And I don't know many people of color or of other ethnic backgrounds. Does Paul think we should deliberately try to reach out to people who are different? The question in the book was, "If we cannot get along with people not like us, does that mean we are not living out the power of the gospel?" I'll have to think about that. So far I have not had much chance to really talk with people who do not think or act like I do.

*Entry from student role-playing Aurelia, from the church in the house of Prisca and Aquila

simply lectured and allowed time for questions. Yet another challenge is keeping up with scholarship on Romans and adjusting the simulation accordingly.[16]

While the simulation approach may make it difficult to cover all the information delivered in a traditional class, it allows students to grasp some key concepts that they may miss given a different class format.

First of all, the early churches did experience conflict, and not all believers agreed on many theological and ethical issues. Contrary to what Nicky thought, if people "come to know the Lord," they will not always get along with each other and experience perfect unity of mind and heart.[17] Understanding how New Testament writings exhibit the human limitations of the earliest believers can make the documents more accessible to students.

Secondly, this method of presenting a new paradigm of interpreting Romans is less threatening to people, especially younger students. During the last twelve years or more, I do not recall having a single student who had heard of the "emerging paradigm" of Romans interpretation, even though various forms of it have been accepted by scholars for years. The traditional paradigm, in which Romans timelessly tells individuals how to get saved by grace through faith and not the law, is what prevails in the church at large. While I agree that this is implicit in Paul's argument, role-playing the letter in its cultural context opens up new ways to look at the text.

Third, by arguing their case for or against the need to continue practicing the Mosaic law, students come to appreciate the value of Jewish covenantal traditions. They learn the difference between religious identity-markers and ethical practices. At times they can feel how easily "grace" can slip into license to do whatever one wants.

Educational research has demonstrated that teaching through constructive controversy is more effective than either lecture or group discussion.[18]

---

16. For example, what if the Jewish believers were still meeting in the synagogues as well as the house-churches? What if Claudius' edict expelling the Jews and Nero's decision to allow it to lapse were not major factors affecting how Paul wrote his letter? No doubt the ethnic and religious disagreements in Rome were far more nuanced than we can simulate. What kinds of problems does that pose?

Virginia Wiles, a Pauline scholar who had been teaching in a more diverse liberal arts college, used my approach for Romans, but included a simulated synagogue of Jews who also reacted to Paul's letter. Wiles also created a web site using the same material but adding more background information that students needed to access for their course. I have found it helpful for my purposes as well.

17. Jewett, *Christian Tolerance, passim.*

18. For example, see David W. Johnson, Roger T. Johnson, and Karl A. Smith, "Constructive Controversy: The Educative Power of Intellectual Conflict," *Change* 1 (2000): 29-37. Also David W. Johnson, Roger T. Johnson, and Karl A. Smith, *Academic Controversy: Enriching Col-*

Even though less material is "covered," more is retained as students wrestle with and provide arguments for or against various positions. Yet students, especially Christian students, have a difficult time vigorously debating their peers for fear of hurting or being hurt. Using role-play first, where they can make their character as obnoxious as they wish, loosens up participants to speak their minds during the subsequent debate and discussion on contemporary application.

Conclusion

There is no question that Paul's letter to the Romans is highly theological and sometimes difficult to understand. One way to use recent research on the theological, rhetorical, and cultural background of the letter is to reconstruct the original situation as accurately as possible in the form of a sustained simulation of the Roman house-church groups who received Paul's letter and (probably) heard it read and interpreted by his co-worker, Phoebe of Cenchreae. Understanding the human believers behind the letter and the questions and disagreements that arose as a result of their diversity can make the text more accessible to today's students. In addition, because of the concrete situation reconstructed behind the text, it often is easier to see contemporary implications of the message of Romans.

Robert Jewett's enthusiasm for Romans obviously has influenced me deeply. His innovative teaching methods have inspired me to improve my own. His endless and challenging assignments have made me feel less guilty when I require significant work from my students. And his creative hermeneutics have pushed me to think of contemporary implications of Romans in ways that otherwise I never would have imagined.

---

lege Instruction through Intellectual Conflict (*ASHE-ERIC Higher Education Report,* Volume 25.3; Washington, D.C.: ERIC Clearing House on Higher Education, Office of Educational Research and Improvement, 1997).

Six-Gun Savior: George Stevens' "Shane" and Paul's Letter to the Romans

L. D. Hurst

> *For the wrath of God is revealed from heaven against all unrighteousness and ungodliness of the human race.*
>
> (ROM 1:18)

Among those working in the field of Biblical studies, none has done more than Robert Jewett to relate his chosen field of the New Testament to a discussion of contemporary American cultural trends. Building on his religious and sociological critiques,[1] he has also given us two innovative and penetrating volumes on film studies: *St. Paul at the Movies* and *St. Paul Returns to the Movies*.[2] There he provides a model that hopefully will be emulated by other biblical scholars — the creation of an "interpretive arch" whereby ancient texts are illustrated and clarified by modern film treatments, and modern film treatments are illustrated and clarified by ancient texts.[3]

---

1. See, e.g., Robert Jewett, *The Captain America Complex* (Philadelphia: Westminster, 1973; Santa Fe: Bear & Company, 1984); *The American Monomyth* (Garden City: Anchor, 1977); *Christian Tolerance: Paul's Message to the Modern Church* (Philadelphia: Westminster, 1982); *Paul the Apostle to America: Cultural Trends and Pauline Scholarship* (Louisville: Westminster John Knox, 1994); and *The Myth of the American Superhero* (Grand Rapids, Mich.: Eerdmans, 2002).

2. Robert Jewett, *Saint Paul at the Movies* (Louisville: Westminster John Knox, 1993), and *Saint Paul Returns to the Movies* (Grand Rapids, Mich.: Eerdmans, 1999).

3. The method is described in Robert Jewett, "Stuck in Time: Kairos, Chronos, and the Flesh in Groundhog Day," 155-65 in *Explorations in Theology and Film* (ed. Clive Marsh and

In joining the chorus of friends and colleagues who are celebrating a multifaceted life and career that has enriched a generation of students (and that shows no sign of slowing down, even in retirement), I wish to extend the dialogue between Biblical texts and film that Bob has so deftly initiated. In doing so, I will look to the religious iconography of one of the past century's foremost American film-makers, George Stevens, and what that might tell us about some of Paul's comments in his Epistle to the Romans, and *vice versa*.

During a period stretching over three decades George Stevens established himself as a member of a select group of America's premier film-makers, a club that included John Ford, Alfred Hitchcock, Cecil B. De Mille, and Howard Hawks. In such features as "Swing Time" (1935), "Gunga Din" (1939), "Woman of the Year" (1942), "A Place in the Sun" (1951), "The Diary of Anne Frank" (1959) and "Giant" (1956), Stevens demonstrated his total devotion to the perfecting of his craft. Despite these landmarks, it is his 1952 masterwork, "Shane," that remains his greatest achievement. There he created and celebrated a mythical western hero who, through constant cable viewings and video rentals, continues to exert a remarkable power on audiences. And, despite the film's age, for many "Shane" continues to represent the high-water mark of the western film — "the greatest of all westerns," as one critic described it.[4]

Following the release of "Shane" in 1952, the mythical American West remained one of the most reliable and popular staples of the Hollywood film, a trend that continued until 1980, when one man's ego almost destroyed the genre for good. Michael Cimino's $45 million epic, "Heaven's Gate," set out to explode the myth of the West, but instead it came close to exploding the western film itself.[5] Since that time, with the exception of a few independent excursions,[6] it is Clint Eastwood who has deliberately and almost single-handedly kept the genre alive. Along the way he also managed to elevate the western to new levels of mythic urgency and gritty realism in the American consciousness.

Here we have two men — Stevens and Eastwood — who reflect radically

Gaye Ortiz; Oxford: Blackwell, 1997), 156: "In the light of the historical-critical method, I understand Pauline texts in the light of their bearing on specific cultural and historical situations, and I look for modern analogies not just to what Paul wrote but also to the situations he addressed. In contrast to a tradition of abstract, dogmatic interpretation that has tended to dominate Pauline studies, I am operating on the assumption that every word of a Pauline letter is embedded in a story of a concrete community in conversation with other faith communities."

4. Alan Starbrook, "The Return of Shane," *Films and Filming* 12 (1966): 40.

5. See Steven Bach, *Final Cut: Dreams and Disaster in the Making of "Heaven's Gate"* (New York: W. Morrow, 1985). I had first-hand experience of the waste that went into this hugely misconceived venture, having played a Harvard undergraduate in the opening sequence of the film.

6. E.g. Lawrence Kasdan's smart-looking "Silverado" (1985); Kevin Costner's "Dances with Wolves" (1990); and George Cosmatos' ultra-violent "Tombstone" (1993).

different visions of the American West. Although "Shane" would be Stevens' most successful and best-remembered work, it would be his only incursion into the genre of the western. Eastwood, on the other hand, has devoted a large part of his career to it. Following the enormous success of the "Spaghetti Westerns" created by Sergio Leone in the 1960's, Eastwood honed his western craft by starring in and directing such fare as "High Plains Drifter" (1972), "The Outlaw Josey Wales" (1976) and, most recently, the Academy Award–winning "Unforgiven" (1992). These works placed him firmly in the saddle as the late-twentieth-century's most successful exponent and deconstructor of the old West.

While the aforementioned films will always remain important in any discussion of Eastwood's life and filmography, it is "Pale Rider," his 1984 homage to "Shane," that restored financial and intellectual viability to the western after Cimino's heaven had turned to hell. "Pale Rider," "'Shane' with an ecological spin,"[7] also remains the film that continues to excite the most comments among those concerned to relate Biblical and theological concerns to the question of the proper response to personal, corporate, and ecological evil.[8] Here Eastwood provides a brisk story laced with Biblical allusions. He invades our collective dreams with a dark-clad savior and leveler of vengeance who appears out of nowhere to settle old scores and to answer our hopes of redressing life's injustices. It is evident that, in "Pale Rider," Eastwood was paying a respectful, if somewhat idiosyncratic, homage to "Shane."[9]

We may now turn back to that "interpretive arch" explored with such success by Robert Jewett, and by which Stevens' and Eastwood's two film treatments might provide some useful insights into Paul's letter to the Romans, and *vice versa*.

The Consequential Wrath of God

According to Paul, "the wrath of God is revealed from heaven against all ungodliness and wickedness of the human race" (Rom 1:18). But what does Paul mean by "the wrath of God" in Rom 1? A number of scholars find the most nat-

---

7. Richard Schickel, *Clint Eastwood* (New York: Random House, 1996), 403.

8. E.g. Robert Jewett, "The Disguise of Vengeance in 'Pale Rider,'" 118-33 in *Saint Paul at the Movies*.

9. Michael Wilmington, "Westerns Return on a 'Pale Rider,'" *Los Angeles Times* (June 28, 1985): Sec. VI, 1 and 15: "Essentially, 'Pale Rider' is a remake of 'Shane' (the plots are virtually identical). . . . By remaking 'Shane' — and finding in it new highlights, new twists, shadings and musical tones — Eastwood takes a fond glance at a slice of the past worth treasuring."

ural meaning to be dictated by what follows, and conclude that God's wrath is identical with the process of "hardening" which Paul goes on to describe in the following paragraphs.[10] The divine wrath is revealed where men and women are passively handed over to endure the consequences of their own folly. This is accomplished when they are "given over" to a hardened mind that is hostile to God.[11]

The "hardening process" is seen in Stevens' film in the respective examples of Wilson (Jack Palance), Ryker (Emile Meyer), and Shane (Alan Ladd). Stevens' cinematic treatment shows a profound attentiveness to the destructive consequences of evil in the human personality. In illustrating this concern, we begin with Wilson, the most obvious case. He is a man completely given over to evil, portrayed by Stevens as living by the gun. For Wilson, killing is not just a profession; it has become a sport. He takes pleasure in the brutal death of Torrey. There is never a hint of regret, for in him the wrath process has spread to every level of his being.[12]

One of the differences between Shane and Wilson is their approach to the gun. For Shane, the gun is just a tool, "as good or bad as the one who uses it." For Wilson, on the other hand, the gun has become an almost permanent extension of his arm, and thus of his character.[13]

Paul's "wrath process" is also present — although not as blunt or obvious — in Rufus Ryker. Here Stevens portrays the "handing over" as indifference to the changing social order. "Your kinda days are over," Shane tells Ryker with prophetic assurance. But Shane agrees that he himself is also part of the old order, and it is his personal tragedy that he cannot answer the demands of this

10. Cf. Rom 1:24, 26, & 28.

11. Cf. C. H. Dodd, *The Epistle of Paul to the Romans* (New York: Harper & Brothers, 1922), 22-24.

12. Lloyd Baugh, *Imaging the Divine: Jesus and Christ-Figures in Film* (Kansas City: Sheed & Ward, 1997), 165, claims "It is . . . in a brief comment that Stevens has [Wilson] make to Ryker that the humanity of Wilson is best revealed. Exasperated by Starrett, Ryker vows, 'I'll kill him if I have to!' Wilson, coffee mug in hand, calmly, with conscious irony, responds, 'You mean *I'll* kill him if you have to.' In that moment of public self-consciousness, Stevens is suggesting that Wilson knows how he is irrevocably trapped in an identity, a destiny of which, it would seem, he might prefer to be free." Humanity? A destiny of which he might prefer to be free? Wilson's comment is nothing more nor less than a crude joke, in which Ryker's inexperience at gunfighting and Wilson's own role as Ryker's surrogate is a subject of sarcasm. In light of this and the observations made above, I find Baugh's assertion of a sense of "humanity" in Wilson to be highly implausible.

13. I reject Bernard Brandon Scott's bizarre reading of sexual imagery into Wilson's gun. Scott claims: "Thus the violence and death of the gun, the male organ, are in sharp contrast to [Marian's] virgin fertility as the mother-goddess" (Bernard Brandon Scott, *Hollywood Dreams and Biblical Stories* [Minneapolis: Augsburg Fortress, 1994], 52).

new world of which he wishes very much to be a part. It is one of Shane's near-supernatural qualities that he is allowed to see the future — that is, that he and others like him are doomed to obsolescence. "The difference [between us]," as Shane says to Ryker, "is that I know it."

Here I might pause and take a step back. Stevens is much too skillful a storyteller (and theologian?) to depict his hero in one-dimensional terms. He never suggests that the wrath process is inactive in Shane. Presenting him as a Christ-figure (see below) does not require that Shane be unscathed by the consequences of his former life. After dispatching Wilson and Ryker, Shane tells little Joe "there's no living with a killing — right or wrong; it's a brand, and a brand sticks." But in Shane the wrath process, or "brand," has been mitigated by something else — a "something" similar to what Paul would call conversion or "grace." Shane regrets his past, turns from it, and resolves to make amends — which in his case means trying to forge a new life apart from the gun (the same process which is seen at work in another crucial character in the story, Chris Callaway [Ben Johnson]). The fact that he ultimately is unsuccessful is beside the point.

Wilson, on the other hand, has allowed the wrath process to run the course to its inevitable, disastrous conclusion. Instead of renouncing the gun, Wilson has made it his life. Shane's reluctance to take up the gun, when contrasted with the brutality with which Wilson kills Torrey, sets in stark relief the difference between the two men's characters. Unfortunately for him, in Wilson's case the wrath process has reached the point of no return and demands the ultimate penalty. Put in simpler terms, "All who live by the sword shall die by the sword" (Matt 26:52). Or as Paul remarks in Gal 6:7, "Whatever a man sows, that shall he reap." In effect, Wilson has allowed his "charge account of evil" to run up to the point where the whole debt is called in. After all, everyone is a debtor to whom God regularly presents a statement of the account, but God is ever ready to remit the debt on the basis of repentance. On the other hand, those who refuse to repent are allowed to run up a long bill against the final day of reckoning. In this way God's wrath takes on a cumulative force unless it continually is translated into grace by forgiveness and repentance. The time eventually comes when Wilson's cumulative debt comes due, and his failure to repent and treat his fellow creatures with respect costs him his life.

By taking the homesteaders' place in the conflict, Shane simultaneously takes his stand against what Paul calls "the principalities and powers and rulers of this age" (Rom 8:38).[14] In Stevens' cinematic version, the "principalities and powers" are the cattlemen who possess the Western land, namely Ryker and his

14. Cf. Col 1:16, 2:10, 15; Eph 1:21, 3:10, 6:12.

gang. Later, in "The Greatest Story Ever Told" (Stevens' epic film portrayal of the life of Christ), they become the religious leaders who control the land of Palestine (also significantly pictured by Stevens as the American West). In "Shane," the homesteaders invite additional parallels to the early Christians in their struggle against the Roman Empire. They are powerless — "no match for them" — when pitted against those who use force to inhabit and control the land. The cattlemen may be wrong, but "they've got it — that's what counts." Shane, on the other hand, while more suited to the life of a cattleman offered him by Ryker, chooses to make the homesteaders' fight his own. Through an act of will, he takes the homesteaders' side to defeat Ryker and his forces. "There are no more guns in the valley" is Stevens' cinematic version of Paul's defeat of "the Powers."

The Timely Death of Christ

For Paul, divine help in the form of God's Son came at a time when the human race should have least expected it. "But God proves his love for us in that while we were yet sinners, Christ died for us" (Rom 5:8). In a similar way, the question "Who are you, Stranger?" takes us to the heart of Stevens' exercise in Christological art. Whether posed by Ryker's man (John Dierkes) at the beginning of "Shane" or by a synagogue official (John Lupton) in "The Greatest Story Ever Told,"[15] it represents the unbelieving world's reaction to the unexpected appearance of divine aid. In "Shane," it comes in the form of the stranger who descends from the mountains to side with the homesteaders. In "The Greatest Story Ever Told," it is the unexpected and dissonant voice in the Jewish synagogue proclaiming God's desire for mercy and love rather than vengeance, or a mysterious figure standing alone in the shadows, silent and unnoticed — except by Stevens' camera.

That last image is one of the most powerful moments in "The Greatest Story Ever Told." An old woman in the street prays for God to send the Deliverer. "You're wasting your time, old woman," a skeptical voice tells her. "If he were coming, he'd be here by now." Stevens then moves his lens to a barely-visible, solitary figure (Max von Sydow) standing in the shadows. It is almost as if Stevens wants his viewers to consider how often divine help has been there when it is most wanted, and yet has gone unnoticed. It comes in unforeseen ways, as in a stranger's unheralded arrival on a Wyoming landscape, giving new

15. Where John Lupton's question (when the crippled boy is healed) is shortened to simply "Who are you?"

hope to the community, or a figure standing silently on a Jerusalem street, heralding the beginning of the fulfillment of ancient promises. "How often has the divine help gone unrecognized and unappreciated, when it was most needed and desired?" is Stevens' version of Paul's startling claim that "While we were yet sinners, Christ died for us."

There remains a significant debate among theologians as to the meaning of Rom 3:25, where Paul claims that God has sent forth Christ as a *hilastērion* or "sacrifice" for human sin. What is the precise meaning of *hilastērion* in this context? Does it involve the divine wrath of Rom 1:18, as in a propitiation? In that case the wrath usually is understood as something poured out on Christ in a penal or substitutionary sense. Christ died not for what he did, but for what sinners have done. Or is Paul saying that Christ's death should be seen more generally, as that which "removes" or "covers" human sin? The commentators remain divided.

Stevens is no professional theologian, and for the purposes of our interpretive arch that may be his greatest value. Nonetheless, while not academically trained in the discipline, he is a theologian, as he attempted to show in "Greatest Story." What he says in story form may help point us in the right direction to understand what Paul is attempting to say in Rom 3:25. In Paul's metaphor Christ's death makes it possible for sinners to live a life free of guilt and judgment. Similarly, Shane makes the ultimate sacrifice, relinquishing his right to remain in the valley. This is no small matter. Shane makes it possible for others in the valley to live a life free of sin and oppression (i.e., the gun), but it costs Shane, even to the shedding of his blood. "It's bloody!" cries Little Joe as he takes Shane's hand. Shane's sacrifice is both personal and bloody. This is Rom 3:25 Western-style. Starrett and the other homesteaders could later say of Shane, as Christians say of Jesus, "Standing in our place, he bore the consequences of our dilemma, and in doing so he exhausted and absorbed the powers, so that their fury should not fall on us."

Had he wished to do so, of course, Stevens could have carried the symbolism further by having Shane's hand shot through, rather than his shoulder, thus making the Christological association more blatant. But Stevens is too good a storyteller for that. He hopes to take his viewers to a deeper level. For him, Shane's real sacrifice entails a return to the life he previously had scorned, that of the wandering gunfighter, which loses him his place in the new society he had come to love and regard as his home. It would be difficult for others to know what such an act might entail for one who has endured what Shane has. "I think we know, Shane," Marian tells the figure standing alone in the rain, alienated from his new friends.

The truth is, she does not know, nor do we. Only one who has experienced the life of a wandering gunfighter could appreciate Shane's experience. And yet, his "otherness" notwithstanding, Shane is more like the homesteaders than different from them simply because he *chooses* to be like them. As he says, for no apparent reason, "I'm a friend of Starrett." And still we get the feeling that the settlers are unworthy of Shane, whether at the beginning or the end of the story. Reminiscent of Paul's view of Jesus — "While we were yet sinners, Christ died for us" (Rom 5:8) — Shane's action is performed before the beneficiaries could understand it. Like Christ, he adopts the settlers as his people, even though we, the viewers, sense that they will never quite understand or appreciate what he will do for them.

In Stevens' version of the story, Shane exhausts the fury of the Ryker gang, and his victory will allow Little Joe to "grow up straight and strong." Growing up "straight and strong" is Stevens' equivalent of Pauline sanctification. It comes at great cost to Shane.

The Divine Claim to Vengeance

In Rom 12:19 Paul exhorts his readers, "Beloved, never avenge yourselves, but leave room for the wrath of God; for it is written, 'Vengeance is mine, I will repay, says the Lord.'" Robert Jewett has addressed this topic at length in his interpretation of "Pale Rider."[16] The dilemma of whether to take personal vengeance or to allow God to execute justice upon wrongdoers through divinely-chosen agents (Rom 13) is a complex one, and has troubled Christians for the past two thousand years. Jewett deals only with Eastwood's version of the story,[17] while Robert Banks extends the discussion to "Shane."[18] For Banks the latter film is superior largely because it can be taken at more than one level, one of which is as a symbolic retelling of the "drama of salvation."[19]

Taken at the level of human conduct, as with most other levels, "Shane" is superior to Eastwood's "Pale Rider." In "Shane" the idea of personal vengeance, if not totally absent, is treated differently. Stevens goes out of his way to show that Shane has no personal ax to grind — no grudge — against Wilson.[20] At

16. Jewett, *Saint Paul at the Movies*, 118-33.

17. Ibid.

18. Robert Banks, "The Drama of Salvation in George Stevens' Shane," 59-72 in *Explorations in Theology and Film* (ed. Clive Marsh and Gaye Ortiz; Oxford: Blackwell, 1998).

19. This approach is similar to that of Lloyd Baugh (*Imaging the Divine*, 171), who published his study simultaneously with that of Banks.

20. In Eastwood's variation of the story, on the other hand, the hero ("The Preacher with No Name") is seen to exact his own personal retribution on his arch-enemy, Stockburn. "Pale

one or two points in the story the viewer even gets the feeling that, had they met years earlier, Shane and Wilson might have been friends (assuming that Wilson was ever capable of friendship). Now, of course, the choices they have made in life have determined that they be deadly rivals.

Yet Stevens would have his audience know that there is a certain mutual regard between the two men — an element totally lacking in Jack Schaefer's novel.[21] In the crucial Fourth of July night scene, while Ryker and Starrett have their overdue confrontation, Stevens diverts the viewers' attention from the speakers to a fascinating pantomime — a wordless interplay between Shane and Wilson in which each views the other warily but with obvious respect. In film terms, the scene lasts a very long time, nearly five minutes. Even after killing Wilson, Shane has nothing negative to say about him. What he feels is the respect of one skilled craftsman for another. "Yes, that was Wilson. He was fast . . . fast on the draw."

What of Shane's taunting words to Wilson, by which he goads him into the fatal confrontation? Does not this indicate hatred of, and personal vengeance against, an enemy? Here it should be noted that Stevens' handling of the critical scene departs significantly from Schaefer's version. Stevens adds some remarkable dialogue which reveals that Shane is not here speaking for himself, but for the slain Torrey.[22]

If we are to explore this in depth we first must go back to Schaefer's version of the original exchange outside Grafton's saloon (in which, incidentally, it is Ernie Wright, not Torrey, who confronts and is killed by Wilson). Then we can turn to the confrontation between Shane and Wilson.

Schaefer's version of Wright versus Wilson:[23]
> "You're a damn fool, Wright. But what can you expect from a breed?"
> "That's a lie!" shouted Ernie. "My mother wasn't no Indian!"
> "Why, you crossbred squatter," Wilson said, quick and sharp, "are you telling me I'm wrong?"
> "I'm telling you you're a God-damned liar!" . . .
> "You'll back that, Wright. Or you'll crawl out of here on your belly."
> [They draw, and Wilson kills Wright.]

Rider" is thus essentially a vengeance story (with biblical allusions thrown in) which is more or less designed to illustrate the old adage that "revenge is a dish best served cold." As Eastwood himself would admit, there is nothing genuinely religious about this.

21. Jack Warner Schaefer, *Shane* (Boston: Houghton Mifflin Co., 1949).

22. Surprisingly, this has been totally overlooked by the previous published discussions of "Shane."

23. Schaefer, *Shane: The Critical Edition* (ed. James C. Work; Lincoln, Neb.: University of Nebraska Press, 1984), 214-15.

Schaefer's version of Shane versus Wilson:[24]

> Wilson's face sobered and his eyes glinted coldly. "I've no quarrel with you," he said flatly, "even if you are Starrett's man. Walk out of here without any fuss and I'll let you go. It's Starrett I want."
>
> "What you want, Wilson, and what you'll get are two different things. Your killing days are done. . . . I'm waiting, Wilson. Do I have to crowd you into slapping leather?"
>
> [They draw, and Shane kills Wilson].

Now compare this with Steven's rendering of both incidents:

Stevens' version of Torrey versus Wilson:

> Wilson: They tell me they call you Stonewall.
> Torrey: Anything wrong with that?
> Wilson: That's just funny. I guess they named a lot of that southern trash after old Stonewall.
> Torrey: Who'd they name you after? Or do you know?
> Wilson: I'm sayin' that Stonewall Jackson was trash himself. Him, Lee, and all the rest of them Rebs. You, too.
> Torrey: You're a lowdown lyin' Yankee.
> Wilson: Prove it.
> [They draw, and Torrey is killed by Wilson.]

Stevens' version of Shane versus Wilson:

> Wilson: My fight ain't with you.
> Shane: It ain't with me, Wilson?
> Wilson: No it ain't, Shane . . .
> Shane: So you're Jack Wilson.
> Wilson: What's that mean to you, Shane?
> Shane: I've heard about you.
> Wilson: What have you heard, Shane?
> Shane: I've heard that you're a lowdown, Yankee liar.
> Wilson: Prove it.
> [They draw, and Wilson is killed by Shane.]

Why, at this critical point, does Stevens have Shane call Wilson "a low-down Yankee liar" — almost exactly echoing Torrey's last words? The intrigue deepens when we notice that earlier in the film Stevens added more dialogue

---

24. Schaefer, *Shane*, 257-58.

not found in the novel, in which he appears to go out of his way to establish that the words between Torrey and Wilson could not have been overheard by Shane or anyone else. The only person in the story who could possibly have heard the crucial words is the Swedish farmer, Shipstead, who returns Torrey's body to the homesteaders after the brutal killing. But this is ruled out. In his broken English Shipstead shouts to the other homesteaders what had happened:

> Shipstead: Torrey is dead. . . . One shot, Torrey dead. . . . We go into town together. . . . Then the anger in their voices I hear. Only the anger, . . . not the words.
> Starrett: Who saw it?
> Shipstead: Just the Ryker men and me.

Stevens, however, would have his audience know that, in some sense which he never explains, Shane "witnessed" the death of Torrey. It is part of Stevens' supernatural underpinnings of the story that Shane is allowed to repeat Torrey's insulting words to Wilson. In the unexpected stranger from the mountains, the voice of Torrey seems again to be heard — as with Abel's blood crying from the ground (Gen 4:10) — but now with a different outcome.[25] While clearly not going as far as Paul, for whom the life he now lived was not his, but Christ living in him (Gal 2:20), Stevens enables Torrey in a sense to come back from the dead in Shane.

In New Testament theology there is a solidarity between the strong and the weak, even extending to the living and the dead. "Inasmuch as you have done it to one of the least of these my brethren, you did it to me" (Matt 25:40). The cry of the martyr does not go unheeded (cf. Rev 6:9-11). Wilson's fight is with Shane, but only because Shane has chosen to make it his fight, and thus to take the place of Torrey and the other oppressed homesteaders. A Biblical-type of solidarity clearly is suggested here.[26] As with the God who repays, Shane's retribution is rooted neither in anger, malice, nor personal vindication. In this way the role of Shane as a true Christ symbol can be perpetuated. There is a moral order to the universe, including a wrath against evil. In Shane that wrath

---

25. It is interesting to note that both Stevens and Eastwood associate the final confrontation scene with a possible return from the dead, although in Eastwood's case there is nothing religious about it.

26. The idea is expressed even more overtly in Stevens' "The Greatest Story Ever Told," where in one unusual shot Stevens depicts the Temple steps strewn with the bodies of Jesus' followers, including the crippled boy (Sal Mineo) whom Jesus had healed in the synagogue. Stevens then superimposes words of Jesus (Max von Sydow): "Where two or three are gathered together in my name, there I am in the midst of them" (Matt 18:20).

is visited upon evildoers, but it is distinctly not malicious. Like that of God himself, Shane's "wrath" is responsible and, to a considerable degree, salvific.

One could point to a number of other elements where Stevens has over-laid Schaefer's story with biblical themes and symbols.[27] Although its comple-tion was delayed until 1965, it is now known that "The Greatest Story Ever Told" was intended by Stevens to be filmed as early as 1960; it is therefore possible, if not likely, that in 1952 he was imbuing his western saga with such Biblical over-tones largely because at that time he was looking ahead to what he hoped would be his greatest cinematic legacy — the story of Christ.

Conclusion: The Continuing Dialogue

As with the parables of Jesus, "Shane" can be understood on at least two levels. It can be viewed as something like a pronouncement story regarding human conduct ("go and do likewise"). In that case, both Stevens' and Eastwood's ver-sions of the story go against Paul's advice in Rom 12–13, thereby setting a dan-gerous precedent. Or at least Stevens' version can be seen as a parable of what God is like and how God has accomplished all that has been done in the drama of salvation, in which case no role model or conscious human imitation would be implied.[28] This is Banks' understanding, and his argument deserves serious consideration. If the former interpretation is adopted — that of a "vengeance story" along the lines of Wister's "The Virginian" — Shane's saga will be re-jected by most Christians as advocating inappropriate conduct. Certainly Jewett is right to see at least the Eastwood rendering as "divinely sanctioned

27. For a helpful list, see Banks, "The Drama of Salvation in George Stevens' Shane." One of the must unusual of these elements concerns Stevens' favorite camera trick, the dissolve shot, during the climactic night sequence in which Shane rides out to confront Ryker and Wilson. As Joey and his dog attempt to keep pace with Shane, they pass through a cemetery, with its tomb-stones and crosses, where earlier in the day Shane had delivered a stirring "sermon" to the set-tlers regarding the importance of family and land. Stevens' camera then dissolves from Joey and his dog to Shane riding on his mount in such a way that, before the previous scene has disap-peared, there is left in the viewer's eye a cross lingering over Shane's palomino. The overall dis-solve lasts almost five seconds, producing a subliminal image of a horse and rider pitted against a dark sky, with the central symbol of Christianity looming ominously overhead. One cannot help but wonder if it was this image that thirty-two years later inspired Eastwood to entitle his retelling of the story "Pale Rider" — but now with associations of a more apocalyptic flavor (cf. Rev. 6:8).

28. Compare a number of Jesus' parables about what God is like (e.g., the Unjust Judge, Luke 18:1-8) which would be equally dangerous if taken as examples of sanctioned human be-havior.

vigilantism,"[29] a potentially dangerous example of the American "Monomyth" or "Captain America Complex." Ultimately Jewett's critique could embrace "Shane" as well — although it is significant that Jewett, intentionally or not, never goes this route.

On the other hand, it must be remembered that the idea of a provisional, substitute justice is, on the face of it, the rationale for the stories of the Old Testament judges, as Banks observes. It is also the essence of the Robin Hood legends, portrayed most ideally in 1938 by Errol Flynn in the Warner Brothers' classic "The Adventures of Robin Hood." The problem is therefore not a uniquely American one. It crosses temporal and national boundaries, and takes many forms — with or without a Christian interpretation added.

The provocative questions raised by "Shane" and "Pale Rider" have created an important dialogue, but one that must end here with the familiar Hollywood phrase "to be continued." Such dialogues tend to force thinking people, Christians or not, to give deeper consideration to their responses to individual, corporate, and ecological evil. Two "Roberts" — Jewett and Banks — already have advanced the discussion a considerable distance by connecting it with similar but different American Western films. It is to be hoped that my comments here, intended to join the celebration of the former's life and work, will serve as well to place some of Paul's most troublesome yet rewarding thoughts in touch with previously untapped aspects of American culture, and thus to bring the Bible and some questions raised by that culture into an even sharper focus.

29. Jewett, *Saint Paul at the Movies*, 119-22.

Vita *Robert Jewett*

Visiting Professor of New Testament, University of Heidelberg
WTS, Kisselgasse 1, D-69117 Heidelberg, Germany
Office phone: 49-06221-54-3320; Fax: 54-3509
Study phone: 49-06275-919-660; Fax: 919-666
E-Mail: Robert.Jewett@urz.uni-heidelberg.de

Education

1960-1964, Doctor of Theology, University of Tübingen
1955-1958, Bachelor of Divinity, University of Chicago, Chicago Theological Seminary
1951-1955, Bachelor of Arts, Nebraska Wesleyan University

Employment Experience

- 2000-present, Guest Professor of New Testament, Wissenschaftlich-Theologisches Seminar, the University of Heidelberg
- 1980-2000, Professor of New Testament Interpretation, Garrett-Evangelical Theological Seminary; 1987-2000, Harry R. Kendail Professor of New Testament Interpretation; 1996-2000, Senior Professor; 2000-present, *Emeritus*
- 1982-2000, Member, Coordinating Faculty of the Joint Garrett/Northwestern Ph.D. Program in Religious and Theological Studies
- Summer 1982-1991, Visiting Professor, Vancouver School of Theology
- Summer 1976-1978, Visiting Professor, Iliff School of Theology
- Summer 1978, Visiting Professor, University of Montana
- Summer 1976, Visiting Lecturer, Wesley Theological Seminary
- 1966-1980, Professor of Religious Studies, Morningside College

- 1964-1966, Minister, the United Methodist Churches at Dakota City and Homer, Nebraska
- 1958-1960, Minister of Education, the Federated Church of Harvey, Illinois

Professional and Religious Associations
- Society of Biblical Literature (Member, the Paul Seminar, 1971-1975; Chair, Pauline Epistles Section, 1976-1981; Member, Program Committee; Chair, Consultation on "Social Sciences and New Testament Interpretation," 1982-1984; Member, advisory committees, Pauline Epistles Section, Social Science and New Testament Interpretation Section, and the Bible in Ancient and Modern Media Group; Chair, Consultation on Pauline Theology, 1985-1990; Member, steering committee, Pauline Theology Group)
- President, Midwest Region SBL, 1986-1988
- Member, advisory committee, joint AAR/SBL Consultation on the History of Interpretation of Romans
- Member, Editorial Board, *The Journal for the Study of the New Testament Supplement Series,* Sheffield Academic Press, 1991-present
- Member, Editorial Board, *Semeia: An Experimental Journal for Biblical Criticism,* 1980-1986
- Member, Editorial Board, *Studies in American Biblical Hermeneutics,* Mercer University Press, 1987-2002
- Member, Editorial Advisory Board, *Jian Dao: A Journal of Bible and Theology,* 1994-2000
- Society of New Testament Studies (Co-Chair, Seminar on Romans, 1997-2000)
- Chicago Society of Biblical Research (President, 1993-1994; Chair, Steering Committee, The "Chicago Bible Translation Project" (with Eerdmans Press)
- Catholic Biblical Association
- American Association of University Professors
- American Academy of Religion (former member, advisory committee, Myth and Symbols consultation and steering committee, American Biblical Hermeneutics section)
- Nebraska Annual Conference of the United Methodist Church

Honors, Fellowships, Grants
- 2003, The American Culture Association John G. Cawelti Book Award, for *The Myth of the American Superhero* ("Best Book of 2002")
- 1999, Honorary Doctor of Divinity degree, Coe College
- 1998, Honorary Doctor of Divinity degree, Kalamazoo College
- 1995, Honorary Doctor of Divinity degree, Morningside College
- 1975, Iowa Board for Public Programs in the Humanities Grant
- 1974, The Unitarian Universalist Association Melcher Book Award for *The Captain America Complex,* for the "most significant contribution to religious liberalism" in 1973

- 1973, Theologian-in-Residence, The American Church in Paris
- 1969, Outstanding Faculty Member Award, Morningside College
- 1968, Outstanding Alumnus Award, Nebraska Wesleyan University
- 1961-1964, DAAD Fellowship (German Academic Exchange program)
- 1960-1961, Chicago Theological Seminary Blatchford Traveling Fellowship

Books

1. *Paul's Anthropological Terms: A Study of Their Use in Conflict Settings* (*Arbeiten zur Geschichte des Antiken Judentums und des Urchristentums* 10; Leiden: E. J. Brill, 1971). Pp. 499.
2. *The Captain America Complex: The Dilemma of Zealous Nationalism* (Philadelphia: Westminster, 1973; rev. ed., Santa Fe: Bear & Company, 1984). Pp. 286. Korean translation by Young-Il Kim (Seoul: Voice, 1996).
3. *The American Monomyth* (with John Shelton Lawrence; Foreword by Isaac Asimov; New York: Doubleday/Anchor, 1977). Pp. 263. Italian translation, Bompiano Press; Japanese version, Kaibun Sha; 2nd ed. (University Press of America, 1988). Pp. 331.
4. *A Chronology of Paul's Life* (Philadelphia: Fortress, 1979). Pp. 160. = *Dating Paul's Life* (London: SCM Press, 1979). German translation by Gisela Koester (Vienna: Kaiser, 1982).
5. *Jesus Against the Rapture: Seven Unexpected Prophecies* (Philadelphia: Westminster, 1979). Pp. 147.
6. *Letter to Pilgrims: A Commentary on the Epistle to the Hebrews* (Berea, Ohio: United Church Press, 1981). Pp. 272.
7. *Christian Tolerance: Paul's Message to the Modern Church* (Philadelphia: Westminster, 1982). Pp. 147.
8. *Romans, Teacher Book* (*Genesis to Revelation Adult Bible Series* 20; Nashville: Graded Press, United Methodist Publishing House, 1986). Pp. 72.
9. *Romans, Student Book* (*Genesis to Revelation Adult Bible Series* 20; Nashville: Graded Press, United Methodist Publishing House, 1986). Pp. 112.
10. *The Thessalonian Correspondence: Pauline Rhetoric and Millenarian Piety* (Philadelphia: Fortress, 1986). Pp. 256.
11. *Romans* (*The Cokesbury Basic Bible Commentary* vol 22; Nashville: United Methodist Publishing House, 1988). Pp. 160. Repr. 1994, *The Basic Bible Commentary* series.
12. *Saint Paul at the Movies: The Apostle's Dialogue with American Culture* (Louisville: Westminster John Knox, 1993). Pp. 186.
13. *Paul the Apostle to America: Cultural Trends and Pauline Scholarship* (Louisville: Westminster John Knox, 1994). Pp. 250.
14. *Saint Paul Returns to the Movies: Triumph over Shame* (Grand Rapids, Mich.: Eerdmans, 1999). Pp. 220.
15. *The Myth of the American Superhero* (with John Shelton Lawrence; Grand Rapids, Mich.: Eerdmans, 2002). Pp. 416.

16. *Captain America and the Crusade against Evil: The Dilemma of Zealous Nationalism* (with John Shelton Lawrence; Grand Rapids, Mich.: Eerdmans, 2003). Pp. 392.

Editorial Projects

1. (Ed., with L. W. Hurtado and P. R. Kiefert) *Christology and Exegesis: New Approaches* (*Semeia: An Experimental Journal for Biblical Criticism* 30; Decatur, Ga.: Scholars Press, 1984). Pp. 233.
2. (Ed., with D. E. Groh) *The Living Text: Essays in Honor of Ernest W. Saunders* (Lanham, Md.: University Press of America, 1985). Pp. 261.
3. (Ed. with Graydon F. Snyder, et al.) *Common Life in the Early Church: Essays in Honor of Graydon F. Snyder* (Harrisburg, Pa.: Trinity Press International, 1998). Pp. xxx; 449.

Articles

1. "Review of R. B. Martin, *Carmen Christi*," *The Journal of Religion* 39 (1969): 306-7.
2. "The Form and Function of the Homiletic Benediction," *Anglican Theological Review* 6 (1969): 18-34.
3. "The Epistolary Thanksgiving and the Integrity of Philippians," *Novum Testamentum* 12 (1970): 40-53.
4. "Conflicting Movements in the Early Church as Reflected in Philippians," *Novum Testamentum* 12 (1970): 363-90.
5. "The Agitators and the Galatian Congregation," *New Testament Studies* 17 (1970-71): 198-212. Repr., 334-47 in *The Galatians Debate: Contemporary Issues in Rhetorical and Historical Interpretation* (ed. M. D. Nanos; Peabody: Hendrickson, 2002).
6. "The Zealot in America," *The Quarterly of the American Interprofessional Institute* 45 (1972): 4-8.
7. "Threshing Sledges of Iron [Sermon for Clergy and Laymen Concerned About Vietnam]," *The Morningside Review* 46 (1972): 57-61.
8. "Enthusiastic Radicalism and the Thessalonian Correspondence," *The Society of Biblical Literature Seminar Papers, One Hundred Eighth Annual Meeting* (1972), Vol. 1: 181-232.
9. "Whispered in Private Rooms . . . Shouted from the Housetops: Reflections on Watergate in Light of Luke 12:2-3," *The Christian Century* 90 (6 June 1973): 648-50.
10. "The Law Is No Respecter of Persons," *The Christian Century* 90 (14 Nov 1973): 1116.
11. "Isaiah: '. . . Truth Has Fallen in the Public Squares,'" *Christian Advocate* 14 (22 Nov 1973): 7-8.
12. "Review of M. Smith, *The Secret Gospel*," *Christian Advocate* 14 (6 Dec 1973): 15-16.

13. "The Gospel as Heresy: Concordia Seminary in Exile," *The Christian Century* 91 (27 Mar 1974): 336-40.

14. "Review of W. Schmithals, *Paul and the Gnostics and Gnosticism in Corinth*," *The Journal of Biblical Literature* 93 (1974): 630-32.

15. "Review of A. C. Cochrane, *Eating and Drinking with Jesus: An Ethical and Biblical Inquiry*," *The Review of Books on Religion* 4 (1975): 5.

16. "Religious Studies and Popular Culture," *Journal of Popular Culture* 9 (Fall 1975): 491-92; repr. *Theories and Methodologies in Popular Culture* (ed. R. B. Browne, et al.; Bowling Green, Ohio: Bowling Green University Press, 1976).

17. "Review of D. B. Kraybill, *Our Star-Spangled Faith*," *The Christian Century* 93 (12 May 1976): 466-67.

18. "Body," 117-18 in *The Interpreter's Dictionary of the Bible, Supplemental Volume* (ed. K. Crim, et al.; New York and Nashville: Abingdon, 1976).

19. "Conscience," ibid., 173-74.

20. "Flesh in the New Testament," ibid., 339-40.

21. "Man, Nature of, in the New Testament," ibid., 561-63.

22. "Spirit," ibid., 839-41.

23. "Norm Demolition Derbies: Rites of Reversal in Popular Culture" (with J. S. Lawrence), *Journal of Popular Culture* 9 (1976): 976-82; repr., 290-97 in *The Popular Culture Reader* (2d ed.; ed. Jack Nachbar, Deborah Weiser, and John L. Wright; Bowling Green, Ohio: Bowling Green University Popular Press, 1978).

24. "Mythic Conformity in the Cuckoo's Nest" (with J. S. Lawrence), *Psychocultural Review* 1 (1977): 68-76.

25. "'Star Trek' and the Bubble Gum Fallacy" (with J. S. Lawrence), *Television Quarterly* 14 (1977): 5-16.

26. "Roots: Black Soap Opera?" (with J. S. Lawrence), *Sunday Des Moines Register* (6 Feb 1977): B1-2.

27. "Review of J. R. McKay and J. F. Miller, eds., *Biblical Studies: Essays in Honor of William Barclay*," *The Circuit Rider* 1, no. 8 (June 1977): 19.

28. "Beyond the Pornography of Violence" (with J. S. Lawrence), *Religion in Life* 46 (1977): 357-63.

29. "Review of J. E. Adams, *Preus of Missouri*," *The Christian Century* 94 (5 Oct 1977): 885-86.

30. "Pop Fascism in Star Wars or Vision of a Better World?" (with J. S. Lawrence), *Sunday Des Moines Register* (27 Nov 1977): 3B.

31. "Psychohistory of the Cinema" (with J. S. Lawrence), *The Journal of Psychohistory* 5 (1978): 512-20.

32. "Review of J. D. Smart, *The Cultural Subversion of the Biblical Faith*," *Religion in Life* 47 (1978): 243-45.

33. "The Redaction of 1 Corinthians and the Trajectory of the Pauline School," *Journal of the American Academy of Religion Supplement* 46 (1978): 389-44.

34. "Review of J. N. Hartt, *The Restless Quest*," *Encounter* 40 (1979): 86-87.

35. "The Sexual Liberation of the Apostle Paul," *Journal of the American Academy of Religion Supplement* 47 (1979): 55-87.
36. "The Problem of Mythic Imperialism" (with J. S. Lawrence), *Journal of American Culture* 2 (1979): 309-20.
37. "Major Impulses in the Theological Interpretation of Romans since Barth," *Interpretation: A Journal of Bible and Theology* 34 (1980): 17-31.
38. "Review of V. P. Furnish, *The Moral Teachings of Paul*," *The Perkins Journal* 33 (1980): 43-44.
39. "U.S. Shows Naivete in Olympic Boycott" (with J. S. Lawrence), *Sunday Des Moines Register* (6 April 1980): C1-2.
40. "Review of J. A. MacCollam, *Carnival of Souls: Religious Cults and Young People*," *Christian Century* 97 (23 Apr 1980): 474-75.
41. "Review of J. C. Beker, *Paul the Apostle: The Triumph of God in Life and Thought*," *Theology Today* 38 (1981): 394-97.
42. "Romans as an Ambassadorial Letter," *Interpretation: A Journal of Bible and Theology* 36 (1982): 5-20.
43. "The Fantasy Factor in Civil Religion: Assassinations and Mass Murder in the Media Age" (with J. S. Lawrence), *Explor: A Theological Journal. Published by Garrett Evangelical Theological Seminary* 7 (Fall 1982): 71-79; repr. *Sunstone* 7 (1982): 28-33; repr. *Mission Journal* 17, no. 2 (1983): 3-7, 17.
44. "Chronology and Methodology: Reflections on the Debate over Chapters in a Life of Paul," 271-87 in *A Time for Reappraisal and Fresh Approaches: Colloquy on New Testament Studies* (ed. B. C. Corley; Macon, Ga.: Mercer University Press, 1983).
45. "Seminar Dialogue with Robert Jewett and Gerd Luedemann," 309-37 in *A Time for Reappraisal and Fresh Approaches: Colloquy on New Testament Studies* (ed. B. C. Corley; Macon, Ga.: Mercer University Press, 1983).
46. "Review of F. J. Ortkemper, *Leben aus dem Glauben. Christliche Grundhaltungen nach Römer 12–13*," *The Journal of Biblical Literature* 102 (1983): 509-11.
47. "Review of H. Moxnes, *Theology in Conflict: Studies in Paul's Understanding of God in Romans*," *The Trinity Journal* 4 (1983): 109-11.
48. "A Covenant with Death," *Christian Century* 100 (1983): 477-78.
49. "American Civil Religion and Ritual Blindness" (with J. S. Lawrence), *Christian Century* 100 (1983): 1075-78.
50. "Review of Bengt Holmberg, *Paul and Power: The Structure of Authority in the Primitive Church as Reflected in the Pauline Epistles*," *The Anglican Theological Review* 66 (1984): 196-98.
51. "Review of Daniel Patte, *Paul's Faith and the Power of the Gospel: A Structural Introduction to the Pauline Letters*," *The Journal of the American Academy of Religion* 52 (1984): 379-80.
52. "Coming to Terms with the Doom Boom," *Quarterly Review* 4, no. 3 (1984): 9-22.
53. "New Testament Christology: The Current Dialogue between Systematic Theologians and Biblical Scholars," *Semeia* 30 (1984): 3-12.
54. "Paul, Saint," *Academic American Encyclopedia* (1984-), Vol. 15: 116-117.

55. "The Redaction and Use of an Early Christian Confession in Romans 1:3-4," 99-122 in *The Living Text: Essays in Honor of Ernest W. Saunders* (ed. with D. E. Groh; Washington, D.C.: University Press of America, 1985).

56. "The Conflict over Sexual Roles in Pauline Churches," *Wesleyan Theology Today: A Bicentennial Theological Consultation* (ed. T. Runyon; Nashville: Kingswood Books, United Methodist Publishing House, 1985), 151-60.

57. "The Law and the Coexistence of Jews and Gentiles in Romans," *Interpretation: A Journal of Bible and Theology* 39 (1985): 341-56.

58. "Chronology, New Testament," *Harper's Bible Dictionary* (San Francisco: Harper & Row, 1985), 165-66.

59. "Review of D. Peterson, *Hebrews and Perfection: An Examination of the Concept of Perfection in the Epistle to the Hebrews,*" *The Journal of Religion* 66 (1986): 72-73.

60. "Following the Argument of Romans," *Word and World: Theology for Christian Ministry* 6 (1986): 382-89; rev. in *The Romans Debate* (ed. K. P. Donfried; Hendrickson, 1991), 265-77.

61. "Review of H. Maccoby, *The Myth-Maker: Paul and the Invention of Christianity,*" *The Philadelphia Inquirer* (26 Oct 1986): S6.

62. "Review of J. L. Kugel and R. A. Greer, *Early Biblical Interpretation,*" *The Christian Century* 103, no. 35 (19 Nov 1986): 1040-41.

63. "Paul the Apostle," 212-21 in *The Encyclopedia of Religion*, Vol. 11 (New York: Macmillan, 1987).

64. "Review of B. J. Malina, *The New Testament World: Insights from Cultural Anthropology,*" *Biblical Theology Bulletin* 17 (1987): 78.

65. "The Woeful Rich," *The Journal of Stewardship* 39 (1987): 36-45.

66. "Review of L. Gilkey, *Creationism on Trial: Evolution and God at Little Rock,*" *New World Outlook* (Apr 1987): 41.

67. "Zeal Without Understanding: Reflections on Rambo and Oliver North," *The Christian Century* 104 (9-16 Sept 1987): 753-56.

68. "Review of J. L. White, *Light from Ancient Letters,*" *Biblical Research* 32 (1987): 46-49.

69. "Review of G. Luedemann, *Apostle to the Gentiles: Studies in Chronology,*" *The Journal of the American Academy of Religion* 55 (1987): 839-40.

70. "Systems Theory and Pauline Anthropology: A Cross-Disciplinary Conversation" (with J. B. Ashbrook), *The Journal of Pastoral Psychotherapy* 1 (1987): 19-37.

71. "Review of N. Hyldahl, *Die paulinische Chronologie,*" *The Journal of Biblical Literature* 107 (1988): 549-50.

72. "Introduction to the Pauline Letters," 1120-29 in *Harper's Bible Commentary* (New York: Harper & Row, 1988).

73. "Paul, Phoebe, and the Spanish Mission," 144-64 in *The Social World of Formative Christianity and Judaism: Essays in Tribute to Howard Clark Kee* (ed. P. Borgen et al.; Philadelphia: Fortress, 1988).

74. "Review of J. Plevnik, *What Are They Saying About Paul?*" *Biblical Theology Bulletin* 19 (1989): 40.

75. "Review of P. Lampe, *Die stadtrömischen Christen in den ersten beiden Jahrhunderten,*" *Interpretation: A Journal of Bible and Theology* 43 (1989): 296-98.

76. "Sin and Salvation: 'Amadeus' in the Light of Romans," *Ex Auditu: An International Journal of Theological Interpretation of Scripture* 5 (1989): 159-69.

77. "Corinth, Corinthian Correspondence," 234-36 in *The Encyclopedia of Early Christianity* (New York: Garland, 1990); rev. ed. (New York: Garland, 1997), Vol. 1: 290-94.

78. "Paul," 699-703 in *The Encyclopedia of Early Christianity* (New York: Garland, 1990); rev. ed. (New York: Garland, 1997), Vol. 2: 881-85.

79. "Jesus as the Apocalyptic Benefactor in Second Thessalonians" (with F. W. Danker), 486-98 in *The Thessalonian Correspondence* (ed. R. F. Collins; Leuven: Leuven University Press, 1990).

80. "A Chance to Affirm the Law of Nations," *Christian Century* 107 (14 Nov 1990): 1054-55.

81. "Numerical Sequences in Paul's Letter to the Romans," 227-45 in *Persuasive Artistry: Studies in New Testament Rhetoric in Honor of George A. Kennedy* (ed. D. F. Watson; Sheffield: JSOT Press, 1991).

82. "A Matrix of Grace: The Theology of 2 Thessalonians as a Pauline Letter," 63-70 in *Pauline Theology. Volume I: Thessalonians, Philippians, Galatians, Philemon* (ed. J. Bassler; Minneapolis: Fortress, 1991).

83. "'Life to the Dead' from the God of Tender Mercies," 1-14 in *Life as Liberty, Life as Trust* (ed. J. R. Nelson; Grand Rapids: Eerdmans, 1992).

84. "Competing in the Creedal Olympics: Pauline Resources for Cross-Cultural Ministry," 23-36 in *Knowledge, Attitude & Experience: Ministry in the Cross-Cultural Context* (ed. Young-Il Kim; Nashville: Abingdon, 1992).

85. "Ecumenical Theology for the Sake of Mission: Romans 1:1-17 + 15:14–16:24," *Society of Biblical Literature 1992 Seminar Papers* (ed. E. H. Lovering Jr.; Atlanta: Scholars Press, 1992), 598-612.

86. "Review of P. Nathanson, *Over the Rainbow: 'The Wizard of Oz' as a Secular Myth of America,*" *Studies in Religion/Sciences Religieuses: A Canadian Journal* 21 (1992): 478-79.

87. "Rambo and the Myth of Redemption" (with J. S. Lawrence), 63-83 in *Transforming Texts: Classical Images in New Contexts* (ed. R. P. Metzger; Lewisburg: Bucknell University Press, 1993).

88. "Paul's Dialogue with the Corinthians . . . and Us," *Quarterly Review: A Journal of Theological Resources for Ministry* 13, no. 4 (1993): 89-112.

89. "Tenement Churches and Communal Meals in the Early Church: The Implications of a Form-Critical Analysis of 2 Thess 3:10," *Biblical Research: Journal of the Chicago Society of Biblical Research* 38 (1993): 23-43.

90. "Tenement Churches and Pauline Love Feasts," *Quarterly Review: A Journal of Theological Resources for Ministry* 14, no. 1 (1994): 43-58.

91. "Gospel and Commensality: Social and Theological Implications of Galatians 2.14," 240-52 in *Gospel in Paul: Studies on Corinthians, Galatians and Romans for*

Richard N. Longenecker (ed. A. Jervis and P. Richardson, *Journal for the Study of the New Testament Supplement* 108; Sheffield: Sheffield Academic Press, 1994).

92. "Review of Jan Lambrecht, *The Wretched 'I' and Its Liberation: Paul in Romans 7 and 8*," *The Journal of Biblical Literature* 114 (1995): 163-64.

93. "Our flag should be honored, not held as sacred" (with C. Collora), *The United Methodist Reporter* (2 Sept 1995): 2.

94. "Review of J. A. Fitzmyer, *Romans: A New Translation with Introduction and Commentary*," *The Journal of Biblical Literature* 114 (1995): 745-47.

95. "Guest Editorial: On Turning the Flag into a Sacred Object" (with C. Collora), *The Journal of Church and State* 37 (1995): 741-52.

96. "Review of R. H. Bell, *Provoked to Jealousy: The Origin and Purpose of the Jealousy Motif in Romans 9–11*," *The Critical Review of Books in Religion* 8 (1995): 170-73.

97. "Review of J. C. Walters, *Ethnic Issues in Paul's Letter to the Romans: Changing Self-Definitions in Earliest Roman Christianity*," *Critical Review of Books in Religion* 8 (1995): 319-20.

98. "Review of D. Aukerman, *Reckoning with Apocalypse: Terminal Politics and Christian Hope*," *Interpretation: A Journal of Bible and Theology* 50 (January 1996): 98-100.

99. "Ecumenical Theology for the Sake of Mission: Rom 1:1-17 + 15:14–16:24," 89-108 in *Pauline Theology*, Vol. 3 (ed. D. M. Hay and E. E. Johnson; Minneapolis: Augsburg Fortress Press, 1995).

100. "Bibliography (on Romans)," 301-29 in *Pauline Theology*, Vol. 3 (ed. D. M. Hay and E. E. Johnson; Minneapolis: Augsburg Fortress Press, 1995).

101. "Review of A. Smith, *Comfort One Another: Reconstructing the Rhetoric and Audience of 1 Thessalonians*," *Critical Review of Books in Religion* 9 (1996): 171-73.

102. "Review of B. B. Scott, *Hollywood Dreams and Biblical Stories*," *Interpretation: A Journal of Bible and Theology* 51, no. 1 (1997): 102.

103. "Honor and Shame in the Argument of Romans," 257-72 in *Putting Body and Soul Together: Essays in Honor of Robin Scroggs* (ed. A. Brown, G. F. Snyder and V. Wiles; Harrisburg, Pa.: Trinity Press International, 1997).

104. "Mapping the Route of Paul's 'Second Missionary Journey' on Previously Undiscovered Roman Roads from Pisidian Antioch to Troas," *Tyndale Bulletin* 48, no. 1 (1997): 1-22; repr. with a "Postscript," 127-34 in *Thetis. Mannheimer Beiträge zur klassischen Archäologie und Geschichte* 4 (ed. Reinhard Stupperich and Heinz A. Richter; 1997).

105. "Review of G. D. Fee, *God's Empowering Presence: The Holy Spirit in the Letters of Paul*," *Interpretation: A Journal of Bible and Theology* 51, no. 3 (1997): 320.

106. "'Babette's Feast' and Shaming the Poor in Corinth," *Dialog: A Journal of Theology* 36, no. 4 (1997): 270-76.

107. "Stuck in Time: Kairos, Chronos and the Flesh in 'Groundhog Day,'" *Explorations in Theology and Film* (ed. Clive Marsh and Gaye Ortiz; Preface by Martin Scorsese; Oxford: Blackwells, 1997), 155-65.

108. "The Basic Human Dilemma: Weakness or Zealous Violence (Romans 7:7-25 and

10:1-18)," *Ex Auditu: An International Journal of Theological Interpretation of Scripture* 13 (1997): 96-109.

109. "Review of J. Murphy O'Connor, *Paul: A Critical Life*," *The Journal of Religion* 78, no. 1 (1998): 107.

110. "The God of Peace in Romans: Reflections on Crucial Lutheran Texts," *Currents in Theology and Mission* 25, no. 3, *Essays in Honor of Edgar Krentz* (1998): 186-94.

111. "Confession as Propaganda," *Pro Ecclesia* 7, no. 4 (1998): 395-97.

112. "The Abandonment of Trust: A Biblical Reflection on Public Lies," *Sojourners* 26, no. 7 (1998): 10-11.

113. "The Gospel of Violent Zeal in Clint Eastwood's 'Unforgiven,'" *Christianity and Literature* 47, no. 4 (1998): 427-42.

114. "Are There Allusions to the Love Feast in Rom 13:8-10?" 265-78 in *Common Life in the Early Church: Essays Honoring Graydon F. Snyder* (ed. Julian V. Hills et al.; Harrisburg, Pa.: Trinity Press International, 1998).

115. "The Bond of Peace and 'Places in the Heart': Reflections on 'The Dialogue on Theological Diversity,'" *Quarterly Review* 18, no. 4 (1998-1999): 355-65.

116. "Confession and Forgiveness in the Public Sphere: A Biblical Evaluation," 53-71 in *Judgment Day in the White House* (ed. Gabriel J. Fackre; Grand Rapids: Eerdmans, 1999).

117. "Chronology, New Testament," 193-98 in *Dictionary of Biblical Interpretation* (ed. J. H. Hayes; Nashville: Abingdon Press, 1999).

118. "The Ethical Legacy of the Impeachment Crisis," *Shalom Papers: Occasional Papers on Theology and Public Policy* (Washington, D.C.: Wesley Theological Seminary, 1999).

119. "The Social Context and Implications of Homoerotic References in Rom 1:24-27," 223-41 in *Homosexuality, Science, and the "Plain Sense" of Scripture* (ed. D. Balch; Grand Rapids, Mich.: Eerdmans, 2000).

120. "The Disguise of Vengeance in 'Pale Rider,'" 243-57 in *Religion and Popular Culture in America* (ed. B. Forbes and J. Mahan; Berkeley: University of California Press, 2000).

121. "Paul and the Caravaneers: A Proposal on the Mode of 'Passing through Mysia' on the 'Second Missionary Journey,'" 74-90 in *Text and Artifact in the Religions of Mediterranean Antiquity: Essays in Honour of Peter Richardson* (ed. S. G. Wilson and M. Desjardins; *Studies in Christianity and Judaism* 9; Waterloo: Wilfrid Laurier Press, 2000).

122. "Response: Exegetical Support from Romans and Other Letters," 58-71 in *Paul and Politics: Ekklesia, Israel, Imperium, Interpretation. Essays in Honor of Krister Stendahl* (ed. R. A. Horsley; Harrisburg, Pa.: Trinity Press International, 2000).

123. "Fourth Sunday of Advent, Year A (Romans 1:1-7)," 10-13 in *The Lectionary Commentary: Theological Exegesis for Sunday's Texts. The Second Readings: Acts and the Epistles* (ed. R. E. Van Harn; Grand Rapids, Mich.: Eerdmans; London: Continuum, 2001).

124. "Ninth Sunday after the Epiphany, Year A (Romans 1:16-17; 3:22b-28, 29-31)," ibid., 14-17.
125. "First Sunday in Lent, Year C (Romans 10:8-13)," ibid., 109-121.
126. "Fifteenth Sunday after Pentecost, Year A (Romans 12:9-21)," ibid., 120-24.
127. "Sixteenth Sunday after Pentecost, Year A (Romans 13:8-14)," ibid., 124-27.
128. "First Sunday of Advent, Year A (Romans 13:11-14)," ibid., 128-31.
129. "Fourth Sunday of Advent, Year B (Romans 16:25-27)," ibid., 142-45.
130. "Leib/Leiblichkeit. I. Biblisch." *Religion in Geschichte und Gegenwart,* 4th ed. (2002), Vol. 5: 215-18.
131. "Impeaching God's Elect: Romans 8:33-36 in Its Rhetorical Situation," 37-58 in *Paul, Luke and the Graeco-Roman World: Essays in Honour of Alexander J. M. Wedderburn* (ed. A. Christophersen, et al.; *Journal for the Study of the New Testament Supplement* 217; Sheffield: Sheffield Academic Press, 2002).
132. "Investigating the Route of Paul's 'Second Missionary Journey' from Pisidian Antioch to Troas," 93-96 in *Actes du Premier Congrès International sur Antioche de Pisidie, Collection d'Archéologie et d'Histoire de l'Antiquité de l'Université Lumière — Lyon 2* (ed. Thomas Drew-Bear, Mehmet Taslialan and Christine M. Thomas; Paris: de Boccard, 2002).
133. "Blood Brothers. Bush's Rambo Delusion. The Myth of the American Superhero" (with J. S. Lawrence), *The San Francisco Chronicle* (25 Aug 2002): D3; article adapted and translated as "Gesetz und Superheldengeist," *Frankfurter Rundschau* (24 July 2002), 19; also in Sweden *(Svenska Dagbladet; Dagens Forskning);* Japan *(Fuku-in to sekai);* Finland *(Suomen Kuvalehti).*
134. "Captain American Takes on Iraq," *Tikkun* 18, no. 1 (2003): 16-20; article adapted and sent to Sweden *(Svenska Dagbladet; Dagens Forskning);* Japan *(Fuku-in to sekai);* Finland *(Suomen Kuvalehti).*
135. "1 and 2 Thessalonians," 1413-27 in *The Eerdmans Commentary on the Bible* (ed. J. D. G. Dunn; Grand Rapids: Eerdmans, 2003).
136. "Romans," 91-104 in *The Cambridge Companion to St Paul* (ed. J. D. G. Dunn; Cambridge: Cambridge University Press, 2003).
137. "The Biblical Sources of the Crusade against Evil" (with J. S. Lawrence), *The On-line Forum Newsletter of Religious Studies News, SBL Edition,* in an issue entitled "Bush's Bible" (ed. Moira Bucciarelli; May 2003).
138. "Paul, Shame and Honor," 551-74 in *Paul and the Greco-Roman World* (ed. J. Paul Sampley; Harrisburg, Pa.: Trinity Press International, 2003).
139. "Bergers Bibelblitz" (with Peter Lampe and Helmut Schwier), *Evangelische Orientierung: Zeitschrift des evangelischen Bundes* 2 (2003): 10-11. Rev. and abbr. as "Paulus ermutigt zur Interkommunion," *Frankfurter Allgemeine Zeitung* (28 May 2003): 8.
140. "Prophezeiung als Stückwerk: Paulus und die Juden in Römer 9–11," 327-37 in *"Ich bin ein Hebräer." Zum Gedenken an Otto Michel* (1903-1993), (ed. Helgo Lindner; Gießen/Basel: Brunnen, 2003).

141. "The Biblical Roots of American Messianism" (with J. S. Lawrence), *The Bible in TransMission: A Forum for Change in Church and Culture* (Autumn 2003): 9-11.
142. "Foreword," xiii-xvi in Peter Lampe, *From Paul to Valentinus: The Christians in the City of Rome of the First Three Centuries* (Minneapolis: Fortress, 2003).
143. "Der Traum von der Erlösung durch den Supermann (Schwarzenegger)," with J. S. Lawrence (trans. and ed. Geiko Müller-Fahrenholz), *Publik Forum* 23 (8 Dec 2003): 20-22.
144. "The Corruption and Redemption of Creation: Reading Romans 8:18-23 within the Imperial Context," 25-46 in *Paul and the Roman Imperial Order* (ed. Richard Horsley; Harrisburg, Pa.: Trinity Press International, 2004).

Studies Completed

1. "Rhetorical Examples from Romans," presented to the SNTS Seminar on NT Rhetoric at the 2002 SNTS annual meeting in Durham, England.
2. "The Question of the 'Apportioned Spirit' in Paul's Letters: Romans as a Case Study," in press for *The Holy Spirit and Christian Origins: Essays in Honour of James D. G. Dunn* (ed. Graham D. Stanton, et al.; Grand Rapids, Mich.: Eerdmans).

Work in Progress

1. *Romans* (*Hermeneia;* Minneapolis: Augsburg Fortress), due 2004.
2. *Paul's Letter to the Romans: A Comprehensive Bibliography,* 2 vols. (*The American Theological Library Association Bibliography series;* Lanham, Md.: Scarecrow), due 2004.
3. *The Corinthian Correspondence: Redaction and Rhetoric* (with Frank Witt Hughes; Minneapolis: Augsburg Fortress), due 2005.
4. *The Letter to the Hebrews* (*The New Cambridge Bible Commentary;* Cambridge: Cambridge University Press), due 2005.
5. *The Fallen Day Star: Superheroism and the Bible* (rev. of the 1980 Rockwell Lectures at Rice University; Grand Rapids, Mich.: Eerdmans).
6. *Essays on Paul's Letter to the Romans: The Genesis of a Commentary* (rev. of *The 1994 Newell Lectures in Biblical Studies;* London: T&T Clark).
7. *Saint Paul and the Movies: Worlds in Collision* (Vol. 3, *Paul and Film;* Grand Rapids, Mich.: Eerdmans).
8. *Love Feasts in House and Tenement Churches: The Discovery of Commensality in Early Christianity;* a collection of already published essays and new chapters, not yet offered for publication.
9. "Paul's Dialogue with the Splintered Congregations in Rome" and "Paul's Opponents and Conversation Partners in the Corinthian Correspondence," for *Paul and His Opponents* (ed. S. E. Porter; Leiden: E. J. Brill).
10. "Review of W. Kraus, *Der Tod Jesu als Heiligtumsweihe: Eine Untersuchung zum Umfeld der Sühnevorstellung in Römer 3,25-26a* (Neukirchen-Vluyn: Neukirchener Verlag, 1991)," for *The Catholic Biblical Quarterly.*

Contributors

Robert A. Atkins (Ph.D. Northwestern University, 1990) is Senior Pastor of Trinity United Methodist Church in Wilmette, Illinois. His recent publications include *The Social World of Saint Paul,* as guest editor of this special Spring 1996 issue of *Listening: Journal of Religion and Culture* (Romeoville, Ill.: Lewis University, 1996); "Pauline Theology and Shame Affect: Reading a Social Location," *Listening* 31 (1996): 137-51; and *Egalitarian Community: Ethnography and Exegesis* (Tuscaloosa: University of Alabama Press, 1991).

Frank W. Hughes (Ph.D. Northwestern University, 1984) is an Episcopal priest of the Diocese of Central Pennsylvania, and currently holds an appointment as Senior Lecturer in New Testament Studies at Codrington in St. John, Barbados. Recent publications include "The Rhetoric of Letters" and "The Social Situations Implied by Rhetoric," 194-240, 241-54 in *The Thessalonians Debate* (Grand Rapids, Mich.: Eerdmans, 2000); "Rhetorical Criticism and the Corinthian Correspondence," 336-50 in *Rhetorical Analysis of Scripture* (Sheffield: Sheffield Academic Press, 1997); and *Early Christian Rhetoric and 2 Thessalonians* (Sheffield: JSOT Press, 1989).

Khiok-Khng (K. K.) Yeo (Ph.D. Northwestern University, 1992) is Henry R. Kendall Associate Professor of New Testament at Garrett-Evangelical Theological Seminary in Evanston, Illinois. His recent publications in English include *Rhetorical Interaction in 1 Corinthians 8 and 10: A Formal Analysis with Implications for a Cross-Cultural, Chinese Hermeneutic* (Leiden: E. J. Brill, 1995); *What Has Jerusalem to Do with Beijing? Biblical Interpretation from a Chinese Perspec-*

tive (Harrisburg, Pa.: Trinity Press International, 1998); and *Chairman Mao Meets the Apostle Paul: Christianity, Communism, and the Hope of China* (Grand Rapids, Mich.: Brazos, 2002).

James D. G. Dunn (Ph.D. Cambridge, 1968; D.D. Cambridge, 1991) is Lightfoot Professor of Divinity at the University of Durham, where he teaches the theology of the New Testament and early Christian history. Recent publications include *The Partings of the Ways Between Christianity and Judaism* (Harrisburg, Pa.: Trinity Press International, 1991), commentaries on several New Testament books, including *Romans* (Word Biblical Commentary 38; Dallas: Word, 1988), and *The Theology of Paul the Apostle* (Grand Rapids, Mich.: Eerdmans/Edinburgh: T&T Clark, 1998).

Jeffrey B. Gibson (D.Phil. Oxford, 1993) is Adjunct Professor of Humanities at Harry S. Truman College in Chicago. His recent publications include "Matthew 6:9-13//Luke 11:2-4: An Eschatological Prayer?" *Biblical Theology Bulletin* 31 (3, 2001): 96-105; "A Turn on 'Turning Stones to Bread': A New Understanding of the Devil's Intention in Q 4.3," *Biblical Research* 41 (1996): 37-57; and *The Temptations of Jesus in Early Christianity* (*Journal for the Society of the New Testament Supplement* 112; Sheffield Academic Press, 1995).

Graydon F. Snyder (Th.D. Princeton Theological Seminary, 1961) was born and raised in West Virginia. Now retired, he was Dean and Professor of New Testament at Bethany Theological Seminary (1959-1985) and Chicago Theological Seminary (1986-1998). His recent publications include *Inculturation of the Jesus Tradition: The Impact of Jesus on Jewish and Roman Cultures* (Harrisburg, Penn.: Trinity Press International, 1999); *Irish Jesus, Roman Jesus: The Formation of Early Irish Christianity* (Harrisburg, Pa.: Trinity Press International, 2002); and *Ante Pacem: Archaeological Evidence of Church Life Before Constantine* (rev. ed.; Macon, Ga.: Mercer University Press, 2003).

William S. Campbell (Ph.D. University of Edinburgh, 1972) is Reader in Biblical Studies at the University of Wales, Lampeter. His recent publications include "Zwischen Synagoge und Staat: Identität und Konflikt in den paulinischen Gemeinden," 151-70 in *Was begegnet sich im religiösen, christlich-jüdischen Dialog? Aktuelle kultur- und religionswissenschaftliche Theorien zur Deutung, Verhältnisbestimmung und Diskursfähigkeit von Religionen;* Stuttgart, Berlin: Kohlhammer, 2003); "Significant Nuances in Contemporary Pauline Interpretation," *Irish Biblical Studies* 24 (2002): 184-200; "Divergent Images of Paul and His Mission," 187-211 in *Reading Israel in Romans: Legitimacy and Plausibility of*

Divergent Interpretations (ed. Cristina Grenholm and Daniel Patte; Harrisburg, Pa.: Trinity Press International, 2000); and "Millennial Optimism for Jewish-Christian Dialogue," 217-37 in *The Future of Jewish-Christian Dialogue* (ed. Dan Cohn-Sherbock; Lampeter and Lewiston, N.Y.: Edwin Mellen, 1999).

James D. Hester (D.Theol. University of Basel, 1968) is Professor of Religion Emeritus at the University of Redlands in Redlands, California, and founding editor of the *Journal for the Study of Rhetorical Criticism of the New Testament* (http://www.rhetjournal.net), an electronic publication sponsored by the Rhetorical New Testament Project of the Institute for Antiquity and Christianity of the Claremont Graduate University at Claremont, California. His recent publications include "Apocalyptic Discourse in 1 Thessalonians," 137-63 in *Intertexture of Apocalyptic Discourse in the New Testament* (Atlanta: Society of Biblical Literature, 2002); "Speaker, Audience and Situations: A Modified Interactional Model," *Neotestamentica* 32, no. 1 (1998): 75-94; and "The Invention of 1 Thessalonians: A Proposal," 251-79 in *Scripture and Theology* (Sheffield: Sheffield Academic Press, 1996).

Wilhelm Wuellner (Ph.D. University of Chicago, 1958) was Professor Emeritus of New Testament at Pacific School of Religion in Berkeley, California. Recent publications include "Paul as Pastor: The Function of Rhetorical Questions in First Corinthians," 49-77 in *L'Apôtre Paul: Personalité, style et conception du ministère* (ed. Albert Vanhoye; *Bibliotheca Ephemeridum Theologicarum Lovaniensium* 73; Leuven: Leuven University Press, 1986); *Paul the Jew: Jewish-Christian Dialogue* (*Hermeneutical Studies* 60; Berkeley: Center for Hermeneutical Studies, 1990), co-authored with Hayim Goren Perelmuter; "Biblical Exegesis in the Light of the History and Historicity of Rhetoric and the Nature of the Rhetoric of Religion," 492-513 in *Rhetoric and the New Testament* (Sheffield: JSOT Press, 1993); and "Rhetorical Criticism and Its Theory in Culture-Critical Perspective: The Narrative Rhetoric of John 11," 171-85 in *Text and Interpretation* (Leiden: E. J. Brill, 1991). He died on February 5, 2004, while this book was in production.

Peter Lampe (Ph.D. University of Bern, 1983), an ordained Lutheran pastor, is University Professor of New Testament Theology at the University of Heidelberg, Germany, where he teaches Biblical studies, early Christian archaeology and epigraphy, the social history of the early church, and the Hellenistic background of early Christianity. The 2001-2004 Director of the Heidelberg Archaeological Surface Survey in Phrygia, his recent publications include "The Language of Equality in Early Christian House Churches: A Constructivist

Approach," 73-83 in David L. Balch and Carolyn Osiek, *Early Christian Families in Context* (Grand Rapids, Mich.: Eerdmans, 2003); "Urchristliche Missionswege nach Rom: Haushalte paganer Herrschaft als jüdisch-christliche Keimzellen," *Zeitschrift für die neutestamentliche Wissenschaft und die Kunde der älteren Kirche* 92, no. 1-2 (2001): 123-27; "Der Briefe an Philemon," 203-32 in Peter Lampe, Eckart Reinmuth, and Nikolaus Walter, *Die Briefe an die Philipper, Thessalonischer und an Philemon* (*Das Neue Testament Deutsch* 8/2; 18th ed.; Göttingen: Vandenhoeck & Ruprecht, 1998); and *From Paul to Valentinus: Christians at Rome in the First Two Centuries* (Minneapolis: Augsburg Fortress, 2003); trans. of *Die stadtrömischen Christen in den ersten beiden Jahrhunderten: Untersuchen zur Sozialgeschichte* (2nd ed.; Tübingen: Mohr Siebeck, 1989).

Carolyn Osiek (Th.D. Harvard University, 1978) is Professor of New Testament at the Brite Divinity School of Texas Christian University in Fort Worth, Texas. Her publications include *The Shepherd of Hermas* (*Hermeneia: A Critical and Historical Commentary on the Bible;* Minneapolis: Augsburg Fortress, 1999); Osiek and David L. Balch, *Families in the New Testament World: Households and House Churches* (Louisville: Westminster John Knox, 1997).

Sheila E. McGinn is Professor of Biblical Studies and Early Christianity in the Department of Religious Studies at John Carroll University, Cleveland, Ohio. Her recent publications include *Bibliographies for Biblical Research: The Book of Revelation* (Lewiston/Queenston/Lampeter: Mellen Biblical Press, 1997); "Internal Renewal and Dissent in the Early Christian World," Vol. 2: 893-906 in *The Early Christian World* (ed. Philip F. Esler; London and New York: Routledge, 2000); "The 'Montanist' Oracles and Prophetic Theology," 128-135 in *Studia Patristica* 31: *Preaching, Second Century, Tertullian to Arnobius, Egypt before Nicaea* (ed. Elizabeth A. Livingstone; Leuven: Peeters, 1997); and "The Acts of Thecla," 854-882 in *Searching the Scriptures,* Vol. 2: *A Feminist Ecumenical Commentary and Translation* (ed. Elisabeth Schüssler Fiorenza; New York: Crossroad, 1994).

Elsa Tamez is President of the Latin American Biblical University in Costa Rica, and responsible for the development of a new campus at that university committed to the development of projects and programs concerning women in Latin America. She is a recipient of the Woman Witness Special Award. Her studies and ministry within the Methodist Church have been shaped by the politics of Central America, and the disappearances, tortures, imprisonments, and massacres that have marked that region. She has published widely on liberation theology, women's rights, and Biblical studies. Recent publications include *When the Horizons Close: Rereading Ecclesiastes* (Maryknoll, N.Y.: Orbis Books, 2000); *The Scandalous Message of James: Faith Without Works Is Dead* (trans. John Eagleson; New York: Crossroad Publishing Company, 1990; 2nd ed., 2002); and *The Amnesty of Grace: Justification by Faith from a Latin American Perspective* (Nashville: Abingdon, 1993).

Pamela L. Thimmes, O.S.F. (Ph.D. Vanderbilt University, 1990) is Associate Professor of Religious Studies at the University of Dayton in Dayton, Ohio, and specializes in Scripture and religion and ecology. Past chair of the Feminist Hermeneutics of the Bible Group of the Society of Biblical Literature and past president of the Eastern Great Lakes Biblical Society, she is the author of numerous articles, as well as *Studies in the Biblical Sea-Storm Type-Scene: Convention & Invention* (Lewiston, N.Y.: Edwin Mellen, 1992), and co-editor of *Escaping Eden: New Feminist Perspectives on the Bible* (Sheffield: Sheffield Academic Press, 1998; New York: New York University Press, 1999).

Keith Augustus Burton (Ph.D. Northwestern University, 1994) is Associate Professor of New Testament at Oakwood College in Huntsville, Alabama. His recent publications include *Rhetoric, Law, and the Mystery of Salvation in Romans 7:1-6* (Lewiston, N.Y.: Mellen, 2001); and "The Millennium: Transition to the Final Aeon," *Andrews University Seminary Studies* 38, no. 2 (2000): 207-22.

Lareta Halteman Finger (Ph.D. Northwestern University, 1997) spent fifteen years as editor of *Daughters of Sarah*, a Christian feminist magazine. Active in the Mennonite Church and the Evangelical and Ecumenical Women's Caucus, she serves as Assistant Professor of New Testament at Messiah College in Grantham, Pennsylvania. Her research interests are the Pauline letters, Acts, and feminist interpretation of the Bible. Recent publications include *Paul and the Roman House Churches* (Scottdale, Pa.: Herald, 1993) and *The Wisdom of Daughters: Two Decades of the Voice of Christian Feminism* (Philadelphia: Innisfree Press, 2001), edited with Kari Sandhaas.

Lincoln D. Hurst is Associate Professor of Religious Studies at the University of California, Davis. Among his various works are *The Epistle to the Hebrews: Its Background of Thought* (Cambridge: Cambridge University Press, 1990; (ed.) *The Glory of Christ in the New Testament: Studies in Christology in Memory of George Bradford Caird* (Oxford: Oxford University Press, 1987); and (with G. B. Caird) *New Testament Theology* (Oxford: Oxford University Press, 1994).

Index of Biblical Citations

270